THE NOAH PLAN®

ENGLISH LANGUAGE CURRICULUM GUIDE

THE PRINCIPLE APPROACH®
KINDERGARTEN THROUGH TWELFTH GRADE

Carole Goodman Adams

The compelling motive for Christian action lies in the nature of God. Christians are obligated to excellence because God himself is supremely excellent. . . . It is because of who and what God is, it is because of the beauty and truth manifest in his Son, it is because of the perfection of his redeeming work, that evangelicals can never be content with the mediocre in aesthetics. Here, as in all else, the call is to the unremitting pursuit of excellence to the glory of the God of all truth.

—Frank Gaebelein

FOUNDATION FOR AMERICAN CHRISTIAN EDUCATION
SAN FRANCISCO, CALIFORNIA • CHESAPEAKE, VIRGINIA

THE NOAH PLAN®

ENGLISH LANGUAGE CURRICULUM GUIDE

THE PRINCIPLE APPROACH®

KINDERGARTEN THROUGH TWELFTH GRADE

Carole Goodman Adams
Edited by Elizabeth L. Youmans

FIRST EDITION © JULY 1998

SECOND EDITION © AUGUST 2000

THIRD EDITION © JULY 2006

FOUNDATION FOR AMERICAN CHRISTIAN EDUCATION

ISBN 978-0-912498-52-2

PUBLISHED BY

THE FOUNDATION FOR AMERICAN CHRISTIAN EDUCATION

P.O. BOX 9588, CHESAPEAKE, VA 23321-9588
1-800-352-FACE
www.face.net

Cover Art

The cover art reflects the fruit of a "writing-oriented school." The student Spenserian poem was written in 1992 by StoneBridge High School sophomore, Heather McCauley. Heather, a commended National Merit Scholar, graduated from Covenant College in the Leadership Program (1998) and will teach high school.

The English binder title page was designed by StoneBridge School kindergartner, Mary Beth Burgher, in 1997. Mary Beth is a true scholar and easily inspired by her favorite subject, literature. She loves to spend time with her family and her little black kitten, Henry.

Editorial Assistant
Aileen J. S. Collins

Layout/Design
David C. Reisch

Acknowledgments

As a college senior with a major in French and an innate love of languages wondering what to do with my liberal arts degree, I took a course called "Materials and Methods of Teaching English." There was no idea of ever actually teaching English, or ever actually teaching for that matter, but graduation was imminent and the need for employment on the horizon. I thought a tool or two towards teaching might not hurt. Thus the course. Underneath this practical choice a more basic need brought me to the door of this particular class in my last semester of college—a lifelong fascination with words and language that wanted to know how exactly does one teach or learn the English language?

The course titled "Materials and Methods of Teaching English" was highly useful to me as a twenty-one-year-old teacher of remedial English the very next year. It was many years before I fully realized what a watershed that one course was. It was taught by a supervisor of English in the city schools fresh from the front lines of the battle to make literate the populations of the city's middle and high schools. His approach was pragmatic and purposeful, effective and common sense.

This forgotten teacher laid a cornerstone in the formation of the system of teaching the English language in classrooms from first grade through high school and in teaching and supervising many teachers of English. While *The Noah Plan*® method goes far beyond that first course to include literature and composition, it remains firmly grounded in a pragmatic approach that causes the student to practice the language in order to learn it.

Language did not come alive for me as a subject I loved to teach until Rosalie June Slater inspired me with the Christian history literature program as I was introduced to the Principle Approach®. Teaching English language through the teaching of literature classics and poetry gave substance, beauty, and purpose—making it a joy to teach and practically letting it teach itself.

The English Language Curriculum was greatly enhanced by the work of Kenneth Oliver in his *Sound Curriculum in English Grammar*. This booklet published by the Council for Basic Education was introduced to me by Jeff Black at American Heritage School in 1979. The simple approach presented by Kenneth Oliver's "Sound Curriculum" is a common sense and direct path to the mastery of English grammar. The text of the booklet is reprinted with permission in our chapter six, "Syntax."

With a very practical approach to grammar from my college professor, and now with the inspiration and elevation of literature, we only need add the component that **more than any other** creates the mastery of English language—composition. The English program that teaches writing, requiring writing skill development as the measure of mastery, is the program that achieves true language mastery. The Principle Approach with its emphasis on writing every subject provides the method of language instruction.

This guide is also the product of my doctoral dissertation entitled "The Educational Foundation of Language in the Mastery of Communication Skills: Reconstructing America's Gospel Purpose through Language Education." In addition, much credit for the method presented here must go to the dozens of teachers at StoneBridge School who over many years have demonstrated how to raise up a generation of Christian scholars. Their creativity and joy of teaching with its obvious fruit made this guide necessary.

Carole Goodman Adams
Chesapeake, Virginia
September, 1997

TABLE OF CONTENTS

TABLE OF CONTENTS

TABLE OF CONTENTS

Foreword

There is a flow to history and culture . . . . " [1] This guide is presented in response to the challenge facing American Christians for a solution to the present madness and chaos threatening twenty-first century education, government, and culture. It is forthrightly the result of a solid and unswerving belief in our sovereign God and His hand of Providence in the affairs of men and of nations. It purports unashamedly Christian Biblical presuppositions of life, faith, and learning. "By presuppositions we mean the basic way an individual looks at life, his basic worldview, the grid through which he sees the world. Presuppositions rest upon that which a person considers to be the truth of what exists (and) also provide the basis for their values and therefore the basis for their decisions." [2]

> Man is only a reed, the weakest in nature,
> but he is a thinking reed. . . .
> Thus all our dignity consists in thought.
> It is on thought that we must depend for our
> recovery, not on space and time,
> which we could never fill.
> Let us then strive to think well;
> that is the basic principle of morality.
> —Pascal, Pensees #347

The primary problem of American education is a philosophical shift from a Biblical worldview, which was the accepted and practiced presuppositional base for American education in its beginnings, to a secular and eclectic philosophical base. The shift created the drift towards the bankruptcy of literacy, and ultimately, of liberty. The solution is simply to re-identify a Biblical Christian philosophy of education, history, and government with which to purge the spoil of "philosophy and vain deceit, after the tradition of men after the rudiments of the world, and not after Christ." [3] When all is said and done, all that is true is "Christ in you, the hope of glory." [4]

The Principle Approach® is the Biblical Christian philosophy, method, and curriculum that re-identifies the impact of Christ in education and government. It builds a Biblical Christian framework of presuppositions into the child's elementary and secondary education along with his reading, arithmetic, science, and literature. The results are measurable; the potential for serving the Lord's purpose for individuals and for our nation is only limited by our courage to respond to the challenge.

The *Noah Plan*® Curriculum presents the solution to the degradation of our times, "the de-Christianization of America [that] has received its greatest impetus through the secularism of education." [5] The Principle Approach offers educators a means of re-establishing a thorough Biblical Christian worldview through every subject.

The role of language in the story of liberty is a fascinating one. The Gospel is basically a relationship that depends upon communication. Language is communication. God used languages and the development of languages for His purposes in the story of liberty.

C. G. A.

---

[1] Schaeffer, Francis A., *How Should We Then Live?*
New York: Fleming H. Revell Co., 1976, p. 19.
[2] Ibid.
[3] Colossians 2:8
[4] Colossians 1:27
[5] Slater, Rosalie J. *Teaching and Learning America's Christian History: The Principle Approach.* San Francisco: F.A.C.E., 1965, p. 52.

The Whole Principle Approach® Curriculum

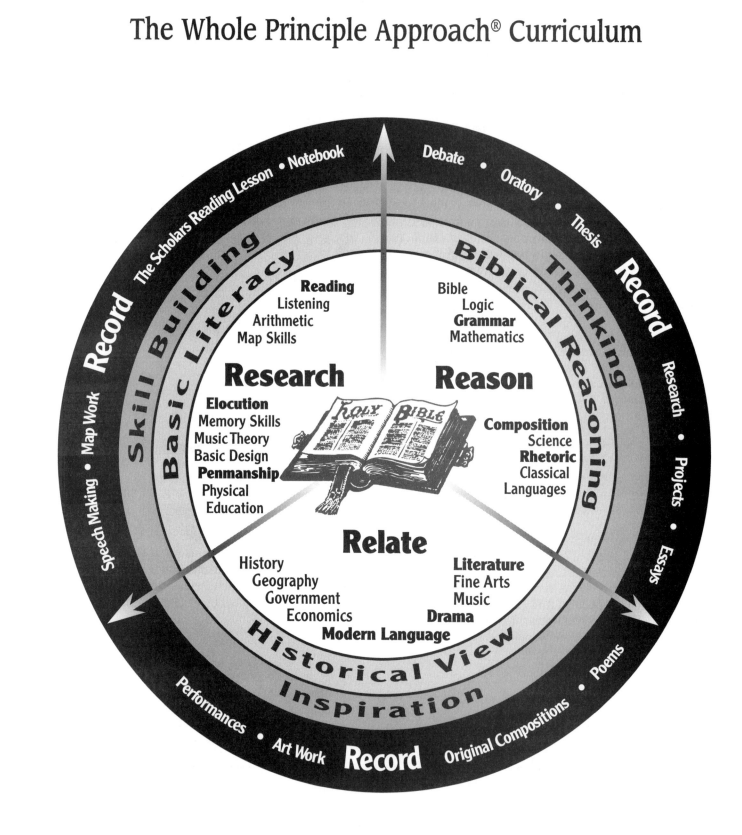

Skill Building · Basic Literacy

Reading
Listening
Arithmetic
Map Skills

Research

Elocution
Memory Skills
Music Theory
Basic Design
Penmanship
Physical
Education

Biblical Reasoning · Thinking

Bible
Logic
Grammar
Mathematics

Reason

Composition
Science
Rhetoric
Classical
Languages

Relate

History
Geography
Government
Economics
Modern Language

Literature
Fine Arts
Music
Drama

Historical View · Inspiration

Record — The Scholars Reading Lesson · Notebook · Debate · Oratory · Thesis

Record — Map Work · Speech Making

Record — Research · Projects · Essays

Record — Performances · Art Work · Original Compositions · Poems

THE NOAH PLAN® © 2006 · FOUNDATION FOR AMERICAN CHRISTIAN EDUCATION

Cultivating Reasoning through the Grades

Grade Level	Metaphor	Research	Reason	Relate	Record
Kindergarten	Planting the seeds of all knowledge	Identifying the subjects by their principles	Understanding symbols (Examples: flag; snowflakes; fingerprints)	Oral language; Mimicry; Narrative;	Recognizing the notebook as a tool of learning
Primary School	Tending the seedlings (sunning; watering; weeding; regulating; fertilizing; guarding; cultivating)	Mastering the basic skills and vocabulary of each subject	Understanding internal to external; Concrete thinking; Using manipulatives; Skill building	Recitation; Rote; Expository (writing); Drama; Guided projects	The notebook as a tool of scholarship—notebook skills practiced and guided by teacher
Middle School	Growing the plant (pruning; guiding; correcting; transplanting; maturing; seasoning; "hardying")	Defining the principles of the subjects	Understanding cause to effect; Questioning; Logic; Critical thinking; Scientific Method	Independent projects; Essays; Original Speech (8th)	Notebook mastery— a tool for lifelong independent learning
High School	Reaping the fruit! (cycling growth and harvesting the fruit)	Expressing the principles in life and learning	Original thinking and actual reasoning from a Biblical worldview	Apprenticeship; Service; Debate; Rhetoric; Creative writing and speech; Independent primary source research; Original science project; Portfolio projects; High School thesis and defense	Habit and spirit of organized learning and Biblical scholarship inculcated

KEY TO ABBREVIATIONS

The Noah Plan® English Language Curriculum Guide continually refers to the resources published by the Foundation for American Christian Education (F.A.C.E.). Following are abbreviations used for these publications in citations and references:

B & C   *The Bible and the Constitution of the United States of America*, Verna M. Hall and Rosalie J. Slater. San Francisco: F.A.C.E., 1983.

C & P   *The Christian History of the American Revolution: Consider and Ponder.* Compiled by Verna M. Hall. San Francisco: F.A.C.E., 1976.

CHOC I   *The Christian History of the Constitution of the United States of America*, Vol. I: *Christian Self-Government.* Compiled by Verna M. Hall. San Francisco: F.A.C.E., 1960, 1975.

CHOC II   *The Christian History of the Constitution of the United States of America*, Vol. II: *Christian Self-Government with Union.* Compiled by Verna M. Hall. San Francisco: F.A.C.E., 1962.

GW   *George Washington: The Character and Influence of One Man.* Compiled by Verna M. Hall. San Francisco: F.A.C.E., 1999.

Rudiments Handbook   *Rudiments of America's Christian History and Government: Student Handbook*, Rosalie J. Slater and Verna M. Hall. San Francisco: F.A.C.E., 1968, 1994.

T & L   *Teaching and Learning America's Christian History: The Principle Approach®*, Rosalie J. Slater. San Francisco: F.A.C.E., 1965.

Webster's 1828 Dictionary   *An American Dictionary of the English Language*, Noah Webster, 1828 facsimile edition. San Francisco: F.A.C.E., 1967.

CHAPTER ONE
TEACHING ENGLISH LANGUAGE:
CURRICULUM AND METHODOLOGY

What Is Language Education?
The Purpose of the English Language Curriculum Guide

The *Noah Plan® English Language Curriculum Guide* answers the question, "What is language?" to show the teacher **how** to teach English and **what** should be taught, prescribing a weekly routine of instruction that will make the student a master of English and a masterful communicator. The teaching of English and the teaching of literature are of one fabric in the Principle Approach®. One is the warp and the other the woof of the fine tapestry that is woven in the mind of the student called mastery of English communication. *My tongue is the pen of a ready writer*, the Psalmist declares. God has ever asked his people to be communicators—writers, penmen, speakers, preachers, prophets, chroniclers, scribes—disciples who teach the nations in propagating the Gospel.

God's Word to us is a document of high literary quality requiring its recipients to be literate; everywhere the Bible is taught, scholarship rises, literacy increases, and language is enhanced. The standard of language, spoken and written, has always been set by the church. Colonial pastors were the oracles sought on election days and by artillery regiments to preach a sermon to prepare and sustain civilization. The monasteries were the repository of learning; the schoolmasters were churchmen, the Bible was the fount of literacy and the means of teaching reading itself.

Today, the teacher finds the results of modern language instruction falling far short of the mark. The ability to articulate coherent ideas, the ability to appreciate and be formed by quality literature including the Bible, the ability to write even simple paragraphs with clarity and effectiveness—basic literacy to former generations—have all been replaced by the popular standard "functional literacy," or the ability to fill out a job application and read the prompts on the computer screen. We live in an age when the need to learn, even to speak, standard English is questioned and doubted.

But God's standards haven't changed; His Word remains forever! This guide presents the teaching and learning of English language, balanced to produce competent and effective and highly literate communicators. It incorporates grammar, composition, and literature in a complete curriculum. Grammar is not an end in itself in this context. Learning parts of speech is only a small step towards this greater purpose.

There are methods and means of achieving the goal of cultivating effective and highly literate communicators that include mastering the basics of grammar, but far exceed the seeming goal of most language books.

English Language Instruction Based on Three Principles

Principle One:
Language Is Both *Impressive* and *Expressive*

" . . . the Word was with God, and the Word was God." (John 1:1)

"Who being the brightness of His glory, and the express image of his person . . ." (Hebrew 1:3a)

God gave us ears to hear, a brain to process articulate sounds and store them in our memories, and a mind to understand, reason, and assimilate information read or heard for future use. This we may call the **impressive** mode of language. God also gave us tongues to speak and fingers to write in order to communicate our thoughts, convictions, conscience, and ideas—*expressive* language. The following definition of language gives the goal of all language instruction.

> **Language**, n. [from French, *langue*, tongue] The *expression* of ideas by words or significant articulate sounds for the *communication* of thoughts. Language consists in the oral *utterance* of sounds, which usage has made the representatives of ideas. When two or more persons customarily annex the same *sounds* to the same ideas, the *expression* of these sounds by one person *communicates* his ideas to another. *This is the primary sense of language, the use of which is to communicate the thoughts of one person to another through the organs of hearing.* (Webster's 1828 Dictionary)

English instruction must fully cultivate both modes—impressive and expressive language. Many language textbooks appear to overload the impressive instruction and allow expression only piecemeal—parts and pieces of language endlessly drilled. *The Noah Plan*® English teacher uses composi-tion, discussion, presentation, debate, and oratory equally with lecture lessons and drills. This idea is fully developed in the composition section, chapter eight.

Principle Two:
Language Is First Learned by Imitation

"*Wherefore I beseech you, be ye followers* [imitators] *of me.*" (1 Corinthians 4:16)

This principle implies both the existence of a model and the fact that children practice from whatever model exists. This makes two important points:

1. All teachers are language teachers ; or (fill in the blank) all _____ are language teachers. (parents, neighbors, grandparents, siblings, etc.)

2. The obvious need in language education is to give children the highest model of language possible in large quantities.

This curriculum guide employs as most essential tools the teaching of the Bible and the classic literature curriculum developed by Rosalie J. Slater beginning in kindergarten and continuing through the twelfth grade. The best models are those that have passed the test of time, particularly the Bible and classic literature.

Principle Three:
Language Is Best Taught by Analysis and Reason

"*Have I not written to thee excellent things in counsels and knowledge. That I might make thee know of the words of truth; that thou mightest answer the words of truth to them that send unto thee?*" (Proverbs 22: 20–21)

When language teaching gives appropriate place to the first and second principles, the content of language teaching focuses on analysis and reason, not rote memory. The contents of the six components of English presented in this guide equip teachers with the methods and materials for imparting a whole and balanced approach. Each of the content chapters—two through eight—presents a reasoning and analytical approach to language.

Books and Materials Needed

The method for teaching English presented in this guide does not require grammar textbooks. Grammar books of drills and exercises as a main text tend to derail the teaching and learning by daily assaults of "busy-work" that tie up time and energy, rather than use instructional time for real language practice—composition writing, literature studies, and opportunities to practice expressive language orally. Grammar books aimed at teaching language by endless pages of fill-in-the-blank and multiple-choice drills of parts and pieces are at best mindless exercises. C. S. Lewis in *The Abolition of Man: Or Reflections on Education with Special Reference to the Teaching of English in the Upper Forms of Schools*, discusses the effect of the "green book," a grammar book.

> The work of amateur philosophers where (we) expected the work of professional grammarians . . . a boy who thinks he is "doing" his "English prep" has no notion that ethics, theology, and politics are all at stake. [The authors of the "green book"] have cut out of his soul, long before he is old enough to choose, the possibility of having certain experiences which thinkers of more authority than they have held to be generous, fruitful, and humane.

Too often the timid or limited teacher surrenders to the bondage of the grammar workbook as a surer choice, rather than liberating the child's language development to the empowerment of literature. The truth is that *classic literature,* *and particularly the Bible, formed the gifts of great masters of language. There is no better way.*

The Noah Plan® English Language Curriculum Guide recommends four essential tools:

1. The F.A.C.E. Christian Literature Program, by Rosalie June Slater, presented in *The Noah Plan Literature Curriculum Guide*. This guide suggests excellent classics for the study of literature for each grade and gives a method of teaching teaching that incorporates composition and grammar.

2. *The Noah Plan Reading Curriculum Guide*, by Martha B. Shirley, which makes the Bible the primary reader for instruction continuing through high school. This guide coordinates perfectly with the literature instruction and the grammar and composition instruction to provide the complete language program for all the grades, kindergarten through twelfth.

3. Strunk and White's *Elements of Style*—to equip the teacher with the simplest and most direct presentation of writing, enabling the teacher to become the model and resource needed by his students. The introduction alone, by E. B. White (*Charlotte's Web*), inspires the reader to teach English with zeal and persistence. This is available in the reference section of any retail book store.

4. Noah Webster's *American Dictionary of the English Language* (Facsimile 1828 ed.). The components of grammar set forth by Webster form the basis of this guide. The dictionary's definitions of the vocabulary of language and grammar contain thumbnail lesson guides for teaching language. (See the word "composition" as an example.)

The English Language Teacher

The simplicity of this approach, without high-tech tools or clever workbooks, may frighten the teacher who does not assess his own abilities to be "masterful" or "highly literate." The teacher who opts for mediocrity on this count is at best a poor steward. "Fortune favors the bold," said conquering Caesar. Education is a lifelong process for the teacher as well as the student. The excellent teacher is one who loves learning and pursues learning lifelong. This teacher will grasp boldly the opportunity to incorporate a language program that will challenge and cultivate his language skills even as he teaches English to his students. The methods put forth in this guide have as sure an effect on the teacher as they have upon the student.

In the school where this method has been developed, a 300-student school including kindergartners through twelfth graders, achievement test scores in reading, spelling, vocabulary, and writing are consistently high, even among average learners. High school students score exceptionally well on the verbal section of the SAT test, averaging in the 1300s over several years. Perfect verbal scores on the SAT have been achieved repeatedly. More importantly, students in this program speak with confidence and authority, write with ease and clarity, debate, persuade, present, and articulate naturally and effectively.

The emphasis in English teaching must be aimed at the most excellent expression of spoken and written English, for as Alice in Wonderland said, "If you don't know where you're going, any road will lead you there."

What Comprises a Good English Program?

by Rosalie June Slater

*Have you kept a
regular Journal?
If you have not,
you will be likely
to forget most
of the Observa-
tions you have
made. If you
have omitted this
Useful Exercise,
let me advise you
to recommence
it, immediately.
Let it be your
Amusement, to
minute every day,
whatever you
may have seen
or heard worth
Notice. One con-
tracts Fondness
of Writing by Use.
We learn to write
readily, and what
is of more impor-
tance, We think,
and improve
our Judgements,
by committing
our Thoughts to
Paper.*

From a letter to
John Quincy Adams
from his father,
John Adams,
May 14, 1783

Basic English Skills

Dr. Donald R. Tuttle, Professor of English, cites the following comment as representative of the multitude of complaints concerning the status of English teaching in American high schools:

One of the kindliest of critics, Derek Colville, quotes a visiting professor from England as saying of American college freshmen, "The class was keen and intelligent. . . . They were excited by the poems we read, and they had insight. . . . But when I asked them to write on those same poems they were lost. Their papers were appalling. They couldn't plan, construct, find words for their meaning, or even punctuate and spell. It was a shattering anti-climax." Later in the article Colville observes that American freshmen of eighteen or nineteen are unable to do what ordinary English schoolboys can do at ten or twelve: "to express their thoughts simply and accurately, to do so in the most reasonable and connected order, and to support and illustrate their comments."

It is evident today that, no matter what field of endeavor an individual enters, the need for command of the written language is basic to success. There are very few jobs which eliminate completely the need for literacy—reading, writing, spelling, and hopefully, basic arithmetic. Even if our interest were purely utilitarian—namely to fulfill college entrance requirements or to permit a young person to hold a white-collar job—we have a long way to go to achieve this proficiency during high school years. Elementary schools today do not send up to Junior High School students who are well-grounded in the rudiments of grammar, spelling, composition, or even reading. Thus we have to be prepared to begin at the beginning again—no matter

how ego-deflating such a program at first appears to new high school pupils. Success in achieving mastery in these fundamentals provides the balm that soothes wounded vanity and constructs the foundation upon which we can then proceed to build. Our regret, of course, is that such teaching has been so long procrastinated—that so many years in school have not produced knowledge of and competence in the basic skills of speaking English, reading English, and writing English.

Literature in High School

It is evident by an examination of high school literature anthologies that, next to American history, this is the subject which has received the most attention from those forces which would destroy the American character and American institutions. Even those friendly critics of the high school literature program have discovered that organization around social rather than literary themes has resulted in more "non-literature" than literature, and has produced huge, unwieldy collections of dubious value to the student.

Much might be said here in criticism, but we would prefer to state our positive premise for a high school literature program. It is simply this: The school's major responsibility is to transmit the rich heritage which belongs to us as Americans and to inspire each new generation to excel and go beyond our greatest and finest literature which has stood the test of many generations, and has eternal value and eternal appeal and interest. We are cognizant of the few years left in the preparation of a young person for an independent life. It is the school's responsibility to stretch the mind and heart—to lift the vision of each student and to enable young men and young women to contemplate life challenges and to see how these same challenges have been met by other individuals like themselves. Literature is the avenue of character and feeling. If it is subverted it projects evil and erroneous models for minds and hearts to feed upon. What a tremendous opportunity to lift the vision of these times from the gutter to the stars!

In a Christian school the demand becomes even more imperative for upgrading the English program. We who are committed to a living Savior cannot afford to walk the multi-laned highways of the world without sacrificing our innocence and our purity, and thus diminishing our usefulness for Him. Feelings need to be evaluated honestly, and we have missed many wonderful opportunities to grow in depth and maturity through our indifference to the quality of literature served up to our youth. Let us rejoice that there are still abroad in this land great teachers from whose minds sparks fly—igniting our hope and conviction that, with careful selection and teaching, we may once again restore truth and beauty to our literature curriculum.

Our American Christian Heritage

The removal of the Bible from our public schools has had a direct effect upon our English program and most particularly on our teaching of literature. When one recognizes that the King James Bible is central to the culture of the English-speaking world, it is evident that to remove the foundation would ultimately bring down its superstructure. Thus, the abandonment of our Christian traditions, our ideals, and our standards of character has followed. It now becomes incumbent upon our Christian schools to lead the nation back to the vision and the purpose of America by restoring to the curriculum the cultural heritage which we have replaced with a "mess of potage." It will not be easy to "restore the years which the locusts hath eaten," but the ultimate goal will be to provide for high school students

a wide and rich sampling of literature that "stretches the mind" and which has been America's link to the Chain of Christianity® moving ever westward.

The English Language Program

The English Language program is divided into three major divisions, each one a two-year block of time, for the six years of Junior and Senior High School:

English IA—Rudiments of Literature: Literary Types (7th grade)

English IB—Rudiments of Literature: Pagan versus Christian Influences (8th grade)

English IIA—English Literature, Part I (9th grade)

English IIB—English Literature, Part II (10th grade)

English IIIA—American literature, Part I (11th grade)

English IIIB—American Literature, Part II (12th grade)

The English Language program has three major aspects—Grammar, Composition, and Literature—each with clearly defined goals. *Reading with Reason* is included throughout the high school years.

Grammar and Composition

The subversion of grammar has been a systematic and sustained effort beginning with the historic attack upon our fundamental American Christian principles.

Yet the study of grammar and the principles of logic enabled generations of Americans to focus their talents in prose, poetry, and oratory, and contribute mightily to American Independence.

We are victims today of an inundation of worthless prose and ineffectual oratory which fails to communicate principles and ideals. It is our conviction that a high school education should enable

Logic—The art of thinking and reasoning justly. "Logic is the art of using reason well in our inquiries after the truth, and the communication of it to others."

—Watts

The purpose of logic is to direct the intellectual powers in the investigation of truth, and in the communication of it to others.

—Hedge

Yet the study of grammar and the principles of logic enabled generations of Americans to focus their talents in prose, poetry, and oratory, and contribute mightily to American Independence.

every student, terminal as well as college preparatory, to achieve effectiveness in the skills of written expression. But such a goal will require careful effort and practice, week by week. The schedule for composition proceeds logically from learning to write illustrative sentences, definitive paragraphs, and expository essays until the student is prepared to achieve success in original writing—both prose and poetry. Constant, consistent practice to achieve specific goals is most necessary.

Spelling is learned through an intensive phonetic approach. It is a horizontal subject, which means it is graded in every subject area when written material is submitted. Penmanship is taught as a part of the Basic English program based upon the Palmer Method of Business Writing. It, too, is a horizontal subject, graded and stressed in every subject area.

Literature in the English Program for Grades Seven through Twelve

A complete six-year program in literature is designed as basic to a high school education—be that education terminal or college preparatory. Such a program might be defined as the most important

and critical subject in the curriculum. It is in literature that ideals, feelings, and character are identified for the student. America is a mirror of the literature which has fed the minds and hearts of America during the past generation. Every evil conception of life and living, every perverted emotion, has been presented as appetizing for contemplation and imitation. If we are to reverse this disastrous trend, we shall have to change the literary fare and begin to nourish faithfully those students entrusted to our stewardship. Minds need to be nourished with beauty and truth, inspired by the ideals and images which have linked us to the Chain of Christianity®. Students need to see evil honestly presented as evil. Affections and emotions, Scripturally-based, will lead us away from our preoccupation as a nation with the salacious, the corrupt, and the hopeless. The Apostle Paul set the standard for the qualities of our literature program when he urged us to think on these things:

Finally, brethren, whatsoever things are true, whatsoever things are honest, whatsoever things are just, whatsoever things are pure, whatsoever things are lovely, whatsoever things are of good report; if there be any virtue, and if there be any praise, think on these things. (Philippians 4:8)

Leading Ideas for Teaching the English Language

English Should Be Taught from a Principle or "Sound" Approach

1. Identify the interrelationship of language and history—English on the Chain of Christianity® and the contribution of the Bible to the language.

2. Relate God's purpose for English in the life of the individual.

3. Exalt the Bible and then literature, our heritage of Christian literature, as the highest standard of language.

4. Instruction and practice must be consistent with use of correct and gracious language.

The Goal of English Instruction

The goal of teaching English is the mastery of language for the communication of the Gospel—effective, lucid expression in speaking and writing—and for successful enterprise in the individual life.

The Method of Teaching English

All teaching begins internally with inspiration and the application of God's Word. The teaching of English begins with inspiring the child's heart to love language and literature, and to delight in effective use of language appreciating a godly standard of expression.

Every Teacher Is an English Teacher

Language is taught by imitation. Every teacher in every subject is a language teacher; therefore, every subject must maintain the standard of excellence in the use of language and the practice of language skills.

The Method of Learning Grammar: Analysis and Reason

Rote memory is a piecemeal approach that fails to produce a sense of relatedness when used as the major method of teaching. English teaching, to be successful, must employ composition as the daily exercise of language.

Order

There is order in language—patterns in words, sentences, and paragraphs. An orderly approach is necessary to effective learning.

Working Definitions of the
Six Components of Teaching English

Foundation of English Language establishes the Biblical worldview and purpose for learning and using language.

Definition of providence: [Fr. from L. providentia] 1. The act of providing or preparing for future use. 2. Foresight. 3. The care and superintendence God gives His creation.

This component lays the foundation for language study in every grade securely upon principles that frame the study of all languages and underpin the development of English language skills. This component provides the Why of language study.

Orthography includes the teaching and learning of basic phonetic reading and writing.

Definition of orthography: [Gr. orthographia; orthos, right, and grapha, writing.] 1. The art of writing words with the proper letters, according to common usage. 2. The part of grammar which treats of the nature and properties of letters, and of the art of writing words correctly. 3. The practice of spelling or writing words with the proper letters.

This component includes the teaching of intensive phonetics through *The Writing Road to Reading*™ with penmanship, spelling notebook, reading, and composition. Elocution is taught and practiced to establish fine speaking skills through reading aloud. This component provides the first level skills of English language mastery.

Etymology includes the mastery of affixes, inflections, and derivatives of Anglo-Saxon and classical root words to expand vocabulary.

Definition of etymology: [Gr. etymos, true, and logos, discourse.] 1. That part of philology which explains the origin and derivation of words, with a view to ascertain their radical or primary signification. In grammar, etymology comprehends the various inflections and modifications of words, and shows how they are formed from their simple roots. 2. The deduction of words from their originals; the analysis of compound words into their primitives.

This component includes the teaching of prefixes, suffixes, affixes, derivatives, inflections, root words of Anglo-Saxon and classical origin, and should include the study of foreign languages. This component provides the tools to acquire rapid vocabulary expansion, reading comprehension, and the ability to articulate ideas with precision.

Syntax teaches the order in language and the patterns of excellent speaking and writing.

Definition of syntax: [L. syntaxis; Gr. syntaxis syn, together, and tasso, to put.] 1. In grammar, the construction of sentences; the due arrangement of words in sentences, according to established usage. Syntax includes concord and regimen, or the agreement and government of words. Words, in every language, have certain connections and relations, as verbs and adjectives with nouns, which relations must be observed in the formation of sentences. A gross violation of the rules of syntax is a solecism. 2. connected system or order; union of things.

This component approaches the mastery of English grammar through the sentence as the basic unit of language, the complete thought. This approach makes the English experience one of learning language to communicate. This component develops ability in composition for writing and speaking effectively.

Prosody creates a love of language that inspires the study and mastery of language.

Definition of prosody: n. [Fr. prosodie; L. prosodia; Gr. prosodia; pros and oda, an ode.] That part of grammar which treats of the quantity of syllables, of accent, and of the laws of versification.

This component cultivates the "inner ear" to appreciate an excellent model of language through literature and poetry. The study of prosody develops the individual style of expression and imparts a love of language in its rhythm, consonance, and artful arrangement. This component produces the tools for vibrant, delightful expression.

Composition equips students to clothe ideas with words for communicating truth and ideals in writing and speaking.

Definition of composition, n. [the act of inventing or combining ideas, clothing them with words, arranging them in order, and in general, committing them to paper, or otherwise writing them.]

This component brings all English language skills to mastery. It provides the practice and refinement of expression that lead to true mastery of English. In the English class, composition is taught as a skill with daily practice to form articulate thinkers and writers and speakers. (Composition is horizontally taught through every subject in the curriculum.) In the English class, composition is taught as a skill with daily practice to form articulate thinkers, writers, and speakers.

THE NOAH PLAN® © 2006 • FOUNDATION FOR AMERICAN CHRISTIAN EDUCATION

The Whole English Language Curriculum

Reading maketh a full man.
Speaking—a ready man.
Writing maketh him exact.

—Sir Francis Bacon, English Essayist

Introducing the English Language Curriculum Charts Forming Language Mastery through the Grades

The teaching of English is an adventure in forming the verbal abilities of the mind to equip our students with one of the greatest life assets—mastery of the mother tongue. The ability to communicate effectively is the foundation of success in any endeavor from personal relationships to the propagation of the Gospel. Inestimable fulfillment comes from the personal expression of ideals as we live our lives. Therefore the mastery of the English language is a foundation block in a solid education.

Building that foundation block into the education of our children begins in kindergarten and continues with careful diligence throughout high school. The components of English presented in this guide work within the context of the literature program and draw upon the teaching of Bible, history, science, and other languages to create a complete and whole experience in English. Composition writing as a discipline to be mastered is the mainstay of the English program and extends into every subject in the curriculum.

Kindergarten and First Grade

Young children possess a natural love of language. They are enraptured by rhyme, rhythm, and "funny" words. They are captivated by stories and "catch" the canter and lilt of the tongue as new words or apt expressions are enjoyed. Kindergarten is the time to provide them with excellent models and inspiration. Children's poetry and classics are read aloud to be shared and relished. English instruction is mostly verbal beginning with The Writing Road to Reading™ and its emphasis upon the correct pronunciation of every sound in the language. At kindergarten we plant the seeds of all knowledge with English as the vehicle. The beginning elements of syntax,

etymology, and orthography are learned, emphasizing the whole sentence. Writing begins first with orthography but many students are writing sentences by the end of the kindergarten year.

Second, Third, and Fourth Grades

In the upper primary grades, English is taught as a subject with careful instruction in orthography, syntax, etymology, prosody, and composition. Testing is done by essay questions in all subjects. The notebook is both the record of learning and the repository of the product of learning. It becomes a reflection of the level of language skill of every child. Therefore great effort is made in the keeping of the notebook and in the teacher's oversight of the development of the notebook habit. Writing now is daily with formal composition instruction and practice. A composition cahier—a black and white stitched notebook—is kept to record composition practice as a permanent record. Compositions are written and presented weekly for grading and to be read aloud for affirmation and gentle critique. The goal of language learning by the end of fourth grade is the mastery of reading and basic writing skills.

Fifth, Sixth, Seventh, and Eighth Grades

Middle school is the time when the content of every subject proliferates, notebook work becomes extensive, and students enter the dialectic stage of questioning, reasoning logically, and taking on independent learning projects. This is the time to emphasize the refinement of language by focusing on the mastery of syntax and etymology. Writing and presenting are daily occupations. Original work is valued and evaluated regularly holding to a worthy standard. Composition writing includes the four steps of pre-writing, drafting, revision, and presentation. It is the goal of middle school that students master basic language skills and enter high school with a broad and substantial vocabulary base.

High School

While in middle school English is a major subject, in high school English is taught through all subjects with the requirement of independent research and original thinking. Syntax instruction is completed with the advanced level of grammar mastery. Etymology, appearing as word analysis, continues to be practiced in every subject. The rich literature program, with two years each of English and American literature, provides the standard and inspiration for language expression. The Bible curriculum, the history and sciences, give breadth and depth to the language experience of high school. Every subject requires research, debate, presentation, and original work. The end result is a rich vocabulary and a facility with language that enables the student to write and defend his thesis, the product of his own interests and passion, before a group of scholars.

The charts on the following pages present a well-balanced and thorough approach to teaching English language.

Teaching and Learning English in Kindergarten

Purpose	Goals
The kindergarten teacher appeals to the child's innate love of language to nurture the competent and confident use of English to develop communication skills using children's classics and the Bible.	• To plant the seeds of language mastery by initiating skill development in orthography, syntax, etymology, composition, prosody. • To engage the child daily in using language towards developing excellent communication skills.

Principles and Leading Ideas

- Introduce language as a gift from God throughout semester one, to learn that language is to help us communicate with Him and with each other. God uses language to communicate with us through His Word. Look for opportunities to reinforce this idea in many lessons, NPEG, 47–49.

- Teach the appreciation of the written Word of God throughout quarter three: God wrote a book to communicate Himself to us, using language, spelling, and sentences.

- Teach England and France on the Chain of Christianity®. God used English to take the Bible to America and, through translation, to the entire world, NPEG, 47, 56, 60, 77.

Books and Materials Essential to Kindergarten English

- *The Noah Plan® English Language Curriculum Guide* (NPEG)
- *The Noah Plan Literature Curriculum Guide* (NPLG)
- *The Noah Plan Reading Curriculum Guide* (NPRG)
- *American Dictionary of the English Language,* Facsimile Edition (Webster's 1828 *Dictionary*)
- The Kindergarten Classics: *Winnie-the-Pooh, Peter Rabbit, Bambi, Little House in the Big Woods, Abraham Lincoln* (d'Aulaire), *Tales of Shakespeare* (Lamb's), *Uncle Remus Stories, Aesop's Fables, A Child's Garden of Verses,* Mother Goose and other nursery rhymes, lullabies, fairy tales, children's poets and poetry.
- Globe, wall map of the physical world
- Classroom Christian history wall timeline
- *Premiers Pas de Français* (the French Primer) or another primary level foreign language program. (Studies show that the study of a foreign language in early childhood and elementary levels affects language skill in the native language as well. Early foreign language introduction enables the child to develop an ear for all future language learning, broadens vocabulary and understanding of the world, which gives the child a growing sense of dominion over God's creation.)

Methodology

- "The pupil is not above his teacher," who teaches his own heart and character foremost. The teacher who loves language and enjoys literature will be more effective in inspiring the student than the teacher who merely possesses the skills. As "the living textbook" and the model of learning and scholarship, the teacher prepares by reading the children's classics and poetry in advance.

- Kindergarten children love language innately and enjoy rhyming, stories, word play, and poetry. The more this love is cultivated and used to elicit the child's own expression and use of language, the better will be the child's language ability.

- The practice of correct and colorful, expressive language daily gives children the confidence and skills for excellent communication.

Quarter One	Quarter Two	Quarter Three	Quarter Four

The **Orthography** and **Etymology** components of English are taught through The Writing Road to Reading™ program and include penmanship, spelling, and reading. See NPRG.

The **Prosody** component of English is taught through the Literature curriculum program. See NPLG.

Syntax

Introduce the structure of the English language and its parts holistically by introducing the complete sentence rather than parts of speech. Practice the sentence as a whole thought in daily speech. Demonstrate the sentence by giving examples of well-phrased sentences from the literature and Bible.

Syntax

Encourage the use of complete sentences in daily speaking and in writing original sentences. Continue demonstrating excellent examples from the literature and the Bible. Introduce simple initial capitalization and end punctuation.

Syntax

Continue teaching the sentence by identifying the subjects and verbs as naming and action words, NPEG, 142–47. Teach the verb as the action word in the sentence by speaking the sentence and asking the student to fid the word that shows action. Teach the subject as the "doer" of the action. Practice until the student can identify the verb and the subject.

Syntax

Continue teaching the sentence by identifying the subjects and verbs as naming and action words and giving the student opportunity to identify these parts daily in the context of the whole sentence, NPEG, 142–147. Continue to encourage the use of complete sentences, demonstrating excellent modes, and reinforcing simple initial capitalization and end punctuation.

Etymology

Identify syllables, NPRG, 111. Build into the student an understanding of syllables and the ability to hear and identify the syllables of any word. Teach the precise meanings of words showing the student the dictionary. Enjoy words that rhyme, describe, and many new words from the Bible, literature, science, history, and geography.

Etymology

Teach the precise meaning of words. Show the dictionary and read the definition aloud to impart precise meaning. Build into the student an understanding of syllables and the ability to identify the syllables of any word, NPRG, 111. Enjoy words that rhyme, describe, and many new words form Bible, literature, science, history, and geography.

Etymology

Continue to teach syllables and the ability to identify the syllables of any word, NPRG, 111. Teach precise meanings of words using the dictionary. Continue enjoying words that rhyme, describe, and many new words from Bible, literature, science, history, and geography.

Etymology

Continue to teach syllables and the ability to identify the syllables of any word, NPRG, 111. Teach precise meanings of words using the dictionary. Continue enjoying words that rhyme, describe, and many new words from Bible, literature, science, history, and geography.

Composition

After the first few weeks of school when the reading routines are established: Introduce composition—the composing of ideas in words, NPEG, 244. Enjoy in all subjects every day picturesque, comical, rhyming, and rhythmic language, sharing excellent models of vivid and effective writing. Cultivate an appreciation of words and language through the enjoyment of them. Create opportunities daily for the child to relate, discuss, and present ideas in complete sentences and good order, preparing to write sentences by mid-year, NPEG, 14–15.

Composition

Continue to plant the seeds of good writing and speaking: lead the student to choose vivid and "telling" words in place of "nice," "pretty," etc.; always require the student to use a complete sentence; create activities that cause the student to observe, notice, describe, and ask questions. Create opportunities daily for the child to relate, discuss, and present ideas in complete sentences and good order preparing to write sentences by mid-year, NPEG, 14–15. Allow the student to retell, imagine, make lists of related ideas, and collect ideas about a subject. Practice making sentences and paragraphs orally together and then independently.

Composition

Practice good verbal syntax using words correctly in sentences in conversation and discussion. Write statements together then independently. This activity should be done several times a week in any subject. Write a group paragraph on the board after discussing the idea or topic (pre-writing), thinking of a topic sentence together (drafting), and forming good supporting sentences (revising). This exercise should be done several times throughout the quarter, NPEG, 244–245.

Composition

Introduce simple initial capitalization and end punctuation. Continue writing group paragraphs to learn paragraph form. Write sentences daily. Write a simple paragraph independently by spring.

Teaching and Learning English in First Grade

Purpose	Goals
• First grade English instruction gives the student opportunity to use language to cultivate excellent communication skills verbally and in writing. Because language is the bedrock of all scholarship, the notebook method upholds a high standard while the enjoyment of language through the children's classics and the Bible inspires creative, articulate expression.	• To nurture the language mastery by practicing skill development routinely in orthography, syntax, etymology, composition, prosody. • To give the child daily opportunity to use expressive language towards developing excellent communication skills.

Principles and Leading Ideas

• Language is a gift from God with a special purpose.

• There is order in God's universe and in language; correct order makes language effective.

• Excellence in using language begins with Christ; language reflects God's character
We are stewards of the gifts God gives us; our use of language reflects our stewardship.

Books and Materials Essential to First Grade English

• *The Noah Plan® English Language Curriculum Guide* (NPEG)

• *The Noah Plan Literature Curriculum Guide* (NPLG)

• *The Noah Plan Reading Curriculum Guide* (NPRG)

• *American Dictionary of the English Language,* Facsimile Edition (Webster's 1828 *Dictionary*)

• The First Grade Classics: *Benjamin West and His Cat Grimalkin* and *Teacher Guide; Heidi* and *Teacher Guide; Pocahontas* and *Benjamin Franklin* (d'Aulaire); *Tales of Shakespeare* (Lamb's); children's poets and poetry

• Globe, wall map of the physical world

• Classroom Christian history wall timeline

• *Premiers Pas de Français* (the French Primer) or another primary level foreign language program. (Studies show that the study of a foreign language in early childhood and elementary levels affects language skill in the native language as well. Early foreign language introduction enables the child to develop an ear for all future language learning, broadens vocabulary and understanding of the world, which gives the child a growing sense of dominion over God's creation.)

Methodology

• The teacher who loves language and enjoys literature will effectively inspire the student. As "the living textbook" and the model of learning and scholarship, the teacher prepares by enjoying the children's classics and poetry in advance and planning carefully.

• First grade children enjoy rhyming, stories, word play, and poetry; the skillful teacher will elicit the child's own expression and use of language daily in response to excellent models in children's classics and the Bible.

• The notebook method is begun in first grade by careful instruction and practice; the teacher plans gradual implementation of the notebook as the child's permanent record of the English, reading, and literature studies.

Quarter One	Quarter Two	Quarter Three	Quarter Four
The **Orthography** and **Etymology** components of English are taught through The Writing Road to Reading™ program and include penmanship, spelling, and reading. See NPRG.			
The **Prosody** component of English is taught through the Literature curriculum program. See NPLG.			
Syntax Demonstrate sentence patterns using sentences from literature and Bible with coding on board. Continue teaching patterns by demonstrating and substituting words in the patterns. Example: S V Birds sing → Birds fly. This exercise begins to set in the understanding the role of different kinds of words in the sentence.	*Syntax* Continue to demonstrate the patterns of sentences by following NPEG, 182. Begin to substitute words until the student recognizes the different uses in a sentence for the different kinds of words. NPEG, 182. The goal for syntax is to demonstrate how sentences work by substituting words in the patterns.	*Syntax* Continue demonstrating sentence patterns until students are able to recognize the different uses in a sentence for the different words, and are able to substitute words at every point in the sentence of the subject-verb, subject-verb-direct object, subject-verb-predicate adjective, and subject-verb-predicate noun types. NPEG, 182. The goal for syntax is learning to name the sentence patterns.	*Syntax* Continue practicing sentence patterns and understanding the uses of words in the sentence. Teach end punctuation and capitalization. The goal for syntax is to recognize the four sentence patterns and how they work.
Etymology Introduce etymology, NPEG, 116, and Webster's 1828 *Dictionary*. Begin to build into the student an understanding of word parts by pointing out easy compound words beginning with ordinal numbers and cardinal numbers.	*Etymology* Teach the parts of words introducing easy prefixes and suffixes to show patterns of words as they appear in the reading or literature. NPEG, 116.	*Etymology* Encourage the acquisition of a rich, extensive vocabulary from all subjects. Define words from the literature classic and poetry, or from science or history class, or record the definitions in student notebooks. Use these contextual words to continue showing patterns and word parts.	*Etymology* Continue writing definitions in the notebook. Continued to show word patterns and parts. Introduce root words and begin to list some common roots. Introduce synonyms and homonyms.
Composition Introduce composition writing by reading samples of excellent primary level composition from the literature classic (a description that first graders appreciate, for example) or from the Bible. Write group compositions of one paragraph by talking through the topic, creating together a topic sentence and support sentences. The teacher writes the composition on the board and the children copy it. Begin the composition *cahier* (a black and white stitched composition book) by regularly writing about experiences, memories, descriptions of special days, Bible lessons, etc.	*Composition* Practice pre-writing (teacher directed) to generate the substance of the paragraph. NPEG, 245. Practice paragraph writing routinely using the "paragraph house" paradigm, NPEG, 249. Write drafts, revise, and present paragraphs weekly. Continue writing in the composition cahier.	*Composition* Continue writing paragraphs emphasizing unity—developing one idea in a paragraph. NPEG, 246. Teach the parts of a letter and regularly practice letter writing. NPEG, 250. Continue regularly writing in the composition cahier.	*Composition* Introduce reason questions and writing essay answers. Use questions from history, science, or literature. See weekly goals, NPL1. Continue writing paragraphs. Teach the oral presentation and give students opportunity to present. NPEG, 99. Continue writing in the composition cahier.

Teaching and Learning English in Second Grade

Purpose	Goals
Second grade English instruction gives the student guided opportunity to use language to cultivate excellent communication skills verbally and in writing. Because language is the medium of all scholarship, the notebook method upholds a high standard while the enjoyment of language through the children's classics and the Bible inspires creative, articulate expression.	• To nurture the language mastery by practicing skill development routinely in orthography, syntax, etymology, composition, and prosody. • To give the child daily opportunity to use expressive language towards developing excellent communication skills.

Principles and Leading Ideas

- Language is a gift from God with a special purpose.
- There is order in God's universe and in language; correct order makes language effective.
- Excellence in use of language begins with Christ; language reflects God's character.
- We are stewards of the gifts God gives us; our use of language reflects our character.
- God uses language to create.

Books and Materials Essential to Second Grade English

- *The Noah Plan® English Language Curriculum Guide* (NPEG)
- *The Noah Plan Literature Curriculum Guide* (NPLG)
- *The Noah Plan Reading Curriculum Guide* (NPRG)
- *American Dictionary of the English Language,* Facsimile Edition (Webster's 1828 *Dictionary*)
- The Second Grade Classics: *Benjamin West and His Cat Grimalkin* and *Teacher Guide; Heidi* and *Teacher Guide; Pocahontas* and *Benjamin Franklin* (d'Aulaire); *Tales of Shakespeare* (Lamb's); children's poets and poetry
- Globe, wall map of the physical world
- Classroom Christian history wall timeline
- *Premiers Pas de Français* (the French Primer) or another primary level foreign language program. (Studies show that the study of a foreign language in early childhood and elementary levels affects language skill in the native language as well. Early foreign language introduction enables the child to develop an ear for all future language learning, broadens vocabulary and understanding of the world, which gives the child a growing sense of dominion over God's creation.)

Methodology

- The teacher who loves language and enjoys literature will effectively inspire the student. As "the living textbook" and the model of learning and scholarship, the teacher prepares by enjoying the children's classics and poetry in advance and planning carefully.
- Second grade children enjoy language and literature; the skillful teacher will elicit the child's own expression and use of language daily in response to excellent models in children's classics and the Bible.
- The notebook method is begun in first grade by careful instruction and practice; the teacher plans gradual implementation of the notebook as the child's permanent record of the English, reading, and literatures studies.
- The *cahier*, a composition-sized stitched notebook, is used for composition practice several times a week for less formal writing such as meditations, descriptions of special days, recording inspiration and things of interest.
- Skill routines are established for weekly practice in spelling, etymology, penmanship, and composition.

Quarter One	Quarter Two	Quarter Three	Quarter Four
*The **Orthography** and **Etymology** components of English are taught through* The Writing Road to Reading™ *program and include penmanship, spelling, and reading. See NPRG, NPL2.*			
*The **Prosody** component of English is taught through the Literature Curriculum program. See NPLG, NPL2.*			
Syntax Syntax instruction begins in quarter two.	***Syntax*** Continuing the learning of the basic sentence pattern analysis: S-V, S-V-dO, S-V-dO-iO, S-V-pA, S-V-pN; able to create sentences of every type with the aid of the coded pattern; able to analyze sentences in the literature and the Bible. NPEG p145–149,182; NPL2.	***Syntax*** Continuing the practice of the basic sentence pattern analysis: S-V, S-V-O, S-V-dO-iO, S-V-pA, S-V-pN; able to create sentences of every type with the aid of the coded pattern; Able to analyze sentences in the literature and the Bible. NPEG p145–149,182; NPL2.	***Syntax*** Continuing the learning of the basic sentence pattern analysis: S-V, S-V-dO, S-V-iO,S-V-pA, S-V-pN; able to create sentences of every type with the aid of the coded pattern; able to analyze sentences in the literature and the Bible. NPEG p145–149,182; NPL2.
Etymology Learning the parts of words and how to analyze words to build vocabulary; derivation of words and dictionary skills. NPEG, 116; NPL2.	***Etymology*** Learning the parts of words and how to analyze words to build vocabulary; derivation of words and dictionary skills; compound words. NPEG, 116; NPL2.	***Etymology*** Learning the parts of words and how to analyze words to build vocabulary; derivation of words and dictionary skills; contractions, possessives, plurals. NPL2.	***Etymology*** Learning the parts of words and how to analyze words to build vocabulary; derivation of words and dictionary skills. NPL2.
Composition Learning to write compositions beginning with practicing paragraph writing to invent or combine ideas, clothe them with words, arrange them in order, and commit them to paper. Use of the four-step writing process, NPEG, 249; NPL2.	***Composition*** Learning to write compositions beginning with practicing paragraph writing to invent or combine ideas, clothe them with words, arrange them in order, and commit them to paper. NPL2.	***Composition*** Reviewing topic sentence and supporting sentences and paragraph unity. Essay answers to reason questions, character sketches from literature notes, and regular letter writing. Learning to paraphrase orally first. Writing in composition cahier. Book review writing. NPL2.	***Composition*** Reviewing topic sentence and supporting sentences and paragraph unity. Essay answers to reason questions, character sketches from literature notes, and regular letter writing. Learning to paraphrase orally first. Writing in composition cahier. Book review writing. NPL2.

Teaching and Learning English in Third Grade

Purpose	Goals
Third grade English instruction gives the student guided opportunity to use language to cultivate excellent communication skills verbally and in writing. Because language is the medium of all scholarship, the notebook method holds a high standard while the enjoyment of language through the children's classics and the Bible inspires creative, articulate expression.	• The love of language of highest quality and appreciation of the artful use of language in story and verse. • Competence in paragraphing and composition. • Growing command of spelling, penmanship, vocabulary, and grammar. • Expanding vocabulary and ability to articulate with persuasion. • Developing critical and logical reasoning skills.

Principles and Leading Ideas

- God reveals Himself through language; our use of language reveals our unique individuality.
- We master the gift of language for God's glory and for the successful stewardship of our abilities.
- Our use of language reflects our individual character and Christian self-government.
- Language has order and is governed by rules and principles.
- The tongue must be subject to conscience, which is governed by Christ.
- Language skill comes by diligent practice daily.
- We conduct our study of language by researching, reasoning, relating, and recording.

Books and Materials Essential to Third Grade English

- *The Noah Plan® English Language Curriculum Guide* (NPEG)
- *The Noah Plan Literature Curriculum Guide* (NPLG)
- *The Noah Plan Reading Curriculum Guide* (NPRG)
- *American Dictionary of the English Language,* Facsimile Edition (Webster's 1828 *Dictionary*)
- The Third Grade Classics: *Hans Brinker and the Silver Skates; Sebastian Bach: The Boy from Thuringia; The Lion, the Witch and the Wardrobe; Tales from Shakespeare* (Lamb's); children's poets and poetry
- *How to Teach Spelling,* Rudginsky & Haskell
- Globe, wall map of the physical world
- Classroom Christian history wall timeline
- *Premiers Pas de Français* (the French Primer) or another primary level foreign language program

Methodology

- The notebook method (dividers for *Foundations, Orthography, Etymology, Syntax, Prosody,* and *Composition*) to record all instruction and daily practice in the skill-building practice routines in spelling, penmanship, composition, sentence analysis, and vocabulary.
- Extraction from the classic literature relevant and useful vocabulary for word study and interesting and engaging sentences for sentence analysis.
- Units of teacher instruction in composition, writing, syntax, and etymology.
- Skill routines are established for weekly practice in spelling, etymology, penmanship, and composition.

Quarter One	Quarter Two	Quarter Three	Quarter Four
Orthography consists of spelling, penmanship, and speaking. Spelling is taught from the book How to Teach Spelling as a practice of dictation in applying spelling rules daily. Penmanship is also a practice of reviewing and building skill using the Palmer method with daily practice. These routines begin in week one and continue throughout the year. The notebook is used each day for recording instruction, recording the dictation and practice. Speaking is taught formally in quarter three. NPL3.			
The **Prosody** component of English is taught through the Literature Curriculum program. See NPLG, NPL3.			
Syntax Syntax instruction begins in quarter two.	**Syntax** Continuing the learning of the basic sentence pattern analysis: S-V, S-V-dO, S-V-dO-iO, S-V-pA, S-V-pN; able to create sentences of every type with the aid of the coded pattern; able to analyze sentences in the literature and Bible. NPEG, 145–149, 182; NPL3.	**Syntax** Continuing the practice of the basic sentence pattern analysis: S-V, S-V-dO, S-V-dO-iO, S-V-pA, S-V-pN; able to create sentences of every type with the aid of the coded pattern; able to analyze sentences in the literature and Bible. NPEG, 145–149, 182; NPL3.	**Syntax** Continuing the sentence analysis with the gradual removal of coding and use of grammatical terms, analyzing sentences in literature and the Bible. NPEG, 145–149, 182; NPL3.
Etymology Reviewing the parts of words; building the word bank through the word analysis method for words found in literature, Bible, history, and science.	**Etymology** Building the word bank through the word analysis method for words found in literature, Bible, history, and science.	**Etymology** Building the word bank through the word analysis method for words found in literature, Bible, history, and science.	**Etymology** Building the word bank using the word analysis method for words found in literature, Bible, history, and science.
Composition Paragraphing as a skill is taught and practiced in quarter one until the student can write a paragraph with correct structure independently. Use of the four-step writing process, NPEG, 249; NPL3.	**Composition** Paragraphing practice continues this quarter with the same goal as quarter one—that the student write a paragraph with correct structure independently.	**Composition** Emphasis on learning and practicing the four steps of the writing process though various methods and weekly practice.	**Composition** Practicing paragraphing using the four-step process. Writing poetry through the "poetry writing workshop," NPL3. End of the year composition.

Teaching and Learning English in Fourth Grade

Purpose	*Goals*
Fourth grade English instruction moves the student from the primary mode of "learning to read" and use rudimentary language skills to the "reading to learn" mode with growing ability. The notebook method provides a tool of study and work habit. The continued study of classic literature and the Bible upholds the highest standard and model of language.	• The love of highest-quality language and the appreciation of literature and poetry continues. • Growing competence in writing composition and essay and in researching. • Increasing mastery of spelling, penmanship, vocabulary, and grammar. • Expanding vocabulary and ability to articulate persuasively. • Developing critical and logical reasoning skills.

Principles and Leading Ideas

- English developed on the Chain of Christianity® as a vehicle for the Gospel.
- One's use of language is a reflection of one's individuality and character.
- God uses individuals to further His purposes: Noah Webster, American Christian lexicographer.
- We conduct our study of language by researching, reasoning, relating, and recording.
- The practice of English skills daily and weekly in writing and in speaking increases the individual's ability to communicate persuasively and effectively.
- Latin influenced English, contributing to its purpose.

Books and Materials Essential to Fourth Grade English

- *The Noah Plan® English Language Curriculum Guide* (NPEG)
- *The Noah Plan Literature Curriculum Guide* (NPLG)
- *The Noah Plan Reading Curriculum Guide* (NPRG)
- *American Dictionary of the English Language,* Facsimile Edition (Webster's 1828 *Dictionary*)
- The Fourth Grade Classics: *Carry On, Mr. Bowditch,* Latham; *Treasure Island,* Stevenson; *Julius Caesar,* Shakespeare; *The Wind in the Willows,* Grahame; Noyes, Longfellow, Wheatley, Wordsworth, Stevenson
- *How to Teach Spelling,* Rudginsky & Haskell
- Globe, wall map of the physical world
- Classroom Christian history wall timeline
- Continued study of French or another foreign language including introductory grammar. Begin study of Latin.

Methodology

- The notebook method (dividers for *Foundations, Orthography, Etymology, Syntax, Prosody,* and *Composition*) to record all instruction and daily practice in the skill-building practice routines in spelling, penmanship, composition, sentence analysis, and vocabulary.
- Extraction from the classic literature relevant and useful vocabulary for word study and interesting and engaging sentences for sentence analysis.
- Units of teacher instruction in composition, writing, syntax, and etymology.
- Skill routines are established for weekly practice in spelling, etymology, penmanship, and composition.

Quarter One	Quarter Two	Quarter Three	Quarter Four
Orthography consists of spelling, penmanship, and speaking. Spelling is taught from the book How to Teach Spelling as a practice of dictation in applying spelling rules daily. Penmanship is also a practice of reviewing and building skill using the Palmer method with daily practice. These routines begin in week one and continue throughout the year. The notebook is used each day for recording instruction, recording the dictation and practice.			
The **Prosody** component of English is taught through the Literature Curriculum program. See NPLG.			
Syntax Review all processes. When it is clear that the structure of basic sentence forms is known and that the parts can be used and named, modifiers are introduced gradually, at first for the S then for the dO, then for the V, then for the pN, and pA, and finally for the iO. Diagramming should be used as a visual aid.	*Syntax* When the student can properly show the modifying relationships of one-word modifiers, phrase modifiers should be introduced. Many exercises are used until the relationship of modifier to the noun or verb it modifies is clearly recognized. Sentences are drawn from the literature studied, and from the student's own writing.	*Syntax* When the student can properly show the modifying relationships of one-word modifiers, phrase modifiers should be introduced. Many exercises are used until the relationship of modifier to the noun or verb it modifies is clearly recognized. Sentences are drawn from the literature studied, and from the student's own writing.	*Syntax* When the student can properly show the modifying relationships of one-word modifiers, phrase modifiers should be introduced. Many exercises are used until the relationship of modifier to the noun or verb it modifies is clearly recognized. Sentences are drawn from the literature studied, and from the student's own writing.
Etymology Word parts receive more emphasis. Stems (or roots or bases) are introduced and a variety of affixes used with them (*tract* = to pull: the stem for de*tract*, con*tract*, pro*tract*, dis*tract*, ex*tract*, ex*tract*ion, ex*tract*able, etc.).	*Etymology* Each word is shown with each prefix and each suffix to build a meaning that is based on the stem. (*spec, spic, spect* from the Latin *specere*, "to see"). Students list prefixes, stems, and suffixes in separate columns.	*Etymology* Word analysis continues to expand vocabulary rapidly since stems are used from several to hundreds of times and the suffixes hundreds of times in words the students will soon need to know.	*Etymology* Word analysis continues to expand vocabulary rapidly since stems are used from several to hundreds of times and the suffixes hundreds of times in words the students will soon need to know.
Composition The use of the four-step writing process, NPEG, 249, should be habit now in fourth grade composition. The Scholar's Reading Lesson should be practiced weekly (NPRG, 69). Types of writing are practiced and research skills.	*Composition* Refinement of paragraphing with emphasis and coherence focused and with transitional words and sentences practiced. The précis, letter writing, essay answer, and creative writing.	*Composition* Sentence variety, using exact nouns and verbs, use of the thesaurus, writing dialogue, usage, formal style. Mastery of punctuation, capitalization, and manuscript style. Proofreading habit required.	*Composition* Sentence variety, using exact nouns and verbs, use of the thesaurus, writing dialogue, usage, formal style. Mastery of punctuation, capitalization, and manuscript style. Proofreading habit required.

Teaching and Learning English in Fifth Grade

Purpose	Goals
In fifth grade English, language skills grow in research, writing, and presentation. The middle grades emphasize the polishing of both writing and research skills in preparation for high school. Fifth grade moves towards the master of basic skills of spelling, grammar, penmanship, and composition by the completion of eighth grade. The notebook method continues to organize and record excellent study and work habits. The continued use of classic literature and the Bible form the most excellent model for inspiring the use of language.	• The use of language to express original thought and to state principles and understandings. • Growing competence in writing composition and essay and in doing research. • Increasing mastery of spelling, penmanship, vocabulary, and grammar. • Expanding vocabulary and ability to articulate persuasively. • Developing critical and logical reasoning skills. • Ability to master the elements of literature, poetry, Shakespeare, biography, and composition.

Principles and Leading Ideas

- The significance of writing and books as demonstrated in both the Bible and in history.
- The influence of other languages on English, including Latin.
- The role of language in furthering God's purposes and our responsibility today in mastering languages.
- The importance of communication skills in propagating the Gospel.

Books and Materials Essential to Fifth Grade English

- *The Noah Plan® English Language Curriculum Guide* (NPEG)
- *The Noah Plan Literature Curriculum Guide* (NPLG)
- *The Noah Plan Reading Curriculum Guide* (NPRG)
- *American Dictionary of the English Language,* Facsimile Edition (Webster's 1828 *Dictionary*)
- The Fifth Grade Classics: *Ruth*—the Bible as literature; *Little Women,* Louisa May Alcott; *Trailblazer of the Sea,* Jean Lee Latham; *Secret Garden,* Frances Hodgson Burnett; *MacBeth,* William Shakespeare; Poets: Frost, Longfellow, Poe, etc.
- *How to Teach Spelling,* Rudginsky & Haskell
- Globe, wall map of the physical world
- Classroom Christian history wall timeline
- Continued study of French or another foreign language

Methodology

- The notebook method (dividers for *Foundations, Orthography, Etymology, Syntax, Prosody,* and *Composition*) to record all instruction and daily practice in the skill-building practice routines in spelling, penmanship, composition, sentence analysis, and vocabulary.
- Extraction from the classic literature relevant and useful vocabulary for word study and interesting and engaging sentences for sentence analysis.
- Units of teacher instruction in composition writing, syntax, and etymology.
- Skill routines are established for weekly practice in spelling, etymology, penmanship, and composition.

THE NOAH PLAN © 2006 • FOUNDATION FOR AMERICAN CHRISTIAN EDUCATION

Quarter One	Quarter Two	Quarter Three	Quarter Four

Orthography consists of spelling, penmanship, and speaking. Spelling is taught from the book How to Teach Spelling *as a practice of dictation in applying spelling rules daily. Penmanship is also a practice of reviewing and building skill using the Palmer method with daily practice. These routines begin in week one and continue throughout the year. The notebook is used each day for recording instruction, recording the dictation and for practice.*

The **Prosody** component of English is taught through the Literature Curriculum program. See NPLG, 18–19.

Quarter One	Quarter Two	Quarter Three	Quarter Four
Syntax Review of basic sentence forms, first without modifiers, then with one-word modifiers, and finally with phrase modifiers. Diagrams of these forms are used as visual aids to reinforce awareness of relationships. Use review as necessary throughout the year.	*Syntax* Formal instruction in sentence patterns should now begin to include modifying clauses (embedded sentences). The diagram provides the important visual aid. These analytical processes will make it possible to achieve a fuller understanding of good literature.	*Syntax* The combining of two short sentences into one is an essential skill for good writing. Examples should be used until there is a full understanding of the process and a realization of how a sentence (which then becomes a clause) may be used to modify any appropriate part of another sentence.	*Syntax* Compound sentences from reading should be diagrammed, and divided into the smaller sentences from which they were constructed. Longer sentences, with three or more clauses, should be analyzed if students ask about them, or if they are difficult to understand, though the two-clause combination is the goal.
Etymology Words with prefixes and suffixes that have been taught are reviewed. Word analysis continues. Compound words are primary.	*Etymology* Word analysis continues. Grammatical terms should be analyzed. NPEG, 184.	*Etymology* Word analysis continues using words from all subjects.	*Etymology* The goal is a good understanding of words, with the specific knowledge of at least fifteen common prefixes, fifteen suffixes, and fifteen to twenty stems.
Composition Establishing a composition writing routine based on the four steps: pre-writing, drafting, revision, and presentation. Proofreading skills developed.	*Composition* Instruction in the basics of paragraphing. Formal book review and oral presentation. Scholar's Reading Lesson. Guided research paper.	*Composition* Guided research project in history and science written and presented. Refinement of writing using the four-step process. Sentence variety, using exact nouns and verbs.	*Composition* Use of the thesaurus, writing dialogue, usage, formal style. Mastery of punctuation, capitalization, and manuscript style. Proofreading habit required.

Teaching and Learning English in Sixth Grade

Purpose	Goals
Sixth grade English moves the student towards mastering spelling, grammar, penmanship, research, essay, and composition by the end of eighth grade. The middle grades emphasize the polishing of both writing and research skills in preparation for high school. The notebook method continues to organize and record excellent study and work habits. The continued use of classic literature and the Bible form an excellent model for inspiring the use of language.	• The use of language to express original thought and to state principles and understandings. • Growing competence in writing composition and essay and in doing research. • Increasing mastery of spelling, penmanship, vocabulary, and grammar. • Expanding vocabulary and ability to articulate persuasively. • Developing critical and logical reasoning skills. • Ability to master the elements of literature, poetry, Shakespeare, biography, and composition.

Principles and Leading Ideas

- The use of language in the propagation of the Gospel
- The role of England and the Bible in English on the Chain of Christianity®
- The Anglo-Saxon love of liberty and struggle with Norman oppression
- Romance languages on the Chain of Christianity

Books and Materials Essential to Sixth Grade English

- *The Noah Plan® English Language Curriculum Guide* (NPEG)
- *The Noah Plan Literature Curriculum Guide* (NPLG)
- *The Noah Plan Reading Curriculum Guide* (NPRG)
- *American Dictionary of the English Language,* Facsimile Edition (Webster's 1828 *Dictionary*)
- The Sixth Grade Classics: *Epistles*—the Bible as literature; *Sir Walter Scott: Wizard of the North*, Pearle Henriksen Schultz; *A Christmas Carol,* Charles Dickens; *Ivanhoe,* Sir Walter Scott; *Twelfth Night,* William Shakespeare; Poets: Longfellow; patriotic poetry by Howe, Holmes, Longfellow
- *How to Teach Spelling,* Rudginsky & Haskell
- Globe, wall map of the physical world
- Classroom Christian history wall timeline
- Continued study of French or another foreign language
- Latin, NPEG, 121–125

Methodology

- The notebook method (dividers for *Foundations, Orthography, Etymology, Syntax, Prosody,* and *Composition*) to record all instruction and daily practice in the skill-building practice routines in spelling, penmanship, composition, sentence analysis, and vocabulary.
- Extraction from the classic literature relevant and useful vocabulary for word study and interesting and engaging sentences for sentence analysis.
- Units of teacher instruction in composition writing, syntax, and etymology.
- Skill routines are established for weekly practice in spelling, etymology, penmanship, and composition.

Quarter One	Quarter Two	Quarter Three	Quarter Four

Orthography consists of spelling, penmanship, and speaking. Spelling is taught from the book How to Teach Spelling *as a practice of dictation in applying spelling rules daily. Penmanship is also a practice of reviewing and building skill using the Palmer method with daily practice. These routines begin in week one and continue throughout the year. The notebook is used each day for recording instruction, recording the dictation and for practice.*

The **Prosody** *component of English is taught through the Literature curriculum program.* See NPLG, 20–21. The literature program is the backbone and basis for all English instruction including vocabulary, composition, and syntax.

Quarter One	Quarter Two	Quarter Three	Quarter Four
Syntax Review essentials from the fifth grade and add analysis of sentences with three and four clauses. If the basics have been learned, progress from this point on will be easy, but it must not be taken for granted.	**Syntax** Continue analyzing sentences, drawing material almost exclusively from two sources: literature and the students' own writing.	**Syntax** Continue sentence analysis. Students are invited to diagram some of their own best sentences and sentences that they have found in their reading.	**Syntax** The teacher should be alert for sentences that might not be completely understood from the literature, the Bible, or other subjects, and analyzes these with the students.
Etymology Words from all subject areas should also be analyzed. A good etymological dictionary should be introduced.	**Etymology** Word analysis continues. Especially interesting words for class analysis and discussion such as *influence* and *influenza* bring special interest to 6th graders.	**Etymology** Emphasis should be on mastering NPEG 120–128 as students collect prefixes, suffixes, and roots upon which to build their analysis skills.	**Etymology** Students should know twenty-five or thirty prefixes, twenty-five or thirty suffixes, and at least forty stems (mostly from Latin but some from Greek and a few from Germanic or other sources).
Composition Establish a composition writing routine based on the four steps: pre-writing, drafting, revision, and presentation. Students should be growing in proofreading skills and in presentation. Book review written first quarter.	**Composition** Review of the basics of paragraphing. Composition writing routine continues. Formal book review and oral presentation required.	**Composition** Composition routine continues. Scholar's Reading Lesson used to develop composition skills. Original speech-making is introduced and practiced.	**Composition** Continue composition routine with presentation. Refinement of writing using the four steps is the goal.

Teaching and Learning English in Seventh Grade

Purpose	*Goals*
Seventh grade English moves the student towards mastering spelling, grammar, penmanship, research, essay, and composition by the end of eighth grade. The middle grades emphasize the polishing of both writing and research skills in preparation for high school. The notebook method continues to organize and record excellent study and work habits. The continued use of classic literature and the Bible form an excellent model for inspiring the use of language.	• The use of language to express original thought and to state principles and understandings. • Growing competence in writing composition and essay and in doing research. • Increasing mastery of spelling, penmanship, vocabulary, and grammar. • Expanding vocabulary and ability to articulate with persuasion. • Developing critical and logical reasoning skills. • Ability to master the elements of literature, poetry, Shakespeare, biography, and composition.

Principles and Leading Ideas

- Language mastery forwards the propagation of the Gospel
- The role of England and the Bible in English on the Chain of Christianity®
- Identifying the literary types in the Bible
- Romance languages on the Chain of Christianity

Books and Materials Essential to Seventh Grade English

- *The Noah Plan® English Language Curriculum Guide* (NPEG)
- *The Noah Plan Literature Curriculum Guide* (NPLG)
- *The Noah Plan Reading Curriculum Guide* (NPRG)
- *American Dictionary of the English Language,* Facsimile Edition (Webster's 1828 *Dictionary*)
- The Seventh Grade Literature Program: literary types including poetry; the essay, speeches, the short story, the novel—*David Copperfield,* Charles Dickens; Drama; Biography—*Abe Lincoln Grows Up,* Carl Sandburg; Autobiography—*The Autobiography of Benjamin Franklin*
- *How to Teach Spelling,* Rudginsky & Haskell
- Globe, wall map of the physical world
- Classroom Christian history wall timeline
- Continued study of French or another foreign language
- Latin, NPEG, 121–125

Methodology

- The notebook method (dividers for *Foundations, Orthography, Etymology, Syntax, Prosody,* and *Composition*) to record all instruction and daily practice in the skill-building practice routines in spelling, penmanship, composition, sentence analysis, and vocabulary.
- Extraction from the classic literature relevant and useful vocabulary for word study and interesting and engaging sentences for sentence analysis.
- Units of teacher instruction in composition, writing, syntax, and etymology.
- Skill routines are established for weekly practice in spelling, etymology, penmanship, and composition.

Quarter One	Quarter Two	Quarter Three	Quarter Four
Orthography *consists of spelling, penmanship, and speaking. Spelling is taught from the book* How to Teach Spelling *as a practice of dictation in applying spelling rules daily. Penmanship is also a practice of reviewing and building skill using the Palmer method with daily practice. These routines begin in week one and continue throughout the year. The notebook is used each day for recording instruction, recording the dictation and for practice.*			
The **Prosody** *component of English is taught through the Literature Curriculum program.* See NPLG, 22–23.			
Syntax The full nature and extent of grammar should be set forth as a body of knowledge to be mastered in seventh grade. The three **grammatical means** (word order, inflections, and function or relational words) should be explained and demonstrated. **Sentence modes** should be identified. The **nine relational functions** (gender, number, person, case, tense, mood, voice, modification, and comparison) are explained and illustrated. NPEG, 162–179.	*Syntax* **Basic sentence types** are reviewed and the grammatical means and relationships shown. Combinations of sentences with subordinate or dependent or relative clauses, with independent or coordinate clauses, and with mixtures of the two are demonstrated. Through the elementary years the emphasis has been on patterns, teaching largely by imitation and authority. Now **understanding** becomes the primary objective.	*Syntax* Understanding is achieved by using the familiar structures and relationships, reinforced with **visual diagrams**. Sentences of considerable complexity from literature should be **analyzed** and explained. Such sentences from literature should be rewritten, reorganized, broken into shorter sentences that are recombined, while questions of form and arrangement are considered.	*Syntax* The students **write often** and rewrite to gain conscious control of sentence patterns, order of clauses, and effective emphasis. **Analyze sentences** with three or four clauses drawing from literature and from students' own writing, diagramming the best selections from literature. Goal: (1) Students can analyze, divide and, in general, freely manipulate sentences with as many as four clauses. (2) Students can write sentences of three clauses effectively.
Etymology Word study should continue at an increased rate. The Germanic origin of English, the three hundred years of French rule of England, and the direct and indirect influx of Latin and Greek words are reviewed.	*Etymology* Word study continues with analysis by prefix, stem, and suffix, with words drawn from texts of all subjects taught in the seventh grade. Mastery of NPEG, 126–131.	*Etymology* Word study continues with analysis by prefix, stem, and suffix, with words drawn from texts of all subjects taught in the seventh grade. Mastery of NPEG, 126–131.	*Etymology* Word study continues with analysis by prefix, stem, and suffix, with words drawn from texts of all subjects taught in the seventh grade. Mastery of NPEG, 126–131.
Composition Pre-writing is a habit by seventh grade with drafting, revising, and presentation forming the writing process. NPEG, 245. Proofreading becomes a habit.	*Composition* Teach types of writing – personal, analytical, persuasive, and précis. Teach usage and formal style, writing dialogue, letter writing, the Scholars Reading Lesson, science project.	*Composition* Research project and presentation is practiced this quarter. Refinement of writing using the four steps is ongoing.	*Composition* Original speechmaking is studied in preparation for the eighth grade and the requirement of the eighth grade speech—the culminating English project of middle school.

Teaching and Learning English in Eighth Grade

Purpose	Goals
Eighth grade brings the student to mastery in spelling, grammar, penmanship, research, essay, and composition. Writing and research skills are polished in preparation for high school. The notebook method continues to organize and record excellent study and work habits. The continued use of classic literature and the Bible form an excellent model for inspiring the use of language with higher levels of abstract thinking, reasoning, and analysis.	• The use of language to express original thought and to state principles and understandings. • Mastery of writing skills and research shown in the final research paper. • Mastery of spelling, penmanship, vocabulary, and grammar. • Expanding vocabulary and ability to articulate with persuasion. • Developing critical and logical reasoning skill. • Literary analysis in the study of literature, poetry, Shakespeare, biography, and composition. • Preparation of the final eighth grade speech to be given before an audience.

Principles and Leading Ideas

- The development of American English and the value of the Webster 1828 *Dictionary*
- The use of word studies in mastering subjects
- Tracing the development of the philosophy of liberty and the role of language
- Comparison of Christianity and chivalry
- Pagan and Christian themes in literature

Books and Materials Essential to Eighth Grade English

- *The Noah Plan® English Language Curriculum Guide* (NPEG)
- *The Noah Plan Literature Curriculum Guide* (NPLG)
- *The Noah Plan Reading Curriculum Guide* (NPRG)
- *American Dictionary of the English Language,* Facsimile Edition (Webster's 1828 *Dictionary*)
- The Eighth Grade Literature Program: *A Wonder Book*, Nathanial Hawthorne; *The Walls of Windy Troy*, Brayer; *Ben Hur: A Tale of the Christ,* Wallace; *The Story of King Arthur and His Knights,* Pyle; *Idylls of the King,* Tennyson; *Hamlet,* Shakespeare; *The Courtship of Miles Standish,* Longfellow
- *How to Teach Spelling,* Rudginsky & Haskell
- Globe, wall map of the physical world; classroom Christian history wall timeline
- Continued study of French or another foreign language

Methodology

- The notebook method (dividers for *Foundations, Orthography, Etymology, Syntax, Prosody,* and *Composition*) to record all instruction and daily practice in the skill-building practice routines in spelling, penmanship, composition, sentence analysis and vocabulary.
- Extraction from the classic literature relevant and useful vocabulary for word study and interesting and engaging sentences for sentence analysis.
- Units of teacher instruction in composition writing, syntax, and etymology.
- Skill routines are established for weekly practice in spelling, etymology, penmanship, and composition.

Quarter One	Quarter Two	Quarter Three	Quarter Four
Orthography consists of spelling, penmanship, and speaking. Spelling is taught from the book How to Teach Spelling *as a practice of dictation in applying spelling rules daily. Penmanship is also a practice of reviewing and building skill using the Palmer method with daily practice. These routines begin in week one and continue throughout the year. The notebook is used each day for recording instruction, recording the dictation and for practice.*			
The **Prosody** *component of English is taught through the Literature Curriculum program.* See NPLG, 24–25. The extensive literature study is the basis of all English instruction in etymology, composition, and syntax. Writing assignments relate to the themes, characterization, and literary analysis of the literature program.			
Syntax The eighth grade fully explores active and passive voice structures. Transformations from active to passive and passive to active are practiced in a variety of tenses. All tenses are clarified and practiced.	*Syntax* Mood is explored, at least the indicative and conditional. The subjunctive is undertaken if the students are ready for it. The direct object in an active voice structure becomes the subject in a passive voice structure.	*Syntax* The subject in the active voice becomes the agent in the passive (if not omitted), and, when present, becomes an indirect object of the preposition *by*. Thus: "The pitcher hurled the ball," becomes "The ball was hurled by the pitcher."	*Syntax* In addition to the active-passive transformation, the diagram should be used to illustrate and clarify modification when it exists in abundance, as it often does in good writing.
Etymology Word study continues, with analysis by prefix, stem, and suffix, with words drawn from texts of all subjects taught in the eighth grade and from the students' own writing.	*Etymology* Assignments in analysis are given, with a good, simple etymological dictionary as a standard tool. By now every student has such a dictionary for regular use and assignments lead him to be familiar with it.	*Etymology* English began as a Germanic language, but most of the new words are of Latin or Greek origin. To ignore this aspect of the study of English is to condemn the student to ignorance or to vague, uncertain knowledge of the language he will be using the rest of his life.	*Etymology* Word study continues with analysis by prefix, stem, and suffix, with words drawn from texts of all subjects taught in the seventh grade. Mastery of NPEG, 116–131.
Composition Formal compositions written, revised, and resubmitted weekly for grading. Usage, formal style, and dialogue writing.	*Composition* Coherence emphasized (transitional words and sentences, order or details—spatial, chronological, importance, etc.). Creative writing for enjoyment.	*Composition* Continue weekly composition assignments for grading. Research paper preparation. Debate introduced.	*Composition* Original eighth grade speech required—the culminating English project of middle school.

Teaching and Learning English in Ninth Grade

Purpose	Goals
English study in the ninth grade is placed upon the major theme of the literature study—*Tracing the Nobler Stream of Liberty.* Through six ages of literature—Anglo-Saxon, Anglo-Norman, Wycliffe-Chaucer, English Reformation, Elizabethan, and Puritan—the student compiles a notebook of literary analysis and writes essays expounding upon the theme.	• Developing an understanding of the progress of the ideals of Christian liberty as seen in the literature from the Anglo-Saxon era through the Puritan. • Writing analysis and essay to develop the theme. • The "Reading with Reason" cultural analysis study • Developing a research paper on a related topic. • The refinement of grammar mastery.

Principles and Leading Ideas

- The nobler strain of liberty seen in Anglo-Saxon literature
- The mastery of themes and ideals through the notebook method
- Literature and poetry were meant for enjoyment through memorization and presentation.

Books and Materials Essential to Ninth Grade English

- *The Noah Plan® English Language Curriculum Guide* (NPEG)
- *The Noah Plan Literature Curriculum Guide* (NPLG)
- *The Noah Plan Reading Curriculum Guide* (NPRG)
- *American Dictionary of the English Language,* Facsimile Edition (Webster's 1828 *Dictionary*)
- *Beowulf,* translated by Raffel; Caedmon; Cynewulf; "The Seafarer"; Selections from Asser's *Life of King Alfred* and Malory's *Morte d'Arthur* and "The Pearl"; Selections from Wycliffe's Bible; Chaucer's Prologue to *Canterbury Tales; Foxe's Book of Martyrs; Faerie Queene,* Spenser; *Voyages of the English Nation,* Hakluyt; *Essays,* Bacon; Poetry of Donne, Herbert; *Richard II,* Shakespeare; *Portable Milton,* Poetry, Essays, Epic; *The Pilgrim's Progress,* Bunyan

Methodology

- The notebook method (dividers for each of the six periods of literature: *Anglo-Saxon, Anglo-Norman, Wycliffe-Chaucer, English Reformation, Elizabethan,* and *Puritan*)
- Extraction from the classic literature relevant and useful vocabulary for word study and interesting and engaging sentences for sentence analysis
- Units of teacher instruction in, syntax and research
- Oral presentation practice regularly

Quarter One	Quarter Two	Quarter Three	Quarter Four

Composition

Weekly essays in literature and assigned research. Writing projects such as the research paper, an allegory, and poetry related to particular selections. Example: the writing of a sonnet, and of a Spenserian stanza. Primary source readings and research.

Literature
See NPLG, 26–27.

Quarter One	Quarter Two	Quarter Three	Quarter Four
Anglo Saxon Literature 450–1066 • Introduction to *Tracing the Nobler Theme of Liberty* • *Beowulf*—notebook study • Caedmon; Alfred the Great; Bede; Boethius's *Consolation; The Anglo-Saxon Chronicle;* "The Seafarer" ***Anglo-Norman Literature 1066–1350*** • Introduction to Anglo-Norman period • Malory's *Morte d'Arthur; When Knights were Bold;* • Magna Charta, "The Pearl"	***Wycliffe and Chaucer 1350–1400*** • Introduction to the age of Wycliffe and Chaucer • *Piers Plowman,* William Langland • John Wycliffe • *The Canterbury Tales* and Geoffrey Chaucer—notebook study ***English Reformation 1400–1550*** • Introduction to the English Reformation • Erasmus, Bilney, Tyndale, Cranmer, Ridley, and Latimer • *Foxe's Book of Martyrs*	***Elizabethan Literature 1550–1620*** • Introduction to the age of Elizabeth • The Geneva Bible • Edmund Spenser, *The Faerie Queene Book I*—notebook study • Michael Drayton, "To the Virginia Voyage" • William Shakespeare and *Richard II*—notebook study • Francis Bacon *Essays* • Richard Hakluyt • Research paper	***Puritan Age 1620–1660*** • Introduction to the Puritan age • John Milton and *Paradise Lost*—notebook study • George Herbert, poetry; John Donne, poetry • John Bunyan's *Pilgrim's Progress*—notebook study and writing an allegory
Syntax Review fundamentals of syntax: the nine relational factors of syntax and the three grammatical means of syntax, stressing case, voice, mood, and modification.	***Syntax*** Moods thoroughly taught: indicative, conditional, subjunctive, and modal.	***Syntax*** Gerunds, participles, and appositives diagrammed. Double function explored. Syntax of a foreign language.	***Etymology*** Continue to develop analytical principles of word formation studying word families.

Reading with Reason: Cultural Analysis NPRG, 31–34: The Reach of Rome; The Hebrew Question; Origins

<u>Books</u>: The life and writings of Cicero, *Pillar of Iron,* Caldewell; *Quo Vadis?* Sienkiewicz; *The Agony and the Ecstasy,* Stone; Virgil; *Death Comes for the Archbishop,* Cather; *The Greek Treasure,* Stone; *The Source,* Michener; *Exodus,* Uris; *The Diary of Anne Frank; Berlin Diary,* Shirer; *The Merchant of Venice,* Shakespeare; *Ivanhoe,* Sir Walter Scott; Darwin; *Genesis Flood,* Morris;

<u>Films</u>: *Ben Hur; Weapons of the Spirit; Inherit the Wind.*

<u>Art</u>: Leonardo da Vinci's masterpieces and inventions; Michelangelo's *Moses, David, Creation,* Sistine Chapel

<u>Music</u>: *The Pines of Rome* and *Messiah*

Teaching and Learning English in Tenth Grade

Purpose	*Goals*
English study in the tenth grade is placed upon the major theme of the literature study—*England Relinquishes Her Christian Heritage* through five ages of literature: Restoration, Eighteenth Century, Romanticism, Victorian, Twentieth Century. The student compiles a notebook of literary analysis and writes essays expounding upon the theme.	• Developing an understanding of the decline of the ideals of Christian liberty reflected in the literature from the Restoration through twentieth century. • Writing analysis and essay to develop the theme. • The "Reading with Reason" cultural analysis study • Developing a research paper on a related topic. • The refinement of grammar mastery.

Principles and Leading Ideas

- Literature reflects the heart of man—from 1660 through the twentieth century, literature reflects the acceptance of secular, atheistic philosophies in place of the Christian ideal.
- The mastery of themes and ideals through the notebook method
- Enjoyment of sharing literature and poetry through memorization and presentation.

Books and Materials Essential to Tenth Grade English

- *The Noah Plan® English Language Curriculum Guide* (NPEG)
- *The Noah Plan Literature Curriculum Guide* (NPLG)
- *The Noah Plan Reading Curriculum Guide* (NPRG)
- *American Dictionary of the English Language,* Facsimile Edition (Webster's 1828 *Dictionary*)
- Locke and Sidney on government; *The Diary,* Pepys; *Principia,* Newton; *Rules for Literature,* Dryden; *Gulliver's Travels,* Swift; *Life of Johnson,* Boswell; *Robinson Crusoe,* Defoe; the writings of Addison, Steele, and Blackstone; poetry of Cowper, Gray, Burns, Blake, Wordsworth, Coleridge, Byron, Shelley, Keats, Lamb, the Brownings, Thompson, Kipling, Conrad, Masefield, Noyes, Housman, Yeats, Auden, Thomas, Eliot; *The Lady of the Lake,* Scott; *Idylls of the King,* Tennyson; *Pride and Prejudice,* Austen; writings of Wells, Galsworthy, Shaw, Synge, Strachey, Lewis, Orwell, Woolf, Mansfield, Forster, Greene, Huxley, Snow, Tolkien; *Peter Pan,* Barrie

Methodology

- The notebook method (dividers for each of the five periods of literature: *Restoration, Eighteenth Century, Romanticism, Victorian,* and *Twentieth Century*)
- Extraction from the classic literature relevant and useful vocabulary for word study and interesting and engaging sentences for sentence analysis
- Units of teacher instruction in syntax and research
- Oral presentation practice regularly

Quarter One	Quarter Two	Quarter Three	Quarter Four

Composition

Weekly essays in literature and assigned research. Writing projects such as the research paper, an allegory, and poetry related to particular selections. Primary source readings and research.

Literature
See NPLG, 28–29.

Restoration Literature 1660–1700 • Introduction to the Restoration • Influence of Puritan writers Milton and Bunyan • John Dryden's *Rules for Literature*; poetry • Algernon Sidney discourses concerning government • John Locke readings • Samuel Pepys, *The Diary* • Newton's *Principia* ***Eighteenth Century 1700–1800*** • Introduction to Eighteenth Century history and the age of prose	***Eighteenth Century, cont.*** • Alexander Pope and classicism • *Gulliver's Travels*, Jonathan Swift • Addison and Steele • Samuel Johnson and the dictionary • *Life of Johnson*, James Boswell • Edmund Burke, Blackstone, Gibbon • Poetry: Gray, Cowper, Burns, Blake • *Robinson Crusoe*, Daniel Defoe ***Romanticism 1700–1850*** • Introduction to Romanticism • Wordsworth, selections; Coleridge; Byron, Shelley, Keats, Lamb	***Romanticism, cont.*** • *The Lady of the Lake*, Walter Scott • *Pride and Prejudice*, Jane Austen ***Victorian Age 1850–1900*** • Introduction to the Victorian Age • *Idylls of the King*, Tennyson; the Brownings, Thompson • *Great Expectations*, Charles Dickens • *Silas Marner, Adam Bede*, George Eliot; Bronte sisters, Robert Louis Stevenson • Macaulay, Carlyle, historians • Ruskin, prose	***The Twentieth Century 1900–Present*** • Influences of socialism in literature • Rise of the Irish school of writers • Kipling, Wells, Galsworthy, Barrie, Conrad, Masefield, Noyes, Housman, Shaw, Yeats, Synge, Strachey, C. S. Lewis, T. S. Eliot, Auden • Thomas, Orwell, Woolf, Mansfield • Forster, Greene, Huxley • Snow, Tolkien • The ideology conflict of Christianity versus socialism
Syntax With the emphasis on great literature and frequent writing, excellent sentences from literature are analyzed.	***Syntax*** With the emphasis on great literature and frequent writing, excellent sentences from literature are analyzed.	***Syntax*** With the emphasis on great literature and frequent writing, excellent sentences from literature are analyzed.	***Syntax*** With the emphasis on great literature and frequent writing, excellent sentences from literature are analyzed.

Reading with Reason: Cultural Analysis NPRG, 31–34: The Second Creation; Revolutions; Frontiers

<u>Books</u>: *The Noah Plan® Reading Curriculum Guide*, Shirley; *The Big Fisherman*, Douglas; *The Robe*, Douglas; *Dear and Beloved Physician*, Caldwell; *The Talisman*, Scott; *A Tale of Two Cities*, Dickens; *The Scarlet Pimpernel*, Orczy; *Three Revolutions*, John Q. Adams (translator); *The Spy*, Cooper; *Christopher Columbus, Mariner*, Morison; *Apollo to the Moon*, Kennedy; *Alone*, Byrd; *Seven Came Through*, Rickenbacker; *Last of the Mohicans*, Cooper; *Out of the Silent Planet*, Lewis; *John of the Mountains*, Muir; *My Antonia*, Cather.

<u>Films</u>: *Chariots of Fire*; *The Manchurian Candidate*; *Amadeus*; *The Man Who Shot Liberty Valence*

<u>Art</u>: Frescoes of Fra Angelico; Paintings of Benjamin West; *Columbus departing from Palos*, Leutze

<u>Music</u>: "The Marseillaise"; *The New World Symphony*; Bach selections

Teaching and Learning English in Eleventh Grade

Purpose	Goals
English study in the eleventh grade is placed upon the major theme of the literature study—*Planting the Seed of the American Christian Republic* through five ages of literature: *Restoration, Eighteenth Century, Romanticism, Victorian,* and *Twentieth Century.* The student compiles a notebook of literary analysis and writes essays expounding upon the theme.	• Developing an understanding of the planting of the American Christian republic reflected in the literature from the Colonial era through the Federal period • Writing analysis and essay to develop the theme • The "Reading with Reason" cultural analysis study • Developing an oration on a related topic

Principles and Leading Ideas

- Literature reflects the heart of man—America's Christian ideals reflected in the planting of the nation
- The mastery of themes and ideals through the notebook method
- Enjoyment of sharing literature and poetry through memorization and presentation

Books and Materials Essential to Eleventh Grade English

- *The Noah Plan® English Language Curriculum Guide* (NPEG)
- *The Noah Plan Literature Curriculum Guide* (NPLG)
- *The Noah Plan Reading Curriculum Guide* (NPRG)
- *American Dictionary of the English Language,* Facsimile Edition (Webster's 1828 *Dictionary*)
- *The Noah Plan Literature Curriculum Guide,* Slater; *T & L; CHOC I & II; C & P; B & C; Captain John Smith's America,* Lankford; *Of Plimoth Plantation,* Bradford; *Good News from Virginia,* Whitaker; "Come Over and Help Us," Slater; "Fundamental Orders of Connecticut, Hooker; *Magnalia Christi Americana,* Mather; *The Works of Anne Bradstreet,* Hensley; *The Bay Psalm Book; New England Primer; The Autobiography of Benjamin Franklin;* "The Rights of the British Colonies," Otis; "Farmer's Letter," Dickinson; "The Rights of the Colonists," Samuel Adams; "Timidity," John Adams; Declaration of Independence; "Give me Liberty," Henry; "Farewell Speech," Washington; Writings of the Revolution: Journal of Major George Washington. Letters of the Revolution: Mercy Warren, John and Abigail Adams; "To His Excellency General Washington," Wheatley; poems of Philip Freneau; "The Battle of the Kegs," Hopkinson; "Hasty Pudding," Barlow; selections from State Papers; *The Sketch Book, Knickerbocker's History of New York, Tales of the Alhambra,* Irving; poems of William Cullen Bryant and Edgar Allan Poe; *The Deerslayer,* Cooper.

Methodology

- The notebook method (dividers for each of the three periods of literature: *Colonial Period, Revolutionary Period,* and *Federal Period*)
- Extraction from the classic literature relevant and useful vocabulary for word study and interesting and engaging sentences for sentence analysis
- Units of teacher instruction in syntax and research
- Oral presentation practice regularly

Quarter One	Quarter Two	Quarter Three	Quarter Four

Composition
Weekly essays in literature and assigned research. Primary source readings and research.

Literature
See NPLG pp 28–29.

Quarter One	Quarter Two	Quarter Three	Quarter Four
Colonial Period 1607–1765 • Introduction to American literature • Captain John Smith • William Bradford, *Of Plimoth Plantation* • William Penn • John Winthrop, "Little Speech on Liberty" • Missionary writers: Whitaker, Eliot, Gookin • Colonial Clergy: Thomas Hooker, Jonathan Edwards, Cotton Mather, Samuel Sewall	***Colonial Period, cont.*** • Poetry and colonial best sellers: Anne Bradstreet; *The Bay Psalm Book; New England Primer* • The influence of the clergy ***Revolutionary Period 1765–1787*** • The pew and the pulpit: election sermons— Mayhew, Davies, Witherspoon • Literature in Statesmanship: James Otis; John Dickinson; Samuel Adams; John Adams; Thomas Jefferson	***Revolutionary Period, cont.*** • Famous Speeches: Henry; Washington • Greatest Statesmen: Benjamin Franklin, *Autobiography; The Journal of Major George Washington* • Letters: Mercy Warren, John and Abigail Adams • Poetry of the Revolution: Wheatley; Hopkinson, Barlow	***The Federal Period 1787–1840*** • First Fruits of the Republic: Washington Irving, biographer and first man of letters • Essayist William Cullen Bryant • Edgar Allan Poe • James Fenimore Cooper, *The Deerslayer*: thorough study of the novel by the notebook method
Syntax With the emphasis on great literature and frequent writing, excellent sentences from literature are analyzed.	*Syntax* With the emphasis on great literature and frequent writing, excellent sentences from literature are analyzed.	*Syntax* With the emphasis on great literature and frequent writing, excellent sentences from literature are analyzed.	*Syntax* With the emphasis on great literature and frequent writing, excellent sentences from literature are analyzed.

Reading with Reason: Cultural Analysis NPRG, 31–34: Wars; Statesmanship; The Purpose of Science

Books: *The Noah Plan Reading Curriculum Guide,* Shirley; *The Tree of Liberty,* Page; *Drums,* Boyd; *Patton: A Genius for War,* d'Este; *An American Life,* Reagan; *The Republic,* Plato; *The Prince,* Machiavelli; *The Glory and the Dream,* Musmanno; *Matthew Fontaine Maury: Scientist of the Sea,* Williams; *Men under the Sea,* Ellsburg

Films: *Bridge on the River Kwai; Casablanca; Mr. Smith Goes to Washington*

Art: The Peale family paintings. Photography

Music: *Hail Columbia; The 1812 Overture; The New World Symphony*

Teaching and Learning English in Twelfth Grade

Purpose	Goals
English study in the twelfth grade is placed upon the major theme of the literature study—*America Falls Away from Her Christian Founding and Character* through three ages of literature: the Civil War period, the National Expansion period, and the Twentieth Century. The student compiles a notebook of literary analysis and writes essays expounding upon the theme.	• Developing an understanding of the falling away from America's Christian founding and character reflected in the literature from the Colonial era through the Federal period • Writing analysis and essay to develop the theme. • The "Reading with Reason" cultural analysis study • Developing an oration on a related topic

Principles and Leading Ideas

- Literature reflects the heart of man—America falls away from her Christian founding and character
- The mastery of themes and ideals through the notebook method
- Enjoyment of sharing literature and poetry through memorization and presentation

Books and Materials Essential to Twelfth Grade English

- *The Noah Plan® English Language Curriculum Guide* (NPEG)
- *The Noah Plan Literature Curriculum Guide* (NPLG)
- *The Noah Plan Reading Curriculum Guide* (NPRG)
- *American Dictionary of the English Language,* Facsimile Edition (Webster's 1828 *Dictionary*)
- *T & L; CHOC I & II; C & P; B & C; How Should We Then Live?* Schaeffer; The Clay-Calhoun Debate; The Hayne-Webster debate; *The Glory and the Dream,* Musmanno; *Evangeline,* Longfellow; *The Oregon Trail,* Parkmen; *The Country of the Pointed Firs,* Jewett; *The Notorious Jumping Frog of Calaveras County,* Twain; *The Outcasts of Poker Flat,* Harte; *The Thread that Runs so True,* Stuart; poetry of Whittier, Holmes, Whitman, Poe, Sandburg, Lanier, Riley, Field, Dickinson, Masters, Longfellow, Robinson, Frost, Eliot, and Millay; essays of Emerson, Thoreau, Audubon; readings from Faulkner, Fitzgerald, Hemingway

Methodology

- The notebook method (dividers for each of the three periods of literature: *The Civil War Period, The National Expansion Period,* and *The Twentieth Century*)
- Extraction from the classic literature relevant and useful vocabulary for word study and interesting and engaging sentences for sentence analysis
- Units of teacher instruction in syntax and research
- Oral presentation practice regularly

Quarter One	Quarter Two	Quarter Three	Quarter Four

Composition

Weekly essays in literature and assigned research. Primary source readings and research for senior thesis assignment. Presentation and defense of the senior thesis before a review committee.

Literature

See NPLG pp 28–29.

The Civil War Period 1840–1876	*The Civil War, cont.*	*National Expansion Period 1876–1925*	*The Twentieth century 1925–Present*
• Political Orators: debating the balance between state and nation • Henry Clay, John Calhoun, Daniel Webster • Abraham Lincoln • Robert E. Lee • Poets: Longfellow, Whittier, Holmes, Lowell, Lanier, Whitman, Emerson	• Prose writers of the Republic: Emerson, Holmes, Lowell, Thoreau, Audubon, Hawthorne • Debating and researching the two great elements of testing the Christian Principle of American Political Union: Local self-government and national union	• Maine: Sarah Orne Jewett, • New York City: O. Henry • The South: Joel Chandler Harris • Mississippi: Mark Twain • Westward movement: Francis Parkman • California: Bret Harte • Midwest: Willa Cather • Poetry: Riley, Field, Dickinson, Lanier, Masters, Sandburg, Frost	• Decline of Biblical standards of life and literature; the lost generation • Novelists: Fitzgerald, Hemingway, Faulkner, Steinbeck, London, Sinclair, Buck • Biography: Booker T. Washington, Carver, Helen Keller, Byrd, Lindbergh, MacArthur • Poets: Millay, Masters, Robinson, Eliot, Frost, Sandburg • Drama: Williams, Wilder, Miller, Anderson, Sherwood
Syntax With the emphasis on great literature and frequent writing, excellent sentences from literature are analyzed.	*Syntax* With the emphasis on great literature and frequent writing, excellent sentences from literature are analyzed.	*Syntax* With the emphasis on great literature and frequent writing, excellent sentences from literature are analyzed.	*Syntax* With the emphasis on great literature and frequent writing, excellent sentences from literature are analyzed.

Reading with Reason: Cultural Analysis NPRG, 31–34: Liberty and Slavery; Letters; Senior Thesis

Books: *The Noah Plan® Reading Curriculum Guide,* Shirley; *Up from Slavery,* Washington; *Narrative of the Captivity and Restoration of Mrs. Mary Rowlandson; The Book of Abigail and John*

Films: *84 Charing Cross Road; To Kill a Mockingbird*

Art: Photography—Brady's photography of the Civil War

Music: Beethoven's *Violin Concerto, Spirituals,* Brahms's *Piano Concerto*

Preparation, research, and presentation of the senior thesis: twenty-five page thesis to be presented and defended before a review committee.

A Teaching Plan for English Language in the Principle Approach

- Review the grade-level guideline in *The Noah Plan® Program Notebook*.

- Highlight the components of English to be developed.

- Examine the English Language Curriculum Chart for the grade level chosen (ex. Third Grade pp. 20–21).

- Highlight the details of each component to be taught in this unit.

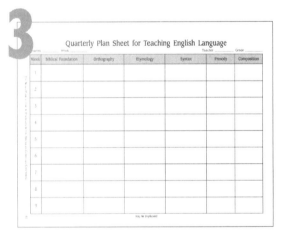

Use the teacher's Plan Sheet (p. 41) for the components of preparing to teach English Language.

Review this curriculum guide for direction in teaching components.

Write lesson plans referring to examples found at the beginning of each chapter.

Quarterly Plan Sheet for Teaching English Language

Quarter _____ Week _____ Teacher _____ Grade _____

Week	Biblical Foundation	Orthography	Etymology	Syntax	Prosody	Composition
1						
2						
3						
4						
5						
6						
7						
8						
9						

May Be Duplicated

Sample English Language Lesson Plan

Grade: _____ Date: _____ Teacher: _____ Component: ☐ Biblical Foundation
☐ Orthography
Skill Taught: _____ ☐ Etymology
☐ Syntax
Principle: _____ ☐ Prosody
☐ Composition
Biblical Reference: _____ Illustration: _____

_____

Materials/Resources: _____

_____

Structure of the Lesson

1. Introduce the purpose and goal of the lesson.

2. Review related skill or concept.

3. Present new principle and idea with appropriate methodology.

4. Require student practice, participation, and presentation.

5. Summarize, review, and evaluate.

THE NOAH PLAN® © 2006 • FOUNDATION FOR AMERICAN CHRISTIAN EDUCATION

Qualities of the Principle Approach Lesson in English

1. The lesson is framed by providential history and rooted in Biblical principles and presuppositions.

2. The methodology of the lesson springs from the Christian idea of the child.

3. The teacher takes the role of living textbook.

4. The lesson's guideposts are principles.

5. The classroom interchange has a reflective and reasoning nature.

6. An excellent vocabulary and literary quality are standard in the lesson.

7. The student records the lesson in a permanent, orderly manner.

8. The lesson's execution has a tutorial approach and expectation.

9. Christian graces and character are in evidence.

10. The student invests personal inquiry and productivity in accomplishing the goals of the lesson that are measurable.

11. The lesson satisfies the need to learn, particularly of furthering the knowledge of God.

Lesson plans to serve as models for each component of English are found in the respective chapters as follows:

For each component, see the following pages:

CHAPTER TWO
FOUNDATIONS OF ENGLISH:
PROVIDENTIAL HISTORY AND
BIBLICAL PRINCIPLES

Yet, O most blessed Spirit, pure lampe of light,
Eterenall spring of grace and wisedom trew,
Vouchsafe to shed into my barren spright
Some little drop of thy celestial dew,
That may my rhymes with sweet infuse embrew,
And give me words equall unto my thought,
To tell the marveiles by thy mercie wrought.

—Edmund Spenser, "An Hymne
of Heavenly Love," lines 43–49.

Sample English Language Lesson Plan

Grade: _____ 7 _____ Date: _4/15/98_ Teacher: _Adams_____ Component:

- ☒ Biblical Foundation
- ☐ Orthography
- ☐ Etymology
- ☐ Syntax
- ☐ Prosody
- ☐ Composition

Skill Taught: _Understanding the Nature of the English Language_

Principle: _God gave the English language a particular purpose._

Biblical Reference: _____ Illustration: _____

_____

Materials/Resources: _"The Foundations of English," ch. 2._

_____

Structure of the Lesson

1. Introduce the purpose and goal of the lesson.

   The English language has a unique history and purpose. The nature of English reflects the Providence of God in preparing a language to carry the Gospel to all parts of the world. The essence of the English language is its dual nature—the Anglo-Saxon and the classical aspects. English literary masterpieces are the best representations of the dual nature of English.

2. Review related skill or concept.

   Review the place of English on the Chain of Christianity® (see CHOC I, p. 6a). Review the role of English among languages. Review the timeline of the English language on page 60 in chapter 2. Notice the three stages of English—Old, Middle, and Modern. Notice the events on the timeline that formed the Old English—the Anglo-Saxon and the Norman invasions.

3. Present new principle and idea with appropriate methodology.

   English possesses a high level of versatility. God provided events and influences to form a language that would carry the Gospel around the world. The two basic aspects of English— the Anglo-Saxon or root language, and the classical elements through Latin and French— give English its versatility (pp. 53–63).

4. Require student practice, participation, and presentation.

   The verse from Beowulf presents the Anglo-Saxon nature of English. Read it several times identifying the Anglo-Saxon words (ch. 4). The verse from Milton represents the classical nature of English. Identify the characteristics of the classical elements.

5. Summarize, review, and evaluate.

   Write selected lines from the two verses evaluating the derivation of the words. Explain the contrast of the two and the value of each of the elements in giving English its versatility.

Introduction to Foundations of English
Providential History and Biblical Principles

Every subject in the Principle Approach® is taught from a Biblical worldview showing the role of the subject on the Chain of Christianity® moving westward as the Gospel progressed across the continents of history. Each subject is identified in the Bible, searching for the principles and setting of the subject in Scripture. This foundation is the stage upon which the subject is taught.

English has a peculiar role among languages and has a distinct history. By studying the role of English in history we can understand its role today and our purpose in teaching and learning it.

The chart of the Chain of Christianity on page 6A of *The Christian History of the Constitution of the United States: Christian Self-Government* shows us that English appeared at a crucial point in the progress of the Gospel. England is positioned at the edge of the continent of Europe both to reap the fruit of western thought and enterprise and to be insulated as a particular nation with a providential purpose.

English as a language developed in stages: Old English during the Anglo-Saxon and Anglo-Norman periods, Middle English in the medieval period, and Modern English after the Reformation and the rise of British supremacy. The language was influenced by battles and invasions, by exploration and industrialization, until it came to its present state standardized by Dr. Johnson's 1755 dictionary.

The Anglo-Saxon root language remains, but both French and Latin have played an important role in bringing English to its full development. According to William J. Long:

> It is this old vigorous Anglo-Saxon language which forms the basis of our modern English. If we read a paragraph from any good English book, and then analyze it as we would a flower, to see what it contains, we find two distinct classes of words. The first class, containing simple words expressing the common things of life, makes up the strong framework of our language. These words are like the stem and bare branches of a mighty oak, and if we look them up in the dictionary we find that almost invariably they come to us from our Anglo-Saxon ancestors.
>
> The second and larger class of words is made up of those that give grace, variety, and ornament to our speech. They are like the leaves and blossoms of the same tree, and when we examine their history we find that they come to us from the Celts, Romans, Normans, and other peoples with whom we have been in contact in the long years of our development.
>
> The most prominent characteristic of our present language, therefore, is its dual character. Its best qualities—strength, simplicity, directness—come from Anglo-Saxon sources; its enormous added wealth of expression, its comprehensiveness, its plastic adaptability to new conditions and ideas, are largely the result of additions from other languages, and especially of its gradual absorption of the French language after the Norman Conquest. It is this dual character, this combination of native and foreign, of innate and exotic elements, which accounts for the wealth of our English language and literature. To see it in concrete form, we should read in succession *Beowulf* and *Paradise Lost*, the two great epics which show the root and the flower of our literary development. (Long's English Literature, p. 29)

Our Literary Development

The Root:

From *Beowulf* (Note the preponderance of Anglo-Saxon words.)

. . . . day after day the music rang
Loud in that hall, the harp's rejoicing
Call and the poets' clear songs, sung
Of the ancient beginnings of us all, recalling
The Almighty making the earth, shaping
These beautiful plains marked off by oceans,
Then proudly setting the sun and the moon
To glow across the land and light it:
The corners of the earth were made lovely
    with trees
And leaves, made quick with life, with each
Of the nations who now move on its face.
    and then
As now warriors sang of their pleasure. . . .

(Translated by Burton Raffel, pp. 88–99)

The Flower:

From Paradise Lost (Note the large number of words derived from Latin and French.)

Now Morn her rosy steps in the eastern
    clime
Advancing, sowed the earth with orient pearl,
When Adam waked, so customed, for his sleep
Was airy light, from pure digestion bred,
And temperate vapors bland, which the only
    sound
Of leaves and fuming rill, Aurora's fan,
lightly dispersed, and the shrill matin song
Of birds on every bough; so much the more
His wonder was to find unawakened Eve
With tresses discomposed, and glowing cheek,
As through unquiet rest. . . .

(John Milton, Book V, Ll. 1–11)

The Study of Language in God's Providence

The study of language shows God's character and purpose for man as His image and glory. Latin, French, and English played particular roles communicating principles of liberty which brought forth the fruit of civil liberty for man.

In the elementary school, we teach the purpose and diversity of language, bringing our children to a love of language in all its delightful nuances and usefulness. Through this study we demonstrate that language reveals to us the character and love of God as He communicates with us and makes it possible for us to enjoy the satisfaction of meaningful communication with our fellow man. It also portrays God's providence as we see His hand in the history of language making His purposes work. The study of the elements of English, along with rudimentary French and, in fourth grade, Latin, defines the distinctive qualities of the languages and lays the foundation for all future language study.

In middle school, Latin is the major study of classic and modern languages, along with a growing command of English and its literary and rhetorical functions. The study of the Biblical foundation and providential history of language shows individuals used by God to bring the Bible into the language of the people and to express principles of liberty. This includes a study of the history of the Bible and the histories of both English and Latin in detail. The student then acquires a sense of God's purpose for the use of English today and thus a greater sense of the importance of language study and a proficiency in communication skills. At this level, language as communication is the emphasis in the classroom through discussion, debate, presentation of information, writing, research, and interpersonal communication.

In high school, the emphasis is on using language for learning and serving. The student will enter high school with the history and purpose of language well-learned and will continue his study of language with the basics mastered through a thorough study of English and American literature. Four years of one classical or modern language are suggested.

Liberty and Language

The two great endowments God gave man are liberty and language. God made man free at Creation by building into man the will, the intellect, the spirit, the conscience, and the image of Himself making it possible for man to have a relationship with God and others (Genesis 1:26, 27, 28; Genesis 2:5). The struggle of Satan to wrestle man's freedom from him is the basic conflict of history and of each life (Genesis 3:1–24; Romans 6:16). God sent Jesus to obtain victory for man in maintaining freedom (John 8:36). God gave language as a measure of making relationships with Himself and others and as a tool for subduing the earth (Genesis 2:19). Language has been used by God in His government of man to control evil (slavery, Genesis 11:7) and to obtain freedom, (Acts 2:7–8).

In God's Providence, language plays an important role on the Chain of Christianity® moving westward. God used Latin, French, and English to communicate principles of freedom and the Christian Scriptures. As American Christians today, we are charged with the task of communicating to the world our heritage of freedom and the Gospel message through our lives, work, and relationships. By studying history, Latin, French, and English we are able to define our role in God's providence personally for the direction of our lives and to refine and educate our use of language, spoken and written, to serve God's purpose.

The study of language has the goal of excellence in communication. Mastery of language is the foundation of excellence in any field of work. The command of language is essential to the propagation of the Gospel.

Language

Human speech: the expression of ideas by words or significant articulate sounds, for the communication of thought. Words arranged in sentences, written printed or engraved, and exhibited to the eye. The speech or expression of ideas of a particular nation. The type or manner of expression. Any manner of expressing thought.

Providence

1) The act of providing or preparing for future use.

2) Foresight.

3) The care and superintendence God gives His creation.

What Is Language?

The purpose of language is to express ideas. (Matthew 12:34) Its goal is to touch others with our thought—to communicate, reach, bring together. (Isaiah 1:18) Its structure is definite.

Language is individual to nations:

Ashdod	(Nehemiah 13:24)
Chaldee	(Daniel 1:4)
Egyptian	(Acts 2:10; Psalm 114:1)
Greek	(Luke 23:38; Acts 21:37)
Latin	(Luke 23:38; John 19:20)
Lycaonia	(Acts 14:11)
Parthia	(Acts 2:9–11)
Syria	(2 Kings 18:26; Ezra 4:7; Daniel 2:4)

There are 5,000 languages in the world today. Each language has a grammar, syntax, spelling system, vocabulary, sound system, and a character of its own. Language is spoken, written, and non-verbal.

The Origin of Language

Language began in eternity with God; He spoke the world into existence and spoke directly with man after Creation. (Genesis 1:26; Genesis 1:3; Exodus 8:1) Language was a gift to man not given to other creatures. (Genesis 2:19) "Human language is absolutely distinct from any system of communication in animals. Non-human vocables . . . do not . . . name, discuss, abstract, or symbolize . . . as true language." (George Gaylord Simpson, "The Biological Nature of Man," Science, Vol. 152, April 1966, p. 476.)

Language was given to man whole, not evolving grunts, signs to words and sentences. The oldest languages known are the most complex with the most complicated grammars. Language has structure which matches the mental structures of man's intellect so that man can learn languages other than his own native language. At the Tower of Babel, languages were confused. The sons of Noah gave their names to the races: Semitic from Shem, Hamitic from Ham, and Caucasian from Japheth.

1. The Caucasian races migrated to Europe into:

   a) Russia (Slavic)

   b) Poland and Germany (Teutonic)

   c) Western Europe (Celtic)

   d) Southern Europe (Italic)

2. The Italic language was Latin and, because Rome became a world power, Latin eventually dominated the Celtic languages in areas Rome conquered.

   a) The Bible was translated into Latin (Vulgate) and remained the Bible of Europe for 1000 years.

   b) French developed from Latin and is called a Romance language.

3. English developed from the Teutonic races because of the Anglo-Saxon conquest of England about A.D. 450.

   a) English was influenced by French because of the Norman conquest of England in A.D. 1066.

   b) French refined English giving it a rich vocabulary of grace, variety, expressiveness, and ability to express abstract ideas.

   c) Because English has been the language of the two greatest western powers, England and the United States, English has a universal character, is the language of diplomacy, has words from many languages, (over 1,000,000) and is very versatile.

   d) The English Bible was the instrument of gaining civil liberty for man by the planting of a Christian republic in America, as the character of liberty was formed in men by the inspiration of the English Bible.

Language as a Tool for Obtaining Liberty

The Written Language

1. God has always directed individuals to write.

   a) Genealogies were kept from Creation. (Genesis 5, 10; Chronicles)

   b) The law was written by Moses. (Numbers 5:23, Deuteronomy 17:18; 31:9, 24, 26; 2 Kings 22:8)

   c) Geography was recorded. (Joshua 18:9)

   d) Chronicles were kept by Jasher, Joshua (10:13; 2 Samuel 1:18); Samuel, Nathan, Gad (1 Samuel 10:25); Iddo (2 Chronicles 12:15; 13:22); Isaiah (2 Chronicles 26:22; 32:32; Isaiah 8:1); of the kings of Judah and Israel (1 & 2 Kings, 1 & 2 Chronicles); Ezra 4:15; Esther (6:1; 9:32); Jeremiah (32:12); and the Acts of the Apostles (19:19).

   e) Prophecies were written.

   f) Books were written.

      (1) Sixty-six in the Bible

      (2) Others lost to us today

      (3) The Book of Life (Exodus 32:32; (Psalm 69:28); Luke 10:20; Philippians 4:3; Revelation 3:5; 13:8; 17:8; 20:12; 21:27; 22:19)

2. Books have directed the events of history.

   a) The force of the Bible is the greatest of all books.

   b) Many books have inspired the best in man (great literature, theology, records of the fruitfulness of great lives and works).

   c) Some books have been used to enslave men (Machiavelli's Prince, Karl Marx, humanist textbooks).

   d) Many writings became instruments for obtaining liberty (John Locke, Montesquieu, Blackwell, the letters of the Committees of Correspondence).

   e) Documents have accompanied every advance in the struggle for liberty (the New Testament, the Magna Charta, the Mayflower Compact, the Declaration of Independence).

3. The key to conversion of anyone to Christianity and freedom is the Bible.

4. The key to converting a nation to liberty is through the written word. From the writings of C. S. Lewis:

   > The challenge today is to subdue the world for Christ by permeating Christian principles of liberty into every area of modern life through writing.
   >
   > I believe that any Christian who is qualified to write a good popular book on any science may do much more by that than by any directly apologetic work. We can make people (often) attend to the Christian point of view for half an hour or so; But the moment they have gone away from our lecture or laid down our article, they are plunged back into a world where the opposite position is taken for granted. As long as that situation exists, widespread success is simply impossible. We must attack the enemy's line of communication. What we want is not more little books about Christianity, but more little books by Christians on other subjects—with their Christianity latent. You can see this most easily if you look at it the other way around. Our faith is not likely to be shaken by any book on Hinduism. But if whenever we read an elementary book on geology, botany, politics or astronomy, we found that its implications were Hindu, that

would shake us. It is not the books written in direct defense of materialism that make the modern man a materialistic; it is the materialistic assumptions in all the other books. In the same way, it is not books on Christianity that will really trouble him. But he would be troubled if whenever he wanted a cheap popular introduction to some science, the best work on the market was always by a Christian. The first step to reconversion of a country is books produced by Christians.

(C. S. Lewis, *God in the Dock: Essays on Theology and Ethics.* Grand Rapids, Mich.: William B. Eerdmans Publishing Co., 1970, p. 93.)

The Role of Latin on the Chain of Christianity®

B.C. 54	A.D. 100s	312	405	455	597	635	735	1000	1384	21st C.
Latin is language of the Roman civilization	Invasion of Britain by Julius Caesar	Jesus Christ Focal Point of All History	Christianity is introduced to Britain	Conversion of Constantine the Great—Christianization of Roman Empire	Jerome translates the Bible into Latin—The Vulgate	Collapse of Rome; vernacular Latin replaces literary Latin as spoken language; becomes foundation of the Romance languages	Augustine brings Roman Catholicism and Latin usage to Britain	Aidan, a Celtic Christian monk, founds Lindisfarne Priory where the Gospels were produced in Latin.	Bede translates Vulgate into Anglo-Saxon	Medieval era—Latin is the language of classical education and the church	Wycliffe translates Vulgate into English	Sixty percent of English is rooted in Latin

The Roman Empire on the Chain of Christianity

(See *CHOC I*, pp. 12, 18; *Rudiments Handbook*, pp. 55–66)

1. Ancient Rome's pragmatic application of the Greek civilization to their culture and language is woven into the tapestry of Western civilization's thinking, politics, systems of law and government, city planning, civil engineering, art, architecture, literature, and languages.

2. God used both the positive and negative aspects of the Roman Empire and its Latin language in directing the westward course of Christianity and the Gospel.

3. Ancient Rome dominated the Mediterranean world politically, culturally, and socially for centuries.

4. Rome was ruled by a "republican" form of government, 509-31 B.C., providing a foundation for America's Christian constitutional republic and her system of law. Rome's military power molded a government of separate powers and checks and balances.

5. Roman culture influenced the western world through its literature, drama, architecture, art, and sculpture. The early Christian church took the Roman basilica as its structural form.

6. Jesus Christ, the Prince of Peace, was born during the Pax Romana, which gave peace and security to a disordered world for a period of time. Christ lived during the reign of Augustus and Tiberius Caesar, was convicted by Pontius Pilate, and was crucified by Roman soldiers. Many of his apostles were also persecuted and killed by the Romans during the first century A.D.

   a) John 11:48—Jewish leaders, fearful that Jesus would gather a powerful following, dreaded even tighter Roman control.

   b) Acts 16:2—Paul and Silas were jailed because they proclaimed ideas that were unacceptable to the Romans.

   c) Acts 18:2—Jews were commanded to leave Rome.

   d) Acts 23:11—Paul was a witness to the power of Jesus Christ in Rome.

   e) Acts 25:11,12—Paul, a Roman citizen, appealed to Caesar.

7. In the Providence of God, Rome's well-constructed roads and water ways stretched throughout the mighty empire which enabled the future spread of the Gospel in Europe.

8. In the first century A.D., the Apostle Paul traveled throughout the Roman provinces in eastern Europe preaching and teaching the Gospel. Christianity was introduced to Britain, a frontier province in the Roman Empire, possibly by Joseph of Arimathea, who had fled the persecution of Emperor Claudius and come to Britain in pursuit of his tin mining interests.

   a) Joseph was a secret disciple and friend of Jesus Christ, who provided the tomb for Jesus' burial. His name is widely known in the legends of Christianity in Britain.

   b) Tradition in Glastonbury, England, history credits Joseph of Arimathea with building the first church in Britain. (*Joseph of Arimathea*, Isabel Hill Elder. Glastonbury, 1996)

   c) As the Celts were converted to Christianity, they established local, independent, decentralized New Testament churches.

9. In the fourth century A.D., Emperor Constantine declared Christianity the official religion of the Empire. God had set the stage for Rome to play a major role in the spread of Christianity westward with or without her consent.

Latin on the Chain of Christianity®

1. Latin was the language of the Roman civilization that dominated the empire after the Old Testament ended and the New Testament began.

2. Latin literature was influenced by Greek forms.

   a) Latin literature is mechanical, complex, inflexible, and projects no intimate feeling.

   b) Although the literature is accurate and interesting, it lacks life and deep thought. It is a reflection of unregenerate man at his best but without Christ.

   c) Catullus (84–54 B.C.) an intense poet, Horace (65–8 B.C.) famous for his Odes, and Virgil's Aeneid are the best examples of Roman ideas combined with Greek skill.

   d) Roman prose writers include: Cicero (106–43 B.C.)—famous orator, letters, speeches; Caesar (102–44 B.C.)—"Gallic Wars"; Livy (A.D. 59–17—"From the Founding of the City."

3. In A.D. 400, the Roman Catholic monk, Jerome, translated the Bible from the Hebrew and Greek languages to Latin.

   a) It is known as the "Vulgate Bible" and was the Bible of medieval Europe for over one thousand years!

   b) The Vulgate was the Bible used by John Wycliffe (1380s) and other early European Bible translators and reformers.

4. After four centuries of Roman domination in Britain, Latin became the language of politics and education. In God's Providence, the arrival in Great Britain of the classic Roman culture and its Latin language was part of His preparation for a future Bible-reading and Bible-reasoning people.

5. In A.D. 563, Columba, an Irish monk and follower of Patrick (A.D. 389–461) brought the Gospels and the Law from Ireland to Iona, Scotland. Before Roman Catholic missionaries (sent by Pope Gregory in A.D. 597) ever reached northern England, Bible-based Celtic missionaries headed by Aidan, one of Columba's Celtic disciples, founded the Lindisfarne Priory in northern England.

   a) The monks produced what are called the Lindisfarne Gospels, superbly beautiful versions of Matthew, Mark, Luke, and John which were written in Latin.

   b) Three hundred years later, these exquisite copies had interlinear translation into Anglo-Saxon and still exist today in the British Museum.

6. In A.D. 597, Pope Gregory sent Augustine and forty Roman Catholic monks as missionaries to Romanize Great Britain.

   a) Churches, monasteries, and schools were established in which the Latin language was used.

   b) At the Synod of Whitby, Roman Christianity nominally triumphed over Celtic Christianity. But it has been noted by many scholars that the strength of the Celtic Church had been very much underestimated by Rome. The Celts emphasized the Bible over the Papacy and held onto their beliefs!

7. Latin was, and still is in many parts of the world, the official language of the Roman church, its liturgy, hymns, and Scripture readings. It was also the language of medieval Roman church documents which maintained the histories of cities and families.

8. Latin was the language of classical education, beginning in the medieval ages and continuing into the founding of America. European and American scholars had to master Latin for reading, understanding, and writing in academic subjects.

9. The Latin language became the foundation of the Romance languages—Portuguese, Spanish, Italian, French, and Romanian. The study of Latin continues to provide an excellent foundation for the study of the Romance languages.

10. Today, sixty percent of the English language is rooted in Latin. Many Latin phrases are incorporated into the language, particularly in the fields of medicine and law.

The Role of French on the Chain of Christianity®

58 B.C.	A.D. 460	800	1000	1400	1550	1685	1748	1775	1789	1958
Roman Conquest	Clovis is converted to Christ	Charlemagne; Birth of French Nation	Crusades; Capet	Jeanne d'Arc; 100 Years War	Calvin; Edict of Nantes; Gaspard de Coligny	Huguenots flee France; Revocation of Edict of Nantes	Montesquieu *L'Esprit des Lois*	Lafayette; France aids American Revolution	French Revolution Napoleon	Fifth Republic DeGaulle

The Individuality of France among Nations

(See *CHOC I*, pp. 406, 414, 424–26.)

1. France is the largest nation in Europe, the continent of development.

2. The diverse geographical features of France—mountains, rivers, fertile plains and valleys—the perfect environment for the development of civilization.

3. The physical position of France on the Atlantic and the Mediterranean made her a maritime nation having close access to other nations and continents for exploration and colonization.

4. France and French culture had the influence of refining other cultures.

    a) Definition of Refine: [raffiner]. To purify, as manners, from what is gross, clownish or vulgar; to polish, to make elegant. To purify, as taste, to give a nice and delicate perception of beauty and propriety in literature and the arts.

    b) French culture excelled in art, music, philosophy, language, science, literature, fashion, and cuisine.

    c) Although French personality is immoderate, France contributed much in a supporting role to the Chain of Christianity moving westward.

A Brief History of France

1. The area of France today was called La Gaule after the tribe, les Gaulois, who descended from the pagan Celts and were the early inhabitants of France.

2. Caesar conquered Gaul in 51 B.C., Rome ruled four and one-half centuries and caused the language to be influenced by Latin.

3. The Franks invaded and adopted the Latin culture and their king, Clovis, became a Christian.

4. Charles Martel, a later Frankish king, who drove the heathen Saracens from France, was called "Sauveur de la Chretiente."

5. Charlemagne, a powerful statesman, who conquered all Gaul, Spain, Italy, and Germany was crowned Holy Emperor by the Pope in A.D. 800.

    a) He encouraged education throughout the empire.

    b) After his death, France was divided by the Treaty of Verdun into three parts: France, Germany, and an area in between.

    c) Norsemen conquered Normandy at this time.

6. Medieval France (10th–14th Centuries)

    a) The Feudal system was the governmental system.

    (1) A lord gathered onto his land peasants, artisans, and soldiers who would obey him in return for his protection.

    (2) Warfare among lords was incessant.

    (3) Each lord had a fortified castle or chateau fort.

    (4) Chivalry reigned as the social system.

b) The Church, though based on mysticism, was the chief force for good.

   (1) Crusades began as an effort to regain the Holy lands.

   (2) St. Louis IX became the example of a just and good king.

   (3) Monasteries were religious centers and also centers of education and industry.

c) The Hundred Years' War

   (1) The English king claimed the French throne.

   (2) Joan of Arc led the French army to victory over the English.

   (3) Joan of Arc was imprisoned at Rouen and burned at the stake by the English as a witch.

7. The Renaissance was inspired by the invention of printing which made possible the spread of the knowledge of former civilizations and cultures.

   a) The crusades and Italian Wars promoted the Renaissance when men returning brought back new ideas, artifacts, books, etc.

   b) Francis I encouraged the Renaissance in France in the arts and letters.

8. Reformation and Wars of Religion

   a) War between Protestants and Catholics was incessant as many French people left the Catholic Church to become Protestant.

   b) Charles IX massacred thousands of Protestants in 1572 and threw the bodies into the Seine River.

   c) Henri IV issued the Edict of Nantes in 1598 guaranteeing freedom of worship to Protestants.

9. Seventeenth Century—(Classicism) and Eighteenth Century (Absolute Monarchy and "Enlightenment")

   a) Richelieu, the prime minister, brilliantly worked to establish the supremacy of France in Europe.

   b) Louis XIV, the Sun King, reigned in "order, majesty and grandeur," built the palace at Versailles and enjoyed an age of classical art and literature.

   c) Montesquieu wrote *L'Esprit des Lois* expounding Christian government.

   d) Certain philosophers brought forth humanistic and atheistic doctrines which they termed "enlightenment" and laid the foundation for depravity in an already tottering empire—Rousseau, Voltaire.

   e) France aided us in our Revolution.

10. Revolution and Empire (1789–1870)

   a) "Liberté, égalité, fraternité" incited the people to storm the Bastille—a symbol of absolute oppression; the Tricolor was raised and an attempt made in constitutional monarchy.

   b) The Reign of Terror became a nightmare to the whole world. The guillotine assassinated thousands as crowds cheered; the Bastille was still a political prison only now in the people's control.

   c) Napoleon Bonaparte took advantage of the chaos, gave strong leadership, united France by making war with all Europe and, after victory, declared himself Emperor.

   d) Retreat from Russia (1814) and the defeat at Waterloo (1815) brought his downfall and exile at St. Helena.

   e) Romanticism in literature, art (impressionism), and music (Debussy) inspire great works.

   f) The Second Republic (1848–1852)

   g) Upheaval, empire, and defeat led up to the Third Republic in 1870.

11. Contemporary France

   a) W.W. I (1914–1918) took the lives of 1,394,000 Frenchmen.

b) W.W. II (1939–1945) divided France into occupied France (the North where the Germans fought a spirited French Resistance Movement) and neutral "Free France" led by Marshall Petain from Vichy (considered cowards by the North).

c) Charles DeGaulle, W.W. I general, inspired the country to greatness again and, in 1958, became president of the Fifth Republic.

d) Colonial Empire included much of Africa, Tahiti, New Caledonia, Tunisia, Morocco, Laos, Vietnam, Algeria; many colonies were freed since 1958, e.g., Algeria in 1962.

e) DeGaulle died in November 1970. France remains stable. France is a member of the Common Market in Europe and enjoys a prominent role in the U.N.

The Contribution of France to the Chain of Christianity® Moving Westward

1. The French language influenced the English language during the Norman occupation of England, adding grace and variety to the Anglo-Saxon tongue and giving it a high quality of flexibility and expression.

2. French explorers went to the New World in the sixteenth and seventeenth centuries.

   a) Jacques Cartier explored Canada and the St. Lawrence River.

   b) Champlain founded Quebec.

   c) Marquette and Joliet explored the Mississippi.

   d) LaSalle explored the Louisiana territory.

3. Early French settlements were made in North America at New Orleans, Quebec, Montreal, St. Louis, and Detroit.

4. The Huguenots sought religious freedom in America in the seventeenth to eighteenth centuries.

5. Montesquieu, a French philosopher, wrote *L'Esprit des Lois* which became an inspiration to our founding fathers concerning the workings of a republic.

6. Defeat of the French in the French and Indian War kept the land area of the North American continent intact.

7. France supported America in her Revolution.

   a) Lafayette resigned from the French army and came to America with arms and ammunition to aid the cause of liberty.

   b) He later procured official French aid for the colonies.

   c) Beaumarchais, a writer, lent a great amount of money for the Revolution which was never repaid though he became impoverished.

   d) Rochambeau and Admiral de Grasse aided the American cause.

8. Napoleon I sold the Louisiana territory to the U. S. in 1803 for $15,000,000 increasing our territory from coast to coast.

9. The French Revolution (1789–1799) served as a warning to the world of a humanistic, man-centered, false liberty which collapsed quickly and ended in oppression and bloodshed for the people.

10. France held to a Republican form of government but lacked the Christian base to make it work. It suffered the collapse of the First Republic (1792–1804), the Second Republic (1848–1851), the Third Republic (1875–1940), and the Fourth Republic (1946–1958). Finally, by strengthening the executive, Charles DeGaulle brought stability through the Fifth Republic (1958–present).

11. France is a member of NATO and an ally of the U.S., though reluctant.

Characteristics of the French Language

1. French developed from Latin and is therefore called a Romance language.

2. Ten languages came from Latin and are closely related to each other. They are:

   a) Provençal   f) Spanish

   b) Catalan   g) French

   c) Sardinian   h) Italian

   d) Rhaeto-Romanic i) Romanian

   e) Dalmatian   j) Portuguese

3. The sons of Noah fathered the three major races: Shem—Semitic; Ham—Hamitic; Japheth—Caucasian.

4. The Caucasians migrated to Russia (Slavics), Poland and Germany (Teutonics), Western Europe (Celtics), and Southern Europe (Italics).

5. The Celtic language spoken by the first inhabitants of France was dominated by Latin after Caesar conquered Gaul in A.D. 51. The natives adopted Vulgar Latin spoken by the Roman soldiers.

6. The name France came from the Franks who invaded France in A.D. 400.

7. The Vikings invaded Normandy in A.D. 900 and absorbed the Latin culture.

8. The first written record of the language is the "Oaths of Strasbourg" in A.D. 842. The language was called "la langue Romane."

9. The priests preached in "la langue Romane" and troubadours wrote songs in it.

10. Modern French dates from Renaissance/Reformation.

    a) Calvin wrote *Institutes de la Religion Chretienne* in 1541.

    b) Psalms were sung in the Protestant churches and by the people (*psaumes*).

11. Standardization of the language came about when the Académie Française was established to preserve the language.

12. A rich and immense body of literature developed characterized by variety and excellence.

Modern French

1. Today eighty million people speak French as their native language.

2. French is one of the official languages of the United Nations and is considered the language of diplomacy.

3. It is the language of Belgium, Switzerland, Haiti, Quebec, and Luxembourg.

4. There are French-speaking areas in Louisiana and Vermont.

5. French is essential for graduate study in science, medicine, and is helpful to the study of art, music, and literature.

6. French literature today has a prominent place among nations, being richly imaginative, innovative, instructive, and diverse.

The Role of English on the Chain of Christianity®

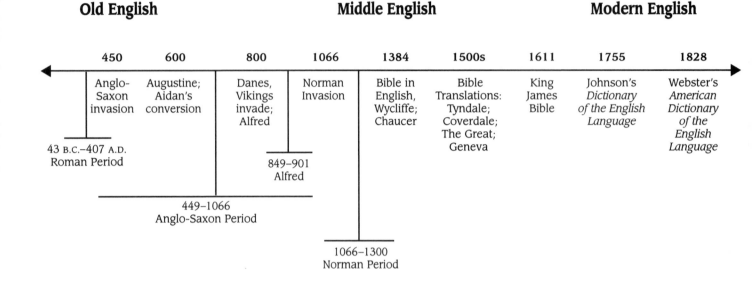

Old English				Middle English		Modern English		
450	600	800	1066	1384	1500s	1611	1755	1828
Anglo-Saxon invasion	Augustine; Aidan's conversion	Danes, Vikings invade; Alfred	Norman Invasion	Bible in English, Wycliffe; Chaucer	Bible Translations: Tyndale; Coverdale; The Great; Geneva	King James Bible	Johnson's *Dictionary of the English Language*	Webster's *American Dictionary of the English Language*

43 B.C.–407 A.D.
Roman Period

849–901
Alfred

449–1066
Anglo-Saxon Period

1066–1300
Norman Period

The Individuality of England among Nations

1. England has distinctive geographical features which make it well-suited for its important role on the Chain of Christianity.

   a) England is set apart from the continent of Europe as an island surrounded by the Atlantic Ocean, the North Sea, and the English Channel.

   b) Her maritime position made England look to the sea for trade, exploration, and protection.

   c) The land is fertile and enjoys a mild climate.

   d) The area of England is 50,327 square miles with population of approximately fifty million today.

   e) The capital is London and is located on the Thames River.

2. The spirit of the English people has always been characterized by independence and a love of personal freedom.

   a) The Anglo-Saxons employed principles of local-government.

   b) The Magna Charta in 1215 limited the power of the monarch.

   c) John Locke and other English philosophers formulated a philosophy of freedom based on Biblical principles.

   d) The English Reformation brought the pure Gospel to the people by putting the Bible in the language of the people for the first time.

   e) Christian influence—early cradle of God.

   f) Anglo-Saxon references to women, hard work, zest for life.

   g) Norman influence

      (1) Lively Celtic disposition

      (2) Vigorous and progressive Latin civilization

      (3) Romance language

      (4) National idea—strong central government

3. English Language

   a) Dual character, two classes of words

     (1) Anglo-Saxon (masculine). Simple words expressing the common things of life make up strong framework (stem and bare branches). Simplicity, strength, directness.

     (2) Norman-Roman-Celt influence (feminine). Words that give grace, variety, and ornament to language (leaves and blossoms). Wealth of expression, comprehensiveness, adaptability to new ideas—from French.

   b) Over 1,000,000 words—versatile

   c) Simple grammar

   d) Rich—words from many languages

   e) Universal character—language of business

Outline Summary of the History of the English Language

Three Spans of Development

1. Old English, A.D. 450–1100

2. Middle, A.D. 1100–1500

3. Modern, A.D. 1500–Present

Old English Period—Anglo-Saxon Influence

1. Julius Caesar attacked Celts, 55–54 B.C.

2. Claudius brought England under Roman Empire—lasted 300 years (A.D. 50.)

   a) Rome built roads, villas, and amphitheaters.

   b) Latin became the official language.

   c) Christianity arrived in England.

   d) Peace—Hadrian's Wall was built across North to protect England from the Picts.

3. Barbarian hordes in the fifth century caused Rome to withdraw from outer posts.

   a) Scots and Picts invaded from North.

   b) Angles, Saxons, and Jutes came to "protect" and conquer.

     (1) They brought their language in A.D. 450.

     (2) They tried to drive out Christianity.

     (3) They worshipped Teutonic gods—Woden and Thor.

       (*a*) Woden's Day

       (*b*) Tuv's Day

       (*c*) Thor's Day

       (*d*) Frig's Day

     (4) There were three Old English dialects:

       (*a*) Northumbrian in the north

       (*b*) Mercian in central England

       (*c*) West Saxon and Kentish in the south

4. In A.D. 597 Pope Gregory sent St. Augustine and forty monks to Kent; King Ethelbert permitted Christianity to be established in Canterbury.

   a) Ethelbert was converted to Christianity.

   b) The Gospel gained a foothold.

5. In A.D. 647 Aidan, a monk from the Scottish Isle of Iona, began preaching in the north.

   a) The country received the Gospel.

   b) Latin had a greater influence on the language.

6. Christian learning spread as the Gospel spread.

   a) The "Venerable" Bede wrote:

     (1) *The Ecclesiastical History of the English People*

(2) It influenced the development of the English language and literature but was written in Latin.

b) King Alfred

(1) Defeated Danes who withdrew from England.

(2) He was a lawmaker and learner, invited scholars to England, and learned Latin.

(3) He translated books into Old English including Bede and the Gospels.

(4) He set up schools to teach Old English.

The Lord's Prayer in Old English

Faeder ure bu de eart on heofonum si bin nama gehalgod
(Father our thou that art in the heavens, be thy name hallowed.)

To becume bin rice. Gerwurde bin willa on eordan swa on.
(Come into being thy kingdom. Be honored thy will on earth as)

hoefonum. Ume gedaeghwamlican hlaf syle us to daeg. And
(in the heavens. Our daily loaf bring us today. And)

foryf us ure gyltas swa we forgyfab urum gylyen-dem. and
(forgive us our sins as we forgive them their sins. And)

ne gelaed bu us on costnunge ac alys us of yfele. So dlice.
(not lead thou us in temptation, but free us from evil. Truthfully)

Notice: word order
  hlaf (loaf)
  "ae" sounds like "a" in 'hat'
  "b" and "j" like "th" sound in 'thin'

---

7. After King Alfred's death, the Danes took over—King Canute. There was a Scandinavian influence on language.

8. Edward the Confessor was friendly with the Norman court. The Normans were Northmen whose ancestors were Vikings but who by living long in France were converted to Latin culture and spoke French.

9. In 1066 William the Conqueror, the Norman king, was crowned king of England on Christmas Day.

a) He divided land, erected fortified castles.

b) He destroyed the Anglo-Saxon culture.

c) Norman French became the official language.

d) The people kept English as their mother tongue.

Middle English—French Influence

1. Two centuries after the Norman Conquest, English gained ground.

a) In A.D. 1258, a proclamation was made in both languages.

b) Universities used English.

c) English was influenced by French but not vanquished.

2. Geoffrey Chaucer was a London poet.

a) He wrote in English.

b) His popularity helped establish the language.

(1) The word order of Middle English is more like modern.

(2) Most words in Middle English were of Old English origin.

Chaucer's English: Middle English

The millere was a stout carl for the nones, Ful byg he was of brawn, and eek of bones: That proved wel, for over al ther he cam, At wrastlynge he wolde have alwey the vam. He was short sholdred, brood, a thikke knavve, There was no dore that he nolde heve of hawe, Or breke it at a rennying with his heed. His berd as any sowe or fox was reed, And therto brood, as though it were a spade. Upon the cope right of hog nose he hade A werte, and theron stood a toft of herys, reed as the bristles of sowes erys; His nosethirles blake were and wyde;

(1) He printed in English.

(2) He printed Chaucer.

(3) Literacy increased.

(4) Spelling was standardized.

(5) Dialects were removed.

(6) Ideas of men spread.

(7) Interest in learning increased.

4. Queen Elizabeth, 1558

   a) English supremacy on sea inspired writing (Drake, Raleigh).

   b) Children were educated.

   c) Shakespeare wrote and literature reached a Golden Age.

   d) King James, in 1611, released the Authorized Version of the Bible.

   e) American settling—Bradford's history *Of Plymouth Plantation*:

c) The London dialect established through Chaucer became the standard.

3. Wycliffe's Bible was the earliest classic Middle English in 1384.

Modern English

1. In Modern English there are sound changes from Middle English.

   a) A final "e" is not pronounced, as formerly (ride, stone, etc.).

   b) This resulted in spelling problems (words not pronounced like they look).

2. Changes in the language were influenced by:

   a) The Anglo-Saxon upheaval;

   b) The Norman invasion;

   c) The influence of Christianity;

   d) Greater vocabulary;

   e) Sound changes.

3. The invention of printing

   a) Up to this time books were so rare (Chaucer owned sixty), that men listed them in wills.

      (1) Copying was done by hand.

      (2) Mistakes were scraped out by knife.

   b) In 1476, William Caxton brought printing press to England.

In these hard and difficult beginnings they found some discontents and murmurings arise amongst some and mutinous speeches and carriages in other; but they were soon quelled and overcome by wisdome, patience, and just and equall carrage of things.

—William Bradford

5. In the eighteenth century, the concern for standardization among literary figures resulted from influence of the Académie Française (1635).

   a) Samuel Johnson's dictionary established a traditional attitude toward dictionaries and standardized English.

   b) Noah Webster's 1828 American dictionary established the American English standard.

Additional Readings on the History of England

1. Charles Dickens: *A Child's History of England*

2. Sir Walter Scott: *Tales of a Grandfather*

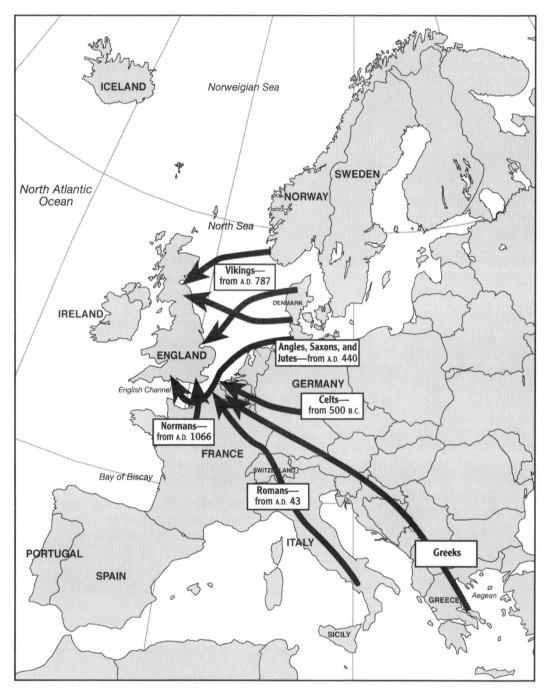

Influences in the Development of the English Language

History of the English Language

From *Lessons in English* by Sara Lockwood.
Boston: Ginn and Company, 1890.

The Celts

It has been conjectured that the first band of people who travelled westward were the Celts or Kelts, since in early times they occupied the countries along the sea-coast—Spain, Gaul (France), and part of Italy—and the adjacent islands of Britain and Ireland. Their position here would seem to indicate that they had been pushed on by other bands until they could go no farther. But this, too, is only a theory. With the story of these early inhabitants properly begins the history of England, though, as we shall see, the Celts were not the ancestors of English people.

The Britons

About fifty-five years before Christ, when Julius Caesar was conquering the Celtic tribes in Gaul, the attention of the Romans was attracted to an unknown land whose shores were dimly seen from the northern coast of Gaul. The Romans were fond of geography and of exploring unknown regions, and their generals had a passion for extending the Roman dominions. Caesar determined to explore the country on the other side of the Channel; and it is to the records of these explorations by the Romans that we owe our knowledge of the early inhabitants of England. It was not then known as England. The Romans named it Britannia, and its inhabitants were called Britons. We must remember that they were Celtic people, like the inhabitants of Gaul. Caesar's own account of his expedition has been preserved. From it we gain a very clear idea of his experiences in this hitherto unknown country. He tells us that the Britons were brave, fierce, and warlike. Strabo, a Greek geographer, says that their houses were made of a conical framework of poles, with long willow branches twisted in and out. There were no windows or chimneys. Another writer compares these dwellings to "huge bee-hives." The chiefs lived in huts which were regarded as extremely elegant, because the branches of which they were woven had been stripped of their bark. The more civilized people, who lived in the southern part of the country, cultivated the land to some extent, but the inland tribes of the North had no knowledge of agriculture. They lived by raising flocks and herds, and by hunting wild animals. They wore coats of skins, and painted their bodies blue with the juice of a plant. Caesar tells us that they looked "dreadful" in battle. These people were pagans. Their priests were called Druids, and their religion is often spoken of as Druidism. Caesar says that they offered human sacrifices to their gods, making "huge images of osier-twigs," into which they put their living victims and then set fire to the cages. The Druids were not only the priests, but the judges of the people and the teachers of the children. At Carnac in France and at Stonehenge in England are works which have been ascribed to the Druids. They consist of large stones set up as if for monuments, or rude pillars for altars and temples. At Carnac the stones are placed in long avenues, but at Stonehenge they were originally arranged in circles. No one knows what purpose they served, or whether the Druids really erected them.

The Romans in England

Julius Caesar did not wholly conquer the warlike Britons, although for nearly five centuries after his invasion the Romans regarded Britannia as one of their provinces. They sent several expeditions to explore the country, but did not demonstrate that it was an island until more than one hundred years after the time of Caesar. Agricola, who was then the ruler of the province, drove the fierce tribes of the North back to their native mountains, and built a wall across the island to prevent them from coming into the southern part of the country. They made roads, established trading-places, drained marshes, and taught the people to build houses, temples, and baths in the Roman fashion. When Italy was invaded by barbarians from the North, the Romans, finding that their capital was in danger, hastily withdrew their army from Britain (A.D. 426).

Effect of the Roman Occupation upon the Language

Besides the soldiers and those directly interested in the government of the province, so few Romans came to live in Britain that there was almost no intermingling of the races. For this reason, the language of the country was but little changed. Many of the Latin words which were introduced into our language by the Roman occupation were greatly changed in form. For example, the proper name Chester, with its compounds such as Dorchester, Manchester, and Winchester, is a corruption of the Latin *castra*, a fortified camp. So also are Worcester and Lancaster. It was in these camps that the Romans established markets to which the Britons brought whatever they had to sell. In the course of time the camps became towns, which still bear the old names. Not more than one hundred Latin words have been added to our language by the five centuries of Roman rule. Most of them are proper names, nearly all ending in *port, caster, cester,* and *chester*. The word street is derived from *strata via,* "paved way," the name applied to the Roman roads. It is estimated that the English language contains at least thirty thousand words of Latin origin; but they were not introduced into England by the Romans.

The Teutons

A second great band of people who made their home in Europe were the Teutons or Germans. They settled north of the Danube River and east of the Rhine; also Denmark and Scandinavia. Here they became separated into various tribes, those of the greatest historical importance being the Goths, the Vandals, the Franks, the Angles, and the Saxons. A Roman historian, Tacitus, the son-in-law of Agricola, gives us a long account of these people. He describes them as having "eyes stern and blue, yellow hair, and huge bodies." They did not live in cities, but each family occupied a little village of its own; and so in time the families grew into tribes, and the tribes into kingdoms. In civilization they were but little in advance of what the Britons had been in the days of Caesar. They spent much of their time in fierce quarrels among themselves, or in battle with the neighboring tribes. In peace they were indolent and fond of carousing. They invaded the neighboring provinces, and killed or drove away the inhabitants, and set up kingdoms of their own.

The Franks settled in Gaul, and from them the name France is derived. The Goths set up a kingdom in Spain and one in Italy. It was when the Goths and the Vandals invaded the Roman provinces that the Romans had to withdraw their legions from Britain to defend their capital. They meant to return, but they never did, for the Roman Empire was destroyed by these barbarians. Three of these Teutonic tribes, the Jutes, the Angles, and the Saxons, lived in Jutland or Denmark and on the seacoast near the mouth of the Elbe. They were bold pirates, who made incursions by water upon the neighboring countries, often ravaging the coasts of Britain. The Britons called them "sea-wolves," and doubtless they richly deserved the name.

The Angles and Saxons in England

After the withdrawal of the Roman forces from Britain, the Picts and Scots—the wild tribes who inhabited the northern part of the island—left their mountain homes and ravaged the lands of their Celtic brethren in the south. The Britons were not so valiant as their ancestors had been; and, despairing of success in their attempts to repel the invaders, they sent a piteous appeal to their Roman masters to come back and help them conquer their enemies. The Romans, however, were too busy with their own troubles to attend to the woes of the Britons. Then Vortigern, a British king, decided to hire his troublesome neighbors, the Angles and the Saxons, to aid him in this time of need, promising to give them money and land in return for their services. They accepted his offer, and helped to drive back the Picts and Scots; but soon complained that he did not pay them well enough, and threatened to plunder the whole island unless he showed more liberality. When it was too late, the Britons repented of having asked help from these "sea-wolves"; for the German tribes made preparations to come over in great numbers and take the land if the Britons would not give it to them.

It was about twenty-five years after the withdrawal of the Romans that these Teutonic invaders came into Britain, led by two chiefs, Hengist and Horsa. The Britons met them at Aylesford, Kent, and a great battle was fought, in which the invaders were victorious. The inhabitants were either slaughtered, enslaved, or driven far to the westward, and the German tribes were left in possession of the greater part of the island. The exiled Britons fled to the mountains of Wales and Cornwall, to the islands adjoining Britain, and to a province in France, which is still known as Brittany. Meanwhile the Jutes, the Angles, and the Saxons continued to come over to Britain, where they formed kingdoms of their own. We can understand now what all this has to do with the history of our language; for England is a contraction of *Engla-land*, and means "the land of the Angles" (or Engles), and these German tribes united to form the *Engle-ish* or English people.

Effect of the Saxon Conquest upon the Language

In order to understand the great change which the coming of the Saxons made in the language of England, let us recall what happened when America was colonized by the nations of Europe. They drove the Indians farther and farther west, exterminating whole tribes of them. This is very much like the way in which the Saxons treated the Britons, in the fifth century. In the United States, the result was that the people who conquered the country adopted but few of the Indian words. Some of them are *tobacco, potato, moccasin, hominy, mush, wigwam,* and *tomahawk*. At first the settlers retained the language of the country from which they came; but in time, as the relations between the colonies became closer, the English, which was spoken in the most influential colonies, became the language of the whole country. In much the same way, the Celtic language was exterminated, so that only a few of our common words can be traced to the speech of the ancient Britons. *Bard*, *glen*, *pool*, *boast*, and *cradle* are among the words which are supposed to be of Celtic origin. In time the dialect of the West Saxons became the language of literature and of law, because the West Saxons were politically the dominant tribe.

The Angles were more numerous and owned larger territory, and so the race and the language were finally named from them. The language of the Teutonic invaders is called sometimes the Anglo-Saxon, sometimes the Saxon, and sometimes the English, and still other names, such as Early English, Old English, and Middle English are used to designate the English of different periods. Still another point of resemblance between the fate of the Britons and that of the Indians may be noted. The remnant of the latter have been driven to the far West, where they retain, to some extent, their old habits of living and of speech. In the same way, the descendants of the Celtic exiles retained, in Wales and in Brittany, the customs and the language of their ancestors.

Compare these two versions of The Lord's Prayer with our modern version:

Old English

Fæder ûre, þû þe eart on heofenum, sî þîn nama gehâlgôd. Tô be-cume þîn rîce. Geweorðr þîn willa on eorðan swâ swâ on heofenum. Ûrne dæghwamlîcan hlâf syle ûs tô dæg. And forgyf ûs ûre gyltâs, swâ swâ wê forgyfað ûrum glytendum. And ne gelæd þû ûs on costnunge, ac âlŷs ûs of yfle. Sôðlice.

Middle English (Wycliffe, 1380)

Oure fadir that art in hevenes Halowid be thi name. Thi kyngdom come to. Be thy wille don in erthe, as in hevene.

Gyve to us this dai oure breed over othir substaunce. And forgyve to us oure dettis as we forgyven to oure dettouris, and lede us not into temptacioun. But delyvere us from yvel. Amen.

We should find it difficult to read the first of these, though we can guess what most of the words mean. It is interesting to notice how the Saxon tongue gradually changed in form, and how our modern English has improved upon the style of the first English translation of the Bible.

Among the poems translated by Longfellow is one from the early English. It is called "The Grave," and was written about the year 1200. Compare the first stanza of the translation with the original:

Original:

De wes bold gebyld
er þu iboren were
ðe wes mold imynt
er ðu of moder come
ac hit nes no idiht
ne þeo deopnes imeten:
nes gyt iloced
hu long hit þe were:
Nu me þe bringæð
þer ðn beon scealt
nu me sceal þe meten
and ða mold seoðða.

þ= th.
ð= dh.

Translation:

For thee was a house built
Ere thou wert born,
For thee was a mould meant
Ere thou of mother camest.
But it is not made ready,
Nor its depth measured,
Nor is it seen
How long it shall be.
Now I bring thee
Where thou shalt be;
Now I shall measure thee,
And the mould afterwards.

Christianity in England

It is not known just how Christianity was first introduced into Britain; but one of the theories is that some of the Roman soldiers who had been led by the preaching of St. Peter or St. Paul to give up the worship of pagan gods taught the new faith to some of the Britons with whom they came in contact. There are traditions, too, that missionaries from Gaul crossed over to Britain before the time of the Anglo-Saxon Conquest. After the Celts had been driven into Wales and Cornwall, the Christian religion continued to spread among them. The English invaders, however, brought with them from their old home on the southern shores of the Baltic the worship of the sun and moon; of Tiw, the god of heaven; of Woden (or Odin), the god of war; of Thor (or Thunder), the god of storms; and of Frea (or Friga), the goddess of peace and plenty. Our names for the days of the week were first given in honor of these gods and goddesses. Seterne is the Old English name for Saturnus, after whom Saturday was named.

More than a century after the settlement of the Saxons in England, they were converted to Christianity by Roman missionaries, chief among whom was Augustine. The story of their conversion is told by the Venerable Bede, an Anglo-Saxon monk who was born about seventy-five years after Augustine went to England, and who wrote the history of the Anglo-Saxon Church. He relates that Gregory, who afterwards became Pope

Gregory the Great, when passing through the marketplace of Rome, noticed among the slaves exposed for sale some remarkably handsome boys. When he was told to what nation they belonged, he said, "With those fair faces, they should be, not Angles, but Angels." The historian goes on to say that when Gregory became pope, he did not rest until he had sent missionaries to convert these people. The church services were conducted in Latin; and not a few words which have come to us from that language were introduced into England by the missionaries, during the sixth and seventh centuries.

The English People

It has already been said that the Teutons did not all come into the country at one time. Gradually their numbers and their power increased, until there were seven prominent kingdoms, which are often called the "Heptarchy," from a Greek word meaning "the rule of seven." But we must not suppose that exactly seven kingdoms existed at one time under one common ruler. The Jutes owned one kingdom, which retained its British name of Kent. The Saxons owned three kingdoms—Wessex, Essex, and Sussex, the names being equivalents of West Saxons, East Saxons, and South Saxons. The Angles owned the largest territory, having three kingdoms—Mercia, East Anglia, and Northumberland. This last means the land north of the Humber. East Anglia, the home of the East Angles, was divided between the North-folk and the South-folk, from which names come Norfolk and Suffolk. The different tribes quarrelled so often among themselves that the number and the boundaries of their kingdoms were continually changing. Nevertheless the English, as we may now call them, made great progress in learning and civilization. In time, the kingdom of the West Saxons became the ruling one. Their most famous king was Alfred the Great, who became the king of Wessex in 871. He was a brave warrior, a persevering scholar, a wise ruler, and a good and noble man.

The Danish Invasions

The enemies whom the English had to fight in the days of Alfred were the Scandinavians, often called simply the Danes, and sometimes the Norsemen or Northmen. They lived in Denmark, in part of Norway and Sweden, and in the very countries from which the English had come. They were savage heathen, as the Saxons had once been. During the ninth and tenth centuries they made many incursions into England, plundering the towns, burning the monasteries and churches, and massacring the people. Sometimes they made alliance with the Welsh and ravaged the adjoining kingdom of Wessex. They were often defeated in battle, but never lost their foothold in the country. Sometimes they obtained control of the kingdom so that in the list of the kings of England during the eleventh century there are several Danish names. Among these Danish sovereigns was King Canute who, according to the well-known story, tried to make the sea retire at his command. The history of this period is full of accounts of wars between the Danes and the English.

Effect of the Danish Invasion upon the Language of England

It must be remembered that the Danes and the Saxons both belonged to the Teutonic race, so it was comparatively easy for the Danes to settle down in England as part of the English people. They were soon converted to Christianity and became almost as civilized as the Saxons. Their language was so closely related to the English that their coming into England made no great change in the speech of that country. Among the words introduced by the Danes are *bait, fling, gust, ransack, rap, whisk, whirl,* and *whim.* Whitby, Derby, Enderby, etc., are Danish names, the termination *by* meaning town.

The Northmen

While some of the Norsemen were plundering England, others of them were making the same sort of trouble in France. They were just such fierce roving pirates as the Saxons had been in the fifth century. Under the leadership of the "Sea-kings," as their chiefs are often called, they made their first visits to the coast of France during the reign of the great Emperor Charlemagne, about the year 800. Again and again they came in ever-increasing numbers, and many times they seized upon portions of the land and dwelt there. Finally the French were obliged to submit to their remaining in the country, just as the English had to share their possessions with the Danes in order to make peace with them. At the beginning of the tenth century the king of France ceded to Rollo, the leader of the Northmen, a large province in the north of France. This was called Normandy, and its inhabitants came to be known as Normans. They soon learned to imitate the manners and customs of the French people, and to speak their language. The ruler of the province became a vassal of the French king and had the title of Duke. When the Normans had lived in France about one hundred years, they were, in some things, superior to the English. As a rule, their manners were more polished and their minds much better cultivated. Being so near neighbors, they became, of course, well-acquainted with the English, and some of the early English kings married the daughters of the Norman nobles.

The Norman Conquest

William, Duke of Normandy, determined to become king of England. He asserted that the throne had been promised him by Edward the Confessor, the English king who built Westminster Abbey. Edward's mother was a Norman lady, and he had spent all of his early life in her native land; so it is not strange that he should have been very fond of the Normans and of their ways. When he became king, he offended his subjects by showing his partiality too plainly. He invited the Norman nobles over to England and appointed them to the highest offices in the kingdom. Edward had no children, and so the Saxon people were very anxious as to who should be his successor. Their choice was Harold,

the brother of Edward's wife and the son of Earl Godwin, one of the Saxon nobles. Not long before this, Harold had been shipwrecked on the coast of France, and had been befriended by William. While Harold was at the court of Normandy, apparently a guest but really a prisoner, William made him promise in the most solemn manner that, in case of Edward's death, he would do all in his power to help William gain the English crown. Edward died in January, 1066, and in spite of his promise to William, Harold made great haste to be crowned in Westminster Abbey. When William heard of this, he spent several months in collecting an army, and then sailed for England. Harold, at the head of the Saxon army, marched to meet him at Hastings; and there a terrible battle was fought, in which the Normans were victorious, and Harold was slain. This battle of Hastings, fought on Oct. 14, 1066, is regarded as one of the most important events in history.

The Normans in England

When William of Normandy, better known as William the Conqueror, became king of England, the Normans came over in great numbers, seized the estates which belonged to the Saxon nobles, and took the political and religious government into their own hands. The Saxons became really the servants of the Normans. William was very severe in dealing with his new subjects. They were heavily taxed and, in order to be exact in the matter, he caused an inventory of each man's personal property and a careful survey of his land to be made, the whole being recorded in the "Domesday Book," which is still in existence. More than this, he massacred all the inhabitants of towns which rebelled against his decrees and laid waste many villages in order to make himself a hunting-ground, "the New Forest," giving the Saxons nothing in return for their land. The Norman barons imitated their king in harshness and insolence towards the conquered Saxons. Much good, however, came out of this evil. With all their faults, the Normans were in some respects superior to the Saxons. They were more enterprising and ambitious, more refined and cultivated. They were better soldiers, too, and better mechanics. Besides, they had broader ideas and knew more about other countries in the world. The two races found that there were many good things they could learn from each other; and so in the course of many generations the old relations of master and servant disappeared, and the two formed a united people. The Saxons ceased to hate their conquerors, and the Normans were proud to call themselves English.

Effect of the Norman Conquest upon the English Language

The Normans tried to have their language become the national speech. It was spoken in the schools, the camps, the courts, and the churches. It was also the language of the higher circles of society. Thus it happens that we have many Latin and French words pertaining the military science, to the law, to art, to poetry, and to the courtesies of social life, most of which were brought in by the Normans. We must remember that they spoke what was called the Norman-French, having adopted not only the religion, but the language of the people in whose land they had come to dwell. The Norman-French was really the Latin language, which had been corrupted by the Celtic speech of the Gauls and by the Teutonic tongue of the Franks, and which was possibly modified by the Norse dialects. It is often called the "unlettered" idiom, in order to distinguish it from the Latin of classical literature. The main reason why the Normans did not succeed in making French the language of England was that the measures by which they sought to gain this end were so harsh that the Saxons

rebelled and stubbornly refused to obey the dictates of their conquerors. Another reason was that the Saxons were so much more numerous than their masters. In their homes and about their daily business they used the familiar Saxon words, instead of the more polished speech of the French. As time went on, Saxon terms came into general use. If we compare some of our Saxon words with those of like meaning which come to us from the Latin or French, we shall notice that the "everyday" words are commonly Saxon; and the more ornamental, "high-sounding" ones of foreign origin. For example, we have—

Saxon:	Foreign:
like	similar
many	numerous
almighty	omnipotent
heavenly	celestial
truth	veracity
happiness	felicity

The greatest effect of the Norman Conquest upon the language was that it introduced the habit of borrowing words from other languages. Before the Conquest the English had hated everything foreign, and had clung to their old forms of speech. When the Normans became a part of the English nation, these prejudices gradually disappeared, until it became the most natural thing in the world to use many foreign words. This habit once formed was not easy to break; so the English have continued to enrich their language in this way. Another result of the Conquest was that it led to great improvements in the structure of the language. To see what a serious thing English grammar used to be, let us compare our adjective pronoun that with the inflection of the Anglo-Saxon poet, as given by Angus:

SINGULAR	Masculine	Feminine	Neutral	PLURAL
Nominative	se	seo	þæt	þâ.
Genitive	þæs	þǽre	þæs	þârâ.
Dative	þam	þǽre	þam	þâm.
Accusative	þone	þâ	þœt	þâ.

Growth of the Language

Since the Norman Conquest there has been no invasion to cause great change in the language. The English of the fourteenth and fifteenth centuries is really the same language which we speak. It does not look like it, to be sure; but, as one writer says, "neither does a child a year old look as he does when he has become a man fifty years old." The language has only "grown up," as the child does. We call Latin and Greek "dead languages," because they are no longer in constant use as the speech of any people. English, on the other hand, is not only a living language, but a growing one. Changes are constantly taking place in the spelling and pronunciation of words, and in grammatical forms. There are fashions in language, as in many other things. If we examine a book published more than one hundred years ago, we find many things that look very odd. Many of the s's look like f's; music and public have k added to the last syllable of each; honor and labor have u in the second syllable.

The following is copied from an article which appeared in the Connecticut Journal of October 19, 1796:

"It cannot be expected, that, if happily, our Judgeſ ſhould be competent to the taſk, they will apply themſelveſ with aſſiduity, to the reduction of our common law from a ſtate of chaotick confuſion to ſyſtematic order; when the Legiſlature at their next ſeſſionſ, without even a plauſible reaſon, may deprive them of their ſeatſ. Thiſ would be, indeed, to labour for the meat that periſheth."

The past tense of speak used to be spake, which is often used in the Bible. In olden times a well-educated man would no more have said *I spoke* than he would have said *I done* and *I seen*. In Shakespeare's time the pronoun its was just coming into the language. Now we should not know how to get along without this useful little word. New words are all the time being introduced; the old words are gaining new meanings. A great many illustrations may be found in the "Supplement" to the large dictionaries. In order to understand how the language came to have its present form, we must notice some of the ways in which it has grown.

Influence of Commerce

As civilization increased, the English became great travelers and traders, and sent out colonies into all parts of the known world. Naturally, the travelers introduced foreign terms in telling the story of the wanderings; and the traders brought back to England, with the strange productions of other lands, the native names for the articles. Sometimes the name was derived from the name of the place whence the merchandise came; for example, damask, from Damascus; calico, from Calicut in India; sardine, from Sardinia. The colonists almost unconsciously introduced into the language many forms of expression which they were in the habit of hearing from the natives about them, just as a child who has a French or a German nurse learns to speak her language without realizing that it is a foreign tongue.

Influence of Education

The growth of our language is mainly due to the increase of learning and to the multiplication of books. In the Middle Ages almost all of the books were written in Latin. The learned men of that time knew more about that language than they did about their own. King Alfred translated several books into the Anglo-Saxon so that the common people could read them; but most of the kings cared too little about learning to take so much trouble. Before the invention of printing, the making of books was almost entirely confined to the monasteries, where the patient monks spent years in copying a single Latin work on philosophy or religion.

A great many Latin words were introduced into our language in this way. Education has now become so general that English scholars are familiar with most of the other languages spoken in the world; and the "making of many books" has brought within the reach of the common people the thought and research of all the centuries. In this way, mainly, has come into use a vast number of foreign words. At first they are distinguished from English words by being printed in italics or inclosed in quotation marks; but in time this distinction ceases to be made, and they are said to be "domesticated." Such words are often Anglicized; that is, the spelling and pronunciation are changed to make them look and sound more like English words. From the Italian we have obtained our musical terms, and from the French our terms of cookery and fashion. Many such words can be traced back to the Latin. We can generally tell whether a word comes directly from the Latin or indirectly through the French, by noticing its form. If the spelling has been changed, it is almost sure to have come through the French. This may be more apparent from the following examples:

Latin	Latin Derivative	Through the French
Populus	popular	people
Fructus	fructify	fruit
Deceptum	deception	deceit
Fidelis	fidelity	fealty
Regalis	regal	royal
Fragilis	fragile	frail

Influence of Science

The prominence that was given to classical studies during the Middle Ages will account for the fact that most of the terms which were peculiar to the sciences then known are of classical origin. In the modern sciences, scholars have followed the same usage, borrowing almost invariably from the Greek. It is estimated that nine-tenths of our scientific terms are Greek. Arithmetic, Geography, Grammar, and History are all Greek names, as are many of the terms which are used in them. With the progress of education, these technical terms, as they are called, have become more and more widely known; and they form an important element in our language.

Influence of Invention and Discovery

Many words have been added to our language as one result of the mechanical ingenuity of the English-speaking people. They seem to be less ingenious in word-making than they are in machine-making; and instead of forming words out of elements in their own language, they go to the Latin or the Greek to find names for their inventions and discoveries. We have, to be sure, such words as steamboat, railroad, typewriter, and oil-well, which were formed from elements already in use; but they are few, as compared with the names of classical origin, such as telegraph, locomotive, bicycle, and petroleum. The Germans, on the other hand, prefer to use homemade names for their inventions. For example, they call the telephone a "far-speaker." They use many of these compounds, too, in place of the classical names in science and literature. Their name for hydrogen may be translated water-substance, and their word for dictionary is the very sensible compound, word-book.

Influence of New Ideas

During the latter half of the nineteenth century not a few words were introduced from other languages, or deliberately coined, to express new ideas in art, science, literature, politics, philosophy, and religion. New subjects of thought occupy the minds of men; new phases of society, new questions of life and duty and destiny. Sometimes there is a word already in use which can be made to express this new thought. We have a host of these old words with modern meanings. For example: social science; differentiation, as used in metaphysics; evolution, as used in geology; free-trader; anarchist; probation after death; realistic, as used in art and literature. Some of the new words which have been introduced in this way are Nihilism, optimist, pessimist, impressionist, as an art term; agnostic, dude, mugwump, and universology.

Number of Words in the English Language

It is estimated that the large dictionaries contain more than one hundred thousand words. Of these, a comparatively small number—Professor Whitney says from three to five thousand—are all that even cultivated people need to use for the ordinary purposes of speaking and writing. It is said that Shakespeare used about fifteen thousand different words.

Elements of the English Language

The English language is said to be "composite," because it is composed of words from other languages. No other tongue is made up of parts taken from so many sources. For this reason, it is very perplexing to foreigners, since the spelling, pronunciation, and meaning of the different classes of words cannot be determined by any one set of rules. There is the advantage, however, in its being made up of so many elements: there are several ways of expressing a single idea, so that variety is easily secured. Besides, we can express more accurately slight distinctions in meaning and delicate shades of thought than is possible in other languages. The most important elements have already been mentioned and their presence in the language explained. We will now review them in the form of a summary.

Elements of the English Language

Celtic: A few words left by the ancient Britons. Some that came through the French, Spanish, and Italian.

Scandinavian: Introduced by the Danes in the ninth and tenth centuries. Some brought by the Northmen into France, and thence into England after the Conquest.

Saxon: Of words in the large dictionaries, less than one-half are Saxon. Of words in common use, about four-fifths are Saxon.

Latin: A few Latin words left by the Romans; all proper names. Ecclesiastical terms introduced by missionaries. Words coming through the French, Italian, and Spanish. Introduced by learned men and education. Nearly one-half of the words in the dictionary are Latin in origin.

Greek: Nine-tenths of all our scientific terms, introduced by scholars and books. Also names for inventions.

Miscellaneous: Introduced mainly by commerce. Either native names for articles of merchandise, or names derived from names of places. Ex. Damask, from Damascus; tariff, from Tarifa; cambric, from Cambray; chestnut, from Castanea, in Pontus; ermine, from Armenia; muslin, from Mosul; florin, from Florence; canary, from the Canary Islands.

Hebrew: Ex. seraphim, cherubim, amen, ephod, jubilee, sabbath, cinnamon, Satan, shibboleth, manna.

Arabic: Ex. algebra, almanac, elixir, zero, talisman, coffee, sugar, lemon, giraffe, gazelle, syrup, alcohol, magazine, cotton, assassin, mosque.

Persian: Ex. caravan, dervish, scarlet, azure, lilac, chess, bazaar, shawl, turban, orange, horde, paradise.

Turkish: Ex. divan, scimitar, dragoman, tulip, ottoman, kiosk.

Chinese: Ex. tea, Bohea, Hyson, china (ware), joss, junk, Nankeen.

Malay: Ex. bantam, sago, ratan, gutta percha, bamboo, gong, mandarin, mango, caddy, cassowary.

Hindu: Ex. calico, chintz, toddy, lac, jungle, banyan, bungalow, pagoda, palanquin, shampoo.

Polynesian: Ex. Taboo, tattoo, kangaroo, boomerang.

West Indian: Ex. tobacco, maize, hurricane, canoe, cannibal, buccaneer.

North American: Ex. squaw, tomahawk, wigwam, mush, opposum, mustang, tomato, permmican, chocolate (Mexican).

South American: Ex. hammock, potato, tolu, caoutchonc, guano, mahogany, pampas, tapioca.

Italian: Ex. banditti, gazette, canto, opera, piano, soprano, piazza, malaria, umbrella, concert, carnival, studio, regatta, volcano, ditto.

Spanish: Ex. mosquito, negro, alligator, cigar, grandee, cork, Creole, desperado, tornado, vanilla, Eldorado, indigo, buffalo.

Portuguese: Ex. palaver, caste, marmalade, molasses, lasso, cocoa-nut, albatross, cobra, fetich.

French: Ex. etiquette, belle, dépôt, penchant, matinée, employé, débris, ennui, trousseau, début, petite, menu, soirée, régime, canard.

Dutch: Ex. yacht, sloop, schooner, yawl, ballast, boor, reef, skates, smack, smuggle.

African: Ex. gnu, gorilla, kraal, zebra, guinea, oasis.

Egyptian: Ex. ammonia.

Russian: Ex. knout, czar, drosky, rouble, steppe.

Indo-European Language Chart

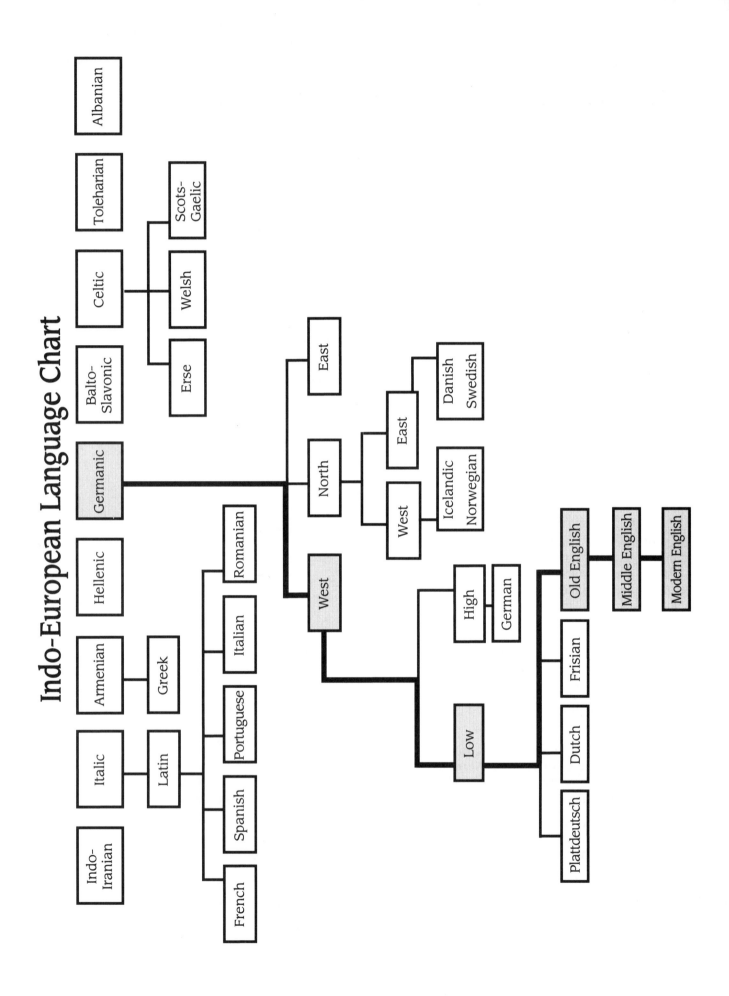

The English Bible and the Language of Liberty

by Rosalie June Slater

The English Bible gave us the language of liberty. Everything connected with our heritage and character of Liberty is related to the appearing of the English Bible, first in the fourteenth century with the Old and New Testaments translated by Wycliffe, and finally coming to its powerful, poetic, and persuasive expression in the 1611 King James Version. This is the greatest classic in the English language.

Owing to the superb beauty of its language, the Bible has an importance in our literature which is unparalleled elsewhere. And note that every advance in the beauty and power of the Bible's translation came when the English language itself had reached a special level of perfection and expression.

The translators who rendered the original languages into English were not only scholars of the language—but their honest character and their love of liberty fashioned their translations into creations of beauty, grace, and comparable phrasing. Moreover, they recognized that English was peculiarly well-developed as a vehicle for the Gospel. Now the language of the Bible would ever be inseparable from the language of liberty; the language of the Bible would become the language of all men. Tyndale set the standard when he stated to one of his Cambridge friends, "If God spares my life, ere many years I will cause the boy that driveth the plough to know more of the scriptures than you do." John Drinkwater writes:

It is almost impossible to exaggerate the influence of Tyndale's version on the English language and on English thought. The Bible made English puritanism; and the Puritan tradition has fostered in the British and American peoples most of their best and distinctive qualities. From the Bible, Milton and Bunyan took the inspiration of their poetry and allegory. In the Bible, Cromwell and the Pilgrim Fathers found that which made them honorable, self-reliant, and steadfast. Bible in hand, Wesley and Whitefield transformed their country. In England all the great Victorians and, in America, men so diverse as Emerson and Walt Whitman showed the direct influence of the Authorized Version. It fashioned the art of Browning and George Eliot, Ruskin and Watts. John Bright, supreme among English orators in the nineteenth century, was essentially a man of one book—The Book. So, too, was Abraham Lincoln, genius alike in statecraft and speech.

The Bible is still the most precious part of the common heritage of the Anglo-Saxon races. The surface of our common culture is littered by transient enthusiasms, vulgar emotions, and moral wreckage, but below strong currents move steadily. In large measure these currents flow from the Bible, which now for five centuries has been the ultimate source of Anglo-Saxon idealism.

The Bible has shaped the English language: but it has also been the supreme spiritually-creative force in the civilization of the British Empire and the American commonwealth.*

There was a time when our statesmen could recite appropriately the prose or poetry of the Bible as they brought to bear Biblical reasoning on their legislative tasks. How long, Lord, O how long before our halls of justice, legislation, and education will echo with the powerful cadences of Thy Word as men and women of character utter the literature of liberty on behalf of thy children?

---

*John Drinkwater, ed., *The Outline of Literature*, pp.74–5.

The Holy Bible in English Timeline

" Heaven and Earth shall pass away: but my words shall not pass away."
— Luke 21:33

The Bible—Source and Seedbed of Life, Learning, and Liberty

Eternity Past

Creation Link

God spoke Creation into existence. Man was created in the image of God with the gift of language. (Genesis 1:2)

The Fall of Man
Pagan Idea of Man and Government
(Reasoning apart from Revelation)

"In the beginning God created . . . and God said . . ." (Genesis 1:1); *"In the beginning was the Word and the Word was with God and the Word was God."* (John 1:1)

1450 B.C.

Moses and the Law Link

Moral Preparation for the Gospel

"And it [copy of the Law in a book] shall be with him and he shall read it all the days of his life: that he may learn to fear the Lord his God, to keep all the words of this law, . . . and to do them." (Deuteronomy 17:19)

Old Covenant Canon:
"The Lord said to Moses, Write this for a memorial in a book." (Exodus 17:14)

Hebrew Old Testament:
Written c. 1450–425 B.C.
Hebrew Bible Divisions: The Law, the Prophets, and the Writings
English Old Testament Divisions: Law, History, Poetry, and Prophecy

425 B.C.

Ezra, the Jewish high priest and educational reformer, compiled Jewish Canon—books with "divine authority."

285 B.C.

Septuagint (LXX), Old Testament translated into Greek, c. 275–150 B.C.; Prepared the way for the coming of Christ in Greek-speaking world; Version from which writers of the New Testament quoted and used.

Readings:
T & L   pp. 332–42
CHOC I   pp. 28–36; 47
C & P   pp. 19–21
B & C   pp. 1–14

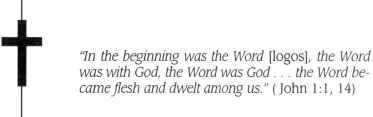

Jesus Christ
Focal Point of All History

Christian Idea of Man
and Government
(Reasoning with Revelation)

"In the beginning was the Word [logos]*, the Word was with God, the Word was God . . . the Word became flesh and dwelt among us."* (John 1:1, 14)

"Study to show thyself approved unto God, a workman who needeth not to be ashamed, rightly dividing the Word of God." (2 Timothy 2:15)

Paul and the Christian Church

The Gospel Is Recorded

A.D. 50

Greek New Testament: The New Testament was written A.D. C. 50–96 in "common" Greek, the language of the people, and traveled westward to Europe on the Roman roads.

405

Latin Vulgate Bible: Jerome translated the Scriptures in Latin from Hebrew and Greek. Called the Latin Vulgate, it was the Bible of Europe for 1000 years.

New Covenant Canon: The Bible, defined as "THE Book," was canonized.

432

Patrick, Celtic pastor, preached the Word of God in Great Britain. God's Word inspired the rule of law and local self-government.

600s

Caedmon, cowherd at Whitby Abbey in Yorkshire where monks illuminated manuscripts in Latin and sang Bible stories in the language of the people.

673

Venerable Bede, Wearmouth Monastery scholar who gave his life to the study of the Scriptures. Also learned science, astronomy, Greek, etc. Wrote *Ecclesiastical History of England*. Translated parts of the Vulgate Bible for the common people into Anglo-Saxon. Finished translating the Gospel of John on his deathbed in 735.

700

Lindisfarne Gospels: The Word struggled to emerge into Anglo-Saxon language.

 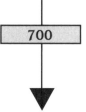

The Bible in English

The Bible in the hands of the individual birthed the Protestant Reformation.

"Scriptures are the property of the people!"

850

Alfred the Great, Christian king and royal scholar, was taught to read by his mother, Judith. Alfred loved learning and at thirteen, translated Psalms and prayers from Latin to Anglo-Saxon. At twenty-two, became King of Wessex and made a law book beginning with the Ten Commandments. Religion and learning were the two most important parts of life to him.

"Ye shall know the truth, and the truth shall make you free." (John 8:32)

1384

Wycliffe Bible, the People's Bible: John Wycliffe, "Morning Star of the English Reformation," translated the Latin Vulgate Bible into English. He thought the church was too rich, and the clergy were not teaching the Word or living for Christ. He taught the Word, sent out followers called Lollards to teach God's Word. Was tried and declared a heretic. His Bible was copied and recopied, taken to read to gatherings of the people.

1456

Gutenberg printing press: Mainz, Germany, first printed Latin Bible. In England, William Caxton set up a printing press.

Columbus

"Christ-bearer to the New World"

1492

Bible prophecy inspired Columbus to sail westward.

1525

Tyndale Translation: Wiliam Tyndale, "Father of the English Bible," translated the Scriptures from Hebrew and Greek; eighty percent of Old Testament and ninety percent of New Testament translations today are from Tyndale's work. He wrote: "I will cause a boy that driveth the plow to know more of Scripture than the pope." Tyndale was inspired by Erasmus. Defied the law to carry on Wycliffe's work. Secretly translated Erasmus's Greek Testament into English. Fled to Antwerp, never to return to England. His translation was smuggled into England. When found, the copies were burned. Tyndale was betrayed, warned, and fled to Worms, Germany. He was imprisoned and eventually martyred. During this era, smaller Bibles were printed. Tyndale's matchless style influenced the English language profoundly with its clear and direct prose. Many of his words and phrases are current today. The later sixteenth-century English Bibles were but improvements on Tyndale's. One-third of the text of the King James New Testament is worded exactly as Tyndale left it. In the remaining parts of the King James Bible, the sentence structure follows Tyndale's pattern.

The English Reformation

Reform "without tarrying for any"

The Hour of Christian Manhood

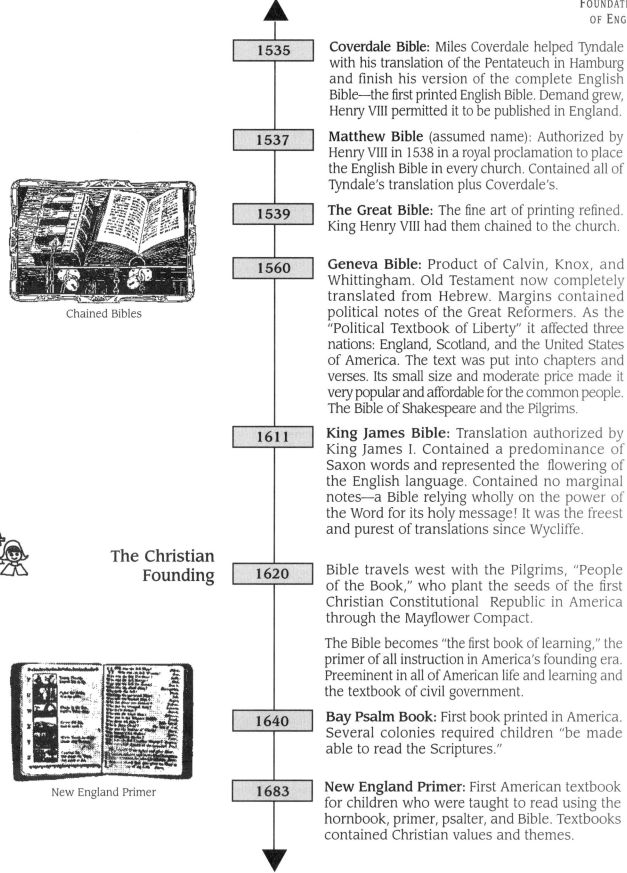

1535 **Coverdale Bible:** Miles Coverdale helped Tyndale with his translation of the Pentateuch in Hamburg and finish his version of the complete English Bible—the first printed English Bible. Demand grew, Henry VIII permitted it to be published in England.

1537 **Matthew Bible** (assumed name): Authorized by Henry VIII in 1538 in a royal proclamation to place the English Bible in every church. Contained all of Tyndale's translation plus Coverdale's.

1539 **The Great Bible:** The fine art of printing refined. King Henry VIII had them chained to the church.

Chained Bibles

1560 **Geneva Bible:** Product of Calvin, Knox, and Whittingham. Old Testament now completely translated from Hebrew. Margins contained political notes of the Great Reformers. As the "Political Textbook of Liberty" it affected three nations: England, Scotland, and the United States of America. The text was put into chapters and verses. Its small size and moderate price made it very popular and affordable for the common people. The Bible of Shakespeare and the Pilgrims.

1611 **King James Bible:** Translation authorized by King James I. Contained a predominance of Saxon words and represented the flowering of the English language. Contained no marginal notes—a Bible relying wholly on the power of the Word for its holy message! It was the freest and purest of translations since Wycliffe.

The Christian Founding

1620 Bible travels west with the Pilgrims, "People of the Book," who plant the seeds of the first Christian Constitutional Republic in America through the Mayflower Compact.

The Bible becomes "the first book of learning," the primer of all instruction in America's founding era. Preeminent in all of American life and learning and the textbook of civil government.

1640 **Bay Psalm Book:** First book printed in America. Several colonies required children "be made able to read the Scriptures."

New England Primer

1683 **New England Primer:** First American textbook for children who were taught to read using the hornbook, primer, psalter, and Bible. Textbooks contained Christian values and themes.

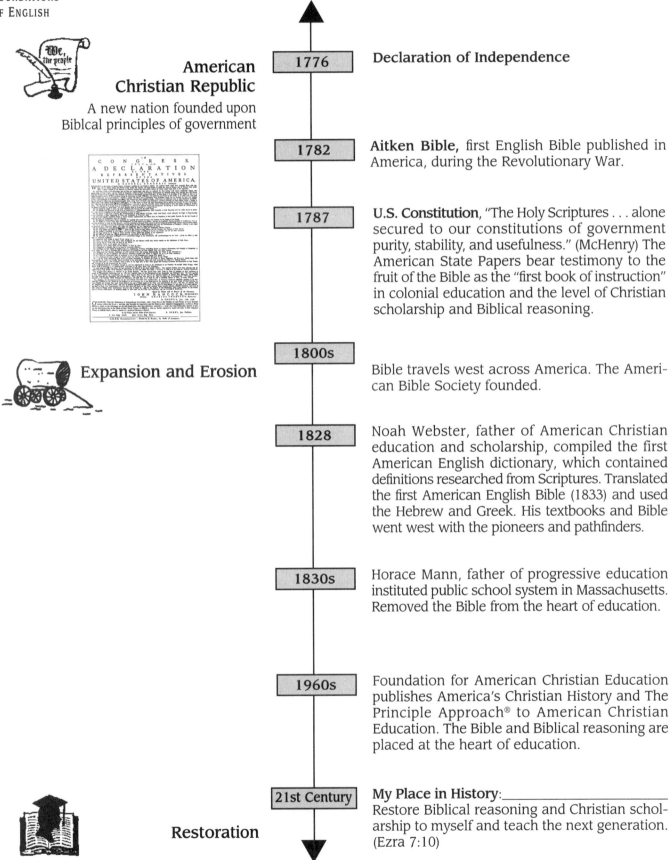

American Christian Republic

A new nation founded upon
Biblcal principles of government

Expansion and Erosion

Restoration

1776 — Declaration of Independence

1782 — **Aitken Bible,** first English Bible published in America, during the Revolutionary War.

1787 — **U.S. Constitution,** "The Holy Scriptures . . . alone secured to our constitutions of government purity, stability, and usefulness." (McHenry) The American State Papers bear testimony to the fruit of the Bible as the "first book of instruction" in colonial education and the level of Christian scholarship and Biblical reasoning.

1800s — Bible travels west across America. The American Bible Society founded.

1828 — Noah Webster, father of American Christian education and scholarship, compiled the first American English dictionary, which contained definitions researched from Scriptures. Translated the first American English Bible (1833) and used the Hebrew and Greek. His textbooks and Bible went west with the pioneers and pathfinders.

1830s — Horace Mann, father of progressive education instituted public school system in Massachusetts. Removed the Bible from the heart of education.

1960s — Foundation for American Christian Education publishes America's Christian History and The Principle Approach® to American Christian Education. The Bible and Biblical reasoning are placed at the heart of education.

21st Century — **My Place in History:**_____
Restore Biblical reasoning and Christian scholarship to myself and teach the next generation. (Ezra 7:10)

Eternity Future

NOTE: *The illustration of the Declaration is used with permission from the Providence Foundation. It is reproduced from* America's Providential History, *Mark A. Beliles and Stephen K. McDowell. Charlottesville, Va.: Providence Foundation, 1989.*

The Influence of the Bible on William Bradford's Literary Style

Of Plimoth Plantation, Our First American Christian Classic

by Rosalie June Slater

Comments on William Bradford's History

"Critics and apologists alike seem content to agree that at least this one work is an 'authentic masterpiece' and an 'American classic.' . . . As a central historical document, and as our first great work of literature, Plymouth Plantation must surely be the most important work of the seventeenth century." (Alan B. Howard, "Art and History in Bradford's *Of Plymouth Plantation*," *The William and Mary Quarterly*, April 1971)

"Wherever it shall go it will be an object of reverent care. I do not think many Americans will gaze upon it without a little trembling of the lips and a little gathering of mist in the eyes, as they think of the story of suffering, of sorrow, of peril, of exile, of death and of lofty triumph which that book tells,—which the hand of the great leader and founder of America has traced on those pages. There is nothing like it in human annals since the story of Bethlehem." (Senator George Frisbie Hoar, in the ceremonies at the State House in Boston, May 26, 1897, upon the return of the Bradford Manuscript to America)

Bradford's Biblical View of Life

1. Satan's battlefield is located in the human heart and mind. (Amsterdam Church, p. 189; Factions of Liford, Oldom, pp. 219–21)

2. Man relying upon his own strength must fail, but by this failure man is forced to acknowledge that his real strength rests in God. (Storm, p. 188; God makes weak to stand, p. 212; Longevity, pp. 239–40)

3. The sustaining hand of God enables man to endure beyond man's natural capacity. (First Winter, pp. 205–06; "All help fails, but ye Lord helped," p. 224)

4. Each new danger or distress draws man closer to God. (Illustrated throughout)

5. Spiritual fruit often comes from the momentary troubles and defeats. (Changes in articles, p. 197; Troubles with Weston, pp. 208–10)

6. Man "by provident care and use of good means" must order his life in strict conformity with "God and His ways." (Years in Holland, pp. 189–91; Preparations for Voyage, pp. 194–95)

7. Human reason anticipates dangers and multiplies problems; man must go forward in faith and trust in God's Providence. (Fears of unknown, pp. 193–94; Sailing the Atlantic, pp. 201–02)

8. The American Wilderness is a perfect symbol of man's earthly pilgrimage. (Description of arrival, pp. 202–03)

9. Christian charity must be exercised toward all men despite how they have used us. (Just one of many examples of Allerton's misconduct, p. 232)

10. The Christian must exercise fully "the gifts of mind and spirit" that God has given him while he lives in the world. (Thus the detail of the financial transactions of the Pilgrims, and of the details of how they repaid their debt to the Adventurers, is an indication of their Christian testimony.)

The Biblical Heritage of Bradford's Style

"Bradford's indebtedness to the English translation of the Bible is clear enough. He was familiar with the Geneva version, first published in 1560, and thereafter for a century the most popular of English Bibles. . . . The differences in style, however, between the Genevan and King James versions are not so great that the strong flavor of the Bible English in Bradford's prose is missed by the modern reader who is more or less familiar only with the language of the King James or Revised versions. Again and again Bradford's words, phrases, and rhythm stir echoes in the reader's memory. At times, indeed, when Bradford quotes, the transition from his words to those of the Bible is so easy and the blending so natural that it is scarcely perceptible where one leaves off and the other begins. A notable example of this is the moving passage at the end of the ninth chapter, where the arrival in Cape Cod Harbor is recounted. . . . The hand is the hand of Bradford, but the voice is the voice of the English Bible." (E. F. Bradford, "Conscious Art in Bradford's History of Plymouth Plantation," The New England Quarterly, Vol. 1, 1928)

The Influence of the Bible on Bradford's Style

1. Bradford's frequent references to Scripture (see pp. 192, 196, 209, 216, 219, 239–40, etc., in CHOC I).

2. Bradford's paraphrasing of Biblical texts (see pp. 191, 203, 212–13, 216–17, 219, etc.).

3. Bradford's use of Biblical parallelism

   ". . . Bradford's description of the Pilgrims' arrival in the new world, where the scriptural types of Paul's shipwreck on Melita and of Israel's wanderings in the desert are drawn, only to be abandoned as somehow inadequate to the particularities of the Pilgrims' situation. . . . This unexpectedly critical and discriminating use of Biblical parallelism extends even to Bradford's handling of the troubles of 1642. The 'outbreak of wickedness' must have tempted him to see these events as a recapitulation of the Old Testament pattern of apostasy and judgment and to voice again Jeremiah's cry for reformation without tarrying. Instead, he first notes that the outbreak may, paradoxically, be either 'intended to subdue and mortify our corrupt natures' or the result of Satan's especial outrage at a holy people, the bitter-sweet reward for the colony's piety." (Howard, "Art and History in Bradford's Of Plymouth Plantation," pp. 264–65)

4. Bradford's words, phrases, rhythm like the language of the Bible.

Though William Bradford began life as a Yorkshire farmer, without formal education, his library contained some 400 volumes in Plymouth. Since Bradford, mind and heart, was educated by the Bible, and since it was for him "his book of all learning," it is not surprising that his masterpiece is a masterpiece of Biblical expression and that it is Christian in its view of life and character.

Literary Devices Used

Alliteration: "The repetition of the initial letter or sound in two or more closely associated words or stressed syllables." (Thrall)

Examples: "ye very roote & rise"; "both scoffed and scorned"; "ye poore people"; "other lands & livings"; "freinds & famillier acquaintance" (all found on p. 185). Alliteration will be found throughout.

Antithesis: "A figure of speech characterized by strongly contrasting words, clauses, sentences, or ideas. A balancing of one term against another for impressiveness and emphasis, i.e., 'Man proposes, God disposes.'" (Thrall)

Examples: "for though they could not stay, yet were ye not suffered to goe." (p. 186), "ye dangers were great, but not desperate" (p.19), "the difficulties were many, but not invincible" (p. 194).

Coupling: Words coupled of similar or nearly identical meaning.

Examples: "occasion and indusment" (p. 185), "strange & uncouth language" (p. 189), "faire & bewtiful cities" (p. 189), "grime & grisly" (p. 189), "bukle & incounter" (p. 189), "both enterprised and overcome" (p. 190).

Metaphor: "A figure of speech based on a comparison which is implied rather than directly used, i.e., " 'He was a lion in the fight.'"(Thrall)

Examples: "armed with faith and patience" (p. 189), "necessitie was a taskmaster" (p. 192), "a sea of troubles" (p. 202), "your honestie & conscience . . . [a] weapon to wound your adversaries" (p. 222).

Simile: "A figure of speech in which a similarity between two objects is directly expressed. Most similies are introduced by like or as, 'He fought like a lion.'" (Thrall)

Example: "povertie . . . like an armed man"

Bradford's Character Portraits

Isaac Allerton: Agent, son-in-law of Brewster. Mismanages their affairs. (pp. 231–32) Note Bradford's own character in his charitable hope that Allerton's motives were better than they seemed in practice.

William Brewster: Beloved Elder Brewster who was a Pilgrim for thirty-six years. He was sixty years old during the winter of 1620 and was a nurse to younger men and women during that fateful winter. (See pp. 205, 232, 238–39.)

Squanto: The Indian whose life God preserved so that he could minister to the Pilgrims and help them survive in the New World. (See pp. 206–07.)

Thomas Weston: "Iron-monger of London, was an 'Adventurer' (promoter and capitalist) . . . a man of enterprise, eager to reap quick profits from the new world, and not very scrupulous as to means." (Samuel Eliot Morison, "Notes") (See

pages 195, 208–09, and also pp. 210–12 which deal with his men.) The Pilgrims always forgave and helped Weston, no matter how badly he treated them, out of their gratitude for his help in financing the Mayflower Voyage.

Ship-Carpenter and Salt-Maker: Contrasting portraits (p. 218)

Edward Winslow: This man's biography should be researched as he is one of the most outstanding of the Pilgrims. His Pilgrimage for Peace with the Indians and his care of Massasoyt is a unique testimony of Pilgrim love.

John Oldom and John Lyford: Other portraits that are noteworthy in their discernment.

Indians: Hobomok and Massasoyt deserve study.

John Robinson: He is mentioned briefly in this selection (p. 190). It is a restrained picture which is felt deeply. His letter to the Pilgrims also gives us a picture of this pastor who was the greatest influence upon the Pilgrim character and testimony. (See pp. 198–201.) In the complete edition the letters of Robinson during the negotiations are insightful, especially his statement, "Lastly, it is not with us as with other men, whom small things can discourage, or small discontentments cause to wish themselves at home again."

William Bradford Writes for Posterity

On p. 197 Bradford indicates one reason why he wishes to include the detail of many of the Pilgrim transactions which might puzzle the non-Christian:

"That their children may see with what difficulties their fathers wrastled in going through these things in their first beginnings, and how God brought them along notwithstanding all their weaknesses & infirmities."

Grandmother Rosalie's Story of
John Wycliffe for Little Boys and Girls

He gave us our First Bible in English.
"The Morning-Star of the Reformation"

Do you know how to find the Morning-Star in the sky? You have to get up very early in the morning—when the sky is still dark. If you go out of doors and look up at the sky, you may see one lone star in the east brightly shining. It is actually the last star we can see before the light of the rising sun brightens the world with light. This is the Morning-star—the first star we saw before the dawn. We call John Wycliffe the Morning Star of the Reformation because he was the first man to give us The Holy Bible in our own language—English.

John Wycliffe loved to learn the truth about everything. He lived in a part of England where he enjoyed freedom. But John Wycliffe did not find the Bible, which is the source of all God's truth, until he was a grown-up man. Would you like to know the story of how John Wycliffe found the Bible for himself?

John Wycliffe loved to study and one day when he was in the great church library, that place where all the books could be found, he pulled out of the shelf a small Book which was entitled *The Holy Bible of God's Word*. John Wycliffe sat down on one of the hard benches in the library and began to read. He sat on that hard bench for a long, long time. What was there about that little Book which fascinated him?

For the first time in his life John Wycliffe was learning how everything in the world—everything he could see and hear and feel—began. The first words of this wonderful Book stated:

"In the beginning, God created the heavens and the earth."

As John Wycliffe read on, he learned that the Great Sovereign God, the One-and-Only God, created or began all of this planet earth which you and I live upon. What do you think about that? Haven't you ever wondered how all this got started?

As John Wycliffe read on in the beginning of The Holy Bible, it was like a great painting which God was filling in. First of all God Himself spoke some Words, Perhaps they were the first Words ever spoken.

"Let there be light—and there was light."

The darkness disappeared and God divided the light from the darkness, and He created day and night.

Rosalie June Slater

CHAPTER THREE
ORTHOGRAPHY: STRONG BASIC SKILLS IN SPELLING, PENMANSHIP, AND SPEAKING

Of all beasts he learned the language,
Learned their names and all their secrets,
How the beavers built their lodges,
Where the squirrels hid their acorns,
How the reindeer ran so swiftly,
Why the rabbit was so timid,
Talked with them whene'er he met them,
Called them "Hiawatha's Brothers."
—Longfellow

Sample English Language Lesson Plan

Grade: _5_ Date: _4/15/98_ Teacher: _Youmans_   Component:
- [ ] Biblical Foundation
- [x] Orthography
- [ ] Etymology
- [ ] Syntax
- [ ] Prosody
- [ ] Composition

Skill Taught: _Speaking-Presenting a Poet and his Poetry._

Principle: _Communicating_

Biblical Reference: _____ Illustration: _____

_____

Materials/Resources: _A poet selected from chapter 6_

_____

Structure of the Lesson

1. Introduce the purpose and goal of the lesson.

The student has studied one of the poets, analyzed his/her poetry and memorized a poem. The student now will use his love of this poet's work to inspire others by making a presentation. The student will be taught, and then practice, guidelines for speaking.

2. Review related skill or concept.

Review the guidelines for speaking on p. 99 in chapter 3. Teacher should demonstrate a good sample of speechmaking to model the guidelines.

3. Present new principle and idea with appropriate methodology.

The student will prepare a speech based on the study of the poet and poetry. The format on pp. 99–100 for elementary speechmaking should be followed. The teacher will guide the student in discovering ways to communicate effectively.

4. Require student practice, participation, and presentation.

The student will practice his speech guided by the teacher incorporating some of the poetry, either as recitation or to demonstrate a point in the speech. When the speech is well-prepared and practiced, it should be presented to a group.

5. Summarize, review, and evaluate.

The speech could be videotaped to give the student opportunity to self-evaluate. In a group of students, peer critique and encouragement can be effective. The speech should be polished to the point that the audience is "reached" effectively, i.e., inspired by the poetry and responsive.

Introduction to Orthography

Basic Skills in Spelling, Penmanship, and Speaking

Orthography includes the teaching and learning of basic phonetic reading and writing. In this Guide, we include basic speaking skills as foundational to language education. While orthography is literally "right writing," language is speaking as much as writing, thus we include various speaking skills along with the basics of phonetics and penmanship.

The beginning-to-read step of language learning rests upon the mastery of phonetics through the method published as *The Writing Road to Reading*™, first developed by Romada and Walter Spalding. It includes penmanship as part of the beginning-to-read program and does an excellent job of integrating all language skills including listening, speaking, writing, and reading. It uses the dictation method based upon mastering the sounds and spellings of the language.

We suggest building upon the penmanship as prescribed by *The Writing Road to Reading*™ by incorporating the *Palmer Method* of penmanship to refine and develop a lovely style.

The content of the Orthography chapter is provided to back up the curriculum charts with material for teaching the other aspects of orthography—speaking and elocution.

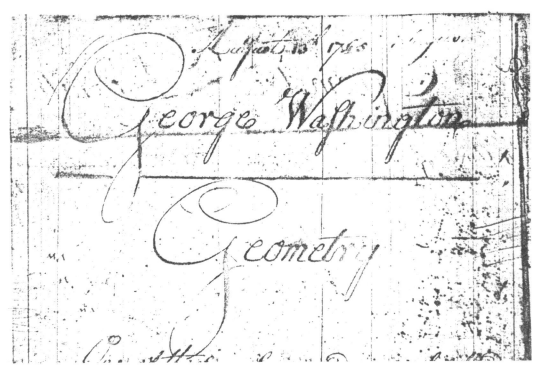

Title Page from Young George Washington's Geometry Copybook

August 15, 1745

Beginning to Read with Phonetic Instruction
The Writing Road to Reading™

Goals for Teaching Reading in The Principle Approach®

1. To teach wholistically, employing all the language skills in the teaching of reading—listening, speaking, syllabication, composition, comprehension, vocabulary, and grammar.

2. Learning is based on reasoning, on logical thinking processes, not solely on drill, recognition, or memorization.

3. Knowledge is not thoroughly mastered until a child can reason from it and express what he has learned—until he can think information through to its explanation to others.

How *The Writing Road to Reading*™ Fits the Goals

1. Reading is taught wholistically along with writing, spelling, speaking, and thinking; and the phonogram system forms the basis of the teaching of spelling throughout the grades.

2. Language is a system of sounds. *The Writing Road to Reading*™ reduces sounds to written symbols and teaches spelling in connection with the sounds of the language, arranging the correct spelling of sounds in a logical sequence.

3. Learning to read must be a reasoning, thinking experience, not just memory work. In *The Writing Road to Reading*™, the writing of words is the skill most fully requiring the mind to think and direct the hand to express thoughts in logical sequence.

The Writing Road to Reading™ integrates the four elements of language—speech, writing, spelling, and reading—to teach phonetics. The great advantage of this is:

1. Spelling is taught from the beginning to reveal the logic of the language;

2. Training is first in written spelling, enabling the child to begin to read with well-written books which interest, educate, and develop a love for reading and a taste for literature;

3. Handwriting and accurate pronunciation are taught from the very start, teaching the saying with the writing of the sounds used in spoken English;

4. Logic and reasoning are developed in applying the knowledge of phonograms;

5. The writing of words is the skill most fully requiring the mind to think and direct the hand to express thoughts in a logical sequence;

6. The sequence of first teaching the writing of phonograms while saying the common sounds before combining them into written and spoken words, and before starting to read books, is reasonable and logical—the proper foundation and pattern for learning.

The Writing Road to Reading™ Method

The purpose of reading is to learn what the author has to say, not to learn phonics.

1. Seventy common phonograms are used to write English on paper. Forty-five basic sounds are used in speaking English.

2. The class learns phonograms by seeing, hearing, saying, and writing them.

3. Then they write from dictation the 150 most used words as they say the phonogram sounds heard in each.

4. They write and read original sentences to show their meanings.

5. Within two months they read books.

6. The 1500 most commonly used words are taught in the order of their frequency of use.

7. Twenty-nine rules of spelling determine which phonogram is used.

8. The method is direct and so organized that children use only paper, pencil, and their minds.

9. By November the first 150 most used words have been studied in the written spelling lessons, and the beginning classes are ready to start reading books—a children's Bible and well-written story books. The students are not dependent on basal readers with a controlled vocabulary.

The Spelling Connection

The failure of most phonics programs is that they do not teach spelling, and they do not teach the saying and writing of the forty-five basic sounds before trying to read.

1. The key to good writing and reading of language is the ability to spell from the spoken word.

2. *The Writing Road to Reading*™ method always indicates the direct relationship of each sound in any spoken word to the written symbol or phonogram which represents it.

3. Words are taught in spelling lessons in the order of their frequency of use in language.

4. The important rules of spelling are taught by example when met in writing of words being studied in twenty-nine rules. Students see and correct areas before they become fixed in their mind.

5. The learning of spelling words from dictation connects at once the written symbols to their spoken sounds.

6. By fifth or sixth grade, students who have mastered the 150 most commonly used words make twelfth grade spelling scores.

Teaching Penmanship

Tools for use in practicing penmanship are found on the following pages and may be duplicated.

1. Lined paper with dotted lines in between for assisting students in learning the proper formation of printed or cursive letters.

2. Paper with slanted lines (one for right-handed and one for left-handed writers) to lay under the sheet of notebook paper to help children with their slant.

The Skill of Speaking

Speaking is a skill and an art. As a skill it includes mastery of diction, elocution, and speaking "presence"—the ability to speak publicly with confidence and poise. We include speaking skills in the orthography component of English language instruction as it is vital to a good education to establish speaking skills early as the child learns to read, write, and reason. The following sections on "Basics of Speaking" and "Elocution" are for elementary grades.

Speaking is an art of composition—inventing or combining ideas, clothing them with words, putting them in order, and committing them to paper. The composition component, in chapter seven, gives the curriculum for developing speaking as an art of composition.

Speaking as a skill and as an art requires practice—opportunities to speak to groups, to discuss, debate, present, or make a formal speech.

In primary grades, speaking should be encouraged throughout the day in all subjects through discussion, presentation, recitation, etc. Opportunity should be made for primary age children to present formal speeches with a simple formula such as:

1. Choose a topic.

2. Have a good beginning.

3. Keep to the subject.

4. Have a good, strong ending.

Basics of Speaking for Elementary Grades

1. Stand straight, but not stiffly. Good posture makes you look better and feel better and helps you to breathe correctly.

2. Breathe correctly. A good breather can feel his waist go in and out as he breathes.

Good breathing is in and out, in and out. It is never up and down. You should be able to breathe deeply without moving your shoulders.

3. Speak loudly enough so that the people in the back of the room can hear you. The more deeply you breathe, the more loudly you can speak.

4. Use the lips and tongue freely. The lips, tongue, and teeth break the voice sounds into words. The voice box cannot make words. It can only make sounds. These sounds are changed by the lips, tongue, and teeth. Try to say the following sentence first while holding your mouth open, and then by using your tongue and lips freely: *Paul's papa put pepper in the peach pudding.*

5. Relax the lower jaw. A relaxed lower jaw is one that is permitted to drop easily as you pronounce such words as bubble, double, trust, and just. It is hard to pronounce words plainly if the jaws are held too close together.

6. Look at your audience. People will pay better attention to a speaker who looks at them than to one who looks at the floor or at the ceiling.

7. Keep your hands at your sides. A speaker who plays with a pencil or some other object in his hands does not get good attention. The listeners watch the hands and forget to listen.

8. Do not make meaningless sounds. Some people say "well," "ah," "uh," or "er" between sentences. These sounds do not mean anything, but it is easy to get into the habit of using them. If you hear yourself using them, try hard to break the habit.

As students rise through the grades, formal speechmaking should be practiced in the English curriculum often, culminating in a public "Eighth Grade Speech." This speech should be given before an assembly of the school with parents to mark the promotion to high school.

How to Teach Student Presentations

Most people usually form their first impressions of us from our appearance, our manners, and our speech. Learning stage presence and the communication skills of making presentations, receiving awards, or singing or playing an instrument in front of an audience while in primary school will serve the student all his life.

Teachers should take every opportunity to instruct students in stage presence and in elocution.

1. Practice entering and exiting the assembly hall with the class.

2. Have assigned positions for each child on stage.

3. Teach students and practice stage presence—where to place their feet, hold their hands, and head.

4. Teach children how to make eye contact with the audience.

5. Practice learning how to shake hands, receive an award or a diploma.

6. Students should be instructed in how to project their voices.

7. Students should be given several opportunities to practice their presentation in the assembly hall with costumes, props, lecterns, sound systems, and cameras.

THE NOAH PLAN® © 2006 • FOUNDATION FOR AMERICAN CHRISTIAN EDUCATION

Elocution

Elocution [from Latin *e*, "out," and *loqui, locutus*, "to speak"] is the art of uttering sentences, either in speaking or reading, with all the agreeableness, feeling, force, and effect of which their meaning is susceptible. Good reading depends on the proper use of the following elements of elocution:

1. Force and Stress
2. Time
3. Pitch
4. Inflections, or Slides
5. Quality
6. Emphasis (union of elements)

Good reading presupposes correct pronunciation in which these elements are included:

1. Articulation
2. Syllabication
3. Accent

Force

Force of voice is the degree of loudness or softness used in vocal utterance. The three principal degrees of force are: **Medium**; **Soft**; and **Loud**.

1. By another mode of naming, the degrees of force are classed as: *(a) Effusive* (as in ordinary conversation); *(b) Expulsive* (with considerable effort); and *(c) Explosive* (with great effort).

2. The varying degree of force may be more minutely denoted by borrowing from the language of music. In the following table the ordinary and the technical names of the degrees of force are set forth in connection with the thoughts and sentiments to the expression of which these degrees of force are applicable.

   Pupils will understand that the Italian names used mean respectively: *piano*, soft; *pianissimo*, very soft; *mezzo forte*, moderate (literally, middling loud); *forte*, loud; *fortissimo*, very loud.

Degrees of Force			Applicable Circumstances
Soft Very Soft	*Piano* *Pianissimo*	*p.* *pp.*	Secrecy, caution, doubt; pity, love, grief, awe . . . . tenderness, plaintive sentiment . . . humility, shame . . . repose; fatigue, prostration.
Medium	*Mezzo forte*	*mf.*	Common conversation . . . plain . . . narrative and description . . . unimpassioned speech.
Loud Very Loud	*Forte* *Fortissmo*	*f.* *ff.*	Certainty . . . anger, rage, hate, ferocity . . . mirth, joy, triumph . . . excited states of the mind generally.

RULE: In the application of force, we must first decide, by an inspection of the general character of the piece, what is the normal degree of force to be used. Applying this degree to words that are not emphatic, we must increase the force in proportion to the importance of the ideas to be expressed. Thus,

He buys - he *sells* - he STEALS - he KILLS for gold.

If I were an American, as I am an Englishman, while a foreign troop remained in my country, I NEVER would lay down my arms—*never*, NEVER, NEVER!

Stress

Stress is the manner of applying emphatic force in the utterance of a syllable. The term *stress*, as distinguished from "force" in general, is used to denote the mode in which force is rendered impressive *in single sounds*. The force of utterance in a sentence may be on one phrase, or even on a single word. In the pronunciation of a word, it may be exclusively on one syllable. In the enunciation of a syllable, the organic force may be chiefly on a single letter. In the sound of a letter, the force of the voice may lie conspicuously on the first or on the last part of the sound, on the middle, or on both extremes, or it may be distributed with an approach to equalizing force over all parts of the sound.

The three principal varieties of stress are:

1. *Initial* (or radical), with the force applied at the beginning of a vowel.

2. *Median*, in which there is an increase of force towards the middle of a vowel.

3. *Final*, with the force applied at the close of a vowel.

The three modes of stress are:

1. *Diminuendo*

2. *Swell*

3. *Crescendo*

We may use the greatest force at the beginning of the word. To indicate this we use the mark >. An instance of this way of applying the force is found where we laugh out heartily, **Ha>** ! **Ha>** ! **Ha>** ! If we now bring out the greatest amount of force in the middle of the word, we mark it <>, as **<oOOOo>**. The most intense feeling or enthusiasm is generally expressed by making the last part of the word the loudest.

Exercise

Soft

Flow, softly flow, by lawn and lea,
A rivulet, then a river;
No more by thee my steps shall be,
For ever and for ever.

Medium

Not enjoyment, and not sorrow,
Is our destined end or way;
But to act that each to-morrow
Find us further than to-day.

Let us, then, be up and doing,
With a heart for any fate;
Still achieving, still pursuing,
Learn to labor and to wait.

Loud

Stand! the ground's your own, my braves!
Will ye give it up to slaves?
Will ye seek for greener graves?
Hope ye mercy still?
What's the mercy despots feel?
Hear it in that battle-peal!
Read it on yon bristling steel!
Ask it—ye who will!

Time

Time is the degree of rapidity in the rate of utterance.

The three principal rates of utterance are:

1. *Medium*
2. *Slow*
3. *Rapid*

The **medium** rate is used in the utterance of unimpassioned speech, that is, when the general character of the piece does not involve the emotions or feelings.

The **slow** rate is used in the utterance of such sentiments and mental states as: solemnity and dignity; deliberation and doubt; grief; and tranquillity.

The **rapid** rate is used in the utterance of such emotions as: cheerfulness, mirth, and gaiety; raillery; anger, hate, and ferocity; and excited states generally.

Exercise

Slow

The curfew tolls the knell of parting day;
  The lowing herd winds slowly o'er the lea;
The plowman homeward plods his weary way,
  And leaves the world to darkness and to me.

Slowly and sadly we laid him down,
  From the field of his fame fresh and gory:
We carved not a line, and we raised not a stone,
  But we left him alone with his glory.

Medium

Yet beautiful and bright he stood,
  As born to rule the storm;
A creature of heroic blood,
  A proud though child-like form.

Rapid

Storm! storm! Riflemen, form!
  Ready, be ready to meet the storm!
Riflemen, riflemen, riflemen, form!

He woke to hear his sentries shriek,
"To arms! they come! the Greek! the Greek!"
He woke to die midst flame and smoke,
And shout and groan and saber-stroke,
And death-shots falling thick and fast
  As lightnings from the mountain cloud.

And rushing and flushing and brushing and gushing,
And flapping and rapping and clapping and slapping,
Amid curling and whirling and purling and twirling,
Advancing and glancing and prancing and dancing,
'Tis this way the water comes down at Lodore.

Under the element of "time" are included **quantity** and **pauses**. The former may be briefly treated: the latter is of great importance.

Quantity determines the character of a syllable, as long, short, or neutral, by regarding its power of being prolonged in pronunciation.

A syllable is long when terminated by a vocal or sub-vocal (go, fear, orb, home, these, bold).

A syllable is short when, containing no sub-vocal, it is terminated by an explosive aspirate (cat, top, pipe, apt).

A syllable is neutral when, terminated by an explosive aspirate, it contains one or more sub-vocals (tract, bank, great); or when terminated by a sustained aspirate, with or without preceding sub-vocals (if, fife, mists, strength, cease, face, grief).

When, for the rhetorical expression of awe, solemnity, grief, etc., a deliberate delivery is required, the prolongation must be made on long syllables. Any attempt to extend those which from their construction are necessarily short or neutral will result in an offensive drawl, and a violation of correct pronunciation.

Pause

A **pause** is a suspension of the voice in reading or speaking, in order to make the meaning clearer or more impressive.

Phrasing is the division of a sentence by pauses into its proper parts in reading.

Pauses are of two kinds—*grammatical*, and *elocutionary* or *rhetorical*.

Grammatical pauses, introduced chiefly for the sake of clearness, are indicated by the punctuation marks.

A very noticeable defect in reading, on the part of young pupils, is the hasty or mechanical delivery of long sentences, complex or compound. As most pupils have been taught to pause at the punctuation marks on the old-fashioned plan, "Stop long enough to count one, and keep your voice up," etc., they form the idea that they must make no pause until some printer's mark is reached. Whenever there is a long or involved sentence, therefore, the teacher should call attention to the different parts of which it is composed, and require a pause at the close of every group of words forming a distinct element of the sentence. Give pupils the general rule: Suspend the voice whenever you think the pause will help you better to understand and express the meaning of what you are reading.

An **elocutionary**, or **rhetorical**, pause is a suspension of the voice for the purpose of rendering words or phrases more impressive or emphatic.

1. The pronunciation marks, which indicate the grammatical relations (of the elements of a sentence) are sufficient for the *eye*, but they are not sufficient for the *ear*. Many more stops than are indicated to the eye ought often to be observed. Good reading depends largely on the judicious use of rhetorical pauses, both as to their position and length.

2. The rhetorical pauses often coincide with the grammatical clauses, but not always. Sometimes a considerable pause is required where no punctuation mark is used; as in the statement:

   He woke to die;

   which should be read,

   He woke   to *die*.

   On the other hand, it often happens that no pause should be made at a comma; as in "Yes, sir," or "No, sir," when a pause at the comma would make the reading stiff and halting.

   In the use of elocutionary pauses, observe the following:

General Rules

1. Pause after a subject which consists of a phrase or a clause, or which is enlarged by adjuncts (modifiers); as,

   > To - be - virtuous / is to be happy.
   > The - blades - of - heroes / fence it round.
   > That - we - ourselves - need - forgiveness /
   > should make us ready to forgive.

2. Pause before an object which consists of a clause which is enlarged by modifers; as,

   > They tell us / that - we - are - weak.
   > The harpies of the shore shall pluck/ the - eagle - of - the - sea.

3. Pause after an element of a sentence placed for emphasis out of its grammatical order; as,

   > Blithe / looked the morning on cottage and spire.
   > Ere the - dark - hunters / the herd have passed by.

> Into - the - jaws - of - death / rode
> the Six Hundred.
> On - Linden when - the - sun was -
> low / all bloodless lay the
> untrodden snow.

4. Pause after words or phrases contrasted in meaning; as,

> It is more blessed to *give* / than to
> *receive.*
> *To - err* / is human ; to - *forgive* /
> divine.

5. Pause where there is an ellipsis (one or more words omitted); as,

> O, thou shalt find, where'er thy
> footsteps roam,
> That land / thy country, and that
> spot / thy home.

Length of Pause

The length of a pause depends on the feeling expressed in a passage: it is long in *solemn* and short in *lively* style. The pauses after emphatic words are longer than after other words.

Pitch

Pitch is the degree of elevation or depression of the voice.

The three most important grades of pitch are:

1. **Medium or Natural**
2. **Low**
3. **High**

The **key-note** of the voice is its *natural pitch.*

The **compass** of the voice is the *range*, from the lowest, to its highest note.

Modulation is the change of the voice from note to note.

1. Even the inflections of speech do not proceed from one perpetual line of pitch as in this diagram:

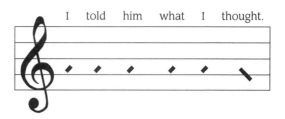

They are diversified by placing them at higher or lower degrees of the scale, as in the following notation of the same sentence:

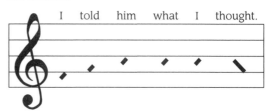

2. Although we may express properly all the pauses, inflections, and degrees of force necessary in a given selection, there will still be an unpleasant monotony of delivery if the voice is kept too long upon the same key, or pitch. To acquire flexibility of voice, there should be frequent changes in the pitch. Certain emotions, as those of joy, hope, or sudden fear, are best expressed in a high key. Ordinary description and general ideas call for the natural or medium pitch, while solemn or deep emotions require a low pitch.

In dialogues it will be found easy, with a little practice, to read the speeches of the different persons in different keys, so that the characters can never be confused or mistaken one for another. In selections in which different persons are quoted or spoken of, much life and interest may be imparted to the reading by changing the pitch or key as the description or speech changes.

To teachers who have a knowledge of musical sounds, the following specific directions will be of value. Let the class sound the syllable "la," upon the key of E, first in one long note, and afterwards in four short ones. Then start them upon a sentence or two in prose or poetry, so as to have them all read upon the same key, even if at first it is a little "sing-song." When this is done, have them continue on another sentence or two, so as to render also the natural sense of the passage while reading on the same key. Practice next on the key of C, in the same way, and afterwards upon the key of G. In this way you will soon train pupils to read naturally on any key that may be desired, from A below middle C to G above. Practice upon the changes in key will develop variety and flexibility of voice.

Exercise

Low Pitch

The curfew tolls the knell of parting day;
    The lowing herd winds slowly o'er the lea;
The plowman homeward plods his weary way,
    And leaves the world to darkness and to me.

Full knee-deep lies the winter snow,
    And the winter winds are wearily sighing;
Toll ye the church bells, sad and slow,
    For the Old Year lies a-dying.

Medium Pitch

All are architects of Fate,
Working in these walls of Time;
    Some with massive deeds and great,
Some with ornaments of rhyme.

In slumbers of midnight the sailor-boy lay;
    His hammock swung loose at the sport of the wind;
But watch-worn and weary, his cares flew away,
    And visions of happiness danced o'er his mind.

High Pitch

Hear the sledges with the bells—Silver bells!
    What a world of merriment their melody foretells!
How they tinkle, tinkle, tinkle,
    In the icy air of night!
While the stars, that oversprinkle
All the heavens, seem to twinkle
With a crystalline delight.

Away, away! through the wide, wide sky,
The fair blue fields that before us lie,
Each sun with the worlds that round him roll,
Each planet, poised on her turning pole,
With her isles of green, and her clouds of white,
And her waters that lie like fluid light!

Inflections or Slides

Inflections are slides of the voice at the close of syllables or words. The slide is a gliding of the voice from one note to another in the scale of speaking tones. Inflections are of two kinds:

1. *Simple*
2. *Compound*

A simple inflection consists of a single slide of the voice in either an upward or a downward direction. There are two simple inflections:

1. *The rising inflection*
2. *The falling inflection*

The rising inflection (marked ´) is a gliding of the voice upward; the falling inflection (marked `) is a gliding of the voice downward.

If we ask a question to which we expect the answer "Yes" or "No," as "Will he go´?" the voice slides or glides upwards on the word "go." In the answer, as "No`," the voice slides or glides downwards.

In the falling inflection, the voice starts above the general pitch of the words in the sentence, and comes down to it as, I say "no`."

Will you go to-day´ or to-morrow`?

Drill on Simple Inflections

One of the best methods of breaking up a monotonous delivery on the part of pupils is to practice them, say five minutes, at the beginning of the reading lesson, on a drill column of words.

Arrange vertically on the blackboard, and mark with the falling inflection, such words as Yes`, No`, Why`, How`, Where`, 1`, 2`, 3` . . .

Then substitute the rising inflection, Yes´, No´, Why´, etc.

Again alternate as—

Yes`	Where`
No`	1´
Why´	2´
How´	3´

Finally for more drill purposes both inflections may be marked and the sounds given: viz., ´Yes` ´No` ´Why`, etc.

These examples of inflection may be practiced first in concert and afterwards individually.

In giving the downward slide, there is a tendency on the part of the pupils to drop the voice *below* the general pitch of the sentence in cases where it should merely come down to that pitch, that is (in exact language) to give the "*full* cadence" where the "*partial* cadence" should be used—to say "I said no" in place of "I said no." In drilling on the falling inflection, in the examples given above, this matter should be carefully watched.

The *compound inflection*, or circumflex, is the union of two simple inflections. The rising may be continued into the falling, or the falling into the rising; and these inflections are named rising circumflex or *falling* circumflex, according to the termination of the slide.

The last part of the circumflex is generally the longer; so that the rising circumflex is a slight downward slide followed by a long upward slide; and the falling circumflex is a slight upward slide followed by a long downward slide.

The rising circumflex (marked ⌣) begins with the falling and ends with the rising slide; the falling circumflex (marked ⌃) begins with the rising and ends with the falling slide.

Rising: Is the servant a dŏg, that he should do this great thing?

Falling: I'm to be queen of the Mây, mother; I'm to be queen of the Mây!

Monotone

When no inflection is used, a monotone, or sameness of tone, is produced. This is suited to sublime or solemn passages, but is out of place in ordinary pieces. *Monotone* improperly used becomes *monotony*.

The unmeaning style so often and justly complained of in school reading is, to a great extent, owing to want of perception in regard to the nature and effect of the inflections. The ability to read aright the plainest passage of narrative or descriptive writing is wholly dependent on the just and discriminating use of the slide.

Exercise

Will they do it´? Dare they do it´?
Who is speaking`? What's the news`?
What of Adams`? What of Sherman`?
God grant they won't refuse`!

If you have tears´, prepare to shed them now`.

What constitutes a state`?

I come to bury` Caesar, not to praise´ him.

Were you ever at sea in a storm´?

Then` the forms of the departed`
Enter at the open door—
The belovéd`, the true-hearted`,
Come to visit` me once more.

Can the dôve live with the hăwk?

Charge, Chester, charge`!  On`, Stanley, on`!

They will give us pêace, yes,
    such pêace as the wŏlf gives to the lâmb!

Quality

Quality of voice is the kind of tones produced by the vocal organs. The two chief tones are:

1. *Pure tones*, when *all* the breath used is vocalized.

2. *Aspirated*, when only *part* of the breath is vocalized.

Orotund

What is called the orotund quality is simply pure tone used in impassioned utterance, by means of volume and energy of voice, combined with ample resonance. This quality of voice is mentioned by Dr. Rush as the highest perfection of the cultivated utterance of the public speaker. It is also regarded by him as the natural language of the highest species of emotion. It characterizes the vivid utterance of children, in their tones of love, and joy, and ecstasy. It belongs to the audible expression of masculine courage, energy, delight, admiration; and to the deliberate language of vengeance, as distinguished from the aspirated and suffocated voice of anger and rage.

Faults in Quality

The following are enumerated by Murdoch as faults which impair purity of tone:

1. ***The guttural tone***—a mode of utterance which seems to make the voice issue from an obstructed throat.

2. ***Nasal tone***—which makes the voice sound as if it came only through the nose.

3. ***The oral tone***—the slight, ineffective voice of indifference, feebleness, or fatigue; or the mincing tone of false taste.

4. ***The pectoral tone***—a fault arising from an imperfect habit of breathing, in consequence of which the lungs are not furnished with a sufficient supply of air to produce full and clear tone.

Of course, all these "faults" in quality may become merits when appropriately used by the professional elocutionist for expressive or imitative effects.

Exercise

Pure

O that this lovely vale were mine!
    Then, from glad youth to calm decline,
My years would gently glide;
    Hope would rejoice in endless dreams,
And Memory's oft-returning gleams
    By peace be sanctified!

There is a land, of every land the pride
    Beloved by Heaven o'er all the world beside,
Where brighter suns dispense serener light,
    And milder moons imparadise the night;
O, thou shalt find, howe'er thy footsteps roam,
    That land—thy country, and that spot—thy home.

Thou, too, sail on, O ship of state!
    Sail on, O Union, strong and great!

Aspirated

Speak softly!
    All's hushed as midnight yet.

Hence, horrible shadow! Unreal mockery, hence!

The citizens whispered, with white lips,
    "The foe! they come! they come!"

Emphasis

Emphasis is the mode of drawing attention to one or more words in a sentence. By the proper use of emphasis we impart interest and animation to reading.

Emphasis, though often confounded with mere comparative force of utterance on an accented syllable, has in reality the wider scope of signification indicated in the preceding and following paragraphs. It is, therefore, not one of the simple elements of vocal expression, but the utilization of two or more of these elements to the end of calling special attention to emphatic words.

Modes of Emphasis

To call special attention to a word in any way, is to emphasize it. Hence a word may be rendered emphatic by the use of extra force, by a change in the inflection, by pauses, or even by uttering it in a very *low* key.

1. Emphasis by Force: A word may be emphasized by uttering it in a *louder* tone (that is, with extra "force").

Exercise

The lowest degree of emphasis is usually marked by italics;
the next higher degree, by SMALL CAPITALS;
the highest degree, by **LARGE CAPITALS.**

Go, ring the *bells*, and fire the *guns*,
    And fling the *starry banners* out;
Shout "FREEDOM" till your lisping ones
    Give back their *cradle* shout.

Come *over*, come OVER the river to me!

Must we but *weep* o'er days more blest?
    Must we but *blush*? Our fathers BLED!

What can alone ennoble *fight*?
    A noble CAUSE!

Not that I loved *Caesar* LESS, but *Rome* MORE.

And if thou saidst I am not peer
To any lord in Scotland here,
Lowland or Highland, far or near,
    Lord Angus, *thou* HAST LIED!

Strike—till the last *armed foe* expires.
    STRIKE—for your *altars* and your *fires*;
STRIKE—for the green graves of your *sires*,
    God, and your *native land*!

An hour passed on—the Turk *awoke*;
    That bright dream was his *last*;
He woke to hear his sentries shriek,
    To *arms*! they *come*! the *Greek*! the GREEK!

2. Emphasis by Inflection: A word may be emphasized by the use of the suitable inflection.

Exercise

Be not like dumb, driven *cattle´*,
    Be a *hero`* in the strife.

Sink´ or swim`, live´ or die`, survive´ or perish`,
    I give my hand´ and my heart to this vote.

Three thousand ducats`
    'tis a good round sum´.

I said an *elder´* soldier, not a *better´*.

In the *one´* writer we most admire the *man´*;
    in the *other`*, the *work`*.

Stand! the ground's your own, my braves!
    Will ye give it up to *slăves*?

He said; then full before their sight
    Produced the beast, and lo! 'twas *whîte*!

Truly, sir, *ăll* that I live by is with the *awl*.

Is thy servant a *dŏg*, that he should do this great thing?

---

3. Emphasis by Time: A word may be rendered emphatic by uttering it more slowly, or by pausing before or after it.

Exercise

I had a brother once—a *g-r-a-cious* boy;
    A lad both *b-r-a-ve* and *g-oo-d*.

H-ai-l, h-o-l-y light!

His sentence was / *death*!

CHAPTER FOUR
ETYMOLOGY

*I believed then, and I believe even more firmly now, that **all words belong to children**. They choose them for their own use by the simple process of taking possession of the ones they need to express what they want to say. If children do not hear speech that has variety and liveliness, and if their books do not have unfamiliar words tucked in like bright little surprises among the everyday ones, how in the world are they ever to accumulate a store of language to draw on, as new experiences and sensations increase the need and desire to communicate with the people they live with? Children, like the rest of us, need to be articulate, and it seems to me a withholding of what is properly theirs, to limit their experience of words (as in the "vocabulary-tested" book) to the vocabulary already possessed by an "average" child of any given age.*

—"Fun with Words," *Bequest of Wings,* Annis Duff

Sample English Language Lesson Plan

Grade: _4_ Date: _4/15/98_ Teacher: _Adams_

Component:
- ☐ Biblical Foundation
- ☐ Orthography
- ☒ Etymology
- ☐ Syntax
- ☐ Prosody
- ☐ Composition

Skill Taught: _Word Analysis_

Principle: _The order in words_

Biblical Reference: _Matthew 13:7–9_ Illustration: _The prevalence of Anglo-Saxon words in the Bible_

Materials/Resources: _The Noah Plan® English Language Curriculum Guide_

Structure of the Lesson

1. **Introduce the purpose and goal of the lesson.**

   To identify the characteristics of Anglo-Saxon words in English by examining a parable in the Bible where thirty-nine out of forty words are of Anglo-Saxon derivation.

2. **Review related skill or concept.**

   Review "root," "prefix," "suffix" the order in words. Review the Anglo-Saxon element in English in contrast to the classical element in ch. 2.

3. **Present new principle and idea with appropriate methodology.**

   Present words distinguished as Saxon by their form, use, and meaning. Identify words of those characteristics in the parable. Present five Anglo-Saxon prefixes or suffixes: -ness, -y, -ly, be-, -less (see pp. 118–121).

4. **Require student practice, participation, and presentation.**

   Students list characteristics of Anglo-Saxon words with examples in notebooks. Words identified in the parable are added. Anglo-Saxon prefixes and suffixes are listed with many examples.

5. **Summarize, review, and evaluate.**

   Using the words identified as having Anglo-Saxon affixes, define the root and the affix in practicing word analysis. Add words to the list as they appear in reading.

Teaching Etymology

Etymology, or the study of the origin and derivation of words, is that aspect of English teaching that dramatically expands vocabulary—giving our children the tools to build their mastery of language. A broad, precise vocabulary is the mark of the educated person. Skill in the use of words makes effective communication. The SAT test required for college entrance rests fifty percent of its score on the verbal segment which tests strictly the knowledge of vocabulary.

Instruction in etymology is directed towards building the word analysis habit. It begins with identifying the parts of words, the knowledge of common prefixes, suffixes, and roots both classical and Anglo-Saxon. Word analysis becomes a habit in every subject as students expand their base vocabularies exponentially by mastering the parts.

The Grammar Curriculum Charts in chapter five give the scope and sequence of teaching etymology throughout the grades. This chapter contains an elementary presentation of the study of etymology and some ideas for teaching it. The etymological dictionary is the major tool needed. The Webster 1828 *American Dictionary of the English Language* serves this purpose well. A modern etymological dictionary is useful with older students, such as *The Oxford Dictionary of English Etymology*, edited by C.T. Onions. Oxford Press, 1995; *An Etymological Dictionary of Modern English*, by Earnest Weekley. Dover Publications, 1967.

The best tool by far, next to Webster's 1828 *Dictionary*, is *Words Every College Student Should Know*, by Kenneth A. Oliver. This is an "analytical dictionary" with each word divided into parts and giving literal meaning of words.

One way to teach word analysis is to have the student set up a simple chart in the notebook for analyzing words:

Definition:
A brief description of a thing by its properties; The explanation of the essence of a thing by its kind and difference; An explanation of a word or term, or of what a word is understood to express.

Prefix	Prefix	Root	Suffix	Suffix	Other Derivations
	dis (apart from or away from)	HEART	en (a verb-forming suffix that makes a verb out of a noun)	ed (makes the past tense of a verb or a participle adjective)	
		SIX	th (a suffix that makes an ordinal numeral)		
	pre (before)	POSIT (put or placed)	ion (that which)		
		SIX	teen (a suffix that makes a cardinal number)		
dis	en	CHANT	ment		

Property:
A peculiar quality of anything; that which is inherent in a subject, or naturally essential to it.

Etymology, n. [Gr. True discourse]
1) That part of philology which explains the origin and derivation of words, with a view to ascertain their radical or primary signification. In grammar, etymology comprehends the various inflections and modifications of words, and shows how they are formed from their simple roots. 2) The deduction of words from their originals; the analysis of compound words into their primitives.

Philology, n. [Gr. to love words]
1) Primarily, a love of words, or a desire to know the origin and construction of language. In a more general sense, 2) That branch of literature which comprehends a knowledge of the etymology or origin and combination of words; grammar, the construction of sentence or use of words in language; criticism, the interpretation of authors, the affinities of different languages, and whatever relates to the history or present state of language. It sometimes includes rhetoric, poetry, history, and antiquities.

The Study of Etymology
From *Lessons in English* by Sara Lockwood.
Boston: Ginn and Company, 1890.

In order to use good English, we must know how to choose our words. To this end, we should learn to tell from looking at a word whether it is originally English or borrowed from some other tongue. We should know, too, just what the word means, so as to be able to use it in the right way. For this reason, we must learn the most important principles of Etymology, the science which treats of the derivation and meaning of words. An explanation of terms used in the science is given below, for the benefit of any who may not be familiar with them.

1. **The Root of a Word**. When a word cannot be reduced to a simpler form in the language to which it belongs, it is called a root, a radical, or a primitive word. Ex. *go, man*.

2. **Compound Words**. When a word is formed by uniting two or more simple words, it is called a compound word. Ex. *butter-fly, rose-bud*.

3. **Derivative Words**. When a word is made by joining to a root either a prefix or a suffix, or both, it is called a derivative word.

4. **Prefix**. A syllable or syllables placed before the root, to vary the meaning of the word; as, *il-legal*, not legal.

5. **Suffix**. A syllable or syllables placed at the end of a root, to vary the meaning of the word; as, *stud-ent*, one who studies.

6. **Affix**. The general name, referring to a syllable fixed to the root. It is, therefore, applied to either a prefix or a suffix.

Two Great Elements of the Language

The English language, as has been shown, is made up of words from many sources; but for convenience, it may be considered as containing two main elements:

1. **Anglo-Saxon**, including also words from other Teutonic tongues, such as the Danish.

2. **Classical**, including the words borrowed from the Latin and the Greek.

Numerical Ratio of the Two Elements

It has been shown in the preceding chapter that of the words in the dictionary, less than one-half are Saxon, nearly one-half Latin, and the remainder Greek and miscellaneous in origin. In common use, however, the number of Saxon words is relatively greater, because almost all the connecting words and the articles, pronouns, and auxiliary verbs are of Saxon origin, and these are used more frequently than any other words. It has been found by actual count that in the writings of about twenty good English authors, thirty-two words in forty are of Saxon origin. In Shakespeare and Milton, thirty-three words in forty are Saxon. The Bible is written in purer English than any other book which we have, some parts of it containing thirty-nine Saxon words in forty.

The Anglo-Saxon Element

The Anglo-Saxon element is the more important, for two reasons:

1. It is the native part of the language;

2. It is the larger element in common use among English-speaking people.

How We Know Saxon Words

Two things help us to determine whether a word is of Anglo-Saxon origin: first, the form of the word; second, the sense in which it is used. It must be borne in mind that there are exceptions to some of the rules which follow. For example, *un* is a Saxon prefix, but we find it in many words of Latin origin. In all doubtful cases, the pupil should consult the etymological dictionary.

Words Distinguished as Saxon by Their Form

1. Articles: a, an, the
   All Pronouns: we, this, which, etc.
   All Auxiliary Verbs: have, may, will
   All Adjectives compared irregularly: good, bad, little
   Nearly all Irregular and Defective Verbs: am, go, ought
   Nearly all Prepositions and Conjunctions: and, with, by, as

2. Nearly all words which, in any of their forms, undergo vowel changes
   Adjectives with two comparisons: old, older, oldest, elder, eldest
   Adjectives changed to nouns: strong, strength
   Nouns changed to verbs: bliss, bless
   Nouns forming plurals by vowel change: foot, feet
   Verbs with strong preterites: fall, fell
   Verbs changed by form from intransitive to transitive: rise, raise

3. Most words of one syllable
   Parts of the body: head, ear, skull, (not face).
   The senses: sight, touch, smell
   Infirmities: blind, lame, deaf
   The elements: fire, wind, frost, (not air)
   Products: grass, corn, bread
   Fuel: coal, wood, peat
   Domestic animals: cat, dog, horse

4. All words beginning with wh, kn, sh: when, know, shine. Most words beginning with ea, ye, gl, th: each, yearn, glad, thus. Most words ending with t, th: beat, truth

5. Most compound and derivative words, the elements of which exist and have a meaning in English: horseback, shipwreck, winsome

6. Most words with Anglo-Saxon prefixes and suffixes

Precise: Exact; nice; definite; having determinate limits; Precision in the use of words is a prime excellence in discourse.

Essence: 1) That which constitutes the particular nature of a being or substance, or of a genus, and which distinguishes it from all others; 2) Formal existence; that which makes anything to be what it is; or the peculiar nature of a thing.

Anglo-Saxon Prefixes:

1. *a* = in, on, at (corruption of on),
   a-bed, in bed; a-board, on board; a-back, at the back

2. *be* = by
   be-cause, by cause
   It is often intensive, as in be-stir, be-deck, be-come.

3. *for* = against, away
   for-bid, to bid against; for-bear, to bear away; for-give, formerly to give away

4. *fore* = before
   fore-tell, to tell before

5. *mis* = denotes wrong, evil
   mis-take, to take wrongly; mis-chance, ill chance

6. *n* = not
   n-ever, not ever
   n-either, not either
   n-one, not one

7. *out* = beyond
   out-law, beyond the law

8. *over* = above, or beyond the limit
   over-spread, to spread above
   over-do, to do too much

9. *up* = up
   up-hold, to hold up; up-land; up-start; up-right

10. *un* = not
    un-truth, not the truth
    un-honored, not honored

11. *under* = beneath
    under-go, to go beneath

12. *with* = against
    with-stand, to stand against

Anglo-Saxon Suffixes:

Noun Suffixes = one who (agent)

1. -ar   li-ar, one who lies
2. -ard   drunk-ard, one who drinks
3. -er   cri-er, one who cries
4. -yer   law-yer, one who understands law
5. -ster   young-ster, one who is young

Noun Suffixes = state, condition, quality

6. -dom   king-dom, state of a king
7. -ship   friend-ship, condition of friends
8. -hood   man-hood, state of man
9. -head   god-head, same as god-hood
10. -ness   good-ness, quality of being good

Noun Suffixes = little

11. -ling   dar-ling, a little dear
12. -kin   lamb-kin, a little lamb
13. -ie   dog-gie, a little dog
14. -ock   hill-ock, a little hill
15. -let   stream-let, a little stream (from the French)
16. -en   chick-en, a little chick

Adjective Suffixes = like, having the quality of, relating to

17. -ful   cheer-ful, having the quality of cheer
18. -ly   king-ly, like a king
19. -ish   boy-ish, having the qualities of a boy
             Engl-ish, originating with the Angles
20. -en   wood-en, having qualities of wood
21. -ern   north-ern, relating to the north
22. -y   gloom-y, having the qualities of gloom
23. -like   god-like, like a god

Miscellaneous Suffixes:

24. -less   loss, hope-less, with loss of hope
25. -some   lone-some, hand-some
26. -teen   ten, four-teen, four and ten
27. -ty (from tig)   decade, for-ty, four times ten
28. -ward   towards, east-ward, towards the east
29. -wise   manner, like-wise, in like manner
30. -en   Forms verbs from adjectives, weak, weak-en.
             Plural nouns: ox-en, child-ren

Words Distinguished as Saxon by Their Use and Meaning

1. Most of the words which we early learn to use, and which are most closely associated with the pleasant memories of childhood and home. Such words have more power over us than have the high-sounding words which we learn later in life. Perhaps this is the reason why we find a simple Saxon style so pleasing.

Among the classes of Saxon words which we learn in childhood are the following:

a) Names of our earliest and dearest associations:

Ex. home, friends, father, mother, husband, wife, son, daughter, brother, sister, fireside, hearth

b) Words expressing our strongest natural feelings:

Ex. gladness (not joy), sorrow (not grief), tears, smiles, blushes, laughing, weeping, sighing, groaning, love, hate (not anger), fear, pride, mirth. So also hungry, thirsty, tired, sleepy, lonesome, homesick, naughty

c) Names of common things, such as a child early notices and learns to talk about:

Ex. sun, moon, star, sky, cloud, earth, water

Animals: horse, cow, dog, cat, calf, pig (beef, veal, and pork are Norman terms)

Objects in the plant world: tree, bush, grass (not flower or vine)

Objects in the mineral world: sand, salt, iron, gold, stone (not rock)

Features of scenery: hill, woods, stream, land, sea (not mountain or valley)

Natural divisions of time, etc.: day, night, morning, evening, noon, midnight, sunset, sunrise, twilight, light, darkness

Kinds of weather, etc: cold, heat, wet, dry, wind, frost, hail, rain, sleet, snow, thunder, lightning, storm

Parts of the body: hand, arm, head, leg, eye, ear, foot, nose (not face)

2. Most of our particular terms. The general terms are mainly from the Latin, as will be seen from the following examples:

Latin-Saxon

motion	slide, creep, walk, fly, swim, etc.
color	white, blue, red, green, yellow, etc.
sound	buzz, speak, whistle, roar, etc.
animal	dog, man, sheep, wolf, etc.
number	all the cardinal numbers to a million and all the ordinal numbers except *second*.

This explains why the Saxon style is more vivid and picturesque, and therefore more pleasing than a style which abounds in words of classic origin.

3. Most of the words used in the common affairs of everyday life. The words which we hear in the home, on the street, in the shops and markets, and on the farm are, to a great extent, Saxon words.

Ex. sell, buy, cheap, dear, high, low, weight (not measure), work, grind, reap, sow, baker, shoemaker, worth, want, wedge, spring, scrape, sweep, wash, rich, poor, business, wages (not salary)

Caution: Notice that many such words are not of Saxon origin. For example, money. In all doubtful cases consult the dictionary.

4. Many colloquialisms; that is, words which are used in familiar conversation. An excited talker does not stop to choose the most elegant word. When a man is angry, he "talks plain English," and uses such words as lazy, shiftless, sly, gawky, shabby, trash, sham.

5. Most words used in our proverbs and maxims.

These "old sayings," or "household words," as they are sometimes called, owe much of their force to their simple Saxon style.

Ex. "Make hay while the sun shines." "A bird in the hand is worth two in the bush." "No pain, no gain." "Look before you leap."

The Classical Element

Latin Prefixes:

1. a, ab, abs = from or away
   ab-solve, to set free from
   ab-duct, to lead away
   a-vert, to turn from
   abs-tract, to draw from

2. ad = to
   Variations: a, ac, af, ag, al, an, ap, ar, as, at, the last letter being usually changed into the first letter of the word to which it is prefixed. This change is for the sake of euphony.

   ad-apt, to fit to
   a-gree, to be pleasing to
   ac-cede, to yield to
   af-fix, to fix to
   ag-grieve, to give pain to
   at-tract, to draw to
   al-lude, to refer to
   an-nex, to tie to
   ap-pend, to hang to
   ar-rive, to come to
   as-sist, to give help to

3. con = with or together
   Variations: co, cog, col, com, cor
   con-nect, to fasten together
   co-here, to stick together
   cog-nate, born together
   col-lapse, to fall together
   com-merce, trading with others
   cor-relative, relative with

4. dis = asunder, apart, opposite of
   Variations: di, dif
   dis-pel, to drive asunder
   dis-please, opposite of please
   di-vert, to turn apart
   dif-fer, to be apart

NOTES

5. se = apart   se-cede, to go apart

6. in = in, into, or on (in nouns and verbs)
    Variations: il, im, ir
    in-clude, to shut in   im-bibe, to drink in
    il-luminate, to throw light on   ir-rigate, to pour water on
    im-migrate, to move into a country

7. intra = intra-tropical, within the tropics

8. intro = within or into   intro-spection, a looking within
    intro-duce, to lead into

9. ex = out or from
    Variations: e, ec, ef
    ex-clude, to shut out   ec-centric, from the center
    e-vade, to get away from   ef-flux, a flowing out

10. contra = against
    Variations: contro, counter
    contra-dict, to speak against   contro-vert, to turn against
    counter-act, to act against

11. ob = against or out
    Variations: o, oc, of, op
    ob-ject, to throw against   oc-cur, to run against
    o-mit, to leave out   of-fend, to strike against
    op-pose, to act against

12. non = not   non-essential, not essential

13. in = not (in adjectives and nouns)
    Variations: ig, il, im, ir
    in-active, not active   il-legal, not legal
    ig-noble, not noble   im-mortal, not mortal
    ir-regular, not regular

14. sub = under or after
    Variations: suc, suf, sug, sum, sup, sus
    sub-scribe, to write under   suc-ceed, to follow after
    sub-sequent, following after   suf-fix, something fixed after
    sug-gest, to bring to mind   sum-mon, to call from under
    sup-press, to press under
    sus-tain, to hold from under

15. subter = under   subter-fuge, a flying under

16. post = after   post-mortem, after death

17. ante = before   ante-cedent, going before

18. pre = before   pre-fix, to fix before

19. pro = for or forward   pro-noun, for a noun
    pro-gress, to move forward

20. re = back or anew   re-pel, to drive back

21. retro = backward   retro-spect, a looking backward

22. extra = beyond   extra-ordinary, beyond ordinary

23. preter = beyond   preter-natural, beyond nature

24. trans = beyond or through   trans-atlantic, beyond the Atlantic
    trans-fix, to pierce through

25. ultra = beyond or extremely   ultra-marine, beyond the sea
    ultra-liberal, extremely liberal

26. per = through   per-spire, to breathe through

27. bi = two   bi-ped, two-footed

28. circum = around   circum-navigate, to sail around

29. inter = between   inter-cede, to go between

30. juxta = near   juxta-position, a placing near

31. sine = without   sine-cure, without care

32. super = over   super-intend, to have care over

33. de = down or off   de-pose, to put down
    de-fer, to put off

Latin Suffixes:

Noun Suffixes = One who (agent); that which

1. -an   artis-an, one who works at a trade
2. -ant   assist-ant, one who assists
3. -ent   stud-ent, one who studies
4. -ary   lapid-ary, one who cuts precious stones
5. -ate   advoc-ate, one who pleads a cause
6. -eer   auction-eer, one who holds an auction
7. -ier   cash-ier, one who has charge of the cash
8. -ist   botan-ist, one who studies botany [orig. Greek]
9. -or   act-or, one who acts
10. -ice   serv-ice, that which serves
11. -ment   induce-ment, that which leads
12. -mony   testi-mony, that which is testified
13. -ure   creat-ure, that which is created

Noun Suffixes = One who is (recipient); that which is

14.	-ate	deleg-ate, one who is sent by others
15.	-ite	favor-ite, one who is favored
16.	-ee	trust-ee, one who is trusted
17.	-ive	capt-ive, one who is taken

Noun Suffixes = State; condition; quality; act

18.	-ance	abund-ance, condition of abounding
19.	-ence	prud-ence, quality of being prudent
20.	-ancy	brilli-ancy, quality of brightness
21.	-ency	despond-ency, state of being despondent
22.	-age	marri-age, act of marrying
23.	-acy	accur-acy, quality of being accurate
24.	-ity	secur-ity, state of being secure
25.	-ty	liber-ty, state of being free
26.	-ion	evas-ion, act of evading
27.	-ism	hero-ism, state of being a hero [originally Greek]
28.	-ment	excite-ment, state of being excited
29.	-mony	matri-mony, state of marriage
30.	-tude	servi-tude, condition of slaving
31.	-ure	depart-ure, act of leaving

Noun Suffixes = Place where

32.	-ary	gran-ary, a place where grain is kept
33.	-ory	fact-ory, a place where things are made
34.	-ery	cemet-ery, a place where the dead sleep

Noun Suffixes = Minute (diminutives)

35.	-cle	parti-cle, a minute part
36.	-cule	animal-cule, a minute animal
37.	-ule	spher-ule, a minute sphere

Adjective Suffixes = Like; being; relating to

1.	-ac	cardi-ac, relating to the heart
2.	-al	leg-al, relating to the law
3.	-an	hum-an, relating to mankind
4.	-ar	circul-ar, like a circle
5.	-ary	milit-ary, relating to the army
6.	-ent	equival-ent, being equal
7.	-ic	hero-ic, like a hero
8.	-ical	histor-ical, relating to history
9.	-ile	puer-ile, like a boy
10.	-id	luc-id, being clear
11.	-ine	femin-ine, relating to a woman
12.	-ory	preparat-ory, relating to preparation

Adjective Suffixes = Abounding in; having the quality of

13. -ate   passion-ate, having the quality of passion
14. -ose   verb-ose, abounding in words
15. -ous   popul-ous, abounding in people
16. -ulent   op-ulent, abounding in wealth
17. -aceous   sapon-aceous, having the qualities of soap
18. -acious   ver-acious, having the qualities of truth

Adjective Suffixes = That may be

19. -able   mov-able, that may be moved
20. -ible   leg-ible, that may be read
21. -ble   solu-ble, that may be dissolved
22. -ile   doc-ile, that may be taught

Adjective Suffixes = Having the power of

23. -ive   negat-ive, having the power of denying

Adjective Suffixes = Causing or producing

24. -ferous   coni-ferous, producing cones
25. -fic   sopori-fic, causing sleep

Adjective Suffixes = Becoming

26. -escent   conval-escent, becoming well

Verb Suffixes = To make; to render; to perform an act

1. -ate   navi-gate, to perform the act of sailing
2. -fy   forti-fy, to make strong
3. -ize   fertil-ize, to render fertile

Words Derived from Latin Numerals

Define each word, so as to show that it contains the idea of the number.

unus (1)	unit, union, unite, uniform, universe, unicorn, unique, university, Unitarian
duo (2)	dual, duel, duplex, duplicate, duplicity
bis, bi(twice)	billion, bisect, bivalve, biscuit, binomial, biennial, bigamist, bidentate
tres (3)	treble, trefoil
tri (thrice)	triangle, tribe, trice, triple, tricolor, trident, trinity, trinomial, triplet, trio, trisect, tripod, triennial
quatuor (4)	quarto, quart, quartette, quadrille, quadruped, quadrilateral, quadrillion, quadruple, quarter
quinque (5)	quintette, quintillion, quintuple, quinquereme, quinquefoliolate, quintessence
sex (6)	sextant, sextillion, sextuple, sexennial
septem (7)	septennial, septillion, septisyllable, September
octo (8)	octave, octillion, octennial, October
novem (9)	novennial, November
decem (10)	decennial, decimeter, decimal, decimate, December
duodecimo (12)	duodecimal, duodecimo (volume)
centum (100)	cent, century, centurion, centigram, centennial, centenarian, centigrade, centiped, percentage
mille (1000)	million, millennium, millimeter, millepede
primus (first)	prime, primary, primal, primeval, primer, primitive
secundus(second)	second, secondary

English Words Derived from Latin Roots

Explain the etymology of each.

1. caput, **n.**   the head
                          cap, cape (geography), capital, captain, chapter, chaplet, chieftain, decapitate, precipitate

2. claudo, clausum, **v.**   to shut, to close, finish
                          clause, close, closet, disclose, include, exclude, seclusion, cloister, recluse

3. duco, ductum, **v.**   to lead, to draw
                          aqueduct, ductile, conduce, induce, conduit, educate

4. fero, latum, **v.**   to bear, to carry, to bring
                          collate, confer, differ, ferry, fertile, oblation, refer, relate, superlative, transfer, legislator

5. gradus, **n.**   a step
   gradior, gressus, **v.**   to step, to go
                          grade, gradual, graduate, congress, degrade, degree, digress, ingredient, transgress

6. mitto, missum, **v.** to send
                          admit, committee, dismiss, intermit, mission, remittance, promise, message

7. pes, pedis, **n.**   foot
                          biped, pedal, expedite, impediment, centiped

8. plico, **v.**   to bend, to fold, to knit
   plecto, plexum   to twine, to weave, to knit
                          apply, duplicate, complex, explicit, implicit, pliant, reply, supplicate, triple

9. pono, positum, **v.** to put, to place, to lay
                          post, postage, repose, depose, impose, composure, deposit, expose, position

10. specio, spectum, **v.**   to see, to look
                          despise, circumspect, respite, special, suspicion, spectacle,   spectre, species, specimen

Principal Greek Prefixes

1.	a, an	without; not	a-pathy, an-omalous
2.	amphi	around; both	amphi-theater, amphi-bious
3.	ana	back; throughout	ana-logy, ana-lysis
4.	anti, ant	against; opposite	anti-pathy, ant-arctic
5.	cata, cat	down; against	cata-logue, cat-arrh
6.	dia	through; across	dia-meter, dia-logue
7.	dis, di	two; double	dis-syllable, di-lemma
8.	dys	ill	dys-pepsia
9.	ec	out of	ec-lectic
10.	en, em	in; on	en-ergy, em-phasis
11.	epi, ep	upon; for	epi-dermis, ep-hemeral
12.	eu, ev	well; good	eu-phonic, ev-angel
13.	hemi	half	hemi-sphere
14.	hyper	over; beyond	hyper-critical, hyper-borean
15.	hypo	under	hypo-thesis
16.	meta, met	beyond; transference	meta-physics, met-onymy
17.	para, par	by the side of	para-site, par-helion
18.	peri	around	peri-meter
19.	pro	before	pro-gram
20.	syn, sy, syl, sym	with; together	syn-thesis, sy-stem, syl-lable, sym-pathy

Words Derived from Greek Words of Number

Define each word so as to show that it contains the idea of the number.

mono (1, single)	monosyllable, monologue, monotony, monarchy, monogram, monolith, monomial, monopoly, monopetalous
deuteros (2, second)	Deuteronomy
dis, di (twice)	dissyllable, diarchy, dilemma, diphthong, diploma
tris (3, thrice).	tripod, trialogue, triarchy, trigonometry, triglyph, trisyllable
pente (5)	pentagon, pentateuch, pentecost, pentameter
hex (6)	hexagon, hexameter
hepta (7)	heptagon, heptarchy
octo (8)	octagon
deka (10)	decagon, decagram, decalogue
dodeka (12)	dodecagon
hekaton (100)	hectometer, hectograph
myria (10,000)	myriad, myriameter
poly (many)	polygon, polysyllable, polygamy, polyglot, Polynesia, polyp, polynomial

English Words Derived from Greek Roots

Explain the etymology of each word.

1. aster, astron   a star   astronomy, asterisk, astrology

2. chronos   time   chronic; chronology, chronicle, anachronism, chronometer

3. ge   the earth   geology, geography, geometry

4. gramma   a letter   grammar, grammatical, anagram, diagram, epigram, monogram, telegram, program

5. graphein   to write   graphic, autograph, biography, photograph, calligraph, geography, lithograph, orthography, phonograph, stenograph, telegraph, topography

6. hudor   water   hydra, hydrant, hydraulic, hydrogen, hydropathy, hydrophobia, hydrostatics

7. logos   speech logic   description, reason, science analogy, catalogue, doxology, etymology, mythology, mineralogy

8. metron   a measure   meter, barometer, thermometer, perimeter, symmetry

9. phone   a sound   euphony, phonograph, telephone, phonic, symphony

10. polis   a city   police, policy, politics, metropolis, necropolis, cosmopolitan, Constantinople

Exercise on the Saxon and Classical Elements

Give Saxon equivalents for the following classical terms:

cohere	nocturnal	inexpensive
exclude	diurnal	diminutive
object (noun)	elevate	assassinate
object (verb)	aqueous	invisible
language	saccharine	injure
puerile	lacteal	crystalline
verbosity	saline	indicate
extravagant	carnivorous	creation
stupendous	luminary	endeavor
magnitude	veracity	fortitude
expansive	precipitate	sanctuary
hilarious	fraternal	omnipotent
eternal	sustain	diffuse
multitude	preservation	mysterious
excite	spectacle	confidence
constellation	dominate	beneficent
promote	contention	

Sample High School Student Assignment
Jane Austen Vocabulary from *Pride and Prejudice*

One hundred words; define each word from Webster's 1828 *Dictionary* and look for each word in *Pride and Prejudice* this year. When you find a word in your reading, write the direct quote next to the definition and identify the source by author, title, and page number. Write an original sentence using the word appropriately.

abominable
absolve
accoutre
acerb
acquit
affability
affront
allude
approbation
arrear
assiduous
augury
audacious

bequeath
blithe
bower

celerity
civility
calrion
colloquialism
compliance
comprise
conciliatory
condescend
conflagration
conjecture
coquetry

dauntless
delectable
diffuse
ductility

efficacy
endeavor

filial
felicity
flaxen
formidable
fray
fortuitous

goad

impertinence
impediment
implacable
impropriety
imprudent
incumbent
invulnerable
incessant

jocund

lugubrious
laconic

mortification
mar
minion
martial
melancholy

obsequiousness
omnivorous
orison

perdition
phantasmagoric
presumptuous
promontory
punctiliously
precipitate

proxy

quell

rabble
rapacity
revelry
repulse
repine
reiterate

silvan
scruples
sequacious
solitude
solace
stint
sublime
succor
shroud
surfeit
surmise
spectra

tacit
timorous
travail
tresses
tuft

unrequited

variance
vexation
vindictive
volubility

wan
wrought

These words were extracted from Jane Austen's *Pride and Prejudice* and assigned throughout the literature study.

Noah Webster's
American Dictionary of the English Language (1828) and How to Use It

In Christian homes the Bible is central, forming the basis of living. It defines the marriage, guides the nurture and growth of the children, and educates every member of the family in the knowledge of God.

In homes that value education, the dictionary has an important role in the intellectual growth of the family. Does your dictionary reinforce and verify Bible study for your family, or does it introduce conflicting values and worldview? More than any other book in the home next to the Bible, the dictionary has an important impact.

Importance of the Dictionary

The dictionary inculcates either a secular or a Christian worldview through word definitions, establishing the system of values by which the family will live. Consider the contrast of the definitions of the word "marriage" taken from a modern dictionary and from the original 1828 Noah Webster dictionary:

Marriage

Modern dictionary (1980)—"The mutual relation of husband and wife; the institution whereby men and women are joined in a special kind of social and legal dependence for the purpose of founding and maintaining a family."

Webster's original dictionary (1828)—"The act of uniting a man and a woman for life; wedlock; the legal union of a man and a woman for life. Marriage is a contract both civil and religious by which the parties engage to live together in mutual affection and fidelity, till death shall separate them. Marriage was instituted by God Himself for the purpose of preventing the promiscuous intercourse of sexes, for promoting domestic felicity, and for securing the maintenance and education of children. 'Marriage is honorable in all and the bed undefiled.' Hebrews 13."

The dictionary imparts either a secular or Christian philosophy of education that will form the attitudes and values concerning education. Consider the definitions of the word "education."

Education

Modern dictionary (1980)—"The action or process of educating or of being educated; a stage of such a process; the knowledge and development resulting from an educational process; the field of study that deals mainly with methods of teaching and learning in schools."

Webster's original dictionary (1828)—"The bringing up, as of a child; instruction; formation of manners. Education comprehends all that series of instruction and discipline which is intended to enlighten the understanding, correct the temper, and form the manners and habits of youth, and fit them for usefulness in their future stations. To give children a good education in manners, arts and science, is important; to give them a religious education is indispensable; and an immense responsibility rests on parents and guardians who neglect these duties."

The dictionary defines the words that expound a theology and the vocabulary with which to describe the knowledge of God. Consider the definitions of the word "sin."

Sin

Modern dictionary (1980)—"An offense against religious or moral law; an action that is thought to be highly reprehensible. Transgression of law of God. A vitiated state of human nature in which the self is estranged from God."

Webster's original dictionary (1828)—"The voluntary departure of a moral agent from a known rule or rectitude or duty, prescribed by God; any voluntary transgression of the divine law, or violation of a divine command; a wicked act; iniquity. Sin is either a positive act in which a known divine law is violated, or it is the voluntary neglect to obey a positive divine command, or a rule of duty clearly implied in such command. Sin comprehends not actions only, but whatever is contrary to God's commands or law. 1 John 3; Matt. 15; James 4." [The definition goes on for another column in the 1828 *Dictionary*.]

The dictionary imparts a philosophy of government either secular or Christian that will form the basis for how every individual in the family will govern himself and expect to be governed. Consider the definitions of "law."

Law

Modern dictionary (1980)—"A binding custom or practice of a community: a rule of conduct or action prescribed or formally recognized as binding or enforced by a controlling authority." [This definition continues for two inches of one column.]

Webster's original dictionary (1828)—"A rule, particularly an established or permanent rule, prescribed by the supreme power of a state to its subjects, for regulating their actions, particularly their social actions. Laws are imperative or mandatory, commanding what shall be done; prohibitory, restraining from what is to be forborne; or permissive, declaring what may be done without incurring a penalty. The laws which enjoin the duties of piety and morality, are prescribed by God and found in the Scriptures." [This definition continues on for twenty-one inches of three columns.]

Home Education: Christian or Secular?

The dictionary is the tool that shapes the thinking and reasoning as words are given precise meanings, as new words are learned by growing children, and as studies are done in the Bible and in every other subject. The writer of the dictionary determines the worldview that is propounded through it. There is one dictionary available today that defines every word both in the original language and from its Biblical usage—a facsimile of the original 1828 Noah Webster's American Dictionary of the English Language. Every modern dictionary reflects the current cultural corruptions and erosion of vocabulary by godless philosophies. The 1828 *Dictionary* is the gold standard of language for the American Christian.

The 1828 Noah Webster dictionary shows the Biblical worldview and vocabulary of the founding generation who were fresh products of the Reformation. This generation practiced Biblical reasoning by assumption and prized Christian character and virtue above all else. Noah Webster was a Christian whose Biblical knowledge and research are seen in his definitions. He researched every word in the original languages to provide the root meanings through his studies of twenty-six languages. Both his scholarship and productivity are without equal in America, earning him the title, "Father of American Christian Education and Scholarship."

Count the Cost: Presuppositions in Word Definitions

Consider the definitions given above. What difference will the definitions of law make to our student today? How will he learn law from the modern definition? What is the implication of "custom" in the first dictionary versus "rule" in the second one? What is the implication of law being defined as "prescribed" or "recognized" rather than "mandatory," "commanding," "prohibitory," or "permissive?"

What will be his view of authority and enforcement based on the two definitions? What will be his sense of responsibility for law? Does the second definition establish a different source and authority for law? What philosophical position will be inculcated by the second definition? What theology?

Christian Scholarship

The home is the primary classroom for every child and, according to Noah Webster, "Education is useless without the Bible." When working with young, pliant minds, it is essential for the parent or educator to establish the habit of beginning the search for principles, answers, and solutions in the Word of God, the *Logos*! It is the Divine Word that consecrates and inspires the mind and builds intellectual virtue. This is why Noah Webster, Father of American Christian education, wrote the first American dictionary and established a system of rules to govern spelling, grammar, and reading. This master linguist understood the power of words, their definitions, and the need for precise word usage in communication to maintain independence. Eager for Americans to be free from the bondage of Old World ideas which were being disseminated through our young nation's educational system, Dr. Webster laid the foundation for uniquely American education and the American usage of English words in his dictionary that defined each word in light of its meanings and usage in the Bible and in the new Christian constitutional republic.

Each learner develops the habit of research by beginning with God's Word through the Word Study, in which words are defined in light of how they are used in Scripture. This process gives preeminence to the Word of God in deducing the Biblical principles of the subject and clothes the learner's ideas with truth. This is the foundation upon which the pathway of logical thinking and just reasoning is established. It produces the acquired habits of Biblical scholarship, thinking cause (internal) to effect (external), and the precise, lucid communication of ideas to others.

The Word Study Defines a Biblical Worldview

The Word Study is more than going to a dictionary and defining a word. It is the method of scholarship that puts the student on the pathway to developing the habits of reflective thinking and deductive reasoning derived from Scripture. The Word Study places the truths of God's Word at the center of all learning, which illuminates the understanding and consecrates the mind. Every home should have a Webster's 1828 *Dictionary* for student homework and adult Bible study.

Benefits Derived from the Word Study

1. Builds vocabulary;

2. Increases reading comprehension and verbal scores;

3. Establishes precise word usage in written and oral communication;

4. Cultivates the habit of critical thinking;

5. Produces deductive reasoning skills—cause (internal) to effect (external);

6. Sharpens discernment of truth from error;

7. Inculcates lifetime habits of scholarship and aids in establishing a Biblical worldview.

The Word Study reveals the Biblical meanings of words and God's principles of knowledge and wisdom for application in every aspect of life through the four steps of learning:

Research:

1. The word is defined and recorded from Webster's 1828 *Dictionary*.

2. Key words within the definition are underlined and also defined.

3. Each word is researched from *Strong's Exhaustive Concordance of the Bible*, and the references that give relevancy to the definition are written out.

Reason:

1. Definition of the assigned word is written by the student in his own words.

2. Biblical principles are then deduced and recorded from the study.

Relate:

The student writes out the application of the definition and deduced principles as they relate to the purpose of the study and to his own life.

Record:

The student's written work, filed appropriately in his notebook, is a permanent record of learning and is easily appropriated for future study.

Sample Student Word Study

8th Grade Rudiments Course   Drew F.

Mr. Ricciardi   April 14, 1998

Petition

Assigned word defined:

petition, noun (Latin, petitio, from peto, to ask, properly to urge or press.) 1. In a general sense, a <u>request</u>, <u>supplication</u> or <u>prayer</u>; a prayer, addressed by a person to the Supreme Being, for something needed or desired. 2. A formal request or supplication, verbal or written, from an inferior to a superior soliciting some favor, grant, right, or mercy.

Key words within the definition defined:

request, noun (Latin, requisitus; requiro; re and quaero, to seek) 1. The expression of desire to some person for something to be granted or done; Esther 7. 2. Prayer; the expression of desire to a superior or to the Almighty. Philippians 4

supplication, noun (French from Latin, supplicatio) 1. Entreaty; humble and earnest prayer in worship. In all our supplications to the Father of mercies, let us remember a world lying in ignorance and wickedness. 2. Petition; earnest request.

prayer, noun (French, prier) 1. In a general sense, the act of asking for a favor with earnestness. 2. In worship, a solemn address to the Supreme Being, consisting of adoration, or an expression of our sense of God's glorious perfections, confession of our sins, supplication for mercy and forgiveness, intercession for blessings on others, and thanksgiving, or an expression of gratitude to God for his mercies and benefits. A prayer, however, may consist of a single petition, and it may be extemporaneous, written or printed.

Relevant Scriptures recorded:

1. "Then Eli answered and said, 'Go in peace: and the God of Israel grant thee thy <u>petition</u> that thou hast asked of him.'" (1 Samuel 1:17)

2. "Then said the king unto her, 'What wilt thou, queen Esther? and what is thy <u>request</u>?' . . . And the king said unto Esther at the banquet of wine, 'What is thy <u>petition</u>? and it shall be granted thee: and what is thy <u>request</u>? even to the half of the kingdom it shall be performed.'" (Esther 5:3 & 6)

3. "Praying always with all <u>prayer</u> and <u>supplication</u> in the Spirit, and watching thereunto with all perseverance and <u>supplication</u> for all saints." (Ephesians 6:18)

Personal definition written:

A petition is a good way to express your thoughts when asking for a change or a favor from those in authority over you or from God. If I only petition God for what I want and give no glory back to Him or forget the needs of others, then I have not learned the true meaning of a personal relationship with Jesus Christ.

CHAPTER FIVE
SYNTAX: A SOUND CURRICULUM
IN ENGLISH GRAMMAR

The important thing to know and convey in teaching grammar is that there are patterns, and that these patterns are the basic forms on which sentences are built.

—Kenneth Oliver

Sample English Language Lesson Plan

Grade: _____ /_____ Date: __4/15/98__ Teacher: __Adams_____ Component:

Skill Taught: __Sentence Analysis_____

Principle: __There is order in language._____

Biblical Reference: __John 11:35__ Illustration: __Analyzing a sentence in the Bible__

Materials/Resources: __The Noah Plan English Language Curriculum Guide__

☐ Biblical Foundation
☐ Orthography
☐ Etymology
☒ Syntax
☐ Prosody
☐ Composition

Structure of the Lesson

1. **Introduce the purpose and goal of the lesson.**

   We will learn four patterns that sentences may have beginning with the S–V pattern.

2. **Review related skill or concept.**

   A sentence is a complete thought.   Give examples of complete sentences and sentence fragments.
   What makes a sentence?   A verb, or action word, and a subject.

3. **Present new principle and idea with appropriate methodology.**

   The first sentence pattern is S–V (Subject–Verb).   This pattern has an action verb.   Explain and
   illustrate.   Example: "Jesus wept." Analysis: Jesus wept. Diagram:

   $$S \qquad V$$
   $$\overline{Jesus \;|\; wept.}$$

4. **Require student practice, participation, and presentation.**

   Practice analyzing sentences with the S–V pattern on the board.   Have student verbally analyze
   in three steps. See p. 146.

5. **Summarize, review, and evaluate.**

   When the student can make up a sentence with the S–V pattern and successfully analyze the
   sentence, the lesson is taught.

Introduction to Syntax
by Elizabeth L. Youmans, Ed.D.

The value of a whole and logical approach to syntax—one that is simple to comprehend, provides order, and teaches the knowledge of the patterns of words and sentences—cannot be overstated. Dr. Kenneth Oliver's English grammar curriculum provides such an approach and is the foundation for teaching syntax in this chapter of *The Noah Plan English Language Curriculum Guide.*

I came to greatly appreciate the merit of Dr. Oliver's grammar curriculum during my first year of full-time classroom teaching at StoneBridge School in 1982. I had taught music and literature the previous founding year of the school and was "promoted" to classroom teacher the following year. As an "apprentice," I lacked the skills and the art of teaching English language. Month by month, I sought the counsel and instruction of Dr. Carole Adams, as she mentored me through my first year of teaching English to my third grade students. I'll never forget her introduction to the teaching of syntax. It was late January, the end of the first semester, and time for me to start teaching syntax. We were gathered one Super Bowl Sunday, and during the intermission Carole taught me Dr. Oliver's approach to grammar and syntax. On a five-by-seven index card, she wrote out the six basic sentence patterns in diagram format. She defined syntax and grammar for me in a simple, logical way and explained Dr. Oliver's approach in a manner that I was instantly able to understand.

As I began to prepare my lesson plans, I recalled my own elementary and high school years of English grammar and syntax as complicated and fragmented. It wasn't until I was taught how to diagram sentences in the seventh grade that I had any clue about the functions of words or their relationships in sentences. After many years of memorizing information about words and sentences that never provided the necessary foundation for understanding syntax, I began to comprehend only after two years of high school Latin.

I had questions as I began teaching. Would Dr. Oliver's whole approach to teaching and learning English grammar spare my StoneBridge students the years of confusion that I had experienced? Would they really be able to diagram sentences with understanding in the third grade? Now, after many years of classroom teaching, I have come to fully appreciate this approach. Not only were my third graders able to diagram English sentences, but I had them diagramming Latin sentences, as well!

The effect of this syntax curriculum, combined with the reflective method of Four R'ing in The Principle Approach, classic literature, Christian history, Bible, and classic and foreign language courses of study, has been high Scholastic Aptitude Test (SAT) scores with three perfect verbal scores out of forty graduates. These same students excelled in their ability to communicate and successfully competed with their peers around the nation for college entrance and scholarship awards. They graduated from high school fully equipped to enter a world of diverse challenges and capable of articulating and defending their Christian worldview.

An Overview for Teaching Syntax
A Sound Curriculum in English Grammar
by Kenneth Oliver

Teaching Patterns of Sentences

Syntax is the due arrangement of words in sentences according to established usage. There are six basic sentence patterns:

1. (S) Subject   Bells (S) RING (V).
    (V) Verb   Trees (S) GROW (V).
                          Birds (S) SING (V).
                          Rivers (S) FLOW (V).

2. (S) Subject   Winter (S) BROUGHT (V) cold (dO).
    (V) Verb   Spring (S) BRINGS (V) showers (dO).
    (dO) Direct Object   Moisture (S) SWELLS (V) buds (dO).

3. (S) Subject   She (S) TOLD (V) Grace (iO).
    (V) Verb   I (S) ASK (V) him (iO).
    (iO) Indirect Object

4. (S) Subject   You (S) GIVE (V) me (iO) apples (dO).
    (V) Verb   I (S) ASK (V) you (iO) a question (dO).
    (iO) Indirect Object He (S) BRINGS (V) her (iO) berries (dO).
    (dO) Direct Object   (dO acted upon)
                          (iO action done for)

5. (S) Subject   That (S) LOOKS (V) good (pA).
    (V) Verb   This (S) LOOKS (V) better (pA).
    (pA) Predicate Adjective

6. (S) Subject   Lillies (S) ARE (V) plants (pn).
    (V) Verb   Plants (S) MAY BE (V) trees (pn).
    (pN) Predicate Noun

---

* This is an overview of an occasional paper published by the Council for Basic Education which is given fully beginning on p. 162. The author, Kenneth Oliver, proposes an approach to grammar that is based on sentence patterns. Used with permission.

Basic patterns are expanded by articles (a, an, the), demonstrative adjectives (this, that, these, those) or other pronoun-adjective forms (anyone's, their, no one's). All these are called **determiners**.

Another way of expanding the basic patterns is by the use of **modifiers**—adjectives or adverbs.

Ex. "All lilies are plants."

"Little boys earnestly covet big bicycles."

Combinations of the basic patterns may produce **compound sentences** joined by a semi-colon (;) or a coordinating conjunction (*and, or, but,* and the like) into a single sentence.

Ex. "Winter brought cold; April brings flowers."

The basic patterns may be combined into a complex sentence in which one part is made dependent on the other by the use of a subordinating conjunction (though, if, when, whenever, and the like).

Ex. "Although all lilies are plants, not all plants are lilies."

"You give me apples, while I give you cherries."

Learning awareness of patterns is just one step toward mastery of language use. For the knowledge of language to reach its full potential, there must be also a **process of questioning how the patterns work and why**, followed **by attempts to use language innovatively** while still in the shelter of the classroom.

The Function of Words: Principles Underlying What Is Taught in Grammar

First Principle: There are different word functions.

Nouns

Nouns name persons, places, things, ideas, processes, and states of being. Examples of these six categories, in the same order, are *Ralph, we, she, I*; *Pittsburgh; bicycle; democracy; development*; and *illness*. It may be noted that pronouns serve the same function as nouns.

Verbs

Verbs identify actions, states of being, or processes, not as static but as something continuing to take place.

Modifiers

Modifiers describe (*warm, blue, stubborn*), limit (*this, those, her, my*), compare (*colder, more, most*), or qualify (*anxiously, eagerly, tenderly*), other words.

Relational or Functional Words

Conjunctions join words, phrases, clauses (*and, but, or, either . . . or, neither . . . nor, if, when, whenever, although*, etc.). **Prepositions** identify relationships between words (*in, on, at, under, over, beyond, beside, until*, etc.). **Auxiliary verbs** assist the main verb of the sentence: examples include *will, shall, can, are* (as is "*are going*", where it's purpose it to assist the verb *going*), *is, am*, etc.

Second Principle: There are three means by which grammar operates, and by which the functions of words in a sentence may be identified—word order, inflections, and relational words.

1. One way grammar conveys meaning is through word order in a sentence.

2. Inflections—the form of words—is the second means of conveying meaning.

Nouns have inflections to show that they are singular or plural, and to show possession. Verbs have inflections to show the third person singular, and to indicate tense. Pronouns have inflections to indicate person, number, and the use of appropriate cases. In some other languages, modifiers are also inflected, and nouns and verbs have many more inflections than occur in English.

Inflections of Verbs

go	goes	went	gone
ride	rides	rode	ridden
sit	sits	sat	sat
set	sets	set	set
lie	lies	lay	lain
lay	lays	laid	laid
want	wants	wanted	wanted

The first column is for all persons and numbers except the third person singular. The second column is the third person singular inflection. The third column is the past tense inflection, which is the same for all persons and numbers. The last column is the past or perfect participle inflection, the form used to make the perfect tenses for all persons and numbers.

Inflections of Pronouns

	1st Person Singular	1st Person Plural	2nd Person Singular	2nd Person Plural	3rd Person Singular	3rd Person Plural
Subjective	I	we	you	you	he, she, it	they
Possessive	my	our	your	your	his, her, its	their
Indirect objective	me	us	you	you	him, her, it	them
Direct objective	me	us	you	you	him, her, it	them

3. Grammar also uses relational words to convey meaning

Relational words help identify the relationships of other words. "Boy goes store." (Does he go into, to, from, around, past, over, under the store?) "Boy goes store buy flour his mother bake cookies." (If the boy goes to the store to buy flour his mother will bake cookies.) Or another possibility: (Although the boy goes to the store to buy flour his mother will not bake cookies.) Still another: (Even if the boy goes to the store to buy flour his mother may not bake cookies.)

Summary: Words have either lexical or grammatical functions. Lexical (defining) functions: nouns, verbs, modifiers, relational. Grammatical (operational) functions: word order, inflections, relational words. For more information, please see 167 in this text.

Making Sentences

The final aspect of grammar concerns the kinds of relationships that make the English language what it is—relationships that the effective speaker or writer uses and the informed listener recognizes. The clarity of a sentence, and the beauty and persuasiveness of it, depend on choices its author makes in three areas—**mode, structure,** and **relationships.**

Mode

There are four reasons for saying something: to tell, to ask, to command, and to exclaim. These four purposes are expressed through four different modes: the **declarative sentence,** which declares or tells; the **interrogative sentence,** which asks a question; the **imperative sentence,** which gives a command; and the **exclamatory sentence,** which most often is only a few words, and which usually does not, but may, have the formal structure of a sentence.

Structure

Simple, compound, complex, and compound-complex sentences, or, "embedded sentences," as modern grammarians say.

Relationships

Number	Voice
Gender	Mood
Person	Modification
Case	Comparision
Tense	

Teaching Sentence Analysis

Traditional English language instruction in American schools teaches parts and pieces of English language as ends in themselves with the goal of promoting basic literacy—if we know our parts of speech! It is assumed, if we can read, if we can spell and write cursive, that we are literate. However, our mission of cultivating the Christian character and leadership of the next generation does not let us settle for just literacy. Our goal must be to produce masterful communicators.

The end goal cannot be to create grammarians or philologists only—masters of grammar or lovers of words—although in the process of producing masterful communicators, we will see grammarians and philologists emerge. Our goal must be consistent with the purpose of Christian education which rests upon nothing less than the Great Commission—the stated purpose of Christian discipleship: to take the Gospel into all the world, teaching all nations. Our mandate.

The goal of English language instruction is the mastery of communication. To accomplish this goal effectively requires "mainstreaming" all areas formerly known as "language arts" into a program aggressively directed towards English as communication. The language arts approach teaches grammar as parts of speech, inflating grammar into a time-consuming end-in-itself that has little to do with the way students speak or write. Moving from this piecemeal approach, to what I will call "mainstreaming" means causing all English language instruction to be directed towards developing communication skills. Therefore, grammar instruction must contribute to improving the way one writes, speaks, and thinks. Six components drive the English language program—orthography, syntax, etymology, prosody, composition, and English language distinctives. There is no wasted time or effort. Each compo-

> *The goal of English language instruction is the mastery of communication.*

nent has a new purpose and a significant contribution to the end goal:

1. Orthography is taught by dictation causing students to apply spelling rules while writing.

2. Syntax is taught by analysis giving students a tool to improve expression by understanding how sentences work to make meaning clear—lucid communication.

3. Etymology is taught by analysis giving students building blocks to expand vocabulary and build word banks.

4. Prosody is taught through a rich curriculum of literature classics and poetry inspiring students with the model of excellent language to form and instruct their own individual expression.

5. Composition is taught as a skill and practiced regularly to develop writing ability, thinking ability, and the means of effectively communicating.

6. English language distinctives inform students of the nature and place of English and give purpose to the study and use of English language today.

Syntax, a Tool of Refining Meaning

Of the six components of English, few are given appropriate emphasis and utility today in English instruction. Syntax is the one most misused and, in part, overworked. In actuality, syntax is valuable in equipping students with sentence-sense and thus communication skill, as the sentence is the whole thought. The approach to syntax presented here, and in *The Noah Plan English Language Curriculum Guide*, gives students an economical tool—without great expense of time or waste of effort. It requires no workbooks and rests upon learning a method of sentence analysis that is then used in any subject. This is especially useful in literature or Bible to get the meaning of a passage fully. Sentence analysis enables students to evaluate their own writing and improve upon their expression through understanding how the language works to communicate thought.

The teacher of this approach masters the method, by practicing with sentences, until he is able to analyze any sentence that appears in the Bible, the newspaper, literature, or in his own writing. The charts will prepare the teacher thoroughly in this chapter.

The sentence analysis method begins with the steps of analysis which must be practiced until they are internalized. The intricacies of English grammar are then built upon the six sentence patterns of English. Here's how to begin:

PART ONE

Kindergarten through Fourth Grades:

Kindergarteners through fourth graders will learn only Part One. Fifth through tenth graders will review Part One and build upon it. The sentences and direction given here are appropriate for middle school, especially for those who have studied Sir Walter Scott's *Ivanhoe*, the classic from which they were taken. Sentences can be pulled from any literature classic for use in presenting the sentence analysis technique.

Methodology:

1. Create a syntax title page for the English notebook:

Define the words "logic," "syntax," and "analysis" and record the definitions.

2. Teach the purpose of sentence analysis.

Explain to the students that sentence analysis is basically thinking logically about how the sentence is structured, and that the purpose of practicing sentence analysis is to improve their writing and expression.

3. Begin with the whole.

a) Introduce the sentence as the complete thought. Teach the students to read the sentence to get its 'sense' or whole thought before beginning to analyze it.

Example. *The Lady Rowena rose and left the table.*

b) Lead the students to envision the action of the sentence in their minds before beginning to identify the pattern. This will enable them to respond to the questions of the six steps. They should envision Lady Rowena rising and leaving.

4. Teach the steps of sentence analysis.

a) Use transparencies made from pages 151–160.

b) Present the six steps of sentence analysis using the overhead projector transparencies, one by one, explaining the examples and drilling the questions of analysis. Students will record the six steps one by one as they are being presented.

5. Present the method.

As each step is introduced and the questions drilled, **it is imperative that this step be methodical and reflective.** The students must copy the steps and think about them sequentially. This allows time to possess the steps.

6. Practice sentences without modifiers.

a) The basic sentences, stripped of modifiers, found on transparency 5, are introduced and practiced to establish mastery of the steps.

b) Practice the first five basic sentences on the board with the students, allowing each of them to name the steps, asking and answering the questions.

c) Then students should be given a few minutes to attempt to analyze the next two or three sentences individually as the teacher moves among them to answer questions and guide. The remaining sentences in the basic set, found on transparency 5, should be given for homework.

7. Practice the sentences with modifiers.

a) The next day, practice sentences with modifiers found on transparency 6. This set should be handled as in Step 6, giving students the same sentences, now with modifiers which are explained as describing words or phrases and marked "M."

The goal of this set is to give the students practice analyzing the patterns of sentences that have additional words. They will mark the modifiers of all types "M" and ignore them for now. The practice sentences with controlled patterns and modifiers are needed until the steps of analysis are mastered.

b) After the steps are mastered, any sentence can be analyzed from literature or from the students' own writing. When the practice sentences are marked according to the directions in the steps, the patterns can be identified as:

S–V	subject-verb
S–V–dO	subject-verb-direct object
S–V–iO–dO	subject-verb-indirect object-direct object
S–V–iO	subject-verb-indirect object
S–V–pN	subject-verb-predicate noun
S–V–pA	subject-verb-predicate adjective

8. Drill the steps of analysis.

a) When the six steps have been introduced and practice sentences completed successfully, students are drilled. Using transparencies 1 and 2, drill students by pointing to the numbers in order and having students snap their fingers as they say the question corporately.

b) Then, when the steps are mastered in order, point to the numbers randomly, eliciting the correct questions. Drill until the questions are crisp and prompt.

9. Add modifiers.

a) At this point, introduce transparencies 3 and 4. One-word modifiers are marked "M."

b) Prepositional phrases are phrase modifiers at this point and are put in parentheses and marked "M."

c) Students copy Step 9, found on transparency 3, into their notebooks reflecting upon the explanation and the examples. It is sufficient at this point for students to recognize prepositions only as words that show relationship between two things such as the cat and the house:

Anything the cat can be to the house is a preposition. It can be in the house, under the house, over the house, etc.

10. Practice with modifiers.

a) Practice sentences found on transparency 7 should now be introduced following the same method as used with Steps 5 and 6.

b) When the sentence is analyzed and marked, the sentence pattern should be labeled.

Results of Step One

At this point students should be able to go through the analysis steps asking and answering the questions without hesitation, marking the patterns. The modifiers are all marked "M"—both one-word and phrase modifiers. Now sentences can be drawn from the literature and from the students' own writing.

PART TWO

Fifth and Sixth Grades:

At this point, students have mastered the analysis method and are ready to begin to use it to master grammar. We will now introduce sentences that contain two or more sentence patterns and learn to recognize types of modifiers, phrases, and clauses.

A compound sentence has a coordinating conjunction. See example on p. 154.

A complex sentence has a subordinating conjunction. See example on p. 154.

Methodology:

11. Teach compound and complex sentences.

Introduce Step 11 with transparency 8. Have students copy it in their notebooks and reflect on the explanation. The examples are explained and discussed.

Again, it is imperative that students read the sentence and get the sense of it before they attempt analysis. Holding the thought in the mind is essential to recognizing the signal that heralds a compound or complex sentence—two or more patterns each having a subject and a verb.

a) Practice sentences: The sentences found on transparency 8 should be analyzed on the chalkboard, leading students to identify the types of clauses and the patterns. Continue to mark modifiers (one-word or phrase modifiers) with "M."

b) More practice sentences: The practice sentences on transparency 9 are introduced and practiced:

- corporately on the board;

- individually;

- completing them for homework.

12. Identify modifiers.

Now we are ready to learn to identify types of modifiers. The word modify should be defined and recorded:

"modify, v. To change the form or external qualities of a thing."

a) Adjectives are introduced as words that modify nouns and answer the questions "Which one?" "What kind?" and "How many?"

b) Adverbs are introduced as words that modify verbs and answer the questions "How?" "When?" "Where?" and "To what extent?"

c) Return to the practice sentences on transparency 6 and mark the one-word modifiers as adjectives or adverbs.

d) Prepositional phrases are either adjective or adverb phrases. Mark the phrase modifiers in sentences on transparency 6 as adjective or adverb phrases.

13. Practice diagramming.

Present the diagram format as shown on p. 180. Practice diagramming selected sentences from all practice sets. Compound and complex sentences are diagrammed on p. 181.

14. Identify modifying clauses (embedded sentences).

The practice sentences on transparency 9 should be used to demonstrate how a sentence pattern in a subordinate clause may be used to modify any appropriate part of another sentence.

The example on p. 184 should be given on the board: "My heart leaps up when I behold a rainbow in the sky."

Show students how the "when clause" is adverbial, as it modifies leaps (telling when) in the sentence.

Results of Step Two

Sentences with three and four clauses can now be analyzed drawing from literature and the students' own writing.

PART THREE

Seventh through Tenth Grades:

At this level, the full nature and extent of grammar should be set forth as a body of knowledge to be mastered.

15. Teach sentence analysis as the basis of grammatical study.

a) Lexical functions are understood as:

1) Nouns

2) Verbs

3) Modifiers

4) Relational Words—conjunctions, prepositions, auxiliary verbs

b) Grammatical operations are understood as:

1) Word Order—the means through which we give or receive meaning.

2) Inflections—the forms of words including verb inflections, pronoun inflections.

3) Relational Words—conjunctions, prepositions, auxiliary verbs

Results of Step Three

With this basis, we now begin to examine all areas of English grammar beginning with sentence modes, sentence structure, and relationships, found on pp. 165–179.

Sentences from literature and the students' own writing are now used to identify all aspects of grammar as sentences are analyzed. Sentence analysis forms the basis of grammatical study.

SENTENCE ANALYSIS

Transparency 1

1. FIND THE **VERB**, and always find the verb <u>FIRST</u>. **ASK . . .**

   "What is the action or being in the sentence?"

   Mark the verb 'V' and underline the verb twice.

   V
   Example: Fangs <u>barked</u>.

2. FIND THE **SUBJECT**. **ASK . . .**

   "Who or what is the doer of the action or being?"

   Mark the subject 'S' and underline the subject once.

   S   V
   Example: <u>Fangs</u> <u>barked</u>.

3. DETERMINE THE **KIND OF VERB**. **ASK . . .**

   "Is the verb an action or a being verb?"

4. IF THE VERB IS AN **ACTION** VERB, LOOK FOR . . .
   DIRECT OBJECT (dO) and/or
   INDIRECT OBJECT (iO).

5. IF THE VERB IS A **BEING** VERB, LOOK FOR . . .
   PREDICATE NOUN (pN) or
   PREDICATE ADJECTIVE (pA).

> **Memorize:**
> *Being verbs or linking verbs are: am, is, are, was, were, be, being, been. Sometimes verbs that imply 'being' are being verbs like 'seem,' 'appear,' 'become,' if they are equivalent to "is."*

SENTENCE ANALYSIS

Transparency 2

6. TO FIND A **DIRECT OBJECT**, ASK . . .

   "Who or what?" after the <u>action</u> verb.

   Mark the direct object '**dO**.'

                   S   V   dO

   Example: <u>Fangs</u> <u>herded</u> swine.

7. TO FIND AN **INDIRECT OBJECT**, ASK . . .

   "To whom or to what? For whom or for what?" after the <u>action</u> verb.

   Mark the indirect object '**iO**.'

                   S   V   iO   dO

   Example: <u>Fangs</u> <u>brought</u> Gurth swine.

8. TO FIND A **PREDICATE NOUN** OR A **PREDICATE ADJECTIVE**, ASK . .

   .

   "Who or what?" after the <u>being</u> verb.

   If the word that answers the question is <u>renaming the subject</u>, mark it **predicate noun (pN)**.

                   S   V   pN   S   V   pN

   Examples: <u>Wamba</u> <u>is</u> a jester.   <u>Gurth</u> <u>is</u> a swineherd.

   If the word that answers the question is <u>describing the subject</u>, mark it **predicate adjective (pA)**.

                   S   V   pA   S V pA   pA

   Examples: <u>Wamba</u> <u>is</u> fantastic.   <u>Gurth</u> <u>is</u> stern and savage.

SENTENCE ANALYSIS

Transparency 3

9. IDENTIFY ALL **MODIFIERS** IN THE SENTENCE.

Modifiers are words that describe or modify other words. To analyze sentences at this point, we will eliminate all modifiers and deal with them later after we have mastered all sentence patterns.

Modifiers can be one word or a phrase (a group of words introduced by a preposition). Put an 'M' over all one-word modifiers. Put prepositional phrases in parentheses and mark an 'M' over top.

```
              M   M    M      S              M           V
Examples: The two human figures (in this landscape) were
                          M
          (of wild and rustic character).


              M  S  V    V      M                M
          The sun was setting (upon one) (of the rich grassy glades)
                  M              M           M
          (of that forest) (in the valley) (of the Don).
```

A preposition cannot stand alone and is always followed by a noun or pronoun. The group of words beginning with a preposition is called a prepositional phrase.

Prepositions

about	above	across	after	against	along
amid	among	around	at	atop	before
behind	below	beneath	beside	between	beyond
by	concerning	down	during	except	for
from	in	inside	into	like	near
of	off	on	onto	out	outside
over	past	regarding	since	through	to
throughout	toward	under	underneath	until	up
upon	with	within	without		

```
              S  V      V     M  dO         M
Examples: I have consulted my legs (upon this matter).


                   M        S  V    M        V
          (From his musing) he was suddenly awakened
                 M           M
          (by the blast) (of a horn).
```

May Be Duplicated

SENTENCE ANALYSIS
Transparency 4

10. COMBINATIONS OF BASIC PATTERNS PRODUCE COMPOUND SENTENCES JOINED BY A SEMICOLON (;) OR A COORDINATING CONJUNCTION (AND, BUT, ETC.) INTO A SINGLE SENTENCE.

S   V   dO   S   V   dO

Examples: <u>Winter</u> <u>brought</u> cold; <u>April</u> <u>brings</u> flowers.

S   V   dO   S   V   dO

<u>Winter</u> <u>brings</u> cold and <u>April</u> <u>brings</u> flowers.

11. THE BASIC PATTERNS MAY BE COMBINED INTO A COMPLEX SENTENCE IN WHICH ONE PART IS MADE DEPENDENT ON THE OTHER BY THE USE OF A SUBORDINATING CONJUNCTION (THOUGH, IF, WHEN, WHENEVER, AND THE LIKE).

C   M   S   V   pN   M   M   S   V   pN

Examples: Although all <u>lilies</u> <u>are</u> plants, not all <u>plants</u> <u>are</u> lillies.

S   V   iO   dO   C   S   V   iO   dO

<u>You</u> <u>give</u> me apples, while <u>I</u> <u>give</u> you cherries.

THE NOAH PLAN® © 2006 • FOUNDATION FOR AMERICAN CHRISTIAN EDUCATION

BASIC PATTERNS SENTENCE ANALYSIS PRACTICE
GRADE SIX

Transparency 5

Mark each sentence as taught following the steps of analysis.

1. The Templar made a reply.

2. The Lady Rowena rose.

3. The troubadour sang songs.

4. Cedric banished Wilfred.

5. Rotherwood was majestic.

6. The Palmer gave him the message.

7. Rotherwood was a house.

8. England was free.

9. Sir Brian had offended.

10. Isaac of York wore a cloak.

11. His dress was plain.

12. The pilgrim listened.

13. The first was Richard the Lion-hearted.

14. The Templar flung a chain.

15. The maidens retired.

SENTENCE ANALYSIS PRACTICE: ADDING MODIFIERS
GRADE SIX

Transparency 6

Mark each sentence as taught following the steps of analysis.

1. The Templar made an angry reply to the Saxon.

2. The Lady Rowena rose from her chair and left the table.

3. The wandering troubadour sang songs of love to the ladies.

4. Cedric banished his only son Wilfred from his home.

5. Rotherwood was majestic in its size.

6. The Palmer gave him the message for Rowena.

7. Rotherwood was an ancient Saxon house.

8. England was free in former times.

9. Sir Brian had offended in his brash speech.

10. Isaac of York wore a cloak of tattered cloth.

11. His humble dress was plain in color.

12. The silent pilgrim listened with rapt attention.

13. The first champion was Richard the Lion-hearted of England.

14. The Templar flung a gold chain unto the boards in tribute to his lady.

15. The young maidens retired for the evening to their rooms.

May Be Duplicated

SENTENCE ANALYSIS: ADDING MODIFIERS II
GRADE SIX

Transparency 7

1. The Palmer threw himself upon his rude couch.

2. The earliest sunbeams found their way through the little grated window.

3. The spectators murmured among themselves.

4. Malvoisin and Front-de-Boeuf were unpopular.

5. The five knights advanced up the platform.

6. At the flourish of clarions and trumpets, they rushed at each other on the full gallop.

7. The antagonist of Front de-Boeuf rolled upon the ground.

8. A second party of knights took the field.

9. Saddle, horse, and man rolled on the ground beneath a cloud of dust.

10. He remained in his tent in an agony of despair.

11. The Disinherited Knight declined their request.

12. The yeoman stood the angry glance of the Prince with steadiness.

13. In a country house near the village of Ashby lived a wealthy Israelite.

14. In a small apartment of the house, richly furnished with decorations of an

    Oriental taste, Rebecca was seated on a divan.

15. Gurth's appearance was rather suspicious.

SENTENCE ANALYSIS: COMPOUND AND COMPLEX
GRADE SIX

Transparency 8

1. His suit of armor was formed of steel richly inlaid with gold, and the device on his shield was a young oak tree pulled up by the roots, with the Spanish word Desdichado, Disinherited.

2. When the two champions stood opposite each other at the extremities of the lists, the public expectation was strained to the highest pitch.

THE NOAH PLAN® © 2006 • FOUNDATION FOR AMERICAN CHRISTIAN EDUCATION

SENTENCE ANALYSIS: COMPOUND AND COMPLEX II
GRADE SIX
Transparency 9

1. When the jester stood before the portal of the castle of Front-de-Boeuf,

   the warder demanded of him his name and errand.

2. The exchange of dress was now accomplished, when a sudden doubt struck Cedric.

3. When the raft was completed, the Black Knight addressed the besiegers.

4. The followers of the knight had no such shelter; two were instantly shot with crossbow

   bolts; two more fell in the moat; the others retreated back into the barbican.

5. Rowena turned to depart, and Cedric was with her.

6. The Friar bared his brawny arm up to the elbow, and gave the knight a buffet

   with his full strength.

7. The ponderous castle bell had tolled the point of noon when Rebecca heard

   a trampling of feet upon the private stair.

8. He was interrupted by a clattering of horses' feet, and the Black Knight galloped

   into the lists.

9. After the judicial combat, Cedric the Saxon was summoned to the court of

   Richard, which was then held at York.

May Be Duplicated

STEPS OF ANALYSIS
Transparency 10

1.

2.

3.

4.

5.

6.

7.

8.

May Be Duplicated

Diagramming English Sentences

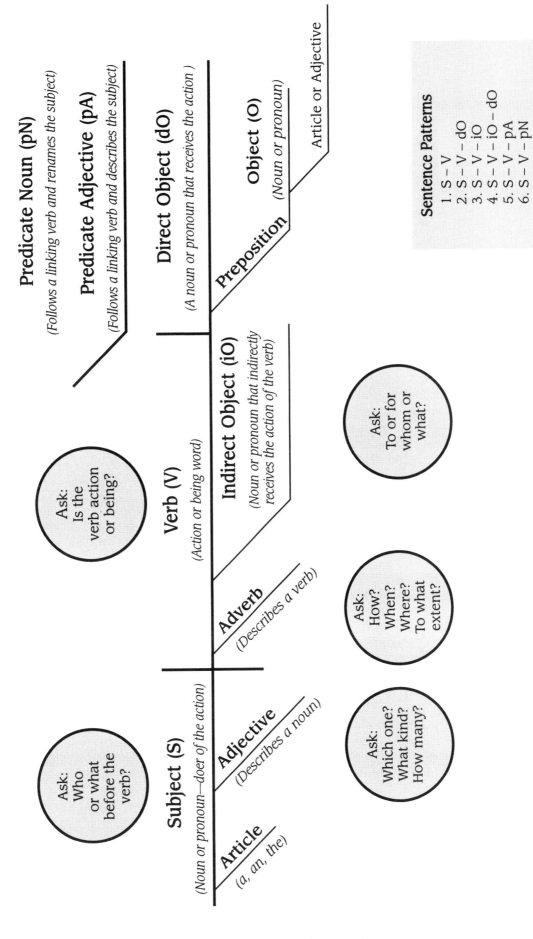

Predicate Noun (pN)
(Follows a linking verb and renames the subject)

Predicate Adjective (pA)
(Follows a linking verb and describes the subject)

Direct Object (dO)
(A noun or pronoun that receives the action)

Object (O)
(Noun or pronoun)

Article or Adjective

Preposition

Sentence Patterns
1. S – V
2. S – V – dO
3. S – V – iO
4. S – V – iO – dO
5. S – V – pA
6. S – V – pN

Ask:
Is the
verb action
or being?

Verb (V)
(Action or being word)

Indirect Object (iO)
(Noun or pronoun that indirectly receives the action of the verb)

Ask:
To or for
whom or
what?

Adverb
(Describes a verb)

Ask:
How?
When?
Where?
To what
extent?

Ask:
Who
or what
before the
verb?

Subject (S)
(Noun or pronoun—doer of the action)

Adjective
(Describes a noun)

Ask:
Which one?
What kind?
How many?

Article
(a, an, the)

May Be Duplicated

A Sound Curriculum in English Grammar

The following is adapted from an occasional paper published by the Council on Basic Education and is used with permission. The author, Kenneth Oliver, Professor of English and Comparative Literature, presents here a sound (healthy, solid) approach to teaching syntax.

By the age of three most children are not only speaking in sentence patterns, but are creating sentences which they have never heard before. Long before they know what grammar is, they are saying whatever they want to say—or at least they think they are—and they are using every, or nearly every, basic sentence pattern that exists.

The human race has learned to speak, to record and read, and to put together how things of the past, present, and future relate to one another, how effect relates to cause, and how one set of causes and effects relates to another. All thinking is relational, and language is the means for perceiving, recording, and using relationships. Language is to the human brain all that a programming system is to a computer, and much more, for the human brain is capable of original thought, esthetic imagination and creativity. But just as the computer must have its coding system, so the brain must have its language, and the more language it has mastered, the more effectively it can work.

The juggler who can keep three balls in the air perfectly is skilled, but not so skilled as one who can manage four. Just so, the child who can handle a vocabulary of a thousand words and every simple sentence structure has achieved something, but not so much as the child who can manage two thousand words and complex sentences. The "mastery" of language is not an absolute skill which one either has or does not have; it is a skill which develops as long as one works at it, whether for a year or ten years or a lifetime.

Words Are the Units of Language

Words are the units of language by which we give names to things, to processes, to emotions, and to ideas. Words are "category tags"; they are like boxes or drawers in which we store things so we will know where to find them. For instance, by calling every animal of one general kind a "horse" we make it possible to recognize all horses, to "know" what they are, and to feel at ease putting them in their proper niche (or stall). Without categories, every horse would have to be called by a separate word. Ten horses would need ten words. With a mastery of categories, we know not only all the horses we have seen, but the millions of them, past, present and future, here and everywhere else in the world, that we will never see.

The child is born with no words, no awareness of categories. Before he begins to speak he recognizes a number of words. By the time he starts school he knows hundreds, more likely thousands, of words, depending on the language used in his environment, including the television shows he watches. Note that he has some knowledge of these words; he does not have absolute knowledge. He may know from visiting a zoo what a rhinoceros looks like, but he will not yet know that the name is made up of separate words used long ago: rhino is from the Greek RHEIN, to run or flow, and was applied to noses (the Greeks must have had a lot of colds and seen a lot of runny noses!); and from the Greek KEROS, or horn. A rhinoceros is a "nose-horn" animal.

As the child grows to adulthood, he should double and redouble his vocabulary until he knows many thousands of words. If the child is well taught, he will come to know the meanings of the parts that have been put together to make each word.

Words go together in sentences, and these too have a rich and wonderful variety. The child learns to construct sentences, just as he learns to use words, by first hearing them and imitating what he

---

The "mastery" of language is not an absolute skill which one either has or does not have; it is a skill which develops as long as one works at it, whether for a year or ten years or a lifetime.

As the child grows to adulthood, he should double and redouble his vocabulary until he knows many thousands of words.

---

hears. The sentences he recognizes and uses give him a means of understanding and expressing ideas, emotions, processes and relationships, and of revealing his own creativity.

Teaching the Patterns of Words and Sentences

Everyone begins learning language the same way, by imitation. The child, of course, learns as language whatever is spoken regularly around him. The same child will learn the language of the Hottentots or Mandarin Chinese with equal ease if he is in one of those linguistic environments from, say, his first month to his third year. When he utters a "word" or syllable—whether or not he knows what he is doing—there is a joyful response and usually some repetition of the word he has pronounced.

If imitation is the easiest way for the child to learn, it is also the hardest to offset later. Characteristics of a language learned through imitation—the precise tonal qualities of speech—may leave life-long traces. Further, the longer an attempt to modify these characteristics is delayed, the harder it will be to do so.

As the child begins (in the first grade if not before, let us hope) consciously to develop his knowledge of words and of sentences, he continues to imitate those around him, but he accepts the teacher as his authority. Because the teacher is in such a strategic position to mold the child's language development, every teacher should be an expert language teacher; he is teaching language even as he teaches arithmetic, science, art, music, social studies, or physical education.

To bolster the mastery of word meanings and basic sentence structures, teachers give what are essentially rote memory assignments. Usually, something like "Learn these five words for tomorrow and use each one in a sentence." The student customarily refers to a dictionary, finds one of the listed definitions—usually the first one given—and makes a sentence.

Thus he looks up inception, finds as a first definition, "beginning, start," and perhaps writes, "At the inception of the story there is a description of an old house." He has done the assignment, and he may recognize the word if he again sees it soon enough and often enough. This is better than nothing, but not an efficient or satisfying or interesting way to develop his vocabulary.

As a grammatical exercise he may be told that a pronoun agrees with its antecedent in person, number, and gender. Example: "If your sister wants to go, she must be ready on time." The teacher may then direct the student to write a similar sentence using a pronoun and its antecedent. The student may write, "My brother wants a bicycle, so he can ride to the swimming pool." This, too, is better than nothing, though the student may have only a vague notion or none at all of what is meant by person, number, or gender. He does what he is told to do, being careful to write only what he can be pretty sure is correct, having learned early that it is better to be right than wrong. At a different level, he may be assigned to write a sentence with a prepositional phrase, and to use his handbook for reference. He finds the section on prepositional phrases, studies the examples and writes, "I want to go to the beach." Has he written one prepositional phrase or two? Unless he has learned about infinitive verbs he may well think he has produced two prepositional phrases.

The point is that rote memory, whether of words or of grammatical rules, is a piecemeal approach. It has the attraction of producing measurable results in a matter of weeks or even days, and when accountability is important there is a strong temptation to use it. Rote memory of words and grammatical structures has, however, two serious disadvantages. It is for most students tedious work which builds knowledge slowly. Also it fails to produce a sense of the relatedness of the materials learned, and fails to give the kind of satisfaction that one might have from putting a simple puzzle together and seeing a completed picture emerge.

There is order in language and the student should become aware of it. He should also become aware of the inconsistencies in the language.

And whatsoever Adam called every living creature, that was the name thereof.
Genesis 2:19b

This must not be taken as a blanket opposition to memorization. It is wonderfully satisfying to memorize a favorite poem or anecdote. What child has not felt the thrill of having learned to count, or to recite all of the alphabet in order, or a multiplication table? Memory is an essential ingredient in the playing of games, in the development of an argument, in the telling of one's adventures, indeed in all structures of knowledge. Moreover, even rote memory may sometimes be the best tool the teacher or the student can command for a part of the learning process. Memorizing combines with and depends upon authority. Appropriately used, memorizing and looking to authority are effective aids for learning language. We must see them as parts of a larger process, not as ends in themselves.

Clearly, at some point the student must begin to understand how language works. There is order in language and the student should become aware of it. He should also become aware of the inconsistencies in the language.

Patterns in Words

Most of the words in English are made up of two or more parts each of which usually contributes something to the meaning. The teacher can move beyond rote memory by showing how compound words are patterned. The word parts are *prefix, stem,* and *suffix.* The stem, for those readers who have been away from their schoolbooks a long time, is the core of the word, and simple words have only a stem. Thus *heart* has only a stem but *disheartened* (dis heart en ed) has one prefix, a stem, and two suffixes. The *-en* is a verb-forming suffix that makes a verb out of the noun *heart,* with the meaning "to give heart," "to strengthen," or "encourage." *Dis* is a prefix meaning "apart from" or "away from"; thus to *dishearten* is to reverse the process of giving heart or courage. The final suffix *-ed* makes the past tense of a verb or a participial adjective. Thus: "He did not win the race and this *disheartened* (verb) him." Or "The *disheartened* (adjective) student may not try so hard the next time."

Patterns in Sentences

What is true of words is also true of sentences. There are patterns which occur over and over again. The simplest, shortest type of sentence is made up of subject – verb.

1. SUBJECT – VERB
S – V "Bells ring." "Trees grow." "Birds sing." " Rivers flow."

Another short pattern is the subject–verb–direct object sentence:

2. SUBJECT – VERB – DIRECT OBJECT
S – V – dO "Winter brought cold." "Spring brings showers." "Moisture swells buds."

A third pattern includes subject–verb–indirect object, such as:

3. SUBJECT – VERB – INDIRECT OBJECT
S – V – iO "She told Grace." "I'll ask him."

A fourth basic pattern includes all of the preceding elements, subject–verb–indirect object–direct object:

4. SUBJECT – VERB – INDIRECT OBJECT – DIRECT OBJECT
S – V – iO – dO "You give me apples." "I ask you a question." "He brings her berries."

The indirect object (dative) differs from the direct object. In the sentence "I throw the dog a bone," the word "dog" is the indirect object, and "bone" is the direct object. One can imagine the bone being thrown and the dog waiting. One does not imagine the dog being thrown and the bone waiting. The direct object is acted upon; the indirect object has the action done for him.

Two further basic types are the subject–verb–predicate adjective sentence, and subject–verb–predicate noun sentence.

5. PREDICATE ADJECTIVE
S – V – pA "That looks good." or "This looks better."

6. PREDICATE NOUN
S – V – pN "Lilies are plants"; and "Plants may be trees."

These basic sentence patterns may be and usually are expanded by the addition of articles (*a, an, the*), demonstrative adjectives (*this, that, these, those*), or other pronoun-adjective forms (*anyone's, their, no one's*). All of these articles, demonstratives, and pronominal adjectives are sometimes called *determiners*. Another way of expanding the basic sentence patterns is by the use of *modifiers*—adjectives or adverbs: "*All* lilies are plants." "*Little* boys *earnestly* covet big bicycles."

The important thing to know and convey in teaching grammar is that there are patterns, and that these patterns are the basic forms on which sentences are built.

Combinations of the basic patterns may produce *compound sentences* joined by a semicolon (;) or a coordinating conjunction (*and, or, but*, and the like) into a single sentence. "Winter brought cold; April brings flowers" is an example. Or the basic patterns may be combined into a *complex sentence* in which one part is made dependent on the other by use of a subordinating conjunction (*though, if, when, whenever*, etc.). "Although all lilies are plants, not all plants are lilies," and "You give me apples, while I give you cherries."

Language by its very nature has patterns. The teacher must be aware of the patterns, and make the students aware of the patterns. As students mature in their awareness of language patterns, they will learn to use them in stories, essays, poetry, musical compositions, and scientific treatises. But awareness of patterns is just one step toward mastery of language use. For the knowledge of language to reach its full potential, there must also be a process of questioning how the patterns work and why, followed by attempts to use language innovatively while still in the shelter of the classroom. Why do words sometimes have only stems? Why do they sometimes have only a prefix and a stem, or only a stem and a suffix? Why does "the bush has red roses" make sense, but "the rose has red bushes" does not?

The Function of Words

Grammar is what distinguishes a sentence from a list of words randomly ordered. There are skills involved in the selection of words, the form chosen for them, and the positioning of them in relation to each other. It is these skills which have probably been mastered by the reader so well they are reflexive, that will be reviewed in this chapter and the next.

A discussion of *what* to teach about grammar needs a brief preface on the how of teaching grammar. Two important schools of thought on teaching grammar are "traditional" and "transformational." Neither has anything to do with what grammar is but rather with how it should be described or presented. Traditional grammar emphasizes categories of words, phrases, and clauses and analyzes how words fit into these categories. Transformational grammar deals more with deep structure and patterns, the meaning of words, and how changes in meaning can change the function of words. What follows in these pages is not approval of one and disapproval of the other. Either method is good—perhaps equally good—if only the teacher understands the

basic principles on which the language is structured. A teacher will fail with either method without a clear understanding of the principles of linguistic structure which make sentences possible. The teacher who does know and understand the basic principles can use any grammatical system that tells the truth about language. Let us look at those basic principles that underlie what is taught:

First Principle: There are Lexical Functions of Words

Some words, called *nouns*, give names to persons, places, things, ideas, processes, and states of being. Examples of these six categories, in the same order, are *Ralph, we, she, I, Pittsburgh, bicycle, democracy, development*, and *illness*. (It may be noted that pronouns are included with nouns, since they also serve to name things or persons. Since they serve the same functions as nouns, there is no need to set up a separate category for them.)

Some words, called *verbs*, identify actions, states of being, or processes, not as static but as something continuing to take place. Examples of the three categories are *shout* or *write, am* or *seem, thrive* or *wilt*.

Some words, grouped here as *modifiers*, describe, limit, compare, or qualify other words. Within this category are two subgroups—adjectives that modify nouns, and adverbs that modify verbs, adjectives and other adverbs. Examples of modifiers that describe are *warm, blue, stubborn*; modifiers that limit are *this, those, her, my*; modifiers that compare are *colder, more, most*; modifiers that qualify are *anxiously, eagerly, tenderly*.

A fourth category of words is relational or functional. Into this category are put conjunctions that join words, phrases, or clauses; prepositions that identify relationships between words, and auxiliary verbs. Examples of conjunctions include *and, but, or, either. . . or; neither. . . nor, if, when, whenever, although*, etc. Examples of prepositions are *in, on, at, under, over, beyond, beside until*, etc. Examples of auxiliary or helping verbs are *will, shall, can, are* (as in *"are going,"* where its purpose is to assist the verb going), *is, am*, etc.

Note again that these categories of words are identified as word *functions*. The word "paper" can function as a noun (*This paper is about as difficult to write as I had anticipated*), as a verb (*We will paper this room if we can fix the holes in the wall first,*) or as an adjective (*America is not a paper tiger*). Some grammarians speak or write of "parts of speech." This is workable only if one recognizes that the same word, as it is used in different sentences, may be a different part of speech at different times.

Second Principle: Words Have Grammatical Functions

There are three means by which grammar operates, and by which the functions of words in a sentence may be identified:

1. **Word order**

2. **Inflections**

3. **Relational words**

Word order is one of the three ways of producing meanings or sentences.

1. Word Order

To take up word order first, look at the three lists below:

a	by	numbers	ordered
a	difference	of	sentence
alphabetically	is	of	the
and	letters	or	what
between	list		words
a	by	what	numbers
a	or	words	ordered
of	the	between	sentence
of	and	letters	difference
is	list		alphabetically
what	between	ordered	of
is	a	alphabetically	letters
the	list	or	and
difference	of	by	a
	words	numbers	sentence

How is each list ordered? Which would be easiest to memorize?

The point, of course, is that word order is one of the means through which we give or receive meaning. Word order is one of the three ways of producing meanings or sentences.

2. Inflections

The second way to convey meaning is through inflections, or the forms of words. Nouns have inflections to show if they are singular or plural and to show possession. Verbs have inflections to show the third person singular and to indicate tense. Pronouns have inflections to indicate person, number, and the use of appropriate cases. In some other languages, modifiers are also inflected, and nouns and verbs have many more inflections than occur in English.

Inflections of Nouns

Singular (uninflected)	Singular Possessive	Plural	Plural Possessive
cat	cat's	cats	cats'
mouse	mouse's	mice	mice's
man	man's	men	men's
deer	deer's	deer	deer's
parent	parent's	parents	parents'
people	people's	peoples	peoples'

The principle then is that inflections are one means of showing grammatical or structural relationships. Inflections combined with word order and often with relational or functional words control meaning.

While the words themselves may have irregular plural forms, the possessive form has a certain consistency. Since mice, men, and the second deer are plural forms, the apostrophe comes before the *s*. People is a collective noun. "The people's choice" is the choice of one unit of people, e.g., American; "The peoples' choices" would represent different choices by different groups of people, or what the Secretary-General of the United Nations has to cope with to earn his daily bread.

Inflections of Verbs

go	goes	went	gone
ride	rides	rode	ridden
sit	sits	sat	sat
set	sets	set	set
lie	lies	lay	lain
lay	lays	laid	laid
want	wants	wanted	wanted

The first column is for all persons and numbers except the third person singular. The second column is the third person singular inflection. The third column is the past tense inflection, which is the same for all persons and numbers. The last column is the past or perfect participle inflection, the form used to make the perfect tenses for all persons and numbers.

While there are irregular forms, they occur mostly in words that are learned in early childhood. Also learned early is the more elaborate set of inflections for the verb to be. Present tense—*I am; you are; he, she, it is; we are; you are; they are.* Past tense—*I was; you were; he, she, it was; we were; you were; they were.* Past or perfect participle—*I, you, he, she, it, we, you, they have been; will have been.*

Inflections of Pronouns

	First Person Singular	First Person Plural	Second Person Sing. & Pl.	Third Person Singular	Third Person Plural
subjective	I	we	you	he, she, it	they
possessive	my	our	your	his, her, its	their
indirect objective	me	us	you	him, her, it	them
direct objective	me	us	you	him, her, it	them

The third way to convey meaning is through relational words which help identify the relationships of other words.

Because the indirect and direct objective case forms are alike, some grammarians combine them, calling all forms simply the objective case. This is unfortunate, since the relationships of the noun or pronoun to the verb or another noun or pronoun are different. In "Kiss *him* for *me*," *him* is direct object and me is indirect object. In "Kiss *me* for *him*," *me* is the direct object and *him* is the indirect object. In the following sentences the italicized word is in the indirect objective case; the capitalized words are direct objects:

Tell me a STORY.
She gave her *mother* a PRESENT.
Give the *devil* his DUE.
I tell *you*, you are wrong.

The last sentence has no direct object. "Wrong" is a predicate adjective; the second "you" is the subject of the second verb (are). The principle then is that inflections are one means of showing grammatical or structural relationships. Inflections combined with word order and often with relational or functional words, control meaning.

3. Relational Words

The third way to convey meaning is through *relational words* which help identify the relationships of other words. While a word like "paper," whether it is used as a noun, adjective, or verb, has approximately the same meaning (a thin sheet of fibrous material), words like "for" and "in" can have many meanings. What is the meaning of "for" in these phrases: "for you," "for an hour," "for once"? What is the meaning of "in" in these phrases: "in a minute," "in that instance," "in a box," "in a hurry," "in all justice"?

The value of relational words can best be realized by looking at two sentences without them: "Boy goes store." (Does he go into, to, from, around, past, over, under the store?) "Boy goes store buy flour his mother bake cookies." (*If* the boy goes *to* the store *to* buy flour his mother *will* bake cookies. Or another possibility: *Although* the boy goes *to* the store *to* buy flour his mother *will not* bake cookies. Still another: *Even if* the boy goes *to* the store *to* buy flour his mother *may not* bake cookies.)

Words have either lexical or grammatical functions.

The clarity of a sentence, and the beauty and persuasiveness of it, depend on choices its author makes in three areas: mode, structure, and relationships.

"We study principles structure we see grammar is interesting." (As we study the principles *of* structure we see *that* grammar is interesting. *If we do* study the principles of structure we *may see that* grammar is interesting. *Since we are about* to study the principles *of* structure we *may see whether* grammar is interesting.)

The reader may have noticed that one word has been ignored so far: namely, *the* is used in some sentences and is not definitely called a relational word. Sometimes, as in "the boy goes to the store," it seems to add no necessary meaning at all (just filling air holes). It is *not* relational in its function. It may be there merely as a matter of linguistic habit. Some languages such as Chinese, Japanese, and Korean have no such word at all. On the other hand, if I say "The reason for my treating it ambiguously. . ." I suggest that there was only one reason for doing so. If I say "A reason for my treating. . .," I suggest that there are others. In such instances *the* and *a* and *an* become important limiting modifiers.

Similarly, the verb *to be* is sometimes essential to meaning and sometimes not. (The Russian language uses it only when it is considered to be necessary.) In "Whatever *is* is right," the first *is*, at least, is necessary; the other may not be (and in Russian would be omitted).

This, then, is the principle reviewed in this chapter: Words have either lexical or grammatical functions.

1. The lexical functions are of four kinds:
   a) nouns
   b) verbs
   c) modifiers
   d) relational (or functional, or structural) words
2. The grammatical functions are of three kinds:
   a) word order
   b) inflections
   c) relational words

Now that these principles have been reviewed, we can go on to review the next, and basically the last, part of grammar: the kinds of relationships that make the English language what it is, relationships that the effective speaker or writer uses and that the informed listener or reader recognizes.

Making Sentences

The clarity of a sentence, and the beauty and persuasiveness of it, depend on choices its author makes in three areas— mode, structure, and relationships.

Mode

There are four reasons for saying something: to tell, to ask, to command, and to exclaim. These four purposes are expressed through four different modes: the *declarative* sentence, which declares or tells; the *interrogative* sentence, which asks a question; the *imperative* sentence, which gives a command; and the *exclamatory* sentence, which most often is only a few words, and which usually does not, but may, have the formal structure of a sentence.

Examples:

Declarative

Birds often sing in the early morning.

I doubt that, on a cold, drizzly morning when most of us feel like staying indoors, reading, tinkering, or huddled around a fire, we would be likely to be listening for the song of a bird.

You ask me whether I want to go out in such weather, and I say emphatically, "No, absolutely not!"

He asked, "Do you want to go out?" To which I replied, "No."

Note that even though doubt is implied in the second example, and an exclamation is inserted in the last sentence, and questions in the last two sentences, the impact of each is to make a statement. All of the examples are declarative. The large majority of all sentences are declarative.

Interrogative

Do you want to go out?
I said I didn't want to go out; didn't you hear me?
Do you understand that I don't want to do it?
Will you please close the door?
Will you please close that door!

The second and third sentences contain declarative elements, but their overall purpose is to ask a question. The last two sentences could be called interrogative (on the basis of form) or imperative (on the basis of purpose) or both. The last sentence could also be called exclamatory (on the basis of force) or all three at once (on all three bases).

Imperative

Close the door (please).
Tell me again what it is you are trying to say.
Son, don't do that!

Characteristic of the imperative sentence is the direct address. Its subject is the usually unspoken "you," which is understood and therefore unnecessary. Even when a noun is used, as in the last example, the "you" is implied: "Son, don't you do that!"

Exclamatory

Ouch!
Never!
Close the door!
I didn't say that!

Note that the exclamation is a short, emotional outburst. Note, too, that it may be either a word or two without the structure of a sentence (no subject, no verb), or it may be declarative and exclamatory (as in "I didn't say that!"), imperative *and* exclamatory ("Close the door!"). Longer sentences may be exclamatory, but to be effective they must make their exclamatory nature clear from the beginning and maintain emphasis. "Listen, friend, what I said was no, and what I mean is no, and you'd better not forget it!" Exclamatory literally says that something is in the nature of shouting out. Clearly, one may "shout out" a short declarative sentence or question or command, but long sentences rarely work very well as exclamations.

Structure

Modern grammarians rarely speak of simple, compound, complex, and compound-complex sentences. Instead, they speak of sentences and embedded sentences. By whatever name they are called, sentence structures have certain *principles* which are easy to state and illustrate.

Three ways of expressing the *first principle* are these:

A sentence has a subject and a predicate.

A sentence has a subject element and a verb element.

A sentence has a noun phrase and a verb phrase.

The *second principle* is that two or more sentences may remain independent, but be combined into one sentence simply by joining them together. The "joiners" are the semi-colon and coordinating conjunctions, such as *and, or, but, either . . . or, neither . . . nor*. These combined clauses are called compound sentences.

The *third principle* is that two or more sentences may be combined in such a way that one of them depends on the other, or is "dependent" or "subordinate." A few subordinating conjunctions are these: *if, when, whenever, although*, and such conjunctive phrases as *to which, of which, of all that*. It should be noted that the relationship between clauses or simple sentences is a matter of degree rather than absolute.

*First Principle—
A sentence has
a subject and a
predicate.*

*Second Principle—
A sentence may
be compound.*

*Third Principle—
A sentence may
be complex.*

Coordinate Clauses

He went to the movies; she stayed home.

He went to the movies and she stayed home.

He went to the movies but she stayed home.

Now look at the different results using subordinating conjunctions:

Subordinate Clauses

He went to the movies while she stayed home.

He went to the movies because she stayed home.

He went to the movies whenever she stayed home.

One might even comment that the sentences become more dependent in proportion as the relationship between the "he" and the "she" becomes worse.

A *fourth principle* is that there is no theoretical limit to the number of clauses that may be united into a single sentence, and, in practice, much excellent writing includes numbers of carefully combined dependent and independent clauses. One familiar example is the opening sentence of the Declaration of Independence:

When in the course of human events it becomes necessary for one people to dissolve the political bands which have connected them with another and (it becomes necessary) to assume among the powers of the earth the separate and equal station to which the Laws of Nature and of Nature's God entitle them, a decent respect to the opinions of mankind requires that they should declare the causes which impel them to the separation.

This is a complex sentence, having only one independent clause. The compound-complex sentence has at least two independent clauses and at least one dependent clause. These may be short or long. Example: *She likes to swim and she goes to the pool every day*, EVEN WHEN THERE IS A COLD WIND BLOWING. The italicized clauses are independent; the capitalized clause is dependent.

Relationships

While being able to identify dependent and independent clauses is important, it is somewhat of a parlor trick compared to what is really essential—being able to join clauses into effective combinations. The rest of this section will examine nine components that determine the effectiveness of the choices made in word order, inflection, and relational words. The nine components are *number, gender, person, case, tense, voice, mood, modification,* and *comparison.*

1. *Number* is simply the distinction of singular or plural among nouns, pronouns, and verbs. English has both weak and strong (or regular and irregular) means for showing number in nouns and pronouns:

Weak (Regular)		Strong (Irregular)	
Singular	**Plural**	**Singular**	**Plural**
house	houses	mouse	mice
car	cars	goose	geese
hero	heroes	woman	women
onion	onions	he, she, it	they

Number is the distinction of singular or plural.

For showing number in verbs the language has a special form only for the third person singular, aside from the distinctive form of the irregular verb to be. It is practical simply to regard the third person singular as a special inflected form: *go (goes), stand, (stands), see (sees).* Of course, *to be* is irregular in the singular: *I am; you are; he, she, it is.*

2. *Gender* in English is natural (some languages base gender on the form of the word, i.e., have grammatical gender). The four natural genders are masculine, feminine, neuter, and common, the last category being collective words which by their nature include both male and female, and perhaps neuter. *People, persons, group*, and *mob* are common gender words. The identification, then, is based on the relationship to life or to nature. But note that *it* may be used where there *is* gender (sex), when the gender is not a matter of importance: "Where is your dog?" "It's in the back yard." (In this instance the gender could become important if the dog is in heat and there is no fence around the yard.) The selection of pronouns is based on gender in order to keep references clear:

As Meg and Harry walked along, *he* swung *his* book back and forth.

She watched *it* as an excuse to look at him.

My physics teacher was good; *she* was also pretty.

The *Adirondack* was a good ship. *She* . . . (ships are generally referred to with the feminine pronoun even when they have non-feminine names, giving rise to such odd-looking news stories as this Associated Press release: "At age 10, she is retiring. Bidding 'ciao' to the Statue of Liberty, the sleek, white Italian luxury liner *Michelangelo* has begun her last trip home.")

Gender is masculine, feminine, neuter, or common.

3. *Person* is a means of keeping references among people and things clear. The three "persons" are the first (*I, me, we, us,* and nouns in apposition or agreement with one of these); the second (*you,* and any noun in direct address such as "Fortune, smile upon me now" in which Fortune is a second person noun); and the third (all nouns, common and proper, except in direct address or when in apposition to a first or second person noun or pronoun). It may help to think of the person relationship in terms of a circle, with a smaller circle as center:

Person is first, second, or third.

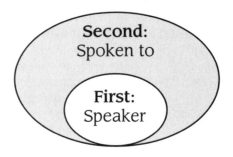

Note that person may shift in regard to an individual or thing, but does so in a way that keeps relationships understandable:

Henry (3rd) said to me (1st): "I (Henry becomes 1st person) wouldn't do that if I (still Henry, 1st person) were you (refers to me which here shifts to 2nd person)."

4. Case identifies the relationships of a noun or pronoun to a verb, or to another noun or pronoun. The four standard cases in English are *subjective*, for the subject of a verb; *possessive*, showing ownership of one noun by another noun, or by a pronoun; *indirect objective*, applied to the indirect object of a verb, or to the object of a preposition; and direct objective, showing the *direct object* of a verb.

Examples:

Subjective
"I think . . ."; "Glen works . . ."; "The *majority* of those present believe . . . "

Possessive
"*Her* attitude . . . "; the *dawn's* early light . . . "; "In regard to *their* proposal . . . "

Indirect objective
"Tell *me* a story about . . ."; "To *him* who in the *love* of *nature* holds communion with her visible *forms*, she speaks a various language . . . "; "I gave my *sister* a quick look."

Direct objective
"I gave my sister a quick *look*." "Of all the stories I have read, I like *that* best." "That is the one *which* I like best."

A *fifth* case, rarely identified anymore in English grammars, is actually used quite often: the case of *direct address*, sometimes called the *vocative*. "Friend, will you . . ."; "Mother, please . . . " While no different form of the noun appears, the relationship is clearly different from any of those in the standard four cases.

5. *Tense* refers to time, and with the use of helping or auxiliary forms, a complex set of time relationships is possible— and is in fact commonly used. (Some "modern" grammarians speak of English as having only two tenses, present and past. This is because there are only two forms of the verbs themselves, except for irregular verbs, such as *go, went, gone; see, saw, seen*). Tense is the grammatical device by which time-relationships are established, not in terms of calendar or clock, but in terms of the whens, thens, and nows of the speaker or writer. "Caesar, about a half century before Christ's birth, wrote, 'I came, I saw, I conquered.'" *Wrote* tells us that the *speaker* was looking back on Caesar's times; *came, saw, conquered* tell us that *Caesar* was looking back upon his own activities.

Tenses are formed by inflection, and the use of function-words. The simple present is the most flexible of the tenses. In addition to the basic reference to the time of the speaking or writing, it may reach so far into the past and future as virtually to encompass all time. An example is the sentence "The earth revolves around the sun." This is clearly the present, but it refers to an action which goes on over an indefinitely long range of centuries. The present tense may also be used for what is a distinctly future reference: "He is going to Europe next summer." Or, in what is called the "historical present," it may be used for past action: "The fisherman *stands* for a moment looking out over the swirls and still pools of the stream. Then he *casts* his line. For a moment the bright feather *touches* the water; then it *skips* like a helpless insect trying to raise a wet wing once again into the dry air." Not only is some unwary fish being deceived; the reader is being made to put himself back into the past to see it as if it were present; this is a standard literary use of the present tense. Note that in the foregoing examples, there are two sets of relationships being established. One is the relationship of time in reference to *now* or to some *then* which may be either defined or left vague; the other is a grammatical adherence of the verb to established tense-patterns.

When we use verbs in a shifting time-sequence, it is important that we relate them to one another so that the shift of time is reasonable. "I shall see tomorrow what I shall never see" violates reason in that both time-references put us in the future, although the second future denies the reality of the first. ". . . what I shall never see *again*," on the other hand, does not violate reason. Good writing demands that the connection of one time or tense with another in a sentence or in a sequence of sentences be understandable, and represent some possible actual time situation.

The past tense refers to some previous time, or, in a general way, to what has gone before. The past perfect also refers backward, either specifically or generally, and then refers backward from *that* time. When you say "The problems *had been solved*," you put the solution before some time, specified or not, which is already in the past, and you leave open the possibility that new factors may have since been introduced which bring the need

for a new and different solution. In the discussion of the present tense, we saw that the continuing present, or present progressive, ("He is going to Europe this summer") could introduce what was actually a future meaning. In the past tense, the progressive form also has a distinct use in addition to the setting forth of a continuation of action. "He *was going*, but he has changed his mind" does not suggest that he was in the process of going, but rather that he *intended* to go. Here the relationship is certainly one of time (the intention existed prior to now), but it is also a relationship of purpose or intention to actuality.

The future tense looks forward to some time after now. ("He will send the box." "They shall not pass.") The future perfect looks forward to some future time *before* which an action is completed. ("Congress *will have adjourned* before that bill can come up for a vote.") The same future perfect meaning, with the same tense-construction, may be achieved without specific time reference. ("Congress will have adjourned without voting on the bill.") The completed action referred to in both sentences is the adjournment. The implied "before which" is the time at which the vote would be taken.

Time, in the world as we know it and live in it, is translated into tense in the composition of sentences. Within the sentence and in a sequence of sentences, tenses relate to one another. The control of these sequences is one important skill of the good writer.

6. *Voice* identifies an active or passive relationship among a doer, a verb, and the thing done. In the *active* voice the *subject* of the verb does the action: "He *throws* the ball." "A man *said* to his neighbor, 'Sir, I *like* your fence.' " In the active voice there may or may not be a direct object for the verb. "*Children play*." "The sun *is shining*."

The passive voice is sometimes called an inferior form, *one that should*

Mood indicates how near, or how far, a statement is from being a positive assertion.

be avoided (a passive voice clause). No such recommendation *would be made* (passive) by anyone who has examined the best literature in the English language with an eye to active and passive structures:

Shakespeare:
". . . that looks on tempests and *is never shaken* . . ."

". . .whose worth's unknown, although his height *be taken*."

"If this be error and upon me *proved* . . ."

(From: "Let me not to the marriage of true minds/Admit impediments")

Emerson:
". . . millions . . . cannot always be *fed* on . . . foreign harvest. . . ."

(From: *The American Scholar*)

Faulkner:
". . . as if he . . . *had been caught.* . . ."

(From: *Barn Burning*)

The examples *could be multiplied* (passive) a thousand times over. In simple truth the passive voice (as with any other form, when well-used) is an important part of effective and beautiful use of language.

The elements that form the active voice can sometimes be transformed into the passive voice. "People use language" becomes "Language is used by people." "My wife baked cookies" becomes "Cookies were baked by my wife." *Only sentences with a transitive verb and a direct object can be transformed into the passive.* But suppose we don't know *who* or *what* did the action. We can't say, "eat rice," without implying an imperative sentence or a crossword puzzle clue. We can say, "Rice is eaten." The passive voice allows us to omit the agent or doer of the action—and often we do not know the agent, or, even if we know, prefer not to identify him. Shakespeare's image would have lost its excellence had he written of love as a star "whose worth we don't

know because no navigator has taken its height." Let's give the passive voice its due and teach it as a standard form to be used, but (like any other form) to be used appropriately and well.

7. *Mood* indicates how near, or how far, a statement is from being a positive assertion. Mood can indicate a statement of fact, or it can introduce an idea of wondering or pondering, or it can suppose what might happen under other circumstances. If the mood indicates a simple assertion, it is indicative; if it introduces *if, when* or *whenever* conditions, it is the conditional mood; and if it supposes what might occur under other conditions, it is the subjunctive mood.

Examples:
Indicative—It is raining.

Conditional—Whenever it rains, the basement leaks.

Subjunctive—If it were raining I would read, but since it isn't, let's go for a walk.

Mood is revealed in two ways—through the form or inflection of the verb and its associated words, and through the meaning of the verb. All verbs in one sentence may be of the same mood, or they may not; each must be considered separately. "*If* birds sing . . ." "*Whenever* birds sing . . ." In each of these a functional word is used, each of which carries a denial that birds sing all the time, and therefore—though they do, in general, sing—they may not be singing now. The present tense function of sing in an absolute sense is brought into question, though it remains in a general sense. This is the *conditional* mood. Some grammarians ignore the conditional mood, preferring only to note the existence of *if, when, whenever* clauses, or simply calling them a part of the indicative mood. The point here is that there is a difference in the force given the verb, and it would be well to recognize it.

Some grammarians also deny the importance of the *subjunctive* mood. At least one has claimed that it no longer exists for practical purposes in English.

The subjunctive is a set of constructions whose purpose is to express conditions contrary to fact. Observe the illustration already given for the subjunctive: "If it were raining I would read, but since it isn't, let's go for a walk." The subjunctive uses a *past tense* form of the verb, but the time or tense reference is not past. Indeed, any use of a verb form other than the standard tense and person expected in a normal indicative sentence or clause is a trademark of the subjunctive. Denial of the verbal implication, or doubt cast on it is also characteristic. "If this *be* treason . . . " implies "It is not treason in my mind, but it may be in yours. . . . " The use of the infinitive form stresses the denial or doubt. This certainly produces a relationship to "fact" which differs from the indicative "this is treason," or the conditional "if this is treason."

There are auxiliary verbs that control mood. These are *can* or *could*, *shall* or *should*, *will* or *would*, *may* or *might*, (*owe*) or *ought*, and *must*. "I can go" is indicative, "I *could go* if I had my work done." This has the past tense form with present or future meaning—characteristic of the subjunctive, with a condition, or more often, a doubt.

"I *could go* if I had my work done, but I don't." This is clearly a denial, also characteristic of the subjunctive. "I *shall go*" and "I *will go*" are indicative future tense.

"I *should go* . . ." or "I *would go* . . ." are subjunctive. The past tense form clearly refers to the present or future, and both introduce doubt or denial. But in "I said I *would go*," the "would go" could be simple past tense.

"I *may go*" and "I *must go*" are indicative.

"I *might go*" and "I *ought to go*" are subjunctive, using past tense forms with present or future meaning, and introducing doubt.

Owe is identified as the present tense form from which *ought* derives. But *owe* has another past form, *owed*, and neither *owe* nor *owed* is a modal (mood controlling) auxiliary. *Ought* is. *Must* is an emphatic auxiliary which lacks the subjunctive past tense form.

8. Modification, literally the act of making or creating a manner, refers to putting into a bare-bones statement words, phrases, or clauses that describe or limit or otherwise give that basic statement or some part of it the exact quality desired.

Modifiers may be divided into *adjectives*, which modify nouns or pronouns, and *adverbs*, which modify verbs, adjectives, and other adverbs. "He eats pancakes" has no modification. "He eats *many* pancakes" and "He eats *many big* pancakes" use adjective modifiers. "He *often* eats pancakes" and "He eats pancakes *for breakfast*" use adverb modifiers.

Modification is the art of molding what you have to say to achieve an effect, using factors which describe, limit, direct, and apply the meaning. The relationship of the modifier to what is modified must not merely be discoverable on careful search, but so apparent that the mind of the reader does not need to be given over directly to the search for that relationship.

Note the difference in these sentences:

John is *only* your friend; sometimes he wants you to know that he . . .

John is your *only* friend; sometimes he wants you to know that he . . .

John is your friend, *only* sometimes he wants you to know that he . . .

John is your friend; sometimes *only* he wants you to know that he . . .

John is your friend; sometimes he *only* wants you to know that he . . .

John is your friend; sometimes he wants *only* you to know that he . . .

Modifiers describe or limit or give an exact quality to a statement.

John is your friend; sometimes he wants you *only* to know that he . . .

John is your friend; sometimes he wants you to know *only* that he . . .

John is your friend; sometimes he wants you to know that *only* he . . .

Phrases and clauses also need to be placed carefully. Note the difference between "The cat *in the coalbin* has black feet" and "*In the coalbin* the cat has black feet." Or the difference between "*When I have the leisure*, I think of going to sea" and "I think of going to sea *when I have the leisure*."

There is a difference apart from that of directly and clearly controlled denotation. "My crotchety old uncle met me at the train" gives the same facts as "My uncle, old and crotchety, met me at the train," yet the second sentence gives a much more favorable impression of the uncle. The art of choosing and placing modifiers is essential to good writing. The misplacement of modifiers is one of the signs of careless or bad writing.

9. *Comparison* is a device for applying varying degrees of the same modification to different things. It has three standard forms:

Comparison communicates varying degrees of modification.

Positive	Comparative	Superlative
hot	hotter	hottest
easy	easier	easiest
terrible	more terrible	most terrible
friendly	more friendly	most friendly
friendly	friendlier	friendliest

These are ordinarily mastered very early. Yet it may be worth calling to attention that although English has only the positive and the two inflected forms (-er, -est) plus the "more" and "most" forms, the actual possibilities of comparison are virtually endless. Think, for example of a row of ten apples, selected and arranged so that at the left end is a completely rotten one, near the middle is the one that is ripe to perfection, and at the right end is one that is too green to be edible. As we go from left to right, each apple is greener than the one before it. As we go from right to left, each one is successively riper. As we go from either end toward the middle, each one is better than the one before it. But note that while the apple second from either end is better than the one at the end, it is still not "good," and that the "best" of the first three is less good than the middle ones. Thus "better" or "best" may be less than "good." In this way the comparative forms make possible

degrees of comparison far richer, far more complex and effective than would seem to be implied with only three standard grammatical forms. We may also, of course, compare things by *description* without the use of the comparative forms: "The tall, slim man is too quiet, giving the effect of a powder keg about to explode. The short one is noisy."

Refinements to Principles of Grammar

There are many refinements to the principles of grammar set forth in the foregoing pages.

Consider the sentence "Seeing is believing." *Seeing* is the gerundive form of the verb *to see*. A gerund is a word which is both verb and noun. The noun form dominates grammatically, so it stands here properly as the subject of a verb, though it still implies the action of a verb. *Is* is a verb. *Believing* is also a gerund. In effect we have a sentence made up of three verbs, yet also having a subject, a verb, and a predicate noun. "To see is to believe" is similar except that it has infinitive verbs, instead of gerunds, to function as nouns.

In some instances, a diagram of the components of a sentence helps us to understand how the components function. Diagrams are useful for showing case, modification, and voice (in that cases change in the active-passive transformation) but they are not useful for analyzing number, gender, person, tense, mood, or comparison. Since case and modification offer serious difficulties to many students, it is worthwhile to be able to give visual reinforcement to explanations of these two sets of relationships. Examples of simple diagramming follow on the next page.

The "which" in the dependent clause of the sentence could also be called a pronominal conjunction, or a relative pronoun. In like manner, the "to my sister" could also be called an adverbial modifying phrase. The whole clause "which belongs to my sister" is an adjective clause modifying the noun "bird."

On page 167 is a diagram of a complex sentence, in which are illustrated all of the cases and a variety of modifying words, phrases, and clauses:

If the precise details of diagramming here presented differ from those the reader is accustomed to, the reader should feel free to change them. The exact form is not sacred. The use of some effective visual aid is what is important. Partly for reasons of space limitation, and partly because the proponents of transformational analysis have not been able to agree on the best way to illustrate their ideas, no attempt is made here to include transformational trees. The transformational tree can be helpful for some aspects of sentence analysis, and should be used if and when it is understood, to clarify and reinforce instruction.

The elements of grammar covered in these chapters apply to all Standard English, whether written or spoken. Punctuation applies only to written language, where it serves to replace the uses of the voice and of pauses to show relationships. Space does not allow the presentation here of all the uses of punctuation. Handbooks of English grammar do, however, give this special subject the detailed treatment necessary.

Diagram of Simple Sentences

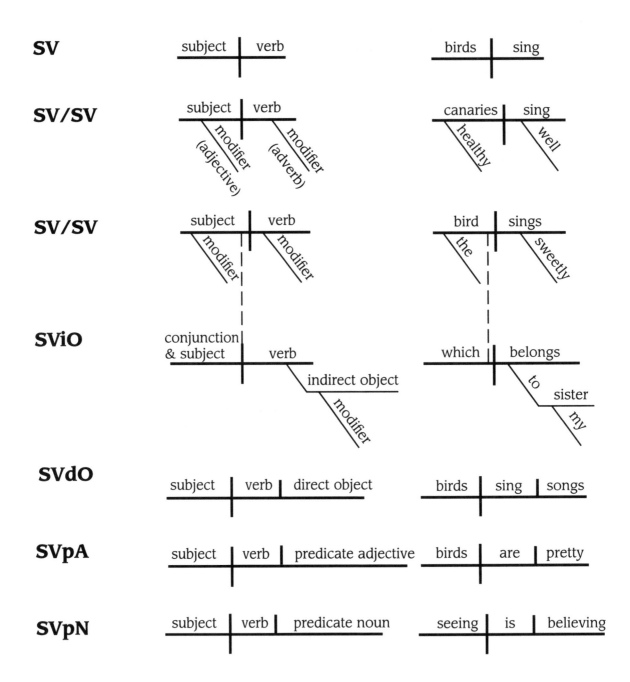

SV

| subject | verb |
| birds | sing |

SV/SV

subject | verb
modifier (adjective) | modifier (adverb)

canaries | sing
healthy | well

SV/SV

subject | verb
modifier | modifier

bird | sings
the | sweetly

SViO

conjunction & subject | verb
indirect object
modifier

which | belongs
to sister
my

SVdO

| subject | verb | direct object |
| birds | sing | songs |

SVpA

| subject | verb | predicate adjective |
| birds | are | pretty |

SVpN

| subject | verb | predicate noun |
| seeing | is | believing |

Diagram of a Complex Sentence

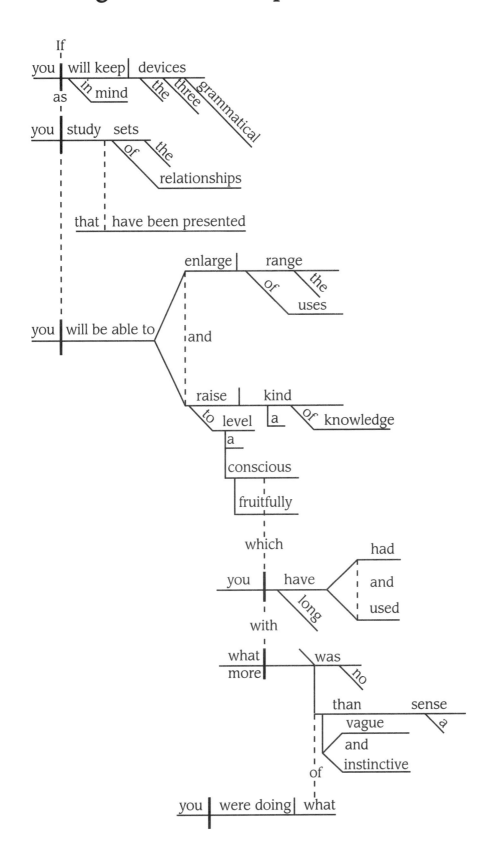

Grammar Curriculum Charted

Grade 1-2

Syntax/Sentence Study

- The emphasis in first and second grade is on learning phonics and reading.
- All the basic sentence patterns are used and written frequently on the board using coding (different colors of chalk, underlining, script, block letters, and parentheses in a code system).

subject (S)
direct object (dO)
predicate noun (pn)
modifiers (M)
(R)

verb (V)
indirect object (iO)
predicate adjective (pa)
relational or functional words such as prepositions, conjunctions, auxiliary

- Grammatical terms are used sometimes, but the *pattern* is the essential thing at this point.
- As patterns become familiar, exercises in changing the words are introduced:

The (M) bird (S) SINGS (V).
The (M) robin (S) FLIES (V).
Who (S) SINGS (V)?
We (S) SING (V) *songs* (dO).

First Grade Goal: Children should recognize the different uses in a sentence for the different kinds of words, and are able to substitute words at every point in sentences of the subject–verb, subject–verb–direct object, subject–verb–predicate adjective, and subject–verb–predicate noun types.

Second Grade Goal: Children recognize the subject–verb–indirect object and subject–verb–direct object sentences as well as others, and are able to create sentences of every type, at least with the aid of coding. The coding is used throughout the first and second years, and at the beginning of the third year.

Etymology/Word Study

Easy compound words are shown, beginning with the ordinal numbers fourth, fifth, etc., and the cardinals thirteen, fourteen, etc. Other easy prefixes and suffixes are shown, in each case with comparison of uses, e.g.: He (S) WAS (V) (quick) (pa). He (S) RAN (V) quickly (M). She (S) IS (V) (careful) (pa). She (S) RUNS (V) carefully (M). I (S) TIE (V) my (M) *shoe* (dO). I (S) UNTIE (V) my (M) *shoe* (dO). Prefixes and suffixes are identified at this stage, but an awareness of the patterns of words is of primary importance to develop at this early level.

Grade 3

Syntax/Sentence Structure

- Review structures of words and sentences of the first two years.
- Gradually eliminate coding, first the S–V, then pa, then pn, then dO, then iO, finally R.
- Modifiers should continue to be coded (because they will offer the most complexity) until the other forms can be recognized consistently. This removal of coding is gradual.
- The grammatical names are introduced before the coding is abandoned and exercises are given with each function form until it is mastered before the next function form is introduced without coding.
- The goal of the third grade should be to replace recognition by coded forms with recognition by names for all of the basic one-clause sentence forms.

Etymology/Word Study

Prefixes and suffixes are taught, e.g., *re-*: *re-read*, *return*, *redo*, etc., *in-*: *inside*, *into*, *insect*. Suffixes might include *-er*: *worker*, *teacher*, *reader*, etc.; *-able*: *readable*, *erasable*, etc.

Grammar Curriculum Charted

Grade 4

Syntax/Sentence Study

- The fourth grade begins with a review of all processes.
- When it is clear that the structure of basic sentence forms is known and that the parts can be used and named, modifiers are introduced gradually, e.g., at first for the S then for the dO, then for the V, then for the pn, and pa, and finally for the iO.
- At this point the diagram should be used as a visual aid:

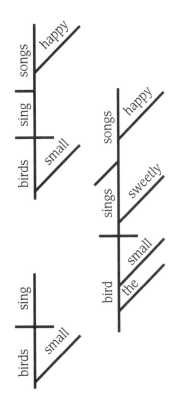

- When this much is mastered so that the children can properly show the modifying relationships of one-word modifiers, phrase modifiers should be introduced:

- Many exercises are used until the relationship of modifier to the noun or verb it modifies is clearly recognized.
- Sentences with this kind of structure are drawn from the literature studied, and from the student's own writing.
- Sentences written by the children are put on the board for the class to add modification (with the teacher's help when necessary).

Etymology/Word Study

- Word parts receive more emphasis.
- Stems (or roots or bases) are introduced and a variety of affixes used with them, e.g., TRACT = to pull, the stem for exTRACT, deTRACT, conTRACT, pro-TRACT, disTRACT, exTRACTion, ex-TRACTable, TRACTion, deTRACTion, disTRACTing, etc.
- The teacher explains each word, showing just what each prefix and each suffix does to build a meaning that is based on the stem.
- The teacher demonstrates with several stems, such as MOVE, MOT, MOB (all mean "move"); FAC, FIC, FACT, FECT, FICT (all from Latin FACere "to make or do"); SPEC, SPIC, SPECT (from the Latin SPECere, "to see"), etc.
- Lists of prefixes, stems, and suffixes in separate columns make a good exercise for students to put together with the teacher reviewing the words assembled.
- In the fourth grade vocabulary development begins a rapid expansion, and this analytical method is the best single method for doing it, since stems are used from several to hundreds of times, and the affixes hundreds of times in words the students will soon need to know.
- Word games of other sorts should of course also be used.

Grammar Curriculum Charted

Grade 5 | Syntax/Sentence Study

- The fifth grade begins with a **review** of basic sentence forms, first without modifiers, then with one-word modifiers and finally with phrase modifiers.
- **Diagrams** of these forms are used as visual aids to reinforce awareness of relationships.
- Some review should be used whenever necessary throughout the year.
- Words and sentences are drawn **from literature** and from the students' writing.
- As a general rule, whenever a word or sentence that is encountered in reading seems not to be thoroughly understood, an analysis is in order.
- These **analytical processes** will make it possible to achieve a fuller understanding of good literature, and good literature is far more effective in meeting and expanding interest than are stories that have been written down to the children's supposed language level.
- Formal instruction in sentence patterns should now begin to include **modifying clauses (embedded sentences)**.
- The diagram is again an important visual aid. Examples: "My sister told me that story." "She is in the seventh grade." These two sentences may become one: "My sister, who is in the seventh grade, told me that story." Or: "My sister, who told me that story, is in the seventh grade."

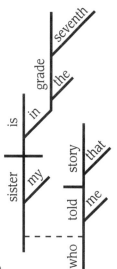

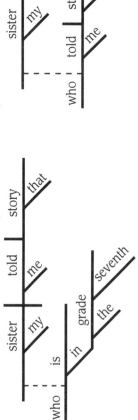

- The **combining of two short sentences** into one is an essential skill for good writing. Examples should be used until there is a full understanding of the process and a realization of how a sentence (which then becomes a clause) may be used to modify any appropriate part of another sentence.
- **Compound sentences** from reading should be diagrammed, and also divided into the sentences from which they were combined:

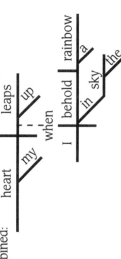

- Here we clearly have two sentences: "My heart leaps up." "I behold a rainbow in the sky." The when clause is adverbial, modifying leaps (telling when the leaping takes place).
- Longer sentences, with three or more clauses, should be analyzed if students ask about them, or if they are difficult to understand, though the responsibility for learning, at this stage, should center on the **two-clause combinations**.

Etymology/Word Study

- Words, especially those with prefixes and suffixes that have been taught, are reviewed.
- Word analysis continues.
- Compound words are a center of attention. Some grammatical terms should be analyzed too, e.g.:
- **prePOSITion** (that which) (is put or placed) (before) and note that prepositions do come before their objects —*on* the table, *for* me, *to* school, etc.;
- **conJUNCTion** (that which) (joins) (together). The teacher should point out that we speak of pencil *and* paper (joining nouns), the dog ran *and* jumped (joining verbs): I like to swim *but* he likes to play baseball (joining clauses or sentences); etc.
- A **comPOUND** word is a word that is (put) (together), that a **preFIX** is (attached or hooked on) (before), while a **sufFIX** is (attached) (behind). The *suf* is a combining form of Latin *sub* which means "under"— subMARine (belonging or going) (under) (the sea).
- The goal for fifth grade is that students can combine and divide sentences, diagram them (as a way of demonstrating this ability), and show a good understanding of words, with the specific knowledge of at least fifteen common prefixes, as many suffixes, and perhaps fifteen or twenty stems.

Grammar Curriculum Charted

Grade 6	Syntax/Sentence Study	Etymology/Word Study
	• The sixth grade first **reviews** essentials from the fifth grade and then adds analysis of sentences with three and four clauses. • If the basics have been learned, progress from this point on will be easy, but it must not be taken for granted. • The essential difference is that the materials used are now drawn almost exclusively from two sources: literature and the students' own writing. • Students are invited to diagram some of their own best sentences and sentences which they have found in their reading. • The teacher should scan books of all subjects at that grade level for sentences which might not be completely understood, and should analyze these or have students do it.	• Words from all subject areas should also be analyzed. • Sixth grade students are shown how to use a good etymological dictionary. • A few simple problems in word analysis should be given for completion in the library. • The teacher should keep a file of words for such assignments and a file of especially interesting words for class analysis and discussion—words, for example, such as *influence* and *influenza* (which have identical analyses), astronomy and disaster (both from Latin ASTER, star), *lord, lady, steward,* and *marshall* (which are of interesting Germanic origins). • The goal of sixth grade is that students can analyze, divide, and in general freely manipulate sentences with as many as four clauses, and can write sentences of three clauses effectively. They know some twenty-five or thirty prefixes, as many suffixes, and at least forty stems (mostly from Latin but a few from Greek and a few from Germanic or from other sources).

Grammar Curriculum Charted

Grade 7 — Syntax/Sentence Study

- The seventh grade with its strong sense of "growing up" for the child entering adolescence should reflect this movement toward the adult world where knowledge, understanding, and communication are of paramount importance.
- At this point the full nature and extent of grammar should be set forth as a body of knowledge to be mastered; a definition of grammar as a systematic (though not necessarily rigid or even wholly consistent) means of producing meaning out of words.
- The three grammatical means (word order, inflections, and function or relational words) are explained and demonstrated.
- Sentence modes should be identified.
- The nine relational functions (gender, number, person, case, tense, mood, voice, modification, and comparison) are explained and illustrated.
- Basic sentence types are reviewed and the grammatical means and relationships shown. Combinations of sentences with subordinate or dependent or relative clauses, with independent or coordinate clauses, and with mixtures of the two are demonstrated.
- Through the elementary years the emphasis has been on patterns, and the means for teaching have been largely imitation and authority. Now, using the familiar structures and relationships, reinforced with visual diagrams, **understanding becomes the prime objective.**
- Sentences of considerable grammatical complexity from reading (textbooks from any or all subjects) are analyzed and explained, with the students doing as much as possible and the teacher ready to answer questions and complete the process.
- Such sentences are rewritten, reorganized, broken into shorter sentences that are then recombined, while the question of most effective form or arrangement is considered.
- The students write often and rewrite to gain conscious control of sentence patterns, order of clauses, and effective emphasis.
- Punctuation, up to now largely a matter of imitation and authority, should be considered not only as a convention, but as a means of controlling or guiding the reader.
- Among the relational factors, mood and voice will not have been stressed before and even now may be given no more attention than is called for by chance selection of sentences or by student inquiry. But they should not be completely brushed aside if questions arise.

Etymology/Word Study

- Word study should continue at an increased rate.
- The Germanic origin of English, the three hundred years of French rule of England, and the direct and indirect influx of Latin and Greek words are reviewed.
- Let it be clearly understood that the **understanding of principles is the goal, not the learning of rules,** not an absolutist or "purist" view of "the way the language should be," but the way it is when effectively used by authors of recognized stature. Let it be noted and accepted that these authors use dialect, slang, ellipses—but that they use them on a foundation of Standard English and that they are effective precisely as variations on Standard English, just as a musician's variations on a theme depend on that theme for effect.
- The preceding paragraph applies not only to the seventh grade, but with equal or increasing emphasis to all English instruction that follows.

Grammar Curriculum Charted

Grade 8 — Syntax/Sentence Study

- The eighth grade fully explores active and passive voice structures. Transformations from active to passive and passive to active are practiced in a variety of tenses.
- All tenses are clarified and practiced.
- Mood is explored, at least the indicative and conditional.
- The subjunctive is undertaken if the students are ready for it. The direct object in an active voice structure becomes the subject in a passive voice structure.
- The subject in the active voice becomes the agent in the passive (if not omitted), and, when present, becomes an indirect object of the preposition by. Thus: "The pitcher hurled the ball" becomes "The ball was hurled by the pitcher."
- In addition to the active-passive transformation, the diagram should be used to illustrate and clarify modification when it exists in abundance, as it often does in good writing.

Etymology/Word Study

- Word study continues, with analysis by prefix, stem, and suffix, with words drawn from texts of all subjects taught in the eighth grade and from the students' own writing.
- Assignments in analysis are given, with a good, simple etymological dictionary as a standard tool.
- By now every student has such a dictionary for regular use, and assignments lead him to be familiar with it.
- English began as a Germanic language, but most of the new words are of Latin or Greek origin. To ignore this aspect of the study of English is to condemn the student to ignorance or to vague, uncertain knowledge of the language he will be using the rest of his life.

Grammar Curriculum Charted

Grade 9

Syntax/Sentence Study

- In the ninth grade the fundamentals stressed for the preceding year are reviewed including the three grammatical means and the nine relational factors.
- Case, voice, mood, and modification are stressed.
- The moods are given thorough attention: indicative, conditional, subjunctive, and the uses of the modal (or "mood forming") auxiliaries.
- Gerunds, participles, and appositives (nouns, phrases, or clauses used in apposition to a noun in any position or function) should all be taught and illustrated with diagrams.
- Double functions should be explained, illustrated, diagrammed, and assigned for diagramming. Examples:
- Double function with a gerund: *Hearing the wind blow down that tree gave me an exciting moment. Note that hearing,* as a noun and verb takes a direct object, *wind;* that *wind* also has a double function, as direct object of the verb *blow;* and that the entire gerundive phrase is the subject of the verb *gave.*

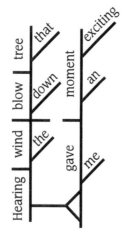

- Subject-Object double function: *I like whoever said that.* Note that *whoever* is the direct object of *like* and subject of *said,* and that the clause *whoever said that,* as a whole, is the direct object of *like.*

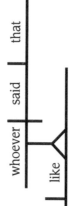

- Example of an appositive clause: My sister, *the girl who saw the fire,* was excited. Note that *girl who saw the fire* is in apposition to *sister* and that *who saw the fire* is an adjective clause modifying *girl.*

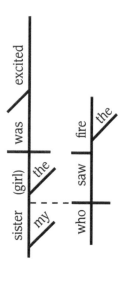

Etymology/Word Study

- The ninth grade continues to develop analytical principles of word formation.
- Word families (those based on a single stem or on the various forms of a single stem) are introduced.
- How many English words are developed, for instance, on the stem forms of Latin SPECere, to see? For a start: SPECial, SPECious, conSPICuous, SPECTacles, inSPECTor, deSPICable (also, via French, deSPISE and deSPITE), exPECT, exPECTation, etc.
- Those students who are to become good adult readers need to raise their vocabularies from the couple of thousand words with which they began school to many thousands.

Grammar Curriculum Charted

Grade 10 — Syntax/Sentence Study

- In the tenth grade English class, the emphasis is on great literature and frequent writing.
- Excellent sentences, from poetry as well as from prose, should be analyzed grammatically.
- Students are encouraged—even assigned—to "tamper with greatness." Rewrite Milton? Yes! Try rewriting:

  "When I consider how my light is spent
  Ere half my days in this dark world and wide,
  And that one talent which is death to hide
  Lodged with me useless, though my soul more bent
  To serve therewith my Maker, and present
  My true account, lest He returning chide,
  'Doth God exact day-labour, light denied?'
  I fondly ask: But Patience, to prevent
  That murmur, soon replies, 'God doth not need
  Either man's work or His own gifts. Who best
  Bear His mild yoke, they serve Him best. His state
  Is kingly: thousands at His bidding speed,
  And post o'er land and ocean without rest;
  They also serve who only stand and wait.'"

- The first ten lines are one sentence, one magnificent sentence, as any serious effort at rewriting will soon demonstrate. Such a sentence may be analyzed grammatically for clauses (and the kind of each as an embedded sentence: is it subject–verb, subject–verb–direct object, or what?), for the mood and voice of each verb, etc. Great literature should be an experience in mastery of the unmodified elements and those that modify. We should not assume that only English teachers need to know how to use the language, and we should not allow in any classroom teachers who lack a mastery of it. In their language as well as in ideas, imagination, emotion, and the senses—and the one type of experience should and can enhance the other.

Etymology/Word Study

- The tenth graders learn the origins and development of the English language. They saw examples of Old English and Middle English in ninth grade, and they know Shakespeare's language. They learned of the 300-year period of French influence, and of the British trade and scholarship which later produced an enormous growth of vocabulary.
- They should learn how science and technology still later made further demands on language, and some of the new words coined to fill the new needs.
- They should learn about dialects, slang, and the melting-pot nature of American English, which has absorbed elements of the speech of immigrants from Europe, Asia, Latin America, and Africa.
- The emphasis is writing—learning to cast words they know more than superficially into effective sentences and these into effective paragraphs and essays. Because the processes of thought depend on the processes of language, they should discover style to express their thoughts as accurately as possible: loose and periodic sentences, parallel structures, balance, and the uses of rhetorical devices.

The curriculum proposed here has put emphasis on mastery of language; it has not stressed the marking of errors. These should be corrected, but they should not be allowed to dominate the instruction or the students' attention. Students should learn that errors are distractions to the reader, sometimes interfering with the transmission of ideas, and are therefore undesirable, but not that they are sure signs of failure. Imperfect excellence is much better than perfect mediocrity if one has to choose. With a sense of competence in structure and a sure mastery of a growing vocabulary, hopefully there will come the desire to make every aspect of the writing as good as possible. And, most important: we should not assume that only English teachers need to know how to use the language, and we should not allow in any classroom teachers who lack a mastery of it. In their years of schooling, students progress far from the imitation through which they first learned English, but they never completely leave imitation behind. All teachers teach language.

CHAPTER SIX
PROSODY

He that would hope to write well hereafter in laudable things, ought himself to be a true poem; that is, a composition and pattern of the best and most honorable things.

—John Milton

Sample English Language Lesson Plan

Grade: _____8_____ Date: _4/15/98_ Teacher: _____Adams_____

Skill Taught: _____Figures of Speech_____

Principle: _____Colorful language communicates effectively._____

Biblical Reference: _____Psalm 72_____ Illustration: _____Literary history_____

Component:
- ☐ Biblical Foundation
- ☐ Orthography
- ☐ Etymology
- ☐ Syntax
- ☒ Prosody
- ☐ Composition

Materials/Resources: _____Bradford's Literary Style, p. 83–85, ch. 2, CHOC 1, pp._____

_____184–240._____

Structure of the Lesson

1. **Introduce the purpose and goal of the lesson.**

   The identification of Bradford's literary style in Of Plimoth Plantation, particularly his use of various figures of speech to make effective description, and the influence of the Bible and its literary style upon his own. History as literature.

2. **Review related skill or concept.**

   Review of figures of speech: alliteration, antithesis, coupling, metaphor, simile—define and give examples. The figures that are not familiar should be given several illustrations.

3. **Present new principle and idea with appropriate methodology.**

   This lesson assumes that pages 184–240 in CHOC 1 have been previously read and the Biblical view of life and the influence of the Bible on his style identified. Each figure of speech is then identified in the excerpt beginning with alliterations. Students should look for the figures by silent reading and recording, then by discussion. They should share their findings and add classmates' findings to their records.

4. **Require student practice, participation, and presentation.**

   The notebook record should include notes identifying Bradford's style with excerpts recorded to illustrate each of the figures of speech. Further reading and analysis verbally referring to Bradford's writing.

5. **Summarize, review, and evaluate.**

   Student writes an essay entitled "The Influence of the Bible on Bradford's Literary Style," analyzing the excerpt from Of Plimoth Plantation to show Bradford's Biblical view of life, the Biblical heritage of Bradford's style, and literary devices used in his writing that give it color.

Introduction to Prosody
"Words in Tuneful Order"

Twice five years or less, I might have been, when first my mind
*With conscious pleasure, opened to the charm of words **in tuneful order** and for the better part of*
Two delightful hours we strolled along repeating favorite verses with one voice.

—William Wordsworth, "The Prelude"

Prosody is "that part of grammar which treats of the quantity of syllables, of accents, and of the laws of versification" according to Webster's original definition. In *The Noah® Plan English Language Curriculum Guide*, Prosody is that element of language that gives grace and force to verbal and written expression. It includes all the various devices of prose and poetry that give language its delightful appeal. Rudyard Kipling in *A Book of Words* tells us that "the magic of literature lies in words, and not in any man. Witness, a thousand excellent, stenuous words can leave us cold or put us to sleep, whereas a bare half-hundred words breathed upon by some man in his agony, or in his exultation, or in his idleness, ten generations ago, can still lead whole nations into and out of captivity . . . or stir us so intolerably that we can scarcely abide to look at our own souls." What makes that difference? The difference is "not the assertion that something is true, but the making of that truth more fully real to us," said T. S. Eliot. Prosody is largely responsible.

The study of Prosody is greatly dependent upon the vast treasury of literature in prose and poetry to model the "magic of literature." The Prosody chapter of the Guide provides first a study of Figures of Speech as a survey of various devices of language. The second part of the chapter is a primer for teaching and learning Poetry that can free the teacher and the student to undergird the development of language skill from kindergarten through graduation.

Figures of Speech are variations of the literal or ordinary forms of expression, the intention being to make the thought more attractive or more striking.

Adapted from
Lessons in
English *by Sara*
E. H. Lockwood.
Boston: Ginn &
Company, 1890.

Literal Examples	Figurative Examples
1. Misfortunes never come singly.	1. When sorrows come, They come not single spies, But in battalions. *Shakespeare*
2. Time seems short when we are happy.	2. How noiseless falls the foot of Time That only treads on flowers! *W. R. Spencer*
3. Why cannot I go to sleep?	3. O, gentle sleep, Nature's soft nurse, how have I frightened thee? *Shakespeare*
4. The king lay wounded and helpless.	4. So, like a shattered column, lay the king. *Tennyson*

Figures of Speech are of many different kinds. The principal Figures will be considered in order.

Figures of Speech

Simile

Simile is an expression of resemblance between two different things. It is usually introduced by such words as *like* and *as*.

Not all expressed comparisons are Similes. The tiger is as brave as the lion is not a Simile, because the things compared have too many points of resemblance. The best Similes are such as compare things which are in most respects unlike; but which have at least one strong point of resemblance in appearance or qualities or actions or in the effects which they produce.

Exercise

What things are compared?
Where does the resemblance lie?
How is the comparison expressed?

1. How far that little candle throws its beams!
   So shines a good deed in a naughty world. *Shakespeare*

2. As the mountains are round about Jerusalem, so the Lord is round about
   his people, from henceforth even forever. *Psalms 125:2*

3. The wild geese fly,
   Storm-sent, from Arctic moors and fells,
   Like a great arrow through the sky. *Whittier*

4. Religion is to the soul what light is to nature.

5. The covetous man pines in plenty, like Tantalus, up to
   the chin in water and yet thirsty. *Adams*

6. It is with words as with sunbeams—the more they are
   condensed, the deeper they burn. *Southey*

7. Her hair drooped round her pallid cheek
   Like sea-weed on a clam. *Holmes*

8. To be mixed in parish stirs
   Is worse than handling chestnut-burrs. *Saxe*

9. The hooded clouds, like friars,
   Tell their beads in drops of rain. *Longfellow*

10. Human life may be compared to a river,
    flowing ever towards the sea of Eternity.

Metaphor

Metaphor is another Figure which is founded upon the resemblance of one thing to another. It differs from Simile in that the comparison is implied instead of being formally expressed. In Metaphor we speak of one thing in such language as suggests a picture of something else. As in Simile, the things compared should not be alike in too many particulars. There is no Metaphor in saying, *That man is a hero*.

The following examples illustrate the difference between Simile and Metaphor:

Simile	**Metaphor**
1. Life is like an isthmus between two eternities.	1. Life is an isthmus between two eternities.
2. Habit may be likened to a cable; every day we weave a thread, and soon we cannot break it.	2. Habit is a cable; every day we weave a thread, and soon we cannot break it.
3. Happiness is like sunshine; made of very little beams.	3. The sunshine of life is made up of very little beams.

Exercise

What things are compared?
Show wherein lies the resemblance.
Change each Metaphor to form a Simile.

1. Kindness is the golden chain by which society is bound together. *Goethe*

2. This [snow] is the poem of the air,
Slowly in silent syllables recorded. *Longfellow*

3. By the street called By-and-by you reach a house called Never.

4. What is pride?
A whizzing rocket
That would emulate a star.

5. We cannot all be cabin passengers in the voyage of life. Some must be before the mast.

6. Aloft on sky and mountain wall
Are God's great pictures hung. *Whittier*

7. Silently, one by one, in the infinite meadows of heaven, Blossomed the lovely stars, the forget-me-nots of the angels. *Longfellow*

8. In the bright lexicon of youth, there's no such word as fail. *Bulwer*

9. A certain amount of opposition is a great help to a man. Kites rise against and not with the wind.

10. Spare moments are the gold-dust of time.

Allegory

Allegory is also founded upon resemblance; but the comparison is more extended than in Simile and Metaphor. An Allegory is a fictitious story designed to teach some abstract truth by the use of symbolic language. Short Allegories are called Fables or Parables.

The difference between Simile, Metaphor, and Allegory may be illustrated by these three ways of representing life as a day's journey.

Examples

Simile

Life may be compared to a day's journey from our Father's house "into a far country" and home again.

Metaphor

From the cradle to the grave is but a day's journey.

Allegory

One bright morning a child left his father's house and wandered out into the wide world. Birds sang in the tree-tops and gay butterflies fluttered among the flowers which grew on every side. The child ran here and there, chasing the butterflies. He gathered the flowers until his hands could hold no more. So the morning wore on.

As the sun rose higher, the birds ceased their songs. Noon found the child hot and weary with chasing butterflies. The flowers in his hands drooped and faded. The way became rougher and steeper as he went on, and often he stumbled over the stones in his path.

After a time he noticed that many of the stones around him contained gleams of gold and veins of silver, and sometimes a sparkling gem firmly imbedded in the coarse rock.

"I will gather these beautiful stones," said he, "for they will not fade as did the flowers."

But the jewels were fast in the rocks, and, with all his strength, he could not loosen them. Tears came to the child's eyes when he found that all these precious things must be left behind, because he was not strong enough to carry the stones in which they were fixed. Presently he grew braver, and said to himself, "Perhaps among the little stones I may find some jewels." So, as the afternoon wore away, he filled his handkerchief with shining pebbles, and carried the precious bundle on his back, while with his one free hand he grasped every little stone that glistened in his path.

As the shadows grew longer, his strength began to fail. His feet were bleeding from contact with the sharp rocks, and the burden on his back seemed crushing him to the earth. Stopping occasionally to rest, he examined the pebbles which he had collected and found that most of them were worthless; so, a few at a time he threw them all away.

As the dew began to fall he sighed, "I am so tired! How pleasant it must be now at home; and how far away I have wandered! I must hasten back before night comes."

The stars came out to light him on his way, and, empty-handed, he went home, to find rest and shelter in his father's house.

Examples of Allegory

The Parables of the Bible; *Aesop's Fables*
Bunyan's *Pilgrim's Progress*
The Mountain and the Squirrel, Emerson
Little Daffydowndilly, Hawthorne

Exercise

1. What do you understand by the expression, "his father's house"?

2. What period of life is meant by the morning?

3. What is represented by the birds and butterflies?

4. What by the flowers?

5. Give a literal expression for "As the sun rose higher."

6. What is pictured by the fading flowers?

7. Explain what is meant by "stones in the path."

8. Why is it proper to speak of the way as growing steeper?

9. What is meant by noon?

10. What do you understand by the gold and jewels among the rocks?

11. What experience of human life is expressed in the sentence beginning, "Tears came to the child's eyes"?

12. What is meant by the pebbles?

13. Explain the expression, "As the shadows grew longer."

14. What was the burden which he carried?

15. What is meant by his throwing away the pebbles?

16. What is meant by the falling of the dew?

17. Express in literal language the quotation beginning, "I am so tired."

18. What is meant by the stars coming out to light him?

19. What is the special significance of the expression "empty-handed"?

20. Tell the story in literal language.

Personification

Personification consists in attributing life to inanimate things. There are three chief kinds of Personification:

First: That produced by the use of adjectives. In this form of Personification, the qualities of living beings are attributed to inanimate things.

Ex. The hungry flames. The whistling wind. A treacherous calm.

This form of Personification is much like Metaphor, and is sometimes so called.

Second: That produced by the use of verbs. Here inanimate things are represented as performing the actions of living beings.

Ex. The winds howled. "Our bugles sang truce." "Hope enchanted smiled."

Third: This is the highest form of Personification. In this, inanimate things are directly addressed, as if they could answer. It is a combination of Personification with another figure, Apostrophe.

Ex. "Violet, sweet violet! Thine eyes are full of tears."

Personification and Metaphor are often combined. A peculiar form of Personification is common in fables, where animals and plants are represented as thinking and talking like men.

Exercise

Where is Personification suggested?

What form of the figure is used?

1. Kind Fancy plays the fairy god-mother.   *Lowell*

2. Scowling turrets and frowning battlements.

3. The years between.
   Have taught some sweet, some bitter lessons.   *Lowell*

4. Fair Science frowned not on his humble birth, And Melancholy marked him for her own.   *Gray*

5. Creaking with laughter swings the old barn door, At little winking seeds upon the floor, Dropped from four hungry barrels in a row.   *Cordner*

6. Procrastination is the thief of time.   *Young*

7. Angel of Peace, thou hast wandered too long.   *Holmes*

8. Joy and Temperance and Repose
   Slam the door on the doctor's nose.   *Longfellow* (Translation)

9. O Nature, how fair is thy face
   And how light is thy heart!   *Owen Meredith*

10. All day the sea-waves sobbed with sorrow.   *Whittier*

Antithesis

Antithesis is a figure founded upon unlikeness. Things are contrasted or opposed to each other.

The best examples of Antithesis are those in which the contrast is the most forcible. Contrast verbs with verbs, adjectives with adjectives, nouns with nouns, etc.

Ex. "Deeds show what we are; words, what we should be." Often there is a double or even a triple contrast in the same sentence.

Ex. "Silence is deep as Eternity; speech is shallow as Time."

Here silence and speech are contrasted; deep and shallow; Eternity and Time.

Exercise

What things are contrasted?

Is there more than one contrast?

1. Better to reign in hell than serve in heaven. *Milton*
2. Fools rush in where angels fear to tread. *Pope*
3. Character is what we are; reputation is what others think we are.
4. The weary to sleep and the wounded to die. *Campbell*
5. Thoughts that breathe and words that burn. *Gray*
6. To err is human; to forgive, divine. *Pope*
7. Strain out a gnat and swallow a camel. *Matthew 23:24*
8. As sad as earth, as sweet as heaven. *Holmes*
9. From grave to gay, from lively to severe. *Pope*
10. God made the country, and man made the town. *Cowper*

Epigram

Epigram formerly meant an inscription on a monument—an epitaph. It is used now with reference to a brief, pointed saying that is in the nature of a proverb. The best Epigrams are those in which there is an apparent contradiction between the intended meaning and the form of the expression.

Ex. "Well begun is half done."

Here the intended meaning is, that if we once undertake a task, it is comparatively easy to complete it.

Like Antithesis, Epigram is founded upon contrast. Puns are often expressed by Epigrams.

Exercise

1. Great truths are often said in the fewest words.

2. He is the richest who is content with the least. *Socrates*

3. The more we do, the more we can do;
   the more busy we are, the more leisure we have. *Hazelett*

4. The child is father of the man. *Wordsworth*

5. A little learning is a dangerous thing. *Pope*

6. Verbosity is cured by a wide vocabulary.

7. Beauty, when unadorned, adorned the most. *Thomson*

8. The fastest colors are those that won't run.

9. A new way to contract debts—pay them off!

10. Beneath this stone my wife doth lie;
    She's now at rest, and so am I. *Old Epitaph*

Metonymy

Metonymy means a change of name. It is somewhat like Metaphor, but it commonly lies in a single word, whereas Metaphor is usually more extended.

Metaphor is founded upon resemblance. The thing spoken of and the thing meant are alike in some respect which is important to the thought.

Ex. "The Lord is my Shepherd." His care is the point illustrated.

Metonymy is founded upon relation. The thing spoken of and the thing meant may be wholly unlike, but the relation between them is such that the mention of one suggests the other.

Ex. "The drunkard loves his bottle." Here there is no resemblance, but very close relation.

There are several kinds of Metonymy. The following are among the most common:

1. Container for thing contained   Ex. The kettle boils, i.e., the water in the kettle.

2. Sign for thing signified   Ex. He deserves the palm, i.e., the victory.

3. Cause for Effect   Ex. Have you read Shakespeare? i.e., his works.

4. Effect for Cause   Ex. Gray hairs should be respected, i.e., age.

Exercise

Point out the figure.

What kind of Metonymy is it?

1. Our ships opened fire.
2. Streaming grief his faded cheek bedewed.
3. There is too much red tape about this system.
4. He addressed the Chair.
5. The bench, the bar, the pulpit.
6. His steel gleamed on high.
7. He is an excellent shot.
8. All flesh is grass. *Isaiah 40:6*
9. He beheld a sea of faces.
10. Let us gather around the festive board.

Some authorities regard as Metonymy the putting of the name of the material of which an object is made for the name of the thing itself. Others regard this as an example of Synecdoche. The connection in which the word is used will commonly determine which figure it constitutes.

Is there any figure of this kind in the Exercise?

Synecdoche

This figure consists in putting a part for the whole, or the whole for a part. It is saying more or less than we mean.

Ex. "Give us this day our daily bread," i.e., all things needful for us. Here a part is put for the whole.

Ex. "The world knows his worth," i.e., the part of the world which knows him. Here the whole is used for a part.

Exercise

Point out the figure.

Why is it Synecdoche?

1. We have tea at six o'clock.
2. He employs fifty-seven hands.
3. I will not be paid in paltry gold.
4. The Assyrian came down like a wolf on the fold. *Byron*
5. The cattle upon a thousand hills. *Psalm 50:10*
6. A maiden of sixteen summers
7. The canvas exhibited by this artist is a marvelous production.
8. A life on the ocean wave, a home on the rolling deep
9. Ten thousand fleets sweep over thee in vain. *Byron*
10. She bestowed her hand and heart upon a worthy man.

Apostrophe

Apostrophe is direct address to the absent as if they were present, to the dead as if they were living, or to inanimate things as if they had life. It is often combined with Metaphor and Personification.

Exercise

What is addressed?

Is there any other figure?

1. Gentle Spring, in sunshine clad,
   Well dost thou thy power display. *Longfellow*

2. Thou hast taught me, Silent River,
   Many a lesson, deep and long. *Longfellow*

3. [To the sun]
   O thou that rollest above, round as the shield of my fathers! *Ossian*

4. Thus, O Genius, are thy footprints hallowed. *Longfellow*

5. Toll! toll! toll!
   Thou bell by billows swung. *Sigourney*

6. My country, 'tis of thee,
   Sweet land of liberty,
   Of thee I sing. *Sam F. Smith*

7. You moon, have you done something wrong in heaven,
   That God has hidden your face? *Jean Ingelow*

8. Go, little book, whose pages hold
   Those garnered years in loving trust.

9. O Death, where is thy sting.
   O Grave, where is thy victory? *1 Corinthians 15:55*

10. Ye winds of memory, sweep the silent lyre. *Holmes*

Exclamation

Sometimes a statement, instead of being made in a declarative form, is made more forcible by being expressed in an exclamatory tone. When the thought springs from real emotion, we may call the figure Exclamation. Not every exclamatory sentence, however, contains the rhetorical figure Exclamation.

Ex. "Oh, yes! what a pity" is exclamatory, but does not contain the figure.

Exercise

Show why this is Exclamation.

Change to declarative form.

1. Farewell, a long farewell, to all my greatness! *Shakespeare*

2. How poor are they that have not patience! *Shakespeare*

3. But oh, for the touch of a vanished hand,
   And the sound of a voice that is still! *Tennyson*

4. How dear to this heart are the scenes of my childhood,
   When fond recollection presents them to view. *Wordsworth*

5. O strong hearts and true! Not one went back in the
   Mayflower. *Longfellow*

6. Oh, what a tangled web we weave
   When first we practise to deceive! *Scott*

7. A horse! A horse! My kingdom for a horse! *Shakespeare*

8. Oh, the glorious Thanksgivings
   Of the days that are no more! *Smuller*

9. Oh that the rules of our living
   More like to the golden would be! *Nourse*

10. Ah! vainest of all things
    Is the gratitude of kings. *Longfellow*

Interrogation

When a question is asked, not for the purpose of obtaining an answer, but for rhetorical effect, there is the figure of Interrogation. Not every interrogative sentence, however, contains the figure.

Peculiarities of Rhetorical Interrogation:

An affirmative interrogation is an emphatic form of denial.

Ex. "Am I Rome's slave?" is understood to mean, You well know that I am not Rome's slave.

A negative interrogation is an emphatic affirmation.

Ex. "Am I not an apostle? am I not free?" means, I *am* an apostle, etc.

Exercise

What is the effect of the Interrogation?

Change to literal form of expression.

1. What man is free from sin?

2. Am I my brother's keeper? *Genesis 4:9*

3. Who is not proud to be an American?

4. Hast thou a charm to stay the morning star
   In his steep course? *Coleridge*

5. Shall mortal man be more just than God? *Job 4: 17*

6. Hath he not always treasures, always friends—
   The good, great man? *Coleridge*

7. Can the Ethiopian change his skin or the leopard his spots? *Jeremiah 13:23*

8. Is life so dear, or peace so sweet, as to be purchased at the price of chains and slavery? *Patrick Henry*

9. Can honor's voice provoke the silent dust?
   Or Flattery soothe the dull cold ear of death? *Gray*

10. Hast thou entered into the treasures of the snow? or hast thou seen the treasures of the hail? *Job 38:22*

Hyperbole

Hyperbole is exaggeration. It is sometimes effective in descriptions of the grand and sublime. Often, however, it is absurd, and has the opposite effect from that intended.

The extravagant use of strong adjectives is a bad habit in conversation and in writing. Extravagant comparisons also should be avoided.

Examples of "School-girl hyperbole": I am "tired to death"; "tickled to pieces" ; "hot as fire"; "cold as ice"; "crazy with the toothache"; "awfully glad"; "excruciatingly hungry"; "a perfectly magnificent time"; "an exquisitely lovely pug dog"; "a divine moustache."

Exercise

Point out the Hyperbole.

Select the best examples.

1. Waves mountain-high broke over the reef.

2. They were swifter than eagles; they were stronger than lions. *2 Samuel 1:23*

3. The tumult reaches the stars.

4. Rivers of water run down my eyes because they keep not thy law. *Psalms 119:136*

5. Every sentence began or closed with the name of Priscilla. *Longfellow*

6. I've been looking all over creation for you.

7. A rescued land
   Sent up a shout of victory from the field,
   That rocked her ancient mountains.

8. He was so gaunt that the case of a flageolet would have been a mansion for him.

9. And it shalt come to pass in that day that the mountains shall drop down new wine, and the hills shall flow with milk. *Joel 3:18*

10. Here at Concord once the embattled farmers stood, And fired the shot heard round the world. *Emerson*

Climax

Climax is an ascending series of thoughts or statements which gradually increase in importance.

In true Climax a weaker or less important thought should never follow a stronger one.

Anti-Climax reverses the order of the expressions, ending with the weakest or least important thought or circumstance. This is often used in humorous writings.

Exercise

Is this Climax or Anti-Climax?

Why?

Is the Climax well-arranged?

1. Since concord was lost, friendship was lost; fidelity was lost; liberty was lost,—all was lost!

2. Here I stand for impeachment or trial! I dare accusation! I defy the honorable gentleman! I defy the government! I defy their whole phalanx!

3. The enemy is now hovering upon our borders, preparing to press the knife to our throats, to devastate our fields, to quarter themselves in our houses, and to devour our poultry.

4. How then shall they call on him in whom they have not believed? and how shall they believe in him of whom they have not heard? and how shall they hear without a preacher? *Romans 10:14*

5. Oh dear! oh dear! what shall l do? I've lost my wife and seed corn too!

6. David was a great warrior, a great statesman, a great poet, and a skillful performer on the harp.

7. Great men, such as Washington, Adams, Jefferson, Arnold, and the friend of my worthy opponent.

8. He lost his wife, his child, his household goods, and his dog, at one fell swoop.

9. I am thinking, if Aunt knew so little of sin,
   What a wonder Aunt Tabitha's aunt must have been!
   And her grand-aunt,—it scares me! *Holmes*

10. The arm of the Lord is as fixed as fate, as sure as eternity, as strong as the rock of Gibraltar.

Irony

Irony is disguised satire. When we praise a thing and really mean to ridicule it, we make use of this figure.

Exercise

Explain the Irony in these extracts:

1. What has the gray-haired prisoner done ?
   Has murder stained his hands with gore?
   Not so; his crime is a fouler one—
   God made the old man poor.   *Whittier*

2. Although I would have you early instill into your children's hearts the love of cruelty, yet by no means call it by its true name, but encourage them in it under the name of fun.

3. Have not the Indians been kindly and justly treated?
   Have not the temporal things, the vain baubles and filthy lucre of this world, which were too apt to engage their worldly and selfish thoughts, been benevolently taken from them? and have they not instead thereof, been taught to set their affections on things above?

4. Here under leave of Brutus, and the rest,
   (For Brutus is an honourable man;
      So are they all, all honourable men;)
   Come I to speak in Caesar's funeral.
   He was my friend, faithful and just to me:
   But Brutus says he was ambitious;
      And Brutus is an honourable man.

   Good friends, sweet friends, let me not stir you up
   To such a sudden flood of mutiny.
   They that have done this deed, are honourable!
   What private griefs they have, alas! I know not,
   That made them do it; they are wise and honourable,
   And will, no doubt, with reasons answer you.   *Shakespeare*

5. Cry aloud: for he is a god; either he is talking, or
   he is pursuing, or he is in a journey, or peradventure
   he sleepeth, and must be waked!
   (Elijah to the priests of Baal, 1 Kings 18:27)

Additional Figures

Vision

Vision consists in describing past, absent, or imaginary scenes as if they were actually before our eyes. It is frequently combined with Personification and Apostrophe.

> Ex. I see before me the gladiator lie; He leans upon his hand—his manly brow
> Consents to death but conquers agony, And his drooped head sinks gradually low.
> *Byron*

Euphemism

Euphemism is the mention of disagreeable things by agreeable names.

> Ex. "She certainly displays as little vanity in regard to her personal appearance as any young lady I ever saw," is a delicate way of saying, "She is untidy."
>
> "She suffers from an overactive imagination," meaning, "She is inclined to exaggerate."

Onomatopoeia

Onomatopoeia is adapting the sound to the sense.

> Ex. Poe's poem "The Bells" contains fine examples of this figure; as does also Southey's "Cataract of Lodore."

How they tinkle, tinkle, tinkle,
In the icy air of night!
While the stars that oversprinkle
All the heavens seem to twinkle
With a crystalline delight,—Keeping time, time, time,
In a sort of Runic rhyme,
To the tintinnabulation that so musically wells
From the bells, bells, bells, bells,
Bells, bells, bells, —From the jingling and the tinkling of the bells. *Poe*

Litotes

This figure consists in making a statement by denying its opposite.

> Ex. "The immortal names
> That were not born to die," i.e., that will live.

Parallel

Parallel is a continued comparison of two similar objects, showing the points of resemblance and of difference. It is an extended Antithesis.

> Ex. The style of Dryden is capricious and varied; that of Pope is cautious and uniform. Dryden obeys the motions of his own mind; Pope constrains his mind to his rules of composition. Dryden is sometimes vehement and rapid; Pope is always smooth, uniform, and gentle. Dryden's page is a natural field, rising into inequalities, and diversified by the varied exuberance of abundant vegetation; Pope's is a velvet lawn, shaven by the scythe and leveled by the roller. *Johnson*

Allusion

Allusion is a reference to some familiar event in history or romance, or to some familiar expression in literature, for the purpose of explanation, description, or illustration.

> Ex. When I was a beggarly boy,
> And lived in a cellar damp,
> I had not a friend nor a toy,
> But I had Aladdin's lamp.
> When I could not sleep for cold,
> I had fire enough in my brain;
> And builded with roofs of gold
> My beautiful castles in Spain.   *Lowell*

"He was the Achilles of the war."

"The * of his profession, the *type* of honesty, the ! of all; and though the ☞ of death has put a . to his existence, every § of his life is without a

Printers' Toast to Franklin

Alliteration

Alliteration is not strictly a figure of speech, but is sometimes called a figure of emphasis. It consists in the repetition of the same initial letter in successive words. The use of this device was the distinguishing characteristic of early Anglo-Saxon poetry; and modern poetry contains many effective examples. Alliteration occurs in many proverbs. It is employed in titles of books and headings of newspaper articles.

Ex. "Apt Alliteration's artful aid." "Many men of many minds."

Pleonasm

This figure consists in the use of redundant words, for purposes of emphasis. What is ordinarily a fault in construction may make the thought clearer and more forcible.

Ex. "Thy rod and thy staff, they comfort me." "Know ye that the Lord he is God."

Poetry

Nothing cultivates a child's natural propensity towards language more than a love of poetry. Poetry is the home that nurtures the love of language. Children and rhymes go together so naturally. Poetry reading, poetry reciting, poetry, poetry, poetry—a basic need of childhood! It is sheer joy, transcending joy, that graces the ordinary moment with ideals set to music!

To love poetry is to love words in rhythms and melodies. Poetry appeals to the ear, as well as the eye, making words the palette of the imagination! Poetry is an essential ingredient that gives flavor and color to the English language curriculum. Teaching poetry in the elementary classroom unleashes boundless inspiration and elevates the student to excellent language.

God chose the form of poetry as a vehicle for communicating truth to man. More than one-third of the Old Testament is written in poetic form. A sense of the sublime and beautiful is deeply implanted in human nature and through the medium of poetry God appeals to the best of our hearts and minds. "Poetry is the highest style of human speech; . . . [it] is the language of human nature when it has found the sublime and beautiful. . . [I]t is the language of the soul, by which it seeks to rise above itself, to hold sympathetic and congenial brotherhood with all that is true and great, all that is lovely and good in the universe around. . . . [I]t is the language of the emotions and of the imagination." (*Literary Attractions of the Bible*, Halsey)

Storing Images of Magnificence

Annis Duff, in her book, *Bequest of Wings*, relates:

> Once, on the day of the first snow, we read together the One Hundred and Forty-seventh Psalm, because of the memorable verse, "He giveth snow like wool, and scattereth the hoarfrost like ashes." . . . How pleasant to have an eight-year-old accept the Bible, so rich a source of magnificent poetry, as a good book! . . .
>
> Meaning, per se, is a rather secondary consideration in our choice of poetry for sharing (with our young daughter), for it is one of the subtlest and most valuable properties of great poetry that it speaks to the feelings rather than to the intellect. What for the moment has no applicable meaning for the child, because of his limited experience, is often committed readily and joyously to memory for the music of the words and the haunting quality of the images. Years later, it will flower in all the nobility of its intention, to illuminate and enrich experience. James Stephens's "The Poppy Field," for instance, suggests a more penetrating sense of relative values than will concern the small listener, but a seed is dropped, along with the flowers.
>
> This is one of the concrete reasons why we feel that poetry is an essential to the full development of the child's spiritual faculties: memory is in the early years both receptive and tenacious, and if it is stored with images of magnificence, there will be the less room for what is cheap and ugly. Then, too, familiarity with the language of genuine poetry gives breadth and color to the child's speech, and this in itself stimulates a sharpened perception of external beauties and spiritual truths. (pp. 76–7)

Poetry Defined

"Poetry is metrical composition; verse; as heroic poetry; dramatic poetry; lyric poetry; The art or practice of composing in verse." (Webster's 1828 *Dictionary*)

Poetry is a rhythmical and usually regular pattern expressing deeply-felt emotion or experience or imagination. The greatest poetry is that which expresses emotion and experience and imagination. When a piece is rhythmical and regular in form, but lacks the power of emotion, experience, and imagination, it is not poetry, but prose.

"Poetry is imaginative discourse that gives powerful expression to experience, ideas, and emotion in heightened, patterned language." *Lynn Altenbernd*

Other Definitions

"Poetry is simply the most beautiful, the most impressive, and the most effective mode of saying things." *Matthew Arnold*

"I can no more define poetry than a terrier can define a rat, but I think we both recognize the object by the symptoms which it provokes in us." *A. E. Housman*

"The chief work of poetry is not to teach anything, nor to explain anything—although it may both teach and explain—it is to intensify life." *James Stephens*

"Poetry is a sort of musical shorthand capable of expressing in a few words vast areas of experience, as well as the realm of the imagination beyond experience." *Michael Lewis*

Goals of Teaching Poetry

1. Develop the reflective senses: the inner ear, the imagination, subtle responses to suggestions, words.

2. Cultivate a love for beauty—internal and external—and a taste for "images of magnificence."

3. Learn to appreciate the gifts of individual poets, the whole body of their work and their styles, as examples of God's Principle of Individuality and as inspiration to believe that each child can produce poetry.

4. Enrich language and vocabulary, elevate and inspire children to use wonderful words and to express themselves in subtle and precise language.

Characteristics of Poetry

1. "Poetry appeals to both the eye and the ear. . . . It is part of everyday life, capturing the spectacular in mundanity. . . . It is concentrated thought. . . . It is the oldest and most powerful of the arts. . . . It shapes imagination." *Louis Untermeyer*

"I Meant to Do My Work Today"

I meant to do my work today
But a brown bird sang in the apple-tree,
And a butterfly flitted across the field,
And all the leaves were calling me.

And the wind went sighing over the land,
Tossing the grasses to and fro,
And a rainbow held out its shining hand—
So what could I do but laugh and go?
—Richard Le Gallienne

(*Doorways to Poetry* by Louis Untermeyer. New York: Harcourt, Brace & World, 1938, p. 5)

2. Poetry is concentrated thought: it says much in a little.

3. Poetry is basically rhythmical; Verbal music.

4. Poetry has shape and structure (the best and fewest words in the best and shortest order).

5. Poetry suggests; Prose states. There is such a thing as poetic prose and prosaic verse. "The chief work of poetry is not to teach anything, nor to explain anything—though it may both teach and explain—it is to intensify life." *James Stephens*

Basic Distinctions between Prose and Poetry

Prose	Poetry
Little or no regular rhythm.	Basically rhythmical; Definitely measured; Strongly rhythmical.
No particular pattern (shape and structure); The unit is the paragraph; Loose in design.	Definite pattern; The unit is the stanza; Condensed and concise.
Usually quieter and less moving; Rambles leisurely or scientifically; Conversational in tone.	Sharper in accent; Tenser in tone; Dramatic moments and highlights; Intense.
Quality of thought: gives information; Responsive to facts; Informational in purpose.	Expresses emotion; Responsive to feelings; Emotional in effect.
States (observation); Plain and precise.	Suggests (imagination); Gives new meanings to words; Makes the familiar scene take on strangeness; Enlarges ideas with fresh values ("observation plus imagination"); Imaginative and suggestive.

Glossary of Terms

1. **Accent:** The stress of the voice laid on a certain syllable when a word is uttered.

2. **Alliteration:** Repetition of a word's first letter (consonants).

3. **Allusion:** Undeveloped reference to some figure, place, or event outside the immediate framework of the subject discussed; name dropping.

4. **Ballad:** Narrative poem composed to be sung—love, crude humor, strong emotion.

5. **Couplet:** Two consecutive rhyming lines.

6. **Haiku:** Japanese word picture: Three unrhymed lines built on contrasts—five syllables, seven syllables, five syllables.

7. **Imagery:** See mental representation of some aspect of the world.

8. **Metaphor:** Compares the subject and object—"of."

9. **Meter:** The rhythmical arrangement of syllables and words in a verse; number of feet in a verse. Important kinds of English meter are:

> **Monometer:** one foot to a verse.
> $$1$$
> Ex. Lochiel! /

> **Dimeter:** two feet to a verse.
> $$1 \qquad 2$$
> Ex. Of thee / I sing. /

> **Trimeter:** three feet to a verse.
> $$1 \qquad 2 \qquad 3$$
> Ex. My coun/try 'tis / of thee. /

> **Tetrameter:** four feet to a verse.
> $$1 \qquad 2 \qquad 3 \qquad 4$$
> Ex. He pray/eth best / who lov/eth best. /

> **Pentameter:** five feet to a verse.
> $$1 \qquad 2 \qquad 3 \qquad 4 \qquad 5$$
> Ex. Awake, / arise, / or be / for ev/er fall'n! /

> **Hexameter:** six feet to a verse.
> $$1 \qquad 2 \qquad 3$$
> Ex. This is the / forest pri/meval, the /
> $$4 \qquad 5 \qquad 6$$
> murmuring / pines and the / hemlocks. /

> **Heptameter:** seven feet to a verse.
> $$1 \qquad 2 \qquad 3 \qquad 4$$
> Ex. The mel/anchol/y days / have come, /
> $$5 \qquad 6 \qquad 7$$
> the sad/dest of / the year. /

Octameter: eight feet to a verse.

      1   2   3   4   5

Ex. Once up/on a / midnight / dreary, / as I

             6   7   8

        pondered / weak and / weary. /

10. **Ode:** Expresses lofty ideas and serious themes; exalted feeling.

11. **Onomatopoeia:** Imitative harmony, "sizzle."

12. **Pastoral Poems:** Rural setting. Ex. Psalm 23.

13. **Personification:** Giving human characteristics to inanimate objects or abstract ideas.

14. **Poesy:** The art or skill of composing poems; Poetry; metrical composition.

15. **Poetic Foot:** The division of a verse, consisting of one accented syllable and one or more unaccented syllables.

    Kinds of Poetic Feet:

    a) **Disyllabic**

    Trochee: Accent on the first syllable.

        Ex. Tell' me/ not' in / mourn'ful / num'bers. /

    Iambus: Accent on the last syllable.

        Ex. He pray'/eth best' / who lov'/eth best.'/

    Spondee: Accent on both syllables.

        Ex. Blos'somed the / love'ly / stars,' the for/get'-me-/ nots' of the / an'gels. /

    b) **Trisyllabic**

    Dactyl: Accent on the first syllable

        Ex. This' is the / for'est pri/me'val, the / mur'muring / pines' and the / hem'locks. /

    Amphibrach: Accent on the second syllable.

        Ex. Three fish'ers / went sail'ing / out in'to / the west. /

    Anapest: Accent on the third syllable.

        Ex. The Assyri'/an came down' / like a wolf' / on the fold.' /

16. **Prosody:** That part of grammar which treats of the quantity of syllables, of accent, and of the laws of versification. (Webster's 1828 *Dictionary*)

17. **Simile:** Compares the subject and object—"as."

18. **Sonnet:** Fourteen lines, strict form.

    Italian (Petrarchan): Love—describes a problem in love: eight lines, the problem; six lines, the commentary.

    Shakespearean (English or Elizabethan): Three quatrains (3 x 4 = 12); One rhyming couplet (lofty).

19. **Syllable:** A letter or combination of letters uttered with one impulse of the voice.

20. **Verse:** Language composed in metrical form or poetry. A verse is a line of poetry.

    a) **Rhyme:** Verse in which there is a correspondence of sound in the last syllables of two or more lines.

    b) **Blank Verse:** Poetry without rhyme.

    c) **Free Verse:** Verse which has no regular meter or predetermined rhythm.

21. **Versification:** The act or practice of composing poetic verse. Versification is the result of art, labor, and rule, rather than of invention or the fire of genius. It consists in adjusting the long and short syllables, and forming feet into harmonious measure. (Webster's 1828 *Dictionary*)

Common and Uncommon Varieties of Meter

Many varieties of meter are possible, since any one of the five kinds of feet may be used to compose verse in any one of the eight meters. Some forms are much more common in English verse than others. Trochaic and iambic tetrameter, iambic pentameter, and dactylic hexameter are most often found. Iambic pentameter is called heroic verse, because it is most used in epic poetry. Monometer, dimeter, and octameter are very seldom found. The latter is usually written as two lines of tetrameter.

Classes of Poetry

The most important classes of poetry are the epic, the lyric, and the dramatic.

1. Epic Poem:

A narrative poem of elevated character, relating usually the exploits of a hero. Since it deals with the past, it depends solely on imagination and memory for its interest. It is simple in construction and enforces no moral. Usually the action is concentrated within a short time. The long epic poem includes several episodes and much dialogue. The Greek *Iliad* and the Latin *Aeneid* are familiar illustrations of this form. *Beowulf* is perhaps the most important epic in the English language.

2. Lyric Poem:

The lyric differs greatly from the epic. It is subjective, dealing with feelings rather than events. The personality of the lyric writer is of far more importance than the events which occasion the poem. It is concentrated in form and movement as compared with the epic. While the epic has a traditional, uniform meter—dactylic, hexameter, heroic couplet, or heroic blank verse—the lyric has its choice of a hundred forms, but it is not difficult to distinguish.

Forms of the Lyric:

Hymn
Ode
Patriotic Lyric
Love Song
Lyric of Nature
Sonnet

Familiar forms of mixed character: Some important forms of poetry show, in differing degrees, epic, lyric, and dramatic traits. These forms are the legend, the allegory, and the ballad.

a) Legend: A legend is a mythical story which has its foundation in tradition. There are national legends, as Layamon's *Brut*; legends of the Church, as Chaucer's *The Prioress's Tale* in the *Canterbury Tales*; historical legends, as Longfellow's *Evangeline*; and legends depending upon the supernatural, as Coleridge's *The Ancient Mariner*.

b) Allegory: An allegory has already been defined as a prolonged metaphor. The great English example, *The Faerie Queene* of Spenser, is a double allegory, having a political and religious significance beneath the obvious story. Many short poems having a didactic purpose, as Leigh Hunt's "Abou Ben Adhem," are also allegorical in character.

c) Ballad: A ballad, or folk song, gives one incident in the life of the central character. The early English ballads have a rude vigor, a dash, and a charm peculiar to themselves. This may be plainly seen by comparing them with more polished modern ballads. Ballads are sometimes divided into ballads of tradition, as "Sir Patrick Spens," "Chevy Chase," and the "Robin Hood" ballads.

3. Dramatic Poem:

The drama, which is a combination of the other two forms, has been described in the *Literature Guide* (see pp. 201–02).

Comedy
Tragedy

Teaching Poetry through God's Principle of Individuality

When language is limited, I am thereby diminished too. . . . We think because we have words, not the other way around. The more words we have, the better able we are to think conceptually. . . . When language becomes exhausted, our freedom dwindles— we cannot think; we do not recognize danger; injustice strikes us as not more than "the way things are." . . . Where language is weak, theology is weakened.

—From *Walking on Water: Reflections on Faith and Art* by Madeleine L'Engle

Poetry is an essential ingredient that gives flavor and color to the elementary classroom. To teach poetry is to unleash boundless inspiration and to elevate the student to excellent language. We teach poetry to our children because it is sheer joy, transcending joy, that graces the ordinary moment with ideals set to music.

Develop Your Own Poets

Prepare to teach poetry by selecting the poets that you, as teacher, love best. The teacher's enthusiasm for the poet and his poetry will inspire the same love in the children. Each teacher should have a repertoire of poets and their poetry. For the literature curriculum in the primary grades, select at least three poets per year to teach in depth.

Develop your own teacher notebook of poetry. As you research your selected poets, develop your notebook from which to pull treasures at appropriate moments as well as to teach major segments of your literature overview. Read a biography of your poet, getting to know the life, influences, character, and full body of work. Read all the poetry of your poets selecting grade appropriate poetry for your students. Condense your reading into a brief biography to give to students by the notebook method, to build into them a whole sense of this person whose language so delights and enriches them.

Collect pictures of the poet, pictures of his home, family, and nation. Look in National Geographic and old books such as

Great Men and Famous Women, (ten volumes edited by Charles F. Horne), which are filled with biographies and portraits.

Present Your Poets to Children

1. Begin with a poem they will love and teach it lovingly, with many repetitions, inspiring them with its beauty, craftsmanship, worth, and charm.

2. Once they love the poem, introduce them to the person behind the poem giving them as much personal information as appropriate. Put up a bulletin board with pictures of the poet's life and nation and with space for the poems your students will write.

3. Read many of the poems of this poet, memorizing at least one.

4. Lead the children in writing their own poetry, patterned after the poet's style. Allow time for sharing their own poetry and display it.

5. Watch for opportunities throughout the year to recall the poet, relish the favorite poems, and to do further study.

6. Encourage poetry-writing often by reading to your children continually from children's poetry collections. Use snippets of the day—five minutes left before lunch, not enough time to begin something else—read poetry! Always enjoy it, especially the aptness of words, the imagery and ideals, and the melody and rhythm.

7. Invite a poet to school—find those literary dads who would dress up as Robert

Louis Stevenson and put on a Scottish burr for a delightful hour with young children. They are out there!

8. Encourage poetry-reading by the older children—dramatic readings performed after practice and preparation. I remember an inspired sixth grader reading the description of Brian the Hermit from *The Lady of the Lake* to wide-eyed classmates and timing her movement to flip off the light switch just as she arrived at the climax. Walter Scott would have been charmed!

9. Through education one can possess greatness—greatness of truth, of fact, and of beauty. Let poetry be a title deed to your children.

There are poets every child should know and love. The following galleries of English and American poets present small biographies and information to help the teacher in inspiring children to love poetry and write their own.

English Poets

William Blake
Robert Browning
Robert Burns
Christina Rossetti
Robert Louis Stevenson
Alfred Tennyson
Isaac Watts
William Wordsworth

American Poets

William Cullen Bryant
Emily Dickinson
Eugene Field
Robert Frost
Henry Wadsworth Longfellow
James Russell Lowell
John Greenleaf Whittier

NOTE: Biographical material was excerpted from *The Famous Literature of England and America* (Philadelphia: American Book and Bible House, 1899) for the following English poets: Robert Browning, Robert Burns, Robert Louis Stevenson, Alfred Tennyson, Isaac Watts, and William Wordsworth; and the American poets—William Cullen Bryant, Eugene Field, Henry Wadsworth Longfellow, James Russell Lowell, and John Greenleaf Whittier.

The portrait of Robert Browning is reproduced from *The Famous Literature of England and America* (Philadelphia: American Book and Bible House, 1899). *Wheeler's Studies in Great Authors* (Chicago: W. H. Wheeler & Co., 1899) is the source for the portraits of William Cullen Bryant, Robert Burns, Henry Wadsworth Longfellow, James Russell Lowell, Alfred Tennyson, John Greenleaf Whittier, and William Wordsworth.

The portrait of Eugene Field is from the *History of American Literature* by Reuben Post Halleck. (New York: American Book Company, 1911) That of Isaac Watts is from *Divine and Moral Songs for Children*, compiled, arranged, and edited by Carris J. Kocher. (Evensville, Tenn.: Cumberland Missionary Society, 1991)

Gallery of English Poets

William Blake
1757–1827
The Morning Star of the
Romantic Revival

Did He smile his work to see?
Did He who made the lamb make thee?

The works of poet-illustrator William Blake are among the most imaginative in the English language. He is known as the "morning star" of the Romantic Revival.

He was born in London, the son of an Irish hosier who was unable to provide a classical education for the lad. Because of his apparent talent for drawing, he was apprenticed to an engraver in 1771, and it was this trade which was his livelihood throughout his life. After his apprenticeship, he studied at the Royal Academy and began to produce watercolor figure subjects and engraved illustrations for magazines.

By the age of twelve, Blake was writing poetry. Some of his youthful verses were later printed in his first book of poems, *Poetical Sketches*, followed within a decade by his masterpieces, *Songs of Innocence* and *Songs of Experience*, two volumes made entirely by Blake's hands. He wrote the verses, made the drawings, engraved them on copper, made the plates, printed the pages on a hand press, and bound them together. From a critical point of view, the lyrics are some of the most pure in the English language. Philosophically, they express his commitment to freedom of the imagination and his hatred of rationalism and materialism.

Yet despite these intense themes, these Songs are easily appreciated by children because Blake chooses imagery from "child life" and employs simplicity of thought and simplicity of phrase. With the heart of an artist Blake paints word pictures on his pages—colors, forms, vistas, sounds, animals, and birds as in these lines from "The Echoing Green":

The sun does arise, and make happy
    the skies;
The merry bells ring, To welcome
    the Spring;
The skylark and thrush, The birds of
    the bush,
Sing louder around, To the bells' cheer-
    ful sound;
While our sports shall be seen
    On the echoing green.

Selected Works of William Blake:

"Nurse's Song"
"Laughing Song"
"Night"
"The Tiger"
"To the Evening"
"Memory"
"The Clod and the Pebble"
"To the Muses"
"Spring"
"The Lamb"
"Infant Joy"
"A Cradle Song"
"The Little Boy Lost"
"The Little Boy Found"
"The Shepherd"
"On Another's Sorrow"

Robert Browning
1812–1889
Poetic Student of Human Nature

*All the breath and the bloom
    of the year in the bag of one bee:
All the wonder and wealth of the
    mine in the heart of one gem;*

Robert Browning was the son of a clerk in the Bank of England, but had the entire sympathy and support of his father in his choice of literature as a profession. His life is almost without incident, and its details are not much known.

In 1846 he married Elizabeth Barrett, who for many years was the much more famous poet of the two. He and Elizabeth lived principally abroad after their marriage, until her death in 1861, when Robert returned to England to live in London. He died in Venice in 1889.

Robert was at his best as a lyric poet. However, he also enjoyed some of the gifts of the novelist and dramatist. His first great success, *The Ring and the Book*, which appeared in 1863, tells the story of a murder and explores the secret motives of the crime. Elsewhere, in the series of shorter poems, entitled *Men and Women* (1855), he dramatizes personalities of the Italian Renaissance.

Like Tennyson, Robert Browning was a master of words, although he tended to avoid poetic language and adopted a more colloquial idiom. Robert was the wordiest of all Victorian poets, and his critics often accused him of being unnecessarily obscure, and of allowing his attempts to answer the questions he set himself to degenerate into mere argument. He seemed to anticipate later trends in English poetry and his poetic innovations were often strikingly original, such as his use of eloquent monologues in his *Men and Women* series. He possessed an inquiring nature and liked to solve problems.

The subtlety of Browning's poetry, the depth of meaning which is buried sometimes under the most trifling narrative—and sometimes so deeply hidden as to dismay any but the most determined student—has always prevented him from becoming a popular poet. For those who will bestow upon them the necessary thought and study, his poems yield the richest returns. During his own lifetime, a distinguished fellow-poet, Walter Savage Landor, declared that, since Chaucer's day:

*No man hath walk'd along our roads
    with step
So active, so inquiring eye, or tongue
So varied in discourse . . .*

His best-known works are "Paracelsus," "Bells and Pomegranates," "The Blot on the 'Schutcheon," "Pippa Passes," "Men and Women," and "The Ring and the Book." Many of his shorter poems are more popular, and among these "The Ride from Ghent to Aix" is a masterpiece in action and intensity.

Selected Works of Robert Browning:

"Epilogue to Asolando"
"Summer Bonum"
"The Ride from Ghent to Aix"
"Evelyn Hope"
"The Book" (from *The Ring and the Book*)

Robert Burns
1759–1796
Best Loved of Scottish Poets

My heart's in the Highlands,
  my heart is not here;
My heart's in the Highlands,
  a-chasing the deer;

The life of Robert Burns was not a model one. In some ways, and those the most important, its story is more useful for the warnings it conveys than for the example it affords. But we shall not be able to understand his poems if we do not know the story of his life, and not to know and love the poetry of Robert Burns is to miss the rarest, most touching, most thoroughly human note in English verse.

The son of a hard-working, unsuccessful peasant farmer, his early years were spent in the monotonous toil of a laborer on a sterile Scottish farm. He had little education except that which he acquired from his father, who, as is often the case among Scottish peasants, was a man of serious mind, somewhat cultivated, and of noble character.

Burns early began to rhyme. His poems were handed around in manuscript, and he acquired in this way considerable fame. The death of his father, in 1784, laid upon the young man of twenty-five the cares of the head of the family, a burden which he bravely assumed, but which was somehow always too heavy for him. He determined to emigrate to the West Indies, and to procure the necessary funds, published, by subscription, a volume of his poems. This attracted the attention of literary people in Edinburgh, and on their invitation he gave up his proposed emigration and visited that city. His reception was most cordial. He, the uncultured peasant, captivated at once the refined and intelligent people among whom he was thrown. No poet was ever so quickly recognized. He published a new and enlarged edition of his poems, which yielded him nearly five hundred pounds; his new celebrity enabled him to secure the post of exciseman in Dumfriesshire, where he took a farm, having advanced nearly half of his returns from the poems to ease the burdens of his mother and brother, whom he left at Mossgiel.

He was married to Jean Armour, and built, largely with his own hands, the cottage in which they were to live at Ellisland, in Dumfries. Here, "to make a happy fireside chime to weans and wife," he labored with an energy which promised better things, and all the circumstances seemed to indicate that a happy and prosperous life lay before the young poet.

His poetry is not English, but Scottish. Its rollicking fun, as in "Tam O'Shanter's Ride," its touching sentiment, as in "On Turning Up a Mouse's Nest with the Plough," the truth and beauty of its descriptions of homely life, as in "The Cotter's Saturday Night," have rarely been equaled in the poems of any language.

Burns wrote for the people. He knew all their life, their every emotion; he stirred their patriotism by such poems as "Scots Wha ha wi' Wallace Bled," or their affection for Scotland by "Ye Banks and Braes," and moralized in "The Twa Dogs," and many others, upon the circumstances of their life, and well-deserves to be called "the greatest poet that ever sprung from the bosom of the people and lived and died in an humble condition."

Selected Works of Robert Burns

"Letter to a Young Friend"
"For A' That and A' That"
"My Heart's in the Highlands"
"The Banks O' Doon"
"Man Was Made to Mourn"
"Tam O'Shanter"
"Bruce to His Men at Bannockburn"
"The Cotter's Saturday Night"

Christina Rossetti
1830–1894
Sweet Singer of Childhood

There's sweetness in an apple tree,
And profit in the corn;
But the lady of all beauty
Is a rose upon a thorn.

Christina Georgina Rossetti is known as one of England's most important poets in both range and quality of works.

She was born into an artistic and literary family in London, the youngest child of Dante scholar Gabriele Rossetti. Christina was schooled at home, and when she was seventeen her grandfather printed a selection of her *Verses* on his private press. Three years later, seven of her poems were published in a literary journal, *The Germ*. Her finest works, *Goblin Market* and *The Prince's Progress*, were produced in 1862 and were decorated by her brother, painter-poet Dante Gabriel Rossetti. One of the nineteenth century's notable children's books is Christina's charming *Sing Song: A Nursery Rhyme Book*, published in 1872. Literary critic Walter Barnes praised this collection for being "sincere, tender, simple, imaginative, picturesque, and musical"; dealing with "childish themes in an artistic manner."

Due to straitened financial circumstances, for a short time Christina and her mother managed a school in Frome, but that venture soon failed. After her father's death, Christina rejected marriage proposals and devoted herself to the care of her mother and to worship in the High Anglican Church. When forty-one years old, she was stricken by Graves' disease which disfigured her and destroyed her health, but she accepted this affliction with courage, sustained by her deep faith.

Christina's character was marked by a spirit of self-denial, humility, and devotion to God. She also displayed, however, a poet's intense temperament, critical perception, and a delightful sense of humor. These opposing moods appear throughout her poetry. The following poignant lines, often quoted at Christmastime, reveal her commitment to Christ:

> What shall I give him, poor as I am;
> If I were a shepherd, I would bring Him a lamb;
> If I were a wise man, I would do my part;
> Yet what can I give Him?
> I'll give Him my heart.

After her death from cancer in 1894, her brother released a volume of unpublished poetry by Christina entitled *New Poems*.

Works by Christina Rossetti:

"To Lalla"
"A Christmas Carol"

Robert Louis Stevenson
1850–1894
"Tusitala," Teller of Tales
Well-beloved Novelist and Poet

From breakfast on through all the day
At home among my friends to stay,
But every night I go abroad
Afar into the Land of Nod.

There was a quality in the character of Robert Louis Stevenson which created for him a circle of personal friends whose number and devotion can hardly be equaled. His quick sympathy, which was shown in his love for children and his comprehension of them, and in the power which, in the closing years of his life, he acquired over the untutored natives of the Samoan Islands; his acute intelligence; and his noble character, made him, perhaps, the best-loved among contemporary men of letters.

Coming of a race of hard-headed, practical men (his father and grandfather were engineers and famous builders of lighthouses), he determined from the first to turn his back on the more practical professions and devote himself to literature. Deferring to the wish of his father, he studied law, and was actually called to the Bar, but he never engaged in the practice of the profession.

In 1873, at the age of twenty-three, his health broke down, and he was no longer able to endure for any length of time the rigorous climate of his native Edinburgh, but passed the remaining years of his life in an almost constant and courageous battle with pulmonary trouble. He lived in the south of France, in Southern California, at Bournemouth in England, in the Adirondacks, and finally sailed away with his American wife and her family to the South Seas where, in the Samoan Islands, he established himself and, until his death in 1894, lived in continuous literary activity, and free from the frequent relapses and acute suffering which he experienced elsewhere.

The story of his life in this remote corner of the world—how he won the confidence of the natives, the part he took in their affairs, and the succession of exquisite stories, essays, and poems which came to tell the rest of the world that his productiveness had not ceased—all this forms one of the most delightful stories which our literary history affords.

His published works include some thirty titles—poems, volumes of essays, stories for children, and novels. The most famous of his works is *The Strange Case of Dr. Jekyll and Mr. Hyde*, which was one of the most talked of books of its time, and still retains its position as a triumph of invention and artistic work. His own opinion was that *Kidnapped* was his best work; but the *Master of Ballantrae*, particularly its first part, is unsurpassed in its kind. The best known of his other works are: *Treasure Island, The Black Arrow, Prince Otto, Merry Men*, two volumes of essays, *Virginibus Puerisque*, and *Familiar Studies of Men and Books*, and a book of poems, *Underwoods*.

He is buried on the summit of Mount Vaca, a precipitous peak near his Samoan home, where his monument is visible for great distances at sea, like the lighthouses of his fathers. After his death, the chiefs and people of the Samoans came in large numbers to kiss his hand and to bring their customary funeral offering of mats for the burial of their friend, "the Story Teller," and in this character Stevenson's fame will be secure.

Poetic Works of Robert Louis Stevenson:

A Child's Garden of Verses

Alfred Tennyson
1809–1892
The First of Modern Poets

Love that hath us in a net,
Can he pass and we forget?
Many suns arise and set.
Many a chance the years beget.
Love the gift is Love the debt.
Even so.

Other poets have written for particular classes; Browning for the philosophers, Wordsworth for those whose intense love of nature can see beauty and needed truth in the commonest and simplest objects and events. But Tennyson has written for every one who loves the beautiful in nature or the noble in action, or whose heart can be moved by the story of great deeds set to the stirring music of perfect verse.

Tennyson was the son of an English clergyman, and was born in Somersby, Lincolnshire, August 6, 1809. The father was distinguished by a love of learning and by his devotion to music, painting, and literature. These qualities, as well as his fondness for outdoor living, were inherited by his children.

Tennyson's earliest published volume was a little book, the joint work of his brother Charles and himself, entitled *Poems by Two Brothers.* Another volume appeared in 1830—*Poems, Chiefly Lyrical*—which contained the promise of much of his best work.

The first reference to the legends of King Arthur, which furnished the subject of so much of his later work, occurs in the volume published in 1832. Among these poems were "The Lady of Shalott" and "The Miller's Daughter," the chief beauty of which lay in the songs in it.

In 1850 Tennyson had succeeded Wordsworth as poet laureate, and he enjoyed for many years an annual pension of two hundred pounds, granted him when he was comparatively unknown.

Carlyle wrote to Emerson in 1844 that Tennyson was: "One of the finest looking men in the world. A great shock of rough, dusty-dark hair; bright, laughing, hazel eyes; massive, aquiline face—most massive, yet most delicate; of sallow-brown complexion, almost Indian-looking; clothes cynically loose, free, and easy—smokes infinite tobacco. His voice is musical-metallic, fit for loud laughter and piercing wail, and all that may lie between; speech and speculation free and plenteous. I do not meet in these last decades such company over a pipe."

Tennyson lived in and about London until his fortieth year when he married Emily Sellwood and took up his residence at Twickenham, until he removed, in the early fifties, to Faringford, in the Isle of Wight, where he lived for many years. About 1869 he purchased a place at Petersfield, Hampshire, and, afterward, Aldworth House, near Haslemere, Surrey, where he continued to live until he died from old age, October 6, 1892.

His physician, Sir Andrew Clark, says of his deathbed: "In all my experience I have never witnessed anything more glorious. There were no artificial lights in the chamber, and all was in darkness save for the silvery light of the moon at its full. The soft beams of light fell upon the bed and played upon the features of the dying poet like a halo of Rembrandt."

Selections from the Works of Alfred Lord Tennyson:

"Song of the Book"
"Ring Out, Wild Bells"
"The Lady of Shalott"
"Sweet and Low"
"The Here and the Hereafter"
"The Passing of Arthur" ("English Idyls")
"Bugle Song"
"Break, Break, Break"
"Garden Song"
"Tears, Idle Tears"
Prelude to "In Memoriam"

Isaac Watts
1674–1748
Writer of Christian Hymns

The praises of my tongue
I offer to the Lord,
That I was taught and learned so young,
To read his holy word.
—Song VIII

The "Hymns," "Psalms," and "Songs for Children" of Dr. Watts have been more read and committed to memory, have exerted more holy influences, and made more lasting impressions for good upon the human heart than the productions of any other writer of verse. But Isaac Watts does not hold high rank as a poet, and during his lifetime was quite as much known as a philosopher and theologian as for his poetical works. Indeed, his *Logick* and *Improvement of the Mind* may still be regarded as standard books. His poems are all of a religious character, many of them having been written for children. He versified the entire book of Psalms, and many of his "Hymns" find a place in the hymn-books of all Christian denominations. It is their ready adaptation to musical rendering, their broad Christian spirit, and their beautiful and tender simplicity, rather than their artistic merits as poems, which have endeared these hymns to so many and such widely different people.

Isaac Watts was a precocious child; he composed verses, we are told, before he was three years old, began to study Latin at four, and could read easy authors at five. Being a Dissenter, he could not enter one of the Universities, but received a thorough education, and became tutor in a private family. In 1698 he was chosen assistant minister of the Independent congregation in Mark Lane, London, of which he became pastor in 1702. Owing to feeble health he resigned this charge, and in 1712 was invited by Sir Thomas Abney, of Abney Park, near London, to become an inmate of his family. Here he remained during the remaining thirty-six years of his life, preaching not infrequently and writing many books in prose and verse. He continued to receive from his congregation the salary which they insisted upon his accepting, and there were many and continuous evidences of the love and esteem in which he was held, not only by those of his immediate circle, but by the general public. He died in 1748, at the age of seventy-four.

"It is the plain promises of the Gospel," said he, near his death, "that are my support; and I bless God they are plain promises, and do not require much labor and pains to understand them, for I can do nothing now but look into my Bible for some promise to support me, and live upon that."

"He is one of the few poets," says Dr. Johnson, "with whom youth and ignorance may be safely pleased; and happy will be that reader whose mind is disposed, by his verses or his prose, to copy his benevolence to man and his reverence to God."

Selections from the Works of Dr. Isaac Watts:

"The Rose"
"The Earnest Student"
"There Is a Land of Pure Delight"
"Looking Upward"
"My Dear Redeemer"
"Come, We That Love the Lord"
"When I Survey the Wondrous Cross"
"Come, Holy Spirit, Heavenly Dove"
"From All That Dwell"
Psalm LXXII

William Wordsworth
1770–1850
Founder of the Lake School of Poetry

I wandered lonely as a cloud
That floats on high o'er vales and hills,
When all at once I saw a crowd,
A host, of golden daffodils;

It was the mission of Wordsworth to bring back the art of poetry to nature. He contended that the ordinary affairs of daily life are fit subjects for poetry, and that the language of the poet should be that really used by men. He thus violated all the established rules of poetic diction, encountered the most hostile criticism, and drew upon himself and those with whom he was associated showers of ridicule. It was only after fifty years that he was recognized as the first poet of his age. There are golden veins of real poetry running throughout everything he has written, and in some places, as in his "Ode on Immortality," he rises to the perfection of human utterance.

His parents were of the middle class, and he was intended for the church, but as he came near the time when he should have definitely prepared himself for the ministry, he found himself more and more inclined to devote his life to poetry. In this resolution he persevered, and the measure of his devotion may be judged from the fact that for the sake of his chosen vocation he resolutely faced a life of poverty, and contrived to live with his sister for about eight years upon the income of a legacy of nine hundred pounds left him by a friend of his youth.

In 1798 Wordsworth and his sister made a tour of Germany in company with Coleridge. Returning, he took up his residence at Grasmere, in the Lake Region, and afterward at Rydal Mount, which was his home during the remainder of his uneventful life. Coleridge and Southey also made their home in the Lake Region, and thus the three came to be known, somewhat in derision, as the "Lake Poets."

Wordsworth's most extensive work, "The Excursion," appeared in 1814. It was intended to be only a part of an extended poem to be entitled "The Recluse," having for its principal subject "The Sensations and Opinions of a Poet Living in Retirement." It was to be composed of three parts: "The Prelude," not published until 1850, "The Excursion," and a third which was never written.

Wordsworth filled for many years the office of distributor of stamps for Westmoreland, and in 1843 succeeded Southey as poet laureate. His domestic life was unclouded and happy. He had received a pension of three hundred pounds a year, and, resigning his office of stamp distributor to his son, he lived in the quiet seclusion of the beautiful region in which he had fixed his home until his death in 1850. Wordsworth brought back into popularity the sonnet, which since Milton's day had fallen out of English poetry. His fame seems to grow with the lapse of time, and his place among famous poets is a high one.

His best-known poems are "The Excursion," "Heart-leap Well," and "We are Seven." Those which have been most ridiculed are "Peter Bell," "The Idiot Boy," "Alice Fell," and "The Blind Highland Boy."

Selections from the works of William Wordsworth:

"The Daffodils"
"The Happy Warrior"
"The World Is Too Much with Us" (Sonnet)
"She Was a Phantom of Delight"
"Ode on Intimations of Immortality from
    Recollections of Early Childhood"
"To a Skylark"
"Ode to Duty"
"To His Wife"

Gallery of American Poets

William Cullen Bryant
1794–1878
The Poet of Nature

There is a day of sunny rest
For every dark and troubled night;
And grief may bide an evening guest,
But joy shall come with early light.

It is said that "genius always manifests itself before its possessor reaches manhood." Perhaps in no case is this more true than in that of the poet, and William Cullen Bryant was no exception to the general rule. The poetical fancy was early displayed in him. He began to write verses at nine, and at ten composed a little poem to be spoken at a public school, which was published in a newspaper. At fourteen a collection of his poems was published.

"Thanatopsis," one of his most popular poems (though he himself marked it low), was written when the poet was but a little more than eighteen years of age. This production is called the beginning of American poetry.

William Cullen Bryant was born at Cummington, Hampshire Co., Massachusetts, on November 3, 1794. His father was a physician and a man of literary culture who encouraged his son's early ability, and taught him the value of correctness and compression, and enabled him to distinguish between true poetic enthusiasm and the bombast into which young poets are apt to fall.

Bryant was educated at Williams College, but left with an honorable discharge before graduation to take up the study of law, which he practiced one year at Plainfield and nine years at Great Barrington. But in 1825 he abandoned law for literature, and removed to New York where in 1826 he began to edit the *Evening Post*, which position he continued to occupy from that time until the day of his death.

In 1821 Mr. Bryant married Frances Fairchild, the loveliness of whose character is hinted in some of his sweetest productions.

Among his best-known poems are "A Forest Hymn," "The Death of the Flowers," "Lines to a Waterfowl," and "The Planting of the Apple-Tree." One of the greatest of his works, though not among the most popular, is his translation of Homer, which he completed when seventy-seven years of age.

His tenderness of the feelings of others, and his earnest desire always to avoid the giving of unnecessary pain, were very marked.

The grand old veteran of verse died in New York in 1878 at the age of eighty-four, universally known and honored. He was in his sixth year when George Washington died, he lived under the administration of twenty presidents, and had seen his own writings in print for seventy years. During this long life—though editor for fifty years of a political daily paper, and continually before the public—he had kept his reputation unspotted from the world, as if he had, throughout the decades, continually before his mind the admonition of the closing lines of "Thanatopsis" written by himself seventy years before.

Selections from William Cullen Bryant:

"To a Waterfowl"
"Thanatopsis"
"Waiting by the Gate"
"Blessed Are They That Mourn"
"The Antiquity of Freedom"
"Robert of Lincoln"
"Drought"

Emily Dickinson
1830–1886
A Poet Who Was Herself

The mushroom is the elf of plants,
At evening it is not;
At morning, in a truffled hut
It stops upon a spot,

As if it tarried always;
And yet its whole career
Is shorter than a snake's delay,
And fleeter than a tare.

The charming poetry of Emily Elizabeth Dickinson was little known until after her death in 1886. Shunning publicity, the poetess limited distribution of her delightful verses to friends and family members. Today she is recognized as the greatest of all American women poets.

Born into an affluent home in Amherst, Massachusetts, Emily was surrounded with fine furniture, a mahogany piano, and was privileged to have her own bedroom with large windows and little cherry writing table. From this room she could gaze upon the distant hills and beautiful trees which enveloped her home. During walks in the garden she was alert to every shiny blade of grass, fragrant flower, and buzzing bumble bee—all of which eventually became memorialized in her poetry.

In keeping with the dignity of his home, Emily's father was a strict, formal man who required church attendance and compliance with many rules. The few books Emily owned, other than the Bible, she called "lonely" books, such as Young's Night Thoughts, Baxter's Saints' Rest, and Cotton Mather. Other books were surreptitiously brought to her by her father's assistant in the law office who hid them in the hedge. Her teacher at Amherst Academy also provided her with many volumes. Further education at a boarding school was cut short by Emily's delicate health and she returned to Amherst.

Emily at twenty was a lovely young woman with auburn hair described by her as "the color of the sherry the guest leaves in the glass." She was a mischievous, witty girl who enjoyed parties and outings, and she was always a gracious hostess for her father's receptions. Emily's romances seemed doomed to disappointment, however, through her father's intervention or other circumstances, and she never married. Usually dressed in white, Emily became reclusive; her world was her home, garden, and her poetry. She raised beautiful flowers in her greenhouse and often sent cheery bouquets to sick friends with a little note attached. The prolific writer also rolled up her little poems like scrolls, tied with a bit of string, and placed them in a drawer away from prying eyes. Emily Dickinson celebrated life, nature, and understood the human heart, with all its desires and its sufferings.

Selected Poems:

"I'm nobody! Who are you?"
"I started early—Too, my Dog—"
"A Bird came down the Walk"
"Dear March—Come in—"
"A narrow Fellow in the Grass"
"To Make a prairie it takes a clover and one bee"
"A Word is dead"
"Some keep the Sabbath going to church"
"The mushroom is the Elf of Plants"

Eugene Field
1850–1895
The Children's Friend and Poet

Wynken, Blynken, and Nod one night
Sailed off in a wooden shoe—
Sailed on a river of misty light
Into a sea of dew.

On the fourth day of November, 1895, there was many a sad home in the city of Chicago and through America. It was on that day that Eugene Field, the most congenial friend young children ever had among the literary men of America, died at the early age of forty-five. The expressions of regard and regret called out on all sides by this untimely death, made it clear that the character in which the public at large knew and loved Mr. Field best was that of the "Poet of Child Life." What gives his poems their unequaled hold on the popular heart is their simplicity, warmth, and genuineness. This quality they owe to the fact that Mr. Field almost lived in the closest and fondest intimacy with children. He had troops of them for his friends and it is said he wrote his child-poems directly under their suggestions and inspiration.

His association with his fellow-workers was equally congenial. No man who had ever known him felt the slightest hesitancy in approaching him.

One of Field's peculiarities with his own children was to nickname them. When his first daughter was born he called her "Trotty." The second daughter was called "Pinny" after the child opera "Pinafore," which was in vogue at the time she was born. Another, a son, came into the world when everybody was singing "O My! Ain't She a Daisy." Naturally this fellow went by the name of "Daisy." Two other of Mr. Field's children were known as "Googhy" and "Posy."

Eugene Field was born in St. Louis, Missouri, September 2, 1850. Part of his early life was passed in Vermont and Massachusetts. He was educated in a university in Missouri and Colorado. He joined the staff of the Chicago Daily News in 1883 and removed to Chicago, where he continued to reside until his death, twelve years later. Of Mr. Field's books, *The Denver Tribune Primer* was issued in 1882; *Culture Garden* (1887); *Little Book of Western Friends* (1889); and *Little Book of Profitable Tales* (1889).

Mr. Field was not only a writer of child verses, but wrote some first-class Western dialectic verse, did some translating, was an excellent newspaper correspondent, and a critic of no mean ability; but he was too kind-hearted and liberal to chastise a brother severely who did not come up to the highest literary standard. He was a hard worker, contributing daily, during his later years, from one to three columns to the *Daily News*, besides writing more or less for the *Syndicate Press* and various periodicals. In addition to this, he was frequently traveling, and lectured or read from his own writings. After his death, his oldest daughter, Miss Mary French Field ("Trotty"), visited the leading cities throughout the country, delivering readings from her father's works. The announcement of her appearance to read selections from the writings of her genial father was always liberally responded to by an appreciative public.

Selections from the Works of Eugene Field:

"Our Two Opinions"

"Lullaby"

"A Dutch Lullaby"

"The Norse Lullaby"

Robert Frost
1875–1963
Poet of New England

The woods are lovely, dark and deep,
But I have promises to keep,
And miles to go before I sleep,
And miles to go before I sleep.

One of the major American poets of the twentieth century, Robert Frost was the first poet to read a poem at a presidential inauguration—that of President John F. Kennedy in 1961.

Robert Frost was born in San Francisco, but upon his father's death ten years later his mother relocated the family to Lawrence, Massachusetts. It was then that Robert's love for the beautiful New England countryside began. Courses at Dartmouth College failed to motivate the young man to further education, and he dropped out to become a bobbin boy at a local mill so that he could spend more time reading. At twenty, he married and two years later tried higher education once more, at Harvard. But he did not enjoy life as a scholar and for the next dozen years he worked in various jobs—as a farmer, editor of a local newspaper—teacher, all the while writing poems which he had little success in publishing.

In 1912, at the insistence of his wife, the family moved to England where his poetry was immediately appreciated. The three years spent there were marked by friendships with other poets and the publication of his first two volumes: A *Boy's Will* and *North of Boston*. He returned to the United States as a recognized poet, and for the next half-century

his works were enthusiastically accepted and critically acclaimed. Robert Frost taught at Amherst College, the University of Michigan, Harvard University, and Dartmouth College, and was awarded the Pulitzer Prize for poetry four times.

Throughout these long years of productivity, the poet was usually living on a farm, where he always gained strength and inspiration from the land. The charm of Robert Frost's poetry results from his ability to describe the moods, images, aromas, and sounds of America's New England. It has been said by literary critic Charles Barnes that Frost is the portrayer of New England farm life as Millet is the painter of peasant life in France.

Principal Works of Robert Frost:

A Boy's Will (1913)
North of Boston (1914)
Mountain Interval (1916)
New Hampshire (1923)
West-Running Brook (1928)
Collected Poems (1930)
A Further Range (1936)
A Witness Tree (1942)
Come in, and Other Poems (1943)
Steeple Bush (1947)
The Road Not Taken (1951)
You Come Too (1959)
In the Clearing (1962)

Henry Wadsworth Longfellow
1807–1882
Sweet Singer of America

Such songs have power to quiet
The restless pulse of care,
And come like the benediction
That follows after prayer.

Longfellow's life from the very beginning moved on even lines. Both he and William Cullen Bryant were descendants of John Alden, whom Longfellow has made famous in "The Courtship of Miles Standish." The Longfellows were a family in comfortable circumstances, peaceful and honest, for many generations back.

Thus, both "The Tales of a Wayside Inn" and "Evangeline"—as many other of Longfellow's poems—may be called compilations or rewritten stories, rather than creations, and it was these characteristics of his writings which Poe and Margaret Fuller, and others, who considered the realm of poetry to belong purely to the imagination rather than the real world, so bitterly criticized. While they did not deny to Longfellow a poetic genius, they thought he was prostituting it by forcing it to drudge in the province of prosaic subjects; and for this reason Poe predicted that he would not live in literature.

It was natural that Longfellow should write as he did. For thirty-five years he was an instructor in institutions of learning, and as such believed that poetry should be a thing of use as well as beauty. He could not agree with Poe that poetry was like music, only a pleasurable art. He had the triple object of stimulating to research and study, of impressing the mind with history or moral truths, and at the same time to touch and warm the heart of humanity. In all three directions he succeeded to such an extent that he has probably been read by more people than any other poet except the sacred Psalmist; and despite the predictions of his distinguished critics to the contrary, such poems as "The Psalm of Life," (which Charles Sumner allowed, to his knowledge, had saved one man from suicide), "The Children's Hour," and many others touching the everyday experiences of the multitude, will find a glad echo in the souls of humanity as long as men shall read.

Selected Works of Henry Wadsworth Longfellow:

"The Psalm of Life (What the Heart of the Young Man Said to the Psalmist)"
"The Courtship of Miles Standish"
"The Children's Hour"
"The Village Blacksmith"
"I Heard the Bells on Christmas Day"
"The Midnight Ride of Paul Revere"
"The Bridge"
"Resignation"
"God's Acre"
"Excelsior"
"The Rainy Day"
"The Wreck of the Hesperus"
"The Old Clock on the Stairs"
"The Skeleton in Armor"

James Russell Lowell
1819–1891
Poet, Critic, and Essayist

Over our manhood bend the skies;
Against our fallen and traitor lives
The great winds utter prophecies;
With our faint hearts the mountain strives;

James Russell Lowell was born in Cambridge, Massachusetts, February 22, 1819, and died in the same city on August 12, 1891, in the seventy-third year of his age. He was the youngest son of the Rev. Charles Lowell, an eminent Congregational clergyman, and was descended from the English settlers of 1639. He entered Harvard in his seventeenth year and graduated in 1838, before he was twenty. He began to write verses early. In his junior year in college he wrote the anniversary poem, and, in his senior year, was editor of the college magazine. Subsequently, he studied law and was admitted to the bar in 1840; but, it seems, never entered upon the practice of his profession. If he did it is doubtful if he ever had even that *first client* whom he afterwards described in a humorous sketch.

In 1841, the first volume of Lowell's verse appeared, entitled *A Year's Life*.

In 1844 Mr. Lowell married the poetess, Maria White, an ardent abolitionist, whose anti-slavery convictions influenced his after career. Two of Mrs. Lowell's poems, "The Alpine Sheep" and the "Morning Glory" are especially popular. Lowell was devotedly attached to this singularly beautiful and sympathetic poet wife and made her the subject of some of his most exquisite verses. They were both contributors to the *Liberty Bell* and *Anti-slavery Standard*, thus enjoying companionship in their labors.

In 1853, Mrs. Lowell died, on the same night in which a daughter was born to the poet Longfellow, who was neighbor and a close friend to Lowell. The co-incidence inspired Longfellow to write a beautiful poem, "The Two Angels," which he sent to Mr. Lowell with his expression of sympathy.

As a public man, a representative of the United States Government, in foreign ports, he upheld the noblest ideals of the republic. He taught the purest lessons of patriotism—ever preferring his country to his party—and he criticized, with energy, and indignation, political evils and selfishness in public service, regarding these as the most dangerous elements threatening the dignity and honor of American citizenship.

Among scholars, Lowell, next to Emerson, is regarded the profoundest of American poets; and, as the public becomes more generally educated, it is certain that he will grow in popular favor. To those who understand and catch the spirit of the man, noticeable characteristics of his writings are its richness and variety. He is at once a humorist, a philosopher, and a dialectic verse writer, an essayist, a critic, and a masterful singer of songs of freedom as well as of the most majestic memorial odes.

Unlike Longfellow and Holmes, Lowell never wrote a novel; but his insight into character and ability to delineate it would have made it entirely possible for him to assay, successfully, this branch of literature. This power is seen especially in his "Biglow Papers" as well as in other of his character sketches. The last of Lowell's works published was *Latest Literary Essays and Addresses*, issued in 1892, after his death.

Selected Works of James Russell Lowell:

"The Gothic Genius" (from "The Cathedral")
"The Rose"
"The Heritage"
"Act for Truth"
"The First Snow-Fall"
"Fourth of July Ode"
"The Dandelion"

John Greenleaf Whittier
1807–1892
The Poet of Freedom

Blessings on thee, little man,
Barefoot boy, with cheek of tan!
With thy turned up pantaloons,
And thy merry whistled tunes;

In a solitary farmhouse near Haverhill, Massachusetts, in the valley of the Merrimac, on the 17ᵗʰ day of December, 1807, John Greenleaf Whittier was born. Within the same town and Amesbury, nearby, this kind and gentle man, whom all the world delights to honor for his simple and beautiful heart-songs, spent most of his life, dying at the ripe old age of nearly eighty-five, in Danvers, Massachusetts, September 7, 1892.

The early surroundings of the farmer boy were simple and frugal. He has pictured them for us in his masterpiece, "Snowbound." Poverty, the necessity of laboring upon the farm, the influence of Quaker traditions, his busy life, all conspired against his liberal education and literacy culture. This limitation of knowledge is, however, at once to the masses his charm, and, to scholars, his one defect. It has led him to write, as no other poet could, upon the dear simplicity of New England farm life. He has written from the heart and not from the head; he has composed popular pastorals, not hymns of culture. Only such training as the district schools afforded, with a couple of years at Haverhill Academy, comprised his advantages in education.

Mr. Whittier, perhaps, is the most peculiarly American poet of any that our country has produced. The woods and waterfowl of Bryant belong as much to one land as another; and all the rest of our singers—Emerson, Longfellow, Lowell, and their brethren—with the single exception of Joaquin Miller, might as well have been born in the land of Shakespeare, Milton, and Bryon as their own. But Whittier is entirely a poet of his own soil. All through his verse we see the elements that created it, and it is interesting to trace his simple life, throughout, in his verses from the time, when like that urchin with whom he asserts brotherhood, and who has won all affections, he ate his "milk and bread. . . . "

In these reveries, "The Barefoot Boy" and others, thousands of his countrymen have lived over their lives again. Every thing he wrote, to the New Englander has a sweet, warm familiar life about it. To them his writings are familiar photographs, but they are also treasury houses of facts over which the future antiquarian will pore and gather all the close details of the phase of civilization that they give.

Selected Works of John Greenleaf Whittier:

"My Playmate"
"The Changeling"
"The Worship of Nature"
"The Barefoot Boy"
"Maud Miller"
"Memories"
"The Prisoner for Debt"
"The Storm" (from "Snowbound")
"Ichabod"

CHAPTER SEVEN
COMPOSITION

The more a man writes, the more he can write.

—William Hazlitt, English essayist

Sample English Language Lesson Plan

Grade: _9_ Date: _4/15/98_ Teacher: _Adams_   Component:

- [ ] Biblical Foundation
- [ ] Orthography
- [ ] Etymology
- [ ] Syntax
- [ ] Prosody
- [x] Composition

Skill Taught: _Writing a Sonnet_

Principle: _The form and rhythm of expression contribute to its power._

Biblical Reference: _1 Sam. 16:23_ Illustration: _David's harp soothed Saul's spirit. Likewise, poetry with its musical qualities can free and refresh the soul._

Materials/Resources: _Copies of Milton's sonnet "On His Blindness"; Longfellow's sonnet "#29."_

Structure of the Lesson

1. Introduce the purpose and goal of the lesson.

The analysis of the sonnet in its various forms—to appreciate its mode of expressing an idea or emotion with beauty and force. The examination of several sonnets, enjoying their effect and analyzing their form as models for writing a sonnet.

2. Review related skill or concept.

Review the rules of versification including meter, scansion, and rhyme. Review the iambic pentameter pattern. Scan the three model sonnets to identify meter.

3. Present new principle and idea with appropriate methodology.

Introduce the sonnet form. Reread the three model sonnets analyzing form and rhyme scheme. Lead students in selecting one idea or emotion of their own to write in sonnet form.

4. Require student practice, participation, and presentation.

Lead students in drafting their own sonnet. Read other examples of sonnets from the same poets. Allow time and freedom to play with words in expressing their idea in sonnet form. Give liberal encouragement and critique.

5. Summarize, review, and evaluate.

When sonnets are drafted, have students read them aloud, take suggestions, and write a final draft.

The Importance and Place of Composition in the Curriculum

The art and skill of writing belong to Composition in our curriculum. The skill of writing is inaugurated early in the child's education through the very method of teaching basic literacy and by encouraging the child to write to express ideas—first in sentences, then in paragraphs, then in journaling, letter-writing, stories, research, and in the learning of every subject.

The art of writing is not a gift; it is developed by practice and by design. "If you wish to be a writer, write," said Epictetus, the Stoic philosopher. "The more a man writes, the more he can write," echoed William Hazlitt, English essayist. Writing as an art was once a subject in the curriculum developed in every student to give him or her a sound liberal education. Somewhere down the decades writing was abandoned as an art to be taught. Nine out of ten people questioned in our seminars believe that writing is a gift they missed in the distribution of talents. The understanding of writing as an art, not a gift, liberates and enables even adults to discover that they can write. How vital it is to give children the proper training in writing as they learn English.

Teaching and learning in the Principle Approach® develops Biblical reasoning and thinking skills in every subject. Reasoning and thinking are cultivated as students handle ideas in response to their instruction. "Writing makes an exact man," said Francis Bacon, and contributes to the kind of study that produces Christian scholarship, the ability to "rightly divide the word of truth."

Composition is both creative and expository. It develops reflective abilities in helping students link ideas, think logically, and present principles upon which conclusions are based. Composition develops the ability to explain, express, and persuade—vital tools of leadership.

The teaching of composition is inspired by the study of the Bible and classical literature which form the standard and cultivate the taste for excellent writing. Poetry and all the various delights of literature study create a love of language in the first step towards forming the art of writing.

When it comes to the teaching of language, there are two false attitudes that dominate and weaken American education: First, that reading is the key to all later learning; Secondly, that writing is a special art, a talent possessed by a gifted few. The fact is that a reading-oriented curriculum will hand our children up to higher schooling badly equipped to satisfy their most demanding need—the need to compose their thoughts, define their feelings, and communicate with others in speech and writing.

George Reimer, in *How They Murdered the Second R*, says, "Reading and writing, like listening and talking, like inhaling and exhaling, belong together; each makes the other intelligible. They are complementary forms of interpersonal communication. Reading is an extension of listening as writing is an extension of talking. We cannot underexercise or overexercise one without loss to the other. It would be absurd to say inhaling is more important than exhaling, to specialize in inhaling while neglecting exhaling, to regard inhaling as essential for life and exhaling as a rare talent possessed by a gifted few."

Writing is the active, expressive side of language. Reading is receptive, passive. Not denying the importance of reading, listening, and observing, we must assert that writing develops the educative facets of a person. The observer who knows he must report, sees more exactly. The listener who knows he must repeat, hears better. The reader who must write reads slower but more accurately. A nation will be remembered down through the centuries

Composition, *n.*
In literature, the act of inventing or combining ideas, clothing them with words, arranging them in order, and in general, committing them to paper, or otherwise writing them.

Compose, *v.* *To invent and put together words and sentences; to make a discourse or writing; as, to compose a sermon, or a book. To calm; to quiet; to appease. To place in proper form.*

NOTES

*Language
or Speech:
The utterance of
articulate sounds
or voices, ren-
dered significant
by usage, for the
expression and
communication
of thoughts.*

*Grammar:
A collection of
principles and
rules, taken from
the established
usages of the
nation using that
language. These
principles and
rules are derived
from the natural
distinctions of
words, or they
are arbitrary, and
depend for their
authority wholly
on custom.*

not by its listeners, but by its speakers. A nation makes its own mark in history, not through its readers but through its writers.

The English method that is writing-oriented would not only teach writing as a subject in its own right, but would teach most other subjects as well through writing. The method of teaching that is writing-oriented would strive to meet life's communication needs. Life needs both factual and imaginative communication. The writing-oriented approach to English teaches children to think problems through to their explanation to others. It teaches children not only to solve problems but to solve the added problem of communicating their solutions to others.

Writing "maketh an exact man" by requiring students to define their own understanding of relationship: is this part of that or that part of this? Are this and that of equal importance? Do this and that contradict each other? The writer reveals not only what facts and concepts he has acquired, but how he associates them with other ideas.

Dr. Peter F. Drucker, an expert in business and industrial management, tells college students not to wait for papers to be assigned but to volunteer and plead for extra writing and to persuade all teachers to read and criticize what they write. He urges them to write poetry and insists that it will teach them to use language exactly and sensitively. The ability to write clearly is the one enduring profit the student can take with him from college.

The individual unique expression of each child's fullest value is blocked, or at best limited, by the inability to describe original thinking or to present plans persuasively to give leadership to others, or to report research and ideas in clear, usable English. More importantly, the inability to communicate powerfully puts our children at the mercy of those whose skills may be strong but whose ideas and passions are evil. A mind trained to write is a well-disciplined mind able to reason independently and stand firm in a stronghold of truth.

The Elements of Style, by William Strunk, Jr. and E. B. White

There is no better guide to teaching and learning the art of writing than this pithy (eighty-five pages) but powerful exposition. It capsulizes good writing with common sense and a direct approach that reflect the essence of the original author, William Strunk, Jr. Best of all, his own student and editor, E. B. White, in the introduction presents an image of the effective English teacher that alone is worth the price of the book.

The Elements of Style is highly recommended to every teacher of English. Not only does it cut through the trivia of most texts of the genre, it hits directly on the most pressing need of most teachers—how to teach oneself to write so that one can teach others. Don't teach English without this book!

New York: Macmillan Publishing Co., 1979.

Restoring the Art of Writing

This article, by Rosalie June Slater, addresses one of the components of American Christian education's methodology—developing the art of writing as a central skill in Principle Approach® education. The life and testimony of one writer is presented as inspiration for this most important art.

Just a generation ago some of the great novels, plays, histories, and poetry of the twentieth century were being written. Today, the shelves of bookstores are bulging with massive histories, furiously fabricated novels, a few plays, and some poetry. But how many of these are of life-changing value? How many present-day books will be read over and over for their unforgettable prose or poetry, their idealism and inspiration, their style—their art?

A Model of Excellence

Like relay racers, there are still, however, some writers of this century whose work can touch our lives—who can pass on to us the baton of inspiration and excellence—and to whom we can look for direction and purpose in our own research and writing. One such writer, whose life on earth closed during our Bicentennial 1976, was Admiral Samuel Eliot Morison—perhaps the last of our great New England historians, a meticulous scholar, a superb stylist—a master of the *art of writing*.

Dr. Morison believed that the art of writing is related to the art of living. He wrote more than three score volumes of history. But he was an exciting writer. He followed literally in the footsteps of each of the early explorers whom he researched. He was also contemptuous of those writers of history who had never left their armchairs when they wrote about the men whose discoveries opened up our world. He called them "historians down to the water's edge." When Dr. Morison was writing his *Admiral of the Ocean Sea*—a biography of Columbus—he organized the 1942 Harvard Expedition which sailed the exact God-directed route which Columbus took when he carried Christian civilization to the Western Hemisphere. And in World War II when Admiral Morison became the official historian of U.S. Naval Operations, he was on the decks of American ships while they were engaging the enemy in that two-ocean war.

Courage Sustained by Prayer

What spirit animated this great historian whose work captured the respect and admiration of so many—from his own doctoral students of history at Harvard, where he taught for forty years, to men like Alan Villiers who had helped in the reconstruction of the *Mayflower* and had sailed the Pilgrim vessel across the Atlantic? In a volume edited by one of his daughters in 1977, entitled *Sailor Historian: The Best of Samuel Eliot Morison*, there is in the foreword to this book the following conversation between the Reverend G. Harris Collingwood, rector of the Church of the Advent in Boston, and our historian:

Four years ago while crossing the Public Garden, by chance Admiral Morison and I fell into step together. He was about to leave for South America where he planned to retrace the Southern Voyages of Magellan by airplane and by ship. He was excited by the prospect. I remarked on the courage of the early explorers.

He was silent for a moment as we walked along. Then he said, "Courage yes, but a courage sustained by prayer."

He told me in detail about the journals and logs of the early explorers, how they were filled with thanksgivings to God for the daily mercies vouchsafed to them through His Providence. . . .

In his last days as I prayed with him in the hospital, I remembered that incident. Samuel Eliot Morison lived a life of courage, sustained by prayer. . . .

"Would it be possible," he asked, "for you to make a public statement of my thankfulness for God's mercy? Today I finished the volume of the southern voyages, it was a plan of writing I began fifty years ago."

It is a remarkable achievement for any man to persevere for fifty years through a hard plan and bring it to its end. It is even more remarkable to wish to give thanks to Almighty God for the strength to complete the task. I used the example of Samuel Eliot Morison the next day, Good Friday, when I preached on the Sixth Word, "It is finished."

Courage sustained by prayer was a mark of the early explorers of the new world. It was a mark of Samuel Eliot Morison's character, and it is his legacy of wisdom to each of us. (*Sailor Historian*, pp. xxvi–xxvii)

History as Literary Art

One of the most successful of the *Old South Leaflets* was written by Dr. Morison and entitled *History as a Literary Art*. As a professor in America's first established college, now Harvard University, he taught his graduate history students the art of writing. What can we learn from his essay to help us restore the art of writing?

Dr. Morison first commands budding writers to "get writing." No excuse, no amount of research, no unwillingness, will substitute for actual practice in writing. What Morison is seeking in his students and which we must begin to develop first as teachers in ourselves, is what Morison calls a "quick, warm synthesis between research, thinking, and writing." (p. 388)

"The three prime qualities of historical composition—*clarity, vigor, and objectivity*"—become an excellent school of discipline, even for those who wish to write fiction and imaginative rather than *realistic literature.*

Writing is a discipline—just like any sport. And as there is really no sport in which even the individual can ignore the goals or object of the sport, so there is no writing without the ultimate presence of an audience or reader. Can we totally disregard the interest of the *reader?*

Perhaps from our consideration of Samuel Eliot Morison we can agree that there are both internal and external prerequisites to being a good writer. First, Morison discovered the *spiritual impulsion* of those explorers whose deeds so inspired him. Secondly, he believed that he needed to *externally experience the dangers, the unknown challenges* these men faced. He needed to follow their paths, endeavor to think their thoughts, consider how he might have faced the same difficulties in earlier centuries. The willingness to place ourselves in readiness to understand the courage or the compassion of those whose pioneer efforts have blessed us in some way seems to impart a *spirit of reality, of respect* for the individual, or subject about which we are writing.

Lastly, but most importantly, we need to practice the *discipline of writing—its restrains as well as its embellishments.* For this it is always good to try out our field of interest, our story, our poem, our play, on the young. Why, because to be able to communicate on the level of a youthful mind requires that we be both *clear* and *true.* What we deplore today is the *lack of truth* in modern day writing. Perhaps what is written is factually true—it is happening—but if it is not spiritually, morally true, it will not represent beauty, wonder, inspiration, courage—all those qualities which we want to inspire our own lives. And because the young are untried they often can *recognize* what is recorded in Philippians 4:8:

"Finally, brethren, whatsoever things are *true*, whatsoever things are *honest*, whatsoever things are *just*, whatsoever things are *pure*, whatsoever things are *lovely*, whatsoever things are of *good report*; if there be any *virtue*, and if there be any praise, think on these things."

Teaching the Second "R"

Principle Approach® education begins with inspiring the heart to learn and grow, giving the practice of learning a natural impetus. So it is in teaching and learning the art of writing. First we inspire our students with the great literature, with models of excellence like Samuel Eliot Morison, delighting them with the best poetry and creative expression. Then we give them practice in developing their own skill.

The distinction between expository writing and creative writing is an important one for teachers to recognize. It is essential that expository writing skills be thoroughly taught and practiced for creative writing to be given full expression. While we look forward to the flowering of creative writing in our students, if they are not equipped with the essential skills, they do not possess the tools appropriate to creative expression. Therefore composition writing should be a basic skill taught in every English curriculum, giving new meaning to "reading, writing, and arithmetic," and beginning as children learn to read and write in the primary grades.

As composition takes its rightful place in the heart of the curriculum, our students practice the art of writing consistently, writing essays, letters, research, poems, short stories, and plays. They become equipped to lead others in whatever field of endeavor they choose for themselves, because the writer wields a powerful tool—the written word, which in His Story has been the tool of bringing man to a rational knowledge of God. It is our hope in Principle Approach education to restore generations of American Christian children to the art of writing.

(First published in *Principly Speaking*, a newsletter from the Foundation for American Christian Education. Vol. 1, No. 1, January 1991)

Forms of Prose Writing

Adapted from **Composition and Rhetoric for Higher Schools** *by Sara E. H. Lockwood and Mary Alice Emerson. Boston: Ginn & Company, 1903.*

Types of Prose

1. Description

Character Sketches
Caricature

2. Narration

Histories
Biographies
Travels
Short Stories
News
Anecdotes
Diaries
Letters

3. Exposition

Essays
Orations
Debates
Editorial
Book Review
Speeches

The most important forms of prose writing are categorized as description, narration, and exposition.

Description

In a sense, a pen picture of a real or imaginary object, scene, or person. In every instance attention must be given to the point of view, the selection of the essential characteristics, the logical arrangement of details, and the careful choice of words.

1. A **character sketch** differs from a caricature in being a fair and impartial presentation of the underlying motives which seem to control a life.

2. A **caricature** is the intentional exaggeration of one or more qualities of character.

Narration

The most important kinds of narration are histories, biographies, travels, short stories, and novels. The shorter forms are news items, anecdotes, diaries, and letters.

1. **History** is a record of past events, or, more accurately, a connected story of the progress of a nation's civilization. History differs from tradition in dealing only with well-authenticated facts, and not with rumors, beliefs, or impressions of individuals or peoples. The historical spirit implies a strong grasp of epoch-making events and principles, a logical view of cause and results, a fine sense of proportion, and a wise power of selection.

2. A **biography** is the life of one man or woman written by another man or woman. The essentials of a good biography are accuracy, fairness, and proportion. An autobiography is the life of a person written by himself. It is likely to be especially interesting because of its peculiar personal character. But it is, of course, some-

times unreliable because of its lack of perspective.

3. A **book of travels** is a combination of description, narration, and exposition, in which narration prevails to a large extent. The chief interest lies either in the novelty of the matter or in the individuality of the writer's style.

4. The **short story** is a brief tale, which usually has a strong point, a well-constructed plot, lifelike characters, and vigorous dialogue. The theme and its treatment may range from humorous to pathetic or tragic. A judicious use of dialect may be very effective.

5. **News items** are of interest and importance. They should treat facts in a fair and impersonal manner and be written in a clear, direct, and vivid style.

6. An **anecdote** should have one telling point, which is brought out strongly and concisely.

7. A **diary** is a brief and intimate daily record of personal observations, experiences, and impressions.

Exposition

The form of prose which unfolds, defines, explains, or interprets facts and conceptions. It presents the idea of a class, or sums up the legitimate conclusions to be drawn from many examples of a truth. The most important forms of exposition are essays, orations, and debates. Other miscellaneous forms are newspaper editorials, book reviews, and speeches for special occasions.

1. **Essays** are formal or informal. The informal essay is usually more or less descriptive in form. The formal essay is scientific or critical. The purpose of the critical essay is not primarily to find fault, but rather to give a fair view of merits and defects. A critic should have a definite standard of criticism based on his own thorough investigation, keenness in recognizing new truths, and judgment unbiased by personal prejudice.

2. An **oration** is an elaborate public discourse intended to convince the intellect, to arouse the emotions, or to move the will. It consists largely of exposition, which should be clear, strong, rapid, and convincing. The brief appeal is based directly on the exposition and leads rapidly to a strong climax. The most important bases of appeal are personal interest, patriotism, domestic or religious feeling, and a desire for truth. These give rise to the plea, the political speech, the sermon, and the lecture.

The **plea** has four more or less distinct parts: an informal opening, a criticism of the evidence of the other side, a clear and forceful argument based on the evidence of the witnesses, and a conclusion. Clearness and earnestness are important requisites of the lawyer's style. Wit, sarcasm, and pathos are also effective.

The **political speech** varies from the informal, colloquial words of the stump speaker to the carefully polished phrases of the statesman. Its appeal is to expediency, integrity, patriotic, or love of justice.

A **sermon** is a discourse based on a text chosen from Scripture, appealing to conscience and religious feeling. It should be brief, logical, practical, and tinged with quiet reverence and deep feeling.

The **lecture** may vary greatly in theme and treatment, but as a rule it should be logical and scholarly. Since it is intended for delivery rather than for reading, it may be somewhat more familiar in style than the essay.

Editorials comment upon the meaning of the news in any of the departments of thought—politics, education, sociology, dramatic and musical criticism, philanthropy, and sometimes theology.

The object of **book reviews** is to give concisely the general scope and value of recently published books.

Speeches for special occasions should be brief and appropriate.

3. A **debate** furnishes the arguments on both sides of a question. The speakers endeavor to destroy the position of their opponents, as well as to maintain their own. Subjects that have practically but one side, that are likely to arouse bitterness of feeling without securing any valuable end, or that are not definitely limited, are unsuited for augmentation. There are two methods of reasoning: the deductive and the inductive. Each of these is based on a syllogism, usually implied rather than stated. A syllogism consists of a major premise, a minor premise, and a conclusion. In the case of deductive reasoning, the major premise is the statement of a general proposition, and in the case of inductive reasoning it is the statement of individual facts actually observed. If the general proposition is wrong, the conclusion must be false; if the facts observed are too few to form a safe basis of judgment, the conclusion is not proved. Inductive reasoning is the method most commonly employed by modern scientists.

Logic:

The art of thinking and reasoning justly. Logic is the art of using reason well in our inquiries after truth, and the communication of it to others.

Developing the Art of Composition

Grade Level	Inventing and Combining Ideas	Clothing Ideas with Words	Putting Words in Order	Commiting Words to Paper
Kindergarten *"Planting the Seeds"*	Observing, noticing, describing, asking Imagining Retelling Listing Clustering—collecting ideas	Choosing vivid and "telling" words Making sentences, paragraphs	Practicing verbal syntax Writing statements Writing group paragraphs on board with a topic sentence	Initial and end punctuation Paragraph form Writing sentences daily Writing a simple paragraph by spring
First–Third Grades *"Beginning Writers"*	Collecting supporting ideas for a paragraph Thinking up topic sentences Describing in detail Taking ideas from general to specific Clustering—collecting ideas	Discovering hundreds of apt and delightful words for "telling" Using dictionary for precision Recording words and phrases using authors' words in literature Paraphrasing Essay answers—reason questions—from the notebook content in subject areas Using exact nouns and verbs	Mastering the topic sentence and supporting sentences Developing one idea by using a beginning statement with "there is a . . ." or a subject-action statement "Kites fly" or a question-topic sentence answering with parts "What happens when it rains?" Unity—all sentences in the paragraph support the topic. Compositions of several paragraphs developing one topic.	Paragraph form Punctuation and capitalization Beginning correction symbols Proofreading Letter-writing regularly Writing a composition that develops one topic Composition-writing several times a week Essay answers daily Research writing—projects
Fourth–Seventh Grades *"Writing to Learn"*	Pre-writing as a habit Outlining skills Types of writing practiced Research skills for writing	Expanding vocabulary and style in writing Sentence variety Using exact nouns and verbs Using the thesaurus The "Scholar's Reading Lesson" Paraphrasing and precis Emphasis developed	Usage and formal style Writing dialogue Coherence emphasized (transitional words and sentences, order of details *spatial, chronological, importance,* etc.)	Proofreading as a habit Mastery of punctuation, capitalization, manuscript style Research style mastered Letter-writing regularly Composition weekly Essay answers daily Creative writing for enjoyment
Eighth–Twelfth Grades *"Writing to Communicate"*	Pre-writing skills used to solve communication problems	Audience-targeted writing	Style and effectiveness development through revision	Presenting research, thesis, argument, persuasion. Creative writing to inspire, instruct, delight

The Writing Process: Teaching Children to Write

Vigorous writing is concise. A sentence should contain no unnecessary words, a paragraph no unnecessary sentences, for the same reason that a drawing should have no unnecessary lines and a machine no unnecessary parts. This requires not that the writer make all his sentences short, or that he avoid all detail and treat his subjects only in outline, but that every word tell.

—William Strunk, Jr.

The System of Learning to Write		
Pre-Writing	Thinking and talking, discussing, describing Reading, questioning Brainstorming Listing, outlining Clustering—collecting thoughts	*"Inventing or combining ideas"*
Drafting	Designing expression of thought Selecting words and phrases Constructing sentences Structuring paragraphs with coherence, unity, emphasis, style	*"Clothing ideas with words"*
Revising	Correcting usage and grammar Trying out various sentence and paragraph styles to improve communication Finding effective openings and closings Choosing more concrete nouns and verbs Refining the "tell" Proofreading	*"Putting ideas in order"*
Presenting	Correcting spelling, punctuation, manuscript form, syntax; Submit in final written form and/or read aloud to audience.	*"Committing ideas to paper and an audience"*

The Paragraph

The paragraph is a sort of composition on a small scale. Many writers, in fact, insist that a constant practice in writing paragraphs is the surest and most economical way of acquiring the ability to write excellent themes.

Language is the picture and counterpart of thought.
—Mark Hopkins

Definition

The paragraph is a group of related sentences which develop a single topic. It has the essential qualities of unity, coherence, and emphasis. Unity has to do with the choice of material. Coherence has to do with arrangement with a view to clearness. Emphasis has to do with arrangement with a view to proportion.

1. Descriptive
2. Narrative
3. Expository

Unity in Paragraphs

Unity in the paragraph requires that all the sentences composing the paragraph shall bear directly on the central thought of that paragraph. If the group of sentences contains a single sentence which does not contribute its share of meaning toward the object for which the group was written, unity is violated and the group is in not true sense a paragraph.

Hindrances to Unity in the Paragraph

The most important hindrances to unity in the paragraph are:

1. Digression; 2. Shifting the point of view; 3. Making a hazy, uncertain beginning.

Means of Securing Unity in the Paragraph

The chief means of securing unity in the paragraph are:

1. Keeping definitely in mind the central thought or idea which is expressed in the topic sentence;

2. Determining upon the point of view and holding firmly to it;

3. Securing an accurate beginning;

4. Avoiding digressions.

Study the following model paragraph from literature to find the central thought and point of view demonstrating the essential quality of paragraph unity.

Example

Who is that short, sturdy, plainly dressed man who stands with legs a little apart and hands behind his back, looking up with keen gray eyes into the face of each speaker? His cap is in his hands, so you can see the bullet head of crisp brown hair and the wrinkled forehead, as well as the high cheek-bones, the short square face, the broad temples, the thick lips which are yet as firm as granite. A coarse plebeian stamp of man; yet the whole figure and attitude are that of boundless determination, self-possession, energy; and when at last he speaks a few blunt words, all eyes are turned respectfully upon him,—for his name is Francis Drake.

—Charles Kingsley

(*Composition and Rhetoric*, Lockwood and Emerson. Boston, 1903)

Paragraph Coherence

Proper words in proper places.
—Jonathan Swift

Definition

Coherence in the paragraph requires that the material shall be so arranged as to make the meaning unmistakably clear.

Hindrances to Coherence in the Paragraph

1. Lack of definiteness in the logical arrangement

2. Lack of connecting words and phrases to show the relation of the parts

Means of Securing Coherence in the Paragraph

1. Seek definitely a natural and logical order of development of the topic sentence.

2. Wherever they are needed to make the meaning clear, use connecting words and phrases, like *so, therefore, hence, notwithstanding, in the former case*, and many similar expressions as sign-boards, to point the way to the connecting road.

Study the following paragraph to find the order of development, and the connecting words and phrases identifying coherence.

Example

The winter passed. The snow gradually melted in the meadows and the fields, which first grew brown and then displayed patches of green here and there where the sun fell strongest. There was deep, sticky mud in the roads, and the discouraged farmers urged their horses along with the wheels of their wagons sunk to the hub in ooze. Then there were wet days, the wind ruffling the leaden surface of the river, the sound of the rain dripping from the bare tree-boughs, the smell of the wet grass and the clean, thirsty soil. Milder weather came, then blustery days, then chill damp ones, but steadily life grew, here, there, everywhere, and the ever-new miracle of the awakening earth took place once again. Sap mounted in the trees, blood coursed in the children's veins, mothers began giving herb tea and sulphur molasses, young human nature was restless; the whole creation throbbed and sighed, and was tremulous, and had growing pains.

—Kate Douglas Wiggin
Mother Carey's Chickens

Paragraph Emphasis

Definition

Emphasis in the paragraph requires that the ideas be given their proper proportion and that the important sentences be placed at the beginning or the end.

Hindrances to Emphasis in the Paragraph

The chief hindrances to emphasis in the paragraph are:

1. Lack of proportion;

2. A weak beginning; and

3. A weak ending.

Securing Emphasis in the Paragraph

Weigh carefully the relative values of ideas and give them space according to their importance. Details should be kept subordinate and amplified only in proportion to their individual importance to the main idea. Over-amplification and too great illustration of a simple statement will clearly be violations of proportion, and give a false and misleading effect.

Develop the important idea expressed in the topic-sentences so as to govern the beginning and the ending of the paragraph. Arrange a climax when the length and the nature of the paragraph warrant it.

We should manage our thought as shepherds do their flowers in making a garland; first select the choicest, and then dispose them in the most proper places, that every one may reflect a part of its color and brightness on the next.
—Coleridge

Study the following model paragraph to find the quality of emphasis:

Example

By the time our daughter was five years old, we had begun to interlard the "everyday" verses with more spacious poetry. Now I am just as much at a loss to define what I mean by this as A. E. Housman was when he was asked to define poetry in general: "I can no more define poetry than a terrier can define a rat. We both recognize the object by the symptoms which it provokes in us." What our family calls "grand poetry" is recognizable by the symptoms he describes, "a shiver down the spine," "a precipitation of water to the eyes," and "borrowing a phrase from Keats' Letters, where he says, speaking of Fanny Brawne, 'everything that reminds me of her goes through me like a knife.'" It is doubtful whether any child feels these symptoms acutely; doubtful, too, if it is desirable that he should. But if they are present in the parent's response, and if, as a result of them, an almost involuntary gift is made to the child, there is bound to be some communication of the thrilling pleasure. How otherwise can you account for the fact that after once hearing it said, a very little girl will beg, "Say that about 'On a cloud I saw a child,'" and listen as many times as you care to say it, with grave and pleased attention?

—Annis Duff
Bequest of Wings

The Paragraph House

The "Paragraph House" is a visual that is used with primary-aged students to help them remember the structure of a paragraph.

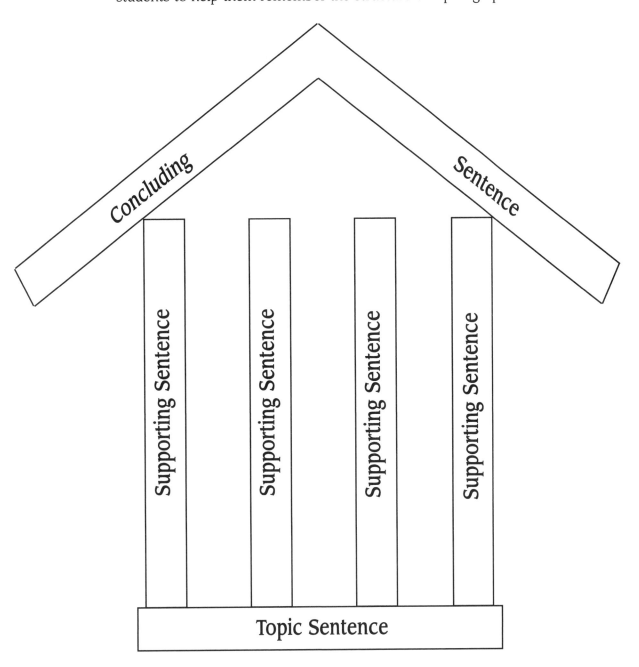

A **paragraph** is a group of sentences that describe one main idea.

A **topic sentence** is the sentence in the paragraph that states the main idea.

Supporting sentences are sentences in the paragraph that relate specific details about the main idea.

A **concluding sentence** is the sentence at the end of the paragraph that restates the topic sentence.

Letter-Writing

Letter-writing is an art and an influence in society. A good letter expresses the individuality of the writer with much accuracy and vividness, and to this fact it chiefly owes its charm. Often people write their thoughts and feelings more easily and precisely than they speak them.

Kinds of Letters

1. Friendly Letters
2. Informal Notes
3. Business Letters
4. Formal Notes

A. The Heading
   1. Place   **Devonshire Terrace**
   2. Date   **March 10, 1843**
   3. Address   **London, England**
   4. Salutation

B. The Introduction   **My Dear Tennyson**

C. The Body of the Letter   (See below)

D. The Conclusion
   1. Complimentary close   **Faithfully, etc.**
   2. Signature

E. The Superscription
   1. Name   **Charles Dickens**
   2. Place

F. Envelope   **(Address on Envelope)**

Devonshire Terrace
March 10, 1843

London, England

My Dear Tennyson,

    For the love I bear you as a man whose writings enlist my whole heart and nature in admiration of their Truth and Beauty, set these books upon your shelves: believing that you have no more earnest and sincere homage then mine.

          Faithfully and gratefully
             your friend,
             Charles Dickens

St. Petersburg
September, 1811

My dear Son,

In your letter of the 18th January to your mother, you mentioned that you read to your aunt a chapter in the Bible or a section of Doddridge's Annotations every evening. This information gave me real pleasure; for so great is my veneration for the Bible, and so strong my belief, that when duly read and meditated on, it is of all books in the world, that which contributes most to make men good, wise, and happy—that the earlier my children begin to read it, the more steadily they pursue the practice of reading it throughout their lives, the more lively and confident will be my hopes that they will prove useful citizens to their country, respectable members of society, and a real blessing to their parents. But I hope you have now arrived at an age to understand that reading, even in the Bible, is a thing in itself, neither good nor bad, but that all the good which can be drawn from it, is by the use and improvement of what you have read, with the help of your own reflection. Young people sometimes boast of how many books, and how much they have read; when, instead of boasting, they ought to be ashamed of having wasted so much time, to so little profit.

I advise you, my son, in whatever you read, and most of all in reading the Bible, to remember that it is for the purpose of making you wiser and more virtuous. I have myself, for many years, made it a practice to read through the Bible once every year. I have always endeavored to read it with the same spirit and temper of mind, which I now recommend to you: that is, with the intention and desire that it may contribute to my advancement in wisdom and virtue. . . .

Let us, then, search the Scriptures; and, in order to pursue our inquiries with methodical order, let us consider the various sources of information, that we may draw from in this study. The Bible contains the revelation of the will of God. It contains the history of the creation of the world, and of mankind. . . . In what light soever we regard it, whether with reference to revelation, to literature, to history, or to morality—it is an invaluable and inexhaustible mine of knowledge and virtue.

I shall number separately those letters that I mean to write you upon the subject of the Bible, and as, after they are finished, I shall perhaps ask you to read them all together, or to look over them again myself, you must keep them on separate file. I wish that hereafter they may be useful to your brothers and sisters, as well as to you.

As you will receive them as a token of affection for you, during my absence, I pray that they may be worthy to read by them all with benefit to themselves, if it please God, that they should live to be able to understand them.

From your affectionate Father,
John Quincy Adams

(From *Letters of John Quincy Adams to His Son on the Bible and Its Teachings*. 1850. As quoted in *The Christian History of the American Revolution: Consider and Ponder*, Verna M. Hall, pp. 614–16.)

Cultivating a Standard of Taste and Imagination

There is between him who writes, and him who reads, a kind of coalition of interests,
a partnership of mental property, a joint stock of tastes and ideas.

—Hannah More

Taste, n. The faculty of discerning beauty, order, congruity, proportion, symmetry or whatever constitutes excellence, particularly in the fine arts and belles lettres. Taste is not wholly the gift of nature, nor wholly the effect of art. It depends much on culture. We say "a good taste" or a "fine taste."

Imagination, n. [L. imaginatio; Fr. imagination.] The power or faculty of the mind by which it conceives and forms ideas of things communicated to it by the organs of sense.

Learning a standard of taste and imagination, of what constitutes the pleasures of taste, takes subjugation of the will and desire, of human inclinations and tastes to the laws of reason and conscience. Childhood is the season of instruction which is granted by Providence. It is the duty of instructors to mould the flexibility to its most durable end, to store the memory with the richest knowledge, to turn inquisitiveness to its noblest intellectual purpose, above converting the impressionability of the heart to its most exalted moral state. Common sense should not be sacrificed to the capricious tastes of a child or to the 'pliant principles' of others nearby. Nothing less than the soundest, most rational, most religious education can counteract the dangers to which they are exposed. . . .

Books alone will never form the character. It is conversation which must unfold, enlarge, and apply the use of books. Without familiar comment on what is read, mere reading might only fill the mind with fallacious models of character, and false maxims of life. It is conversation which must develop what is obscure, raise what is low, correct what is defective, qualify what is exaggerated, and gently and almost insensibly raise the understanding, form the heart, and fix the taste; and by giving just proportions to the mind, teach it the power of fair appreciation, draw it to adopt what is reasonable, to love what is good, to taste what is pure, and to imitate what is elegant. . . .

But above all, there should be a constant, but imperceptible habit of turning the mind to a love of truth in all its forms and aspects; not only in matters of grave morality, but in matters of business, of common intercourse, and even of taste; for there is a truth both in moral and mental taste, little short of the exactness of mathematical truth; and the mind should acquire a habit of seeking perfection in everything. It is not enough that a child should possess truth as a principle; he should cherish it as an object of affection, delight in it as a matter of taste and dread nothing so much as false coloring and artifice.

(Hannah More, *Hints towards Forming the Character of a Princess*, Philadelphia, 1830)

Timeline of Key Writers and Writing

by Penny Paquette

"Led by the Hand of history. . . ."

Eternity Past

Creation

The Beginning of Language

The beginning of rhetoric as illustrated by John Quincy Adams in his *Lectures on Rhetoric and Oratory* is found in the analysis by Aristotle of the division of rhetoric as:

1. **Invention**

   "In the beginning God created the heaven and the earth; and the earth was without form and void."

2. The **Elocution** or speech (style):

   "And God said, Let there be light."

3. The **Disposition** (arrangement):

   "And God divided the light from the darkness: and God called the light day, and the darkness He called night."

Moses and the Law
The Beginnings of the Bible and Classical Literature

1450 B.C.

Moses, the first historian, wrote the Pentateuch; the Books of Law, the account of the Creation, the early history of the world, and of the nation of Israel.

Note: See *Rudiments Handbook*; "Moses and the Moral Law."

Poetry

The Bible, the Word of God, is our model for all literary types, and thus our model for every type and principle of composition and rhetoric. Beauty, sublimity and novelty, the constituents of taste and imagination are illustrated to perfection in the Word of God. "The poetry of the Bible is like the cathedral window through which the rainbow lights of heaven play upon the marbles of impressive and momentous truths. . . . The Book of Job is . . . one of the most sublime poems in all literature. For sublimity of thoughts, lofty spiritual sentiment, breadth and range of vision, as well as for beauty of form and expression, the Book of Psalms . . . stands at the very forefront of the literature of all time." (*Book of Life*, Vol. V, John Rudin and Co., 1936) See *Literature Curriculum Guide*, pp. 70–71.

Proverbs

Chronicles

Biography

Ecclesiastes 1:12–24: "An ideal biography, the life of the greatest king yields no profit, but serves to show that each day brings its own reward." (*Book of Life*, Vol. V)

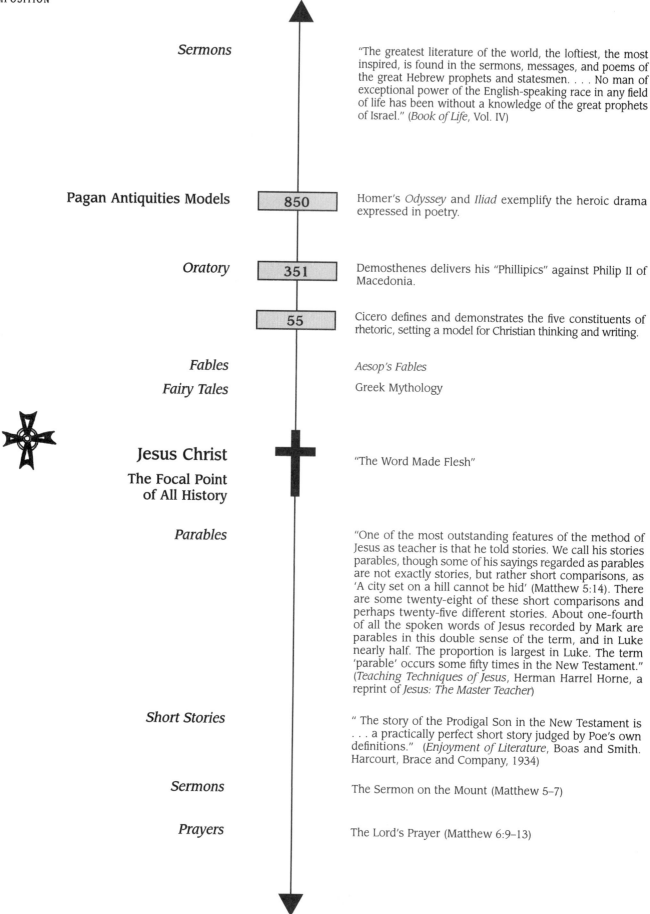

Sermons

"The greatest literature of the world, the loftiest, the most inspired, is found in the sermons, messages, and poems of the great Hebrew prophets and statesmen. . . . No man of exceptional power of the English-speaking race in any field of life has been without a knowledge of the great prophets of Israel." (*Book of Life*, Vol. IV)

Pagan Antiquities Models   **850**

Homer's *Odyssey* and *Iliad* exemplify the heroic drama expressed in poetry.

Oratory   **351**

Demosthenes delivers his "Phillipics" against Philip II of Macedonia.

55

Cicero defines and demonstrates the five constituents of rhetoric, setting a model for Christian thinking and writing.

Fables   *Aesop's Fables*

Fairy Tales   Greek Mythology

Jesus Christ

**The Focal Point
of All History**

"The Word Made Flesh"

Parables

"One of the most outstanding features of the method of Jesus as teacher is that he told stories. We call his stories parables, though some of his sayings regarded as parables are not exactly stories, but rather short comparisons, as 'A city set on a hill cannot be hid' (Matthew 5:14). There are some twenty-eight of these short comparisons and perhaps twenty-five different stories. About one-fourth of all the spoken words of Jesus recorded by Mark are parables in this double sense of the term, and in Luke nearly half. The proportion is largest in Luke. The term 'parable' occurs some fifty times in the New Testament." (*Teaching Techniques of Jesus*, Herman Harrel Horne, a reprint of *Jesus: The Master Teacher*)

Short Stories

" The story of the Prodigal Son in the New Testament is . . . a practically perfect short story judged by Poe's own definitions." (*Enjoyment of Literature*, Boas and Smith. Harcourt, Brace and Company, 1934)

Sermons   The Sermon on the Mount (Matthew 5–7)

Prayers   The Lord's Prayer (Matthew 6:9–13)

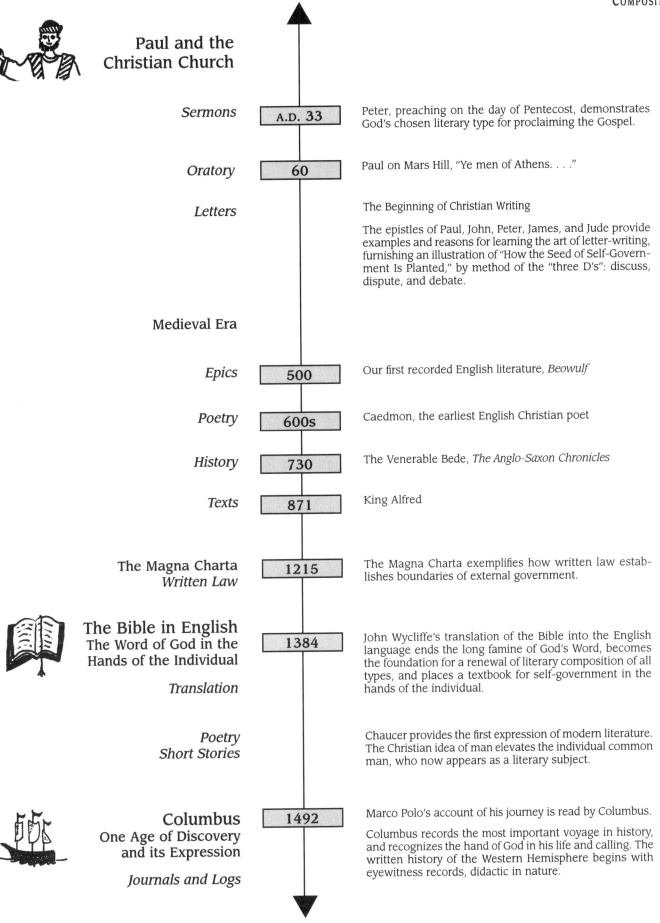

Paul and the
Christian Church

Sermons — A.D. 33 — Peter, preaching on the day of Pentecost, demonstrates God's chosen literary type for proclaiming the Gospel.

Oratory — 60 — Paul on Mars Hill, "Ye men of Athens. . . ."

Letters

The Beginning of Christian Writing

The epistles of Paul, John, Peter, James, and Jude provide examples and reasons for learning the art of letter-writing, furnishing an illustration of "How the Seed of Self-Government Is Planted," by method of the "three D's": discuss, dispute, and debate.

Medieval Era

Epics — 500 — Our first recorded English literature, *Beowulf*

Poetry — 600s — Caedmon, the earliest English Christian poet

History — 730 — The Venerable Bede, *The Anglo-Saxon Chronicles*

Texts — 871 — King Alfred

The Magna Charta
Written Law — 1215 — The Magna Charta exemplifies how written law establishes boundaries of external government.

The Bible in English
The Word of God in the Hands of the Individual — 1384 — John Wycliffe's translation of the Bible into the English language ends the long famine of God's Word, becomes the foundation for a renewal of literary composition of all types, and places a textbook for self-government in the hands of the individual.

Translation

Poetry
Short Stories

Chaucer provides the first expression of modern literature. The Christian idea of man elevates the individual common man, who now appears as a literary subject.

Columbus
One Age of Discovery and its Expression — 1492 — Marco Polo's account of his journey is read by Columbus.

Columbus records the most important voyage in history, and recognizes the hand of God in his life and calling. The written history of the Western Hemisphere begins with eyewitness records, didactic in nature.

Journals and Logs

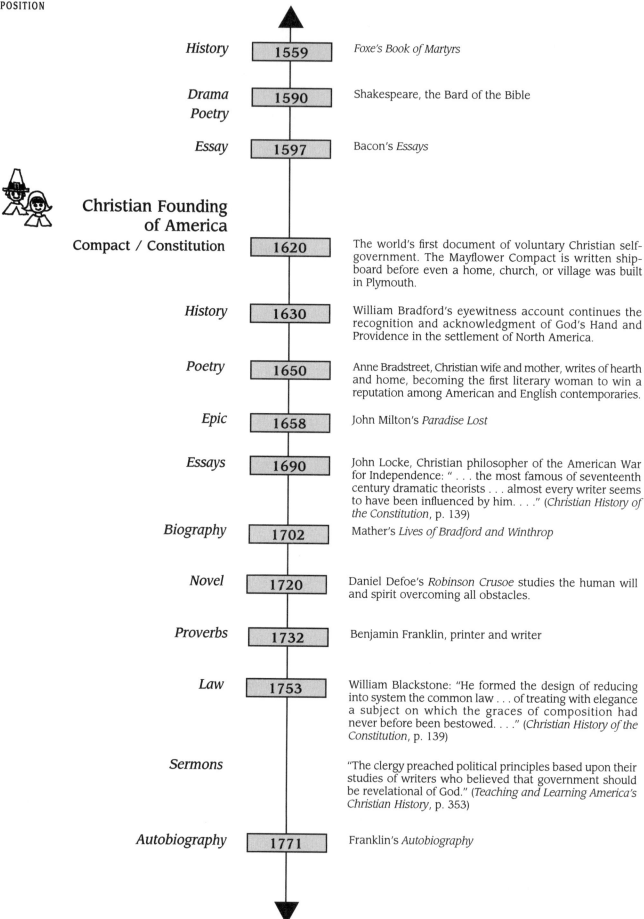

History — 1559 — *Foxe's Book of Martyrs*

Drama — 1590 — Shakespeare, the Bard of the Bible
Poetry

Essay — 1597 — Bacon's *Essays*

Christian Founding of America

Compact / Constitution — 1620 — The world's first document of voluntary Christian self-government. The Mayflower Compact is written shipboard before even a home, church, or village was built in Plymouth.

History — 1630 — William Bradford's eyewitness account continues the recognition and acknowledgment of God's Hand and Providence in the settlement of North America.

Poetry — 1650 — Anne Bradstreet, Christian wife and mother, writes of hearth and home, becoming the first literary woman to win a reputation among American and English contemporaries.

Epic — 1658 — John Milton's *Paradise Lost*

Essays — 1690 — John Locke, Christian philosopher of the American War for Independence: " . . . the most famous of seventeenth century dramatic theorists . . . almost every writer seems to have been influenced by him. . . ." (*Christian History of the Constitution*, p. 139)

Biography — 1702 — Mather's *Lives of Bradford and Winthrop*

Novel — 1720 — Daniel Defoe's *Robinson Crusoe* studies the human will and spirit overcoming all obstacles.

Proverbs — 1732 — Benjamin Franklin, printer and writer

Law — 1753 — William Blackstone: "He formed the design of reducing into system the common law . . . of treating with elegance a subject on which the graces of composition had never before been bestowed. . . ." (*Christian History of the Constitution*, p. 139)

Sermons — "The clergy preached political principles based upon their studies of writers who believed that government should be revelational of God." (*Teaching and Learning America's Christian History*, p. 353)

Autobiography — 1771 — Franklin's *Autobiography*

"'The chief glory of a nation,' says Dr. Johnson, 'arises from its authors.' With this opinion deeply impressed on my mind, I have the same ambition which actuated that great man when he expressed a wish to give celebrity to Bacon, to Hooker, to Milton and to Boyle.

"I do not indeed expect to add celebrity to the names of Franklin, Washington, Adams, Jay, Madison, Marshall, Ramsay, Dwight, Smith, Trumbull, Hamilton, Belknap, Ames, Mason, Kent, Hare, Silliman, Cleaveland, Walsh, Irving, and many other Americans distinguished by their writings or by their science; but it is with pride and satisfaction, that I can place them as authorities, on the same page with those of Boyle, Hooker, Milton, Dryden, Addison, Ray, Milner, Cowper, Davy, Thomson, and Jameson.

"A life devoted to reading and to an investigation of the origin and principles of our vernacular language, and especially a particular examination of the best English writers, with a view to a comparison of their style and phraseology, with those of the best American writers, and with our colloquial usage, enables me to affirm with confidence, that the genuine English idiom is as well preserved by the unmixed English of this country, as it is by the best English writers. . . ." It is true, that many of our writers have neglected to cultivate taste, and the embellishments of style; but even these have written the language in its genuine idiom. In this respect, Franklin and Washington, whose language is their hereditary mother tongue, unsophisticated by modern grammar, present as pure models of genuine English, as Addison or Swift. But I may go farther, and affirm, with truth, that our country has produced some of the best models of composition. The style of President Smith; of the authors of the Federalist; of Mr. Ames; of Dr. Mason; of Mr. Harper; of Chancellor Kent; (the prose) of Mr. Barlow; of the legal decisions of the Supreme Court of the United States; of the reports of legal decisions in some of the particular states; and many other writings; in purity, in elegance and in technical precision, is equaled only by that of the best British authors, and surpassed by that of no English compositions of a similar kind." (Noah Webster, "Preface to the Dictionary," 1828)

Sermons	Election, Artillery, Fast Day, and Commemorative sermons
Letters	Samuel Adams and the Committees of Correspondence; George Washington's letters; the letters of Abigail and John Adams all demonstrate *"How the Seed of Self-Government Is Planted"* by the "3 D's": discuss, dispute, and debate.
News Reports	Benjamin Franklin's *Poor Richard's Almanac*
Poetry 1773	Phyllis Wheatley
Oratory 1775	Patrick Henry
American Christian Republic 1776	Declaration of Independence: Thomas Jefferson articulates the Christian Idea of Man and Government, with the help of John Adams and other patriots.
Law Philosophy Compact/Constitution	

Journal	**1786**	James Madison's records of the Constitutional Convention; Commonplace books are widely used.
Law: Covenant /Constitution	**1787**	The United States Constitution; The protection of writers' property rights in the copyright law, which Noah Webster proposed and actively lobbied to procure, results in the as yet unabated proliferation of American literature. The early American writing is inherently Christian in nature and continues to be so until the first quarter of the twentieth century.
Essays		The Federalist Papers; Anti-Federalist Papers
Oratory	**1796**	Washington's Farewell Address
Journals	**1804**	The Lewis and Clark Expedition
History	**1805**	Mercy Otis Warren
	1828	Bible and dictionary, and textbooks. Webster writes ". . . to refine and establish our language, to facilitate the acquisition of grammatical knowledge, and diffuse the principles of virtue and patriotism. . . . and whether the success should equal my wishes or not, I shall still have the satisfaction of reflecting that I have made a laudable effort to advance the happiness of my country. . . ." (Noah Webster, *An American Selection of Lessons in Reading and Speaking*, 1789)

Expansion and Erosion

"The scriptures, ever abound with sublimity in thought and in language; the two so aptly united in the harmonies of prophetic language, which announce through the poet's tongue, the mission and glories of the Messiah. But the sublime in Scripture is ever present with us from the universal diffusion of the Bible in our country: and illustrations suggest themselves to the daily delight of its readers." (*Elements of Rhetoric*, Henry Coppee, 1860)

Poetry	William Cullen Bryant
Novels	Sir Walter Scott created the historical novel, writing the Waverley Novels, followed in 1821 by James Fenimore Cooper, Jane Austen, Jane Porter, and others.
Short Stories	Washington Irving
Biography	Irving's biographies of Columbus and Washington
Poetry	The English Romantics: Wordsworth, Shelley, Keats, Byron, and Tennyson
	Longfellow, "The Children's Poet"
Oratory	Daniel Webster, Henry Clay, John Calhoun
History	Thomas Carlyle's *Heroes and Hero Worship* and *The French Revolution; Grandfather's Chair* by Nathaniel Hawthorne
Novels	Charles Dickens, Nathaniel Hawthorne, the Brontes

Oratory	**1863**	The Gettysburg Address, Lincoln
Letters		Civil War
Poetry		John Greenleaf Whittier
Journals		Louisa May Alcott's prolific pen produces a significant fiction literature for young people. Her childhood journals are a basis and background for her lifelong writing career.
Short Stories		Mark Twain, Joel Harris, Bret Harte, Sarah Orne Jewett, Nathaniel Hawthorne, O. Henry
Essays		Oliver Wendall Holmes
Novels		Howard Pyle, Lew Wallace, Robert Louis Stevenson
History		Francis Parkman, John Fiske, George Bancroft
Poetry		Emily Dickinson, Walt Whitman

1900s

The Nobler Stream

Novels	Kate Douglas Wiggin, Marguerite Henry, L. M. Montgomery, Willa Cather, George Orwell, Ernest Hemingway, Jack London
Memoirs	Herbert Hoover, Admiral Richard Byrd, Charles Lindbergh, Eddie Rickenbacker, Madeleine L'Engle
Drama	Thornton Wilder, T. S. Eliot
Biography	Jean Lee Latham, Ingri and Edgar Parin d'Aulaire, Douglas Southall Freeman, Lytton Strachey, Catherine Drinker Bowman, Samuel Eliot Morison
Autobiography	Booker T. Washington, Helen Keller, Marguerite DeAngeli
History	Samuel Eliot Morison, Catherine Drinker Bowen
Law	Robert Borke

The Falling Away

" . . . the students who have succeeded that generation of the late fifties and early sixties, when the culture leeches, professional and amateur, began their great spiritual bleeding, have induced me to wonder whether my conviction . . . that nature is the only thing that counts in education is correct. At the very best, it is clear to me now that nature needs the cooperation of convention, just as man's art is needed to found the political order that is the condition of his natural completeness. At worst, I fear that spiritual entropy or and evaporation of the soul's boiling blood is taking place. . . . Today's select students know so much less, are so much more cut off from the tradition, are so much slacker intellectually, that they make their predecessors look like prodigies of culture. . . . I had not . . . paid sufficient attention to what students actually used to bring with them, the education that was once in the air that helped launch them. Most students could be counted on to know the Bible, that ubiquitous source of the older traditions. In America it was not filtered through great national interpreter, but approached directly in the manner of early Protestantism, every man his own interpreter. The Bible was thus a mirror of that indifference to national cultures inherent in the American method. Most students also participated in a remarkable unified and explicit political tradition that possesses one writing known to everyone and probably believed by most, the Declaration of Independence." (*The Closing of the American Mind*, Allan Bloom. Simon & Schuster, 1987)

Twenty-first Century

Restoration

You: the student and the teacher as authors writing inherently Christian literature, displacing and replacing the secular worldview with an ennobled view of man and government.

"What we want is not more little books about Christianity, but more little books by Christians on other subjects—with their Christianity latent. . . . The first step to the reconversion of a country is books produced by Christians." (C. S. Lewis)

Eternity Future

Beholding the Beauty of the Lord

The central idea of providential history is the impact of Christ, the Word of God, through time on a man or a nation. This idea is the essential orientation for every Christian in identifying the purpose of all things. Because literature and the fine arts serve to nourish the spirit of man and to reflect his relationship to God, they serve both as agents of the Gospel and as records of its work. By nature and integrity, therefore, the fine arts have an essential role in the propagation of the Gospel.

The fine arts considered in their whole purpose and providential meaning are more than mere aesthetics. Art for enjoyment and appreciation is the gift of our Creator God who put into man the senses and soul to embrace it. However, a Biblical view of the fine arts proceeds from a commitment to the unfolding revelation of truth in the Scriptures and results in an identification of the interdependence of truth and beauty and faith as the principle of the fine arts.

The single man in Scripture bearing the distinction of being sought of the Lord as a "man after his own heart" revealed what the desires of that heart were in his Psalm 27:

One thing have I desired of the Lord, that will I seek after; that I may dwell in the house of the Lord all the days of my life, to behold the beauty of the Lord, and to inquire in his temple.

David's one desire—to behold the beauty of the Lord—is a statement of the Christian aesthetic making the pursuit of beauty an obligation not an option. The Bible depicts beauty as an attribute or perfection of God; He is the source of beauty, just as He is the source of truth. Our God made provision for the quality of human life, not simply its survival, suggesting that "artistic beauty needs not justification for its existence, any more than a happy marriage does, or a bird, or a flower, or a mountain or a sunset."[1]

How much, then, is the God-shaped inner vacuum that can only be sufficiently filled by the Savior, fed in the tender ages of childhood by the hunger for beauty? Parents and educators must account for this avenue of bringing children to the full stature of Christ, reclaim it, and place it in its proper realm. *We must ask what habits of the heart, mind, and soul, what qualities of character, are encouraged or discouraged by the aesthetic dynamics that influence our children.*[2]

We are so accustomed to thinking of beauty as merely decorative and ornamental that we forget that beauty is a moral necessity. God wrought beauty in the structure of the universe. Beauty is the highest form of righteousness. Beauty and truth are not separated in God's world, and they ought not to be in human thought. God, who gave as much care to painting a lily as to forming the eternal hills, joined truth and beauty in holy union; and what God has joined together, man ought not attempt to put asunder, *because beauty has a moral value for truth.*

This universal love of beauty is one of the resources of human life that Christianity ought to pervade with its spirit and claim its own. It is to this instinctive love of the beautiful that the artist makes his appeal, and gets, therefore, a wider hearing for the truth he presents in this universally loved form.

Art is the interpretation of the great eternal realities of life, and as soon as the artist tries to embody the greatest feelings and aspirations of the human soul, he gets on Biblical ground, for there is no great interest or aspiration of man which the Bible has not treated. It is for this reason that great artists have dealt so largely with Biblical themes. Painting and the Bible could not be

Aesthetic education, therefore, is essentially educating tastes and sensibilities, and is mandatory to the education of the whole child.

kept separate. They are congenial companions, because they have one common characteristic: both deal, not with the immediate and material, but with the eternal and spiritual. The function of art is to embody the universal and the eternal. The function of religion is to help man to discover that his selfhood (soul) is eternal, that he is building it day by day; and that "as a man soweth, so shall he also reap."[3]

To neglect the fine arts in education is to admit ignorance and vulgarity.

For every one pupil who needs to be guarded from a weak excess of sensibility there are three who need to be awakened from the slumber of cold vulgarity. The task of the modern educator is not to cut down jungles but to irrigate deserts. The right defence against false sentiments is to inculcate just sentiments. By starving the sensibility of our pupils we only make them easier prey to the propagandist when he comes. For famished nature will be avenged and a hard heart is no infallible protection against a soft head. [4]

The tendency towards anti-intellectualism that has sometimes appeared in evangelicalism has a less obvious counterpart in anti-aestheticism. Dorothy Sayers speaks of it as "the snobbery of the banal" which snares Christians into depriving our children of the riches of God's grace. This describes those who "look down upon good music as highbrow, who confuse worship with entertainment, who deplore serious drama as worldly yet are contentedly devoted to third-rate television shows, whose tastes in reading run to the piously sentimental, and who cannot distinguish a kind of religious calendar art from honest art."[5] The Bible teaches us that Christianity is an incarnational religion. It is truth embodied in a physical world containing the elements of design—form, shape,

line, color, etc.—and truth embodied in real people to whom God gave the ability to respond to art by his grace. We do respond to art, to good art and to bad art. It imprints itself upon us and our children and becomes a reference point for our most subtle and profound needs. "Culture has very much to do with the human spirit. What we find beautiful or entertaining or moving is rooted in our spiritual life. . . ." T. S. Eliot has noted that aesthetic sensibility and spiritual perception are very closely related.[6] The fine arts in high culture have transcendent properties, taking us beyond ourselves, and teaching through perception of spiritual truth.

This brings us to a realization of the Christian obligation for the stewardship of literature and the fine arts. How do we "irrigate the deserts" to nourish the sensibilities of our children for Christ? Removing or diminishing the swamp of popular culture through television and the nearly-inescapable multimedia that inundate us every day is not the answer. It is a step that creates a vacuum which must be filled with the beauty of the Lord. The birth of a child extracts the most tender and noble sentiments of human nature. The business of Christian parents and educators is to nurture the smallest child in the living Word of God as it appears in the Person of Jesus and in the written language of the Bible, as it is reflected in creation, and as it is recorded in the annals of the fine arts.

The smallest child is naturally alert to all the elements of the arts. Children are delightfully and uninhibitedly creative by the gift of God. They are highly perceptive and receptive visually. They love pictures and respond to them enthusiastically. As children begin to express themselves, drawing and painting, singing and impromptu "instruments" appear. Art education begins here with the home environment, feeding the child through the aesthetic standards of home life.

As a child enters school, too often his curriculum centers on "basics" literacy and a "craft experience" approach to the fine arts that excludes the true nurture of sensibilities and tastes which are left to popular culture for influence. What is needed is a propagation of the Gospel through literature, art, music, and a genuine instruction in the elements of design, in art history and appreciation. The "basics" of design and music theory should be built into the education of children along with phonics and arithmetic. Literature classics, poetry, and masterpieces of art and music should become the intimate acquaintances of our children, establishing the values and high standards early.

Reading classics aloud and the practice of art and music are essential to a child's whole education. Drawing instruction in the early grades was seen as an aid to learning other subjects in pre-progressive American education, and there was evidence that good instruction counted at least as much as "talent."[7] Because the fine arts are channels to the soul, they are healing instruments to many children. The child who struggles with "classroom learning" often finds comfort in having classics read aloud or in the art class where his stronger abilities have expression and affirmation.

The curriculum that combines all these aspects of the fine arts in primary and elementary grades is a rich feast that cultivates talent, imparts a Christian worldview, develops skills, and influences tastes for what is excellent. A recent first grade class art lesson consisted of the study of Michelangelo, his individuality, his character, his contribution, and his work, making notes in their notebook and examining many examples. The children admired especially the Sistine Chapel ceiling which was completely understandable to them as it illustrated their own Bible lessons. The practice of line drawings was reviewed and each child created his own interpretation using the new skills taught in the lesson. The teacher then taped a mural size paper to the underside of their reading table, put a mat under it to cover the floor, and then allowed each child to transfer his line drawing to the "ceiling" just as Michelangelo must have done. The finished product was then attached to the first grade room ceiling for the rest of the year for further appreciation. This lesson is a memorial to high culture and to a great master in the minds and hearts of that class of first graders. It staked a claim on their hearts for the transcending effect of an experience in the fine arts.

The fine arts must have a more adequate place in Christian education and not be treated carelessly in the curriculum. In addressing the aesthetic problem, Frank Gaebelein says,

Yet in actuality they are not marginal, peripheral subjects; they are close to the heart of Christian life and witness. At present evangelical education is strongest aesthetically in music, although even here it has far to go. When it comes to the visual arts such as painting and architecture, and to the other performing arts, including drama, much of evangelical education is like a fallow field that needs both planting and cultivation. Christian schools and colleges must practice the unity of truth they preach by giving the arts a greater place in the curriculum.

The compelling motive for Christian action in the field of aesthetics lies in the nature of God. Christians are obligated to excellence because God himself is supremely excellent. In the Hall of Fame at New York University, these words are inscribed in the place given Jonathan Edwards, the greatest of American Christian philosophers: "God is the head of the universal system of existence from whom all is perfectly derived and on whom all is most absolutely dependent, whose Being and Beauty is the sum and comprehension of all existence and excellence." It is because of who and what God is, it is because of the beauty and truth manifest in his Son, it is because of the perfection of his redeeming work, that evangelicals can never be content with the mediocre in aesthetics. Here, as in all else, the call is to the unremitting pursuit of excellence to the glory of the God of all truth.[8]

Notes

[1] Ryken, Leland. *Triumphs of the Imagination: Literature in Christian Perspective.* Downers Grove, Ill.: InterVarsity Press, 1979.

[2] Myers, Kenneth A., *All God's Children and Blue Suede Shoes: Christians and Popular Culture.* Westchester, Ill.: Crossway Books, 1989.

[3] Maus, Cynthia Pearl, *Christ and the Fine Arts.* New York: Harper & Brothers Publishers, 1938.

[4] Lewis, C. S. *The Abolition of Man,* or *Reflections on Education with Special Reference to the Teaching of English in the Upper Forms of Schools.* New York: Macmillan Publishing Co., 1947.

[5] Gaebelein, Frank E. *The Christian, The Arts, and the Truth: Regaining the Vision of Greatness.* Portland, Oreg.: Multnomah Press, 1985.

[6] Myers, *All God's Children*, p. 27.

[7] Edwards, Betty, *Drawing on the Artist Within.* New York: Simon and Schuster, 1986.

[8] Gaebelein, *The Christian, The Arts, and the Truth*, p. 59.

Creative Writing: A Biblical Approach
Teaching and Learning the Writing of Poetry

The Inspiration: Genesis Chapter One

God as Creator

In the beginning God created the heaven and the earth. And the earth was without form, and void; and darkness was upon the face of the deep. And the spirit of God moved upon the face of the waters. And God said, Let there be light: and there was light. (Genesis 1:1–3)

God as Creator gave form and shape, filled the void (emptiness), spoke light and saw that it was good, divided light from darkness.

Genesis Records All That God Created

". . . the physical world has no meaning except by and for the moral world." (Arnold Guyot, Christian geographer)

". . . remember that the earth was made for man. . . ." (Matthew Fontaine Maury, Christian founder of Oceanography)

Evident Qualities of God

Everything God created was "very good." We can trust and expect continuity. *"And we know that all things work together for good to them that love God. . . ."* (Romans 8:28)

We have faith to receive good. "Everything in God's universe is revelational of God's infinity, God's diversity, God's individuality. God creates distinct individualities. God maintains the identity and individuality of everything which He created." (*Teaching and Learning*, p. 113)

1. **God fills all space**. We cannot get away from **God**. *"Whither shall I go from thy spirit? or whither shall I flee from thy presence?"* (Psalm 139:7)

2. **God** brings **light**. He *distinguishes* between **light** and **darkness**.

The Role of Poetry

Enabling us to become aware of our **Creative God** and His creation.

1. Poetry can become an instructor in the beauty of God's creation, so that our hearts and minds overflow with eagerness to sing, or write of the joy we entertain *within*, of what we behold *without*.

2. The happiness, and inner content of children, can be *nourished* with poetry, as we help them develop an *affection for the creations* of the Lord, that what they see, they can begin to define and describe, put to melody, and put into verse.

3. "Poetry opens the eyes of us all to loveliness in earth and sky and sea, in flower and weed, in tree and rock and stream, in things common and things not alike." (Arlo Bates, *Talks on the Study of Literature*. Houghton, Mifflin and Company, 1900, p. 221)

4. "This is one of the concrete reasons why we feel that poetry is an essential to the full development of the child's spiritual faculties: memory is in the early years both receptive and tenacious, and if stored with 'images of magnificence' there will be less room for what is cheap and ugly. Then, too, familiarity with the language of genuine poetry gives breadth and color to the child's speech, and this in itself stimulates a sharpened perception of external beauties and spiritual truths." (Annis Duff, *Bequest of Wings*)

The Application: Romans 1:20

For the invisible things of him from the creation of the world are clearly seen, being understood by the things that are made, even his eternal power and Godhead.

Cultivating Children's Affection for Our Benevolent Creator

1. The teacher, inspired by this ideal of creativity reflecting the character of the Master Creator, and having purposed to lead her children in writing creatively, begins by following this path of inspiration and revelation:

   a) She asks her students to consider the word *create*, defining it, and leading them to identify Creator and His *creation*.

   b) She describes the goodness, wholeness, order, and beauty found in nature. What does nature show us about God? What does something we create reflect about us? How does nature reflect God's Principle of Individuality?

2. The teacher has chosen a poem to read that celebrates some aspect of the attributes of God seen in creation or nature. She prepares her students in two ways:

   a) To anticipate that this is a "grown-up" poem that they will need to read several times for understanding, but that she will explain it carefully so that they can *appreciate* it and be *enriched* by it.

   b) To practice alertness and awareness with their imaginations as she reads, closing their eyes to *receive* the full effect intended by the poet

Reading Some Poetry about God's Good Creation

1. An excerpt from the Prelude, "June," (from "The Visions of Sir Launfal") by James Russell Lowell *is read in small segments* to the children, *slowly*, allowing frequent pauses for explanation of words and phrases, then reading the segment fluidly several times.

2. The first six lines contain delightful words—"rare," "perfect," "murmur," "glisten"—and a magnificent image—"Heaven" laying her warm ear over earth, "softly," to see if it be "in tune." The children relish the concrete imagery of heaven and earth and are inspired by the aptness and precision of this language.

Discerning the Rhythm of God's Universe

The satisfaction of rhythm; cultivating listening skills.

1. A basic characteristic of God is continuity, constancy, eternity. This is found in the rhythm of God's universe. Where can we find immediate evidence that rhythm is a persistent reminder of our trust in the constancy of God? Where can you first find rhythm in evidence?

2. Ask the children to feel their own pulse, or heartbeat. Discuss how all living things have a pulse or heartbeat. Perhaps you might have the music teacher write down or record a heartbeat. In fact, as you begin to identify rhythm, from the tick, tick, ticking of the clock, to the patter of the rain against the window, to the rhythms of insects, birdsongs, etc., you may want to have a rhythm record in music. And, then, it is important to discuss what sounds and rhythms make us quiet, rested, and renew a right spirit within us. Which sounds alarm us, disturb, or repel us?

3. Rhythm in the poem:

   a) Read the poem to the class again, asking them to listen especially for the rhythm. They could quietly tap their hands on their desks to mark the rhythm of the poem.

b) This is a good time to ask them to listen for rhyme and to identify it.

c) Explain that rhythm is a quality of poetry that makes it very satisfying to our souls because it appeals to our inner sense of rhythm.

d) Read the poem yet again savoring all elements—words, images, rhythm, rhyme, meaning.

Writing Poetry—Creative Writing

1. Ask for a suggestion of a beautiful idea or image or thought about God's creation; put this thought into rhythmic phrases.

2. Ask students to suggest words that are precise or colorful or descriptive of just the right meaning desired.

3. Let students begin now to write their own poem. Give younger ones the key words on the board to help them with spelling.

4. Encourage students to expand their imaginations in visualizing their ideas. Move from child to child, encouraging and providing guidance.

5. Allow children editing time to correct and revise, then allow them to illustrate their poems and read them to the class.

6. The product will reflect a truly Biblical view of God and nature, and a delight in all goodness and beauty.

"Visions of Sir Launfal"
by James Russell Lowell

June
(From the Prelude)

And what is so rare as a day in June?
    Then, if ever, come perfect days;
Then Heaven tries earth if it be in tune,
    And over it softly her warm ear lays;
Whether we look, or whether we listen,
We hear life murmur, or see it glisten;
Every clod feels a stir of might,
    And instinct within it that reaches and towers,
And, groping blindly above it for light,
    Climbs to a soul in grass and flowers;
The flush of life may well be seen
    Thrilling back over hills and valleys;
The cowslip startles in meadows green,
    The buttercup catches the sun in its chalice,
And there's never a leaf nor a blade too mean
    To be some happy creature's palace;
The little bird sits at his door in the sun,
    Atilt like a blossom among the leaves,
And lets his illumined being o'errun
    With the deluge of summer it receives;
His mate feels the eggs beneath her wings,
And the heart in her dumb breast flutters and sings;
He sings to the wide world and she to her nest,
In the nice ear of Nature which song is the best.

Poetry-Writing at StoneBridge School

The first, second, third, fourth, sixth, seventh, and eighth graders participated in this creative writing lesson led by Miss Rosalie Slater and Dr. Carole Adams using the Lowell poem. Each class responded enthusiastically and produced fine poems. The following poems were selected from these classes:

June

June is my favorite month of the year,
    The trees are green and the air is clear.
I hear the birds singing in the trees,
    And on my face I can feel the warm breeze.
Girls in fields of colorful flowers,
    The warm sun in the sky for hours.
Life as free and as wonderful as a dream,
    Rain coming down like a beam.
Eyes dark, piercing and glassy,
    Plains and fields green and grassy.

—Kimberly Watkins
6th Grade

Spring

Spring is a rare and uncommon gift
    of God's love,
The trees and flowers are in bloom
    and the birds are singing,
The animals come out of hibernation,
    The rivers are flowing,
And the world is alive once again.

—Timothy Andrus
4th Grade

The Two Happy Birds

There were birds in the park
    Sitting on a branch
Hatching their egg.
    Listen to the birds
Singing out Joy!

—Bethany O'Connor
1st Grade

Springtime

What is springtime to me in the morn,
    When the robin's tiny egg is now torn.
With dew on the ground, and white clouds in the sky,
    And frogs in the water with a glimmering eye.
There is grass for the fawn to rest and lay.
    It is springtime in the middle of May.

—Dorothy O'Donnel Tullidge
4th Grade

Teaching Writing across the Curriculum

Composition is practiced across the curriculum because writing is at the heart of the methodology of the Principle Approach®. Notebooks are kept in every subject. Tests are mostly essay in format. The strong emphasis on research and reason, relating and recording depends heavily on writing. The mastery of principles and leading ideas comes when the student has personally expressed his understanding in his own words verbally and on paper.

Essay Answer

The Essay Answer test goes beyond knowledge of names, dates, and other isolated facts; it requires that the facts fit together into a logical framework. Essay tests require the student to write a composition quickly. The best aid to quick thinking is organization. The following steps produce clear, effective essay answers:

1. Read all the questions on the test. Decide how much time you have to devote to each and apportion appropriate time.

2. Analyze the question reading every word and noting key words that direct your answer. Here are some examples:

   a) Classify—give the main divisions or classes.

   b) Compare—give likenesses.

   c) Contrast—give differences.

   d) Define—give an extended definition.

   e) Explain—tell how and why.

   f) Illustrate—give examples or incidents.

   g) Summarize—give briefly the main points.

3. Plan your answer before you begin to write. Make a list of your main ideas. Planning is essential in essay answers because one seldom has time to do much, if any, rewriting.

4. Write the essay answer beginning by making a direct reference to the wording of the question. Write a thesis statement that gives your main points.

5. Develop each main idea in a separate paragraph. Use the main ideas as the topic sentences of the paragraphs. Support the topic sentences with examples, illustrations, quotations, etc.

6. Write a brief concluding paragraph reasserting your thesis.

7. Proofread your answer, making neccesary corrections.

Paraphrase

A Paraphrase is a rewording of the meaning of a given passage. To write a paraphrase is not merely to substitute synonyms for each word in the original, but rather to take into one's mind the ideas of another and to send those same ideas forth in a different form. Since the paraphrase retains all the ideas in the original passage, it may be as long as the original, or longer.

Writing paraphrase is valuable because it improves one's writing ability, reading ability, and vocabulary. It sharpens thinking and reasoning skills. For a classical method of teaching writing that has been used for centuries in European schools, see *The Noah Plan® Reading Curriculum Guide* by Martha Shirley. It is called "The Scholar's Reading Lesson," and it incorporates paraphrasing in an exercise that builds good writers.

When writing a paraphrase, follow these suggestions:

1. Study the original carefully, reading it over and over again until understanding is assured. Look up the definitions of any words you don't know.

Adapted from Composition and Rhetoric, Sara Lockwood and Mary Alice Emerson. Ginn and Company, 1903.

2. Use your own words avoiding the author's wording except when there is no satisfactory substitute.

3. Do not omit ideas or add ideas.

4. Conserve the tone of the original, reproducing it as closely as possible whether it is formal, humorous, or serious.

5. Revise and edit your paraphrase.

Example

Original:	One may smile and smile, and be a villain. —Shakespeare
Paraphrase:	A man may affect sincerity and friendliness even while planning evil against another.

Revising and Presenting the Composition for Grading

Before turning in my paper, how does it check on each of the following points?

1. Does the appearance of my paper look like a picture? (framed by proper margins, titled, neat penmanship, etc.?)

2. Is my title on the first line?

3. Did I capitalize all important words in my title? Did I remember that my title must not be underlined nor placed in quotation marks?

4. Are my paragraphs well-developed?

5. Have capitalization rules been observed?

6. Are all words spelled correctly?

7. Is every sentence complete? Have I avoided fragments?

8. Will my reader understand what I am saying? Does each sentence make sense?

9. Does the main idea stand out?

Revision

1. Have I corrected all errors as indicated by grading symbols?

2. Have I revised my ideas, clothing them with the best words, putting them in logical and pleasing order, to reach my reader's understanding?

3. Have I proofread my final draft and corrected all remaining errors?

> Let every man prove his own work,
> and then shall he have
> rejoicing in himself,
> and not in another. (Galatians 6:4)

Composition Grading Scale

Contents: 40 points

Unity _____

Coherence _____

Development _____

Mechanics: 30 Points

Punctuation _____

Capitalization _____

Spelling _____

Manuscript Form: 30 Points

Margins _____

Title _____

Paragraphing _____

Legibility _____

Neatness _____

_____
Student's Name

_____
Title of Composition

_____
Date

_____
Class

_____
Grade

May Be Duplicated

Symbols Used for Marking Errors

1.	cap	Capital letter needed or omitted
2.	sp	Mistake in spelling
3.	p	Mistake in punctuation
4.	¶	New paragraph needed
5.	no ¶	New paragraph not needed
6.	mar	Faulty margin
7.	head	Heading incorrectly placed or incomplete
8.	ill	Illegible handwriting
9.	f	Fragment (not a complete sentence)
10.	ro	Run-on sentence
11.	voc	Vocabulary (poor word choice)
12.	abb	Abbreviation wrong or inappropriate
13.	?	Not clear
14.	^	Something omitted
15.	gr	Faulty grammar
16.	t	Wrong tense or verb
17.	awk	Awkward construction
18.	syl	Word incorrectly or poorly divided
19.	u	Faulty usage (illiterate expression or slang)
20.	//	Lack of parallel structure
21.	#	More space needed between words
22.	df	Comma fault—two sentences joined with a comma
23.	rep	Repetition, word used too often
24.	agr	Agreement
25.	tr	Reverse the order

The Art of Speaking

Speaking is a skill and an art. As a skill it includes mastery of diction, elocution, and speaking "presence"—the ability to speak publicly with confidence and poise. We include speaking skills in the orthography component of English language instruction as it is vital to a good education to establish speaking skills early as the child learns to read, write, and reason. In the Orthography chapter are "Basics of Speaking" and "Elocution" for elementary grades to help the teacher establish the skills of speaking in the student.

Speaking as an art involves composition—inventing or combining ideas, clothing them with words, putting them in order, and committing them to paper. In this chapter on Composition, speaking is presented as an art of composition including Oration, Debate, and Rhetoric.

Speaking as a skill and as an art requires practice speaking, opportunities to speak to groups, to discuss, debate, present, or make a formal speech.

In primary grades speaking should be encouraged throughout the day in all subjects through discussion, presentation, recitation, etc. In upper grades, speaking as an art should be cultivated through composition, giving assignments and opportunities that develop the art of speaking. The following sections on Oratory, Debate, and Rhetoric are for use with upper level students to build upon the skill of speaking as taught in orthography.

A Brief Summary of the Approaches to Rhetoric

Effective speaking requires structured thought. The classical rhetoric identifies five "topics" or approaches to argument designated: definition, comparison, relationship, circumstance, and testimony.

1. Definition attempts to delimit a particular idea or situation to your issue.

2. Comparison argues similarity, difference, and degree.

3. Relationship may be divided into four parts: cause and effect; antecedent and consequence, contraries, and contradictions.

4. Circumstance includes the possible and the impossible, past fact and future fact.

5. Testimony includes authority, testimonial, statistics, maxims, law, and precedent.

For a thorough presentation of persuasion, see *The Art of Persuasion* by Linda Bridges and William F. Ricken-backer, published by National Review, 1991.

Other valuable books for teaching and learning the art of speaking are:

Adler, Mortimer, *How to Speak, How to Listen*. Macmillan Publishing Co.,1983.

Keefe, Carolyn, *C. S. Lewis: Speaker and Teacher*. Zondervan, 1971.

Preparing an Oration

From *Composition and Rhetoric*,
Sara Lockwood and Mary Alice Emerson. Ginn and Company, 1903.

Scope of the Oration

An oration is an elaborate, formal exposition delivered in public and intended to convince the intellect, to arouse the emotions, or to move the will. Formerly great emphasis was laid upon the appeal to the emotions, and far less pains were taken to base that appeal on facts. The tendency of modern oratory is toward logical exposition, and away from emotional appeal. Three bases of appeal are frequently used: appeal to selfish or unselfish personal interests; to intellect; and to patriotic, domestic, or religious feeling.

Material for the Oration

The sources of material for the oration are much the same as those for the theme: (1) Personal observation of events and facts, together with their meaning; (2) Discussion of the facts and their meaning with those who have a wider knowledge of the subject; (3) Careful study of available printed matter as a basis of revision or accentuation of one's own opinion on the subject to be presented. To these may be added a study of human nature as a basis of effective appeal.

Steps in the Preparation of the Oration

The steps in the preparation of the oration are also practically the same as those in the preparation of the theme.

1. Choice and limitation of the subject. The subject chosen should be interesting and reasonably familiar to the writer; suitable both to the audience and the occasion; and of enough importance to make possible future action in regard to the matter discussed of real moment. When the subject has been carefully chosen, by the successive rejection of unsuitable subjects, it should be so limited as to be within the range of treatment in the given time.

2. *Selection of the material.* The special facts to be used will be determined by careful thought and judicious note-taking. The library should be used freely.

3. *Preparation of the outline.* The outline may be brief, but it should be very definite and logical.

4. *Development of the oration.* This follows the plan of the development of the theme outline. *Unity, coherence, and emphasis in the sentence, the paragraph, and the whole oration should, of course, receive the most careful attention.*

5. *Revision.* In the revision the student should criticize his own work closely, to see if he has chosen the best methods of appeal, the most logical arrangement of the parts, and the best possible words.

Suppose, for example, that the student is to write an oration of seven hundred words, on a subject chosen by himself. After the rejection of several subjects, as being uninteresting, hackneyed, or beyond his reach, he may decide to write about The Literary Society. The subject is too broad and general, so he limits it in this way: "The Scope of the High School Literary Society." He may have a strong desire to see such a society started in his own High School. He thinks carefully about his own views and notes them somewhat in this way:

1. Pleasant social discussions,

2. Individual and class competition,

3. Study in a new and attractive form.

He may be invited to attend meetings of the literary societies of other high schools. At one of these meetings he may see the work of a small and exclusive number of congenial young people, who meet to read and discuss modern fiction. At another he observes the more formal work of a society which includes half the school. The rules of parliamentary procedure are carefully observed; the program includes a brief report of current political topics, a paper on the new books of the month, and a debate on the subject, "Resolved that the free public library is a more potent factor in education than the free public school." The student may be somewhat puzzled, thinking that one method of conducting the literary society is too narrow, and the other too broad, to suit him. He next consults his own principal and other men who have observed the working of such societies. When he finds sufficient material to help him, he turns his thought toward making his outline. The following is one pupil's outline on this subject:

Example of Oratory Outline

The Scope of the High-School Literary Society

  A. Membership

  B. Objects

    1. Breadth of culture

    2. Individuality of expression

    3. Social relaxation

  C. Frequency of meetings

  D. Programs

After the development of these topics into paragraphs of suitable length, the work was ready for completion by revision.

Familiar Forms of the Oration

The most familiar forms of the oration are the plea, the political speech, the sermon, and the lecture. Although the student may never be called upon to write just these forms, they are worth studying, since the methods employed may be used whenever needed in any kind of oration.

The Plea

This is most often used by the lawyer when he is trying to influence the verdict of a judge or a jury. There are various types of the modern plea, but some suggestion of the following elements is commonly to be found:

1. An informal opening which will remove any feeling of distance or restraint on the part of the judge or the jury.

2. A criticism of the evidence of the other side, in which it is attacked as much as possible.

3. A summing up of the lawyer's own evidence, in which the fragments given by various witnesses are woven into a clear and forceful argument.

4. A conclusion, which is appropriate to the occasion varying from a concise restatement of the case to an eloquent appeal to the feelings of the hearers. The most important requisites of the plea are earnestness and clearness.

The following quotation from Daniel Webster's plea in the case of the Commonwealth vs. Knapp illustrates an effective restatement of the pleader's case:

Example

I think you cannot doubt that there was a conspiracy formed for the purpose of committing the murder, and who the conspirators were; that you cannot doubt that the Crowninshields and the Knapps were the parties in this conspiracy; that you cannot doubt that the prisoner at the bar knew that the murder was to be done on the night of the 6th of April; that you cannot doubt that the murderers of Captain White were the suspicious persons seen in and about Brown Street on that night; that you cannot doubt that Richard Crowninshield was the perpetrator of that crime; that you cannot doubt that the prisoner at the bar was in Brown Street on that night. If there, then it must be by agreement, to countenance, to aid the perpetrator. And if so, then he is guilty as *Principal*.

Gentlemen, your whole concern should be to do your duty and leave consequences to take care of themselves.

—Daniel Webster

The Political Speech

This form of oration varies from the colloquial sentences of the stump speaker to the polished periods of the statesman. Not all the able political leaders of our own or of any other country have had careful literary training. Not all have had the instinctive power over the minds and hearts of men that belongs to the true orator; but many of them, at least, have possessed this gift. The theme of such a speech is usually some political issue of present and pressing interest. Its purpose is to set forth the speaker's view of the subject as strongly as is at all consistent with fairness, and to make a manly appeal to the listeners to act in the matter as befits intelligent citizens and large-minded men. The basis of appeal is patriotism, love of justice, integrity, or expediency. The beginning and the ending are especially important, as in any theme. The thought expressed in the climax often lives in the hearts of men long after the words have died away. On the following page, an extract from the latter half of a famous speech merits study:

Suggestions for the Political Speech

1. What action is the speaker trying to influence?

2. What methods of appeal does he use?

3. In what particulars does he make use of their common experience?

4. Where and how does he use figures of metaphor, allusion, interrogation, exclamation, and climax?

5. Show the effect of variety in the length of the sentences.

6. What sentences especially well-illustrate the requirements of unity, coherence, and emphasis?

7. Discuss the use of purity, propriety, and precision in the matter of words.

8. What is the proportion of Anglo-Saxon words, and why?

Example

I have but one lamp by which my feet are guided; and that lamp is the lamp of experience. I know of no way of judging the future but by the past. And judging by the past, I wish to know what there has been in the conduct of the British ministry for the last ten years to justify those hopes with which gentlemen have been pleased to solace themselves and the House? Is it that insidious smile with which our petition has been lately received? Trust it not, sir; it will prove a snare to your feet. Suffer not yourselves to be betrayed with a kiss. Ask yourselves how this gracious reception of our petition comports with these war-like preparations which cover our waters and darken our land. Are fleets and armies necessary to a work of love and reconciliation? Have we shown ourselves so unwilling to be reconciled, that force must be called in to win back our love? Let us not deceive ourselves, sir. These are the implements of war and subjugation; the last arguments to which kings resort. I ask gentlemen, sir, what means this martial array, if its purpose be not to force us to submission? Can gentlemen assign any other possible motives for it? Has Great Britain any enemy in this quarter of the world, to call for all this accumulation of navies and armies? No, sir, she has none. They are meant for us; they can be meant for no other. They are sent over to bind and rivet upon us those chains which the British ministry have been so long forging. And what have we to oppose to them? Shall we try argument? Sir, we have been trying that for the last ten years. Have we anything new to offer on the subject? Nothing. We have held the subject up in every light of which it is capable; but it has been all in vain. Shall we resort to entreaty and humble supplication? What terms shall we find which have not been already exhausted? Let us not, I beseech you, sir, deceive ourselves longer. Sir, we have done everything that could be done to avert the storm which is now coming on. We have petitioned; we have remonstrated; we have supplicated; we have prostrated ourselves before the throne, and have implored its interposition to arrest the tyrannical hands of the ministry and parliament. Our petitions have been slighted; our remonstrances have produced additional violence and insult; our supplications have been disregarded; and we have been spurned, with contempt, from the foot of the throne. In vain, after these things, may we indulge the fond hope of peace and reconciliation. There is no longer any room for hope. If we wish to be free—if we mean to preserve inviolate those inestimable privileges for which we have been so long contending—if we mean not basely to abandon the noble struggle in which we have been so long engaged, and which we have pledged ourselves never to abandon until the glorious object of our contest shall be obtained, we must fight! I repeat it, sir, we must fight! An appeal to arms and to the God of Hosts is all that is left us! . . .

It is in vain, sir, to extenuate the matter. Gentlemen may cry peace, peace—but there is no peace. The war is actually begun! The next gale that sweeps from the north will bring to our ears the clash of resounding arms! Our brethren are already in the field! Why stand we here idle? What is it that gentlemen wish? What would they have? Is life so dear, or peace so sweet, as to be purchased at the price of chains and slavery? Forbid it, Almighty God! I know not what course others may take; but as for me, give me liberty, or give me death!

—Patrick Henry
Speech in the Convention of Delegates, March 28, 1775
Richmond, Virginia

The Sermon

In general this form of oration is a discourse based on a text from the Bible, appealing to conscience and religious instinct. The modern sermon is usually brief, logical, practical, and tinged with deep reverence and quiet feeling. Formal divisions, as Firstly, Secondly, etc., are no longer used, but the outline should be so clear in the mind of the speaker, that it may be promptly apparent to the listener. The following extract from a pupil's notebook, giving an outline written the day after the sermon had been heard, illustrates a general plan of this kind of oratory.

Example

Subject: The Opportunities of Youth
Text: "Let no man despise thy youth." 1 Timothy 4:12.

1. Introduction. Ever-increasing prominence of young people in many important fields of usefulness.

2. Youth is a time of special opportunity.

   a) Health and vigor make hard work possible and enjoyable.
   b) Enthusiasm makes all things seem possible.
   c) High ideals have not been lowered by many temptations.

3. The time of opportunity is the time of *responsibility*.

   a) To train patiently and thoroughly under the present leaders for intelligent, faithful service
   b) To carry to a grander development the departments of work already established
   c) To create new lines of work as fast as is expedient
   d) To use popularity for unselfish helpfulness

4. Conclusion. Each young person should ascertain what is his own particular gift, cultivate it carefully, and use it to the best possible advantage. "Neglect not the gift that is in thee."

The Lecture

Many so-called lectures are mere desultory talks, collections of anecdotes strung on a very slender thread afforded by the subject. A good lecture should have as definite and logical an outline, and should be in every way as practical, as any other form of oratory. It often closely resembles an essay, with such modifications as are natural when the words are to be heard instead of read. Its scope is broad; for the subjects may be drawn from every possible field, the appeal may be made to every conceivable motive, and the style may range from the humorous to the sublime. The appeal is rather impersonal, indirect, and subtle. Sometimes, indeed, it is entirely omitted, especially when the subject is merely entertaining. The following selection gives an interesting example of this form of oratory:

Example

When we come to think about the matter, it is plain that industrial partnerships are founded upon the surest principle of human nature—self-interest. There can, I think, be but four motives which can operate upon a workman.

1. Fear of dismissal

2. Hope of getting higher wages or better employment

3. Good-will to his employer, and desire to fulfill his bargain honestly

4. Direct self-interest in the work

The first of these, no doubt, is sufficient to prevent the workman from being much below the average of efficiency, but it cannot do more. The second is a powerful incentive where an employment allows of many grades, and promotion is free and depends on merit. In many of the ordinary handicraft employments, however, both these motives are to a great extent relaxed by the regulations of the unions, which favor the equal payment of all moderately efficient workmen, and yield a strong support to those who are in their opinion wrongfully dismissed. The third motive is really operative to a greater extent than we should suppose, but is not one that we can expect to trust. The fourth motive—direct interest in the work done—is entirely excluded by the present mode of payment, which leaves all profit to the master. It is upon this motive that the partnership principle depends. So far, indeed, is the principle from being a new one, that it lies at the basis of all ordinary relations of trade and private enterprise. The very opponent of industrial partnerships argues upon the ground that the employer must have all the profit because it is requisite to compensate him for all the trouble and skill expended in management; in short, that he must have powerful self-interest in the matter. But it may be safely answered that the men have so many means of injuring it by strikes and contentions, that it is entirely for the interest of the employer to buy their exertions and good-will with a share of profits.

— W. Stanley Jevons
"Industrial Partnerships"

Debate

Scope of the Debate

The debate is based on exposition, but has peculiarities of form which are of so much importance that it is usually classified by itself. A debate furnishes the arguments, or logically reasoned expositions, upon both sides of a question. The reasoning should be as logical and inevitable as possible. The speakers on each side endeavor to show the weakness or falsity of their opponents' position as well as to maintain their own.

Subjects for Debate

Much loss of time and bitterness of feeling would be prevented if disputants remembered that some subjects are unsuited for argumentation. A subject for debate should have two sides, upon either of which much may reasonably be said. Moreover, it should be a subject about which it is possible to get sufficiently reliable facts to form a basis for argument. This requirement, however, does not exclude every subject that calls for the use of the imagination.

It often happens in a debate that the two sides fail to "clinch." The affirmative discusses one phase of the subject, the negative discusses another; the listeners feel that the contestants are not face to face, discussing precisely the same proposition. Such debates often result from failure to limit the subject properly, or from failure to agree on a definition of each term in the subject.

Two Methods of Reasoning

Two methods are in general use: the deductive and the inductive. Each of these may be formally stated by a syllogism. As a matter of fact, this is usually implied instead of being directly stated. By the former method a syllogism consists of a general statement called a major premise, a specific statement called a minor premise, and a resulting proposition called a conclusion. The following is a syllogism arranged according to the deductive method of reasoning:

Major premise: All men are mortal.

Minor premise: John is a man.

Conclusion: John is mortal.

The chief danger with this formal method is that the general statement which constitutes the major premise may be false or inadequate.

The inductive method is much used by scientific men today. In this case the syllogism consists of a major premise, stating individual related facts which have been observed; a minor premise, consisting of a generalization about those facts; and a conclusion drawn from those premises. The following is a correct syllogism of this kind:

Major premise: Oak, pine, maple, ash, etc., will burn.

Minor premise: Oak, pine, maple, ash, etc., are wood.

Conclusion: All kinds of wood will burn.

The chief danger in this method of reasoning is that the reasoner cannot always observe facts enough to warrant an accurate conclusion.

Outline of the Debate

After the choice and limitation of the subject, and the division of the work among the disputants, the next step is the preparation of the outline, or brief, for each side. This outline contains the main points that each side will attempt to prove, and the line of argument to be followed in refuting the arguments of the opposing disputants. Below are given the briefs prepared by the leaders of the affirmative and the negative on the following question: "Resolved that compulsory laws regarding education should be passed."

Outline for the Affirmative

1. Introduction. Nature of the compulsory laws in the state of _____. Right of the state to do all that is necessary for its own safety.

2. Dangers arising from an uneducated citizenry.

3. An educated citizenry cannot be secured if education is left to parental caprice; for some parents are neglectful, others are avaricious, and others criminal.

4. An educated citizenry cannot be secured merely by providing free public schools, for not all will attend voluntarily.

5. An educated citizenry cannot be secured through the private schools, for not all of them teach what children most need to prepare them for the duties of citizenship.

6. Conclusion: Attendance in public schools or in private schools approved by state authorities should be compulsory.

Outline for the Negative

1. Introduction. Every man has the right to independence of action in matters which affect only himself. Results of a contrary doctrine.

2. An educated citizenry can be secured if education is left to parents, for all parents take pride in having their chil-

dren intelligent, prepared to earn good wages, and supplied with new resources and pleasures.

3. A much better education will be secured by pupils who attend school because they are interested in their work than by those who are forced against their will. Provide the schools and make them so interesting and profitable that the pupils will be glad to attend.

4. Conclusion. Compulsory education laws are not needed, and therefore should not be passed.

Order of Procedure in Debate

The order varies somewhat with the number of disputants, but the following is often used when there are four speakers.

1. First speaker on the affirmative, who states the case, outlines the argument for the affirmative, and proves all the points in the direct argument of his side.

2. First speaker on the negative, who outlines the argument for the negative, and proves all of the points in the direct argument of his side.

3. Second speaker on the negative, who refutes or disproves the arguments of the affirmative.

4. Second speaker on the affirmative, who refutes the arguments of the negative, and sums up the case as he thinks it has been proved by his own side. No new arguments are allowed to be introduced by this speaker, as the other side would have no opportunity to answer.

Ideas for Practicing Composition in the Elementary School

Word Artists at Work: Writing Assignments

Read all directions carefully. Follow all directions. Think carefully. Use a dictionary and a thesaurus. Write your thoughts out thoroughly, giving all details and explaining with care. Proofread, make corrections, then have another person proofread. All work submitted must have a title, correct paragraph form, a conclusion, and well-developed ideas. Papers with more than three errors will not be considered until errors vanish. To be a Word Artist, work must be approved for publication.

Work diligently. Use good tools and your imagination. Proofread!

Descriptive Paragraphs

1. Describe one of the four seasons using all your senses.

2. Describe a person with distinctive characteristics.

3. Write a vivid description of the setting sun.

4. Sit outdoors in a woodsy spot and observe—then write your observations.

Exposition

1. Write a "How to _____" article about something you have mastered telling the steps in order, in detail.

2. Write an explanation of simple machines telling all types and giving examples.

3. Write an advice article on:

    a) How to make friends
    b) How to succeed in school
    c) How to organize a notebook

Poetry

Choose two of the following topics and write a poem:

1. Autumn leaves
2. Friends
3. Play
4. Families
5. Free choice

Drama

Write a one-act play or puppet show about: (choose one)

1. The school's rabbits escape

2. A historical incident (Paul Revere's ride)

3. A real-life adventure

Composition

Write a composition in several paragraphs about one of the following:

1. A continent you have studied or researched

2. A day in the life of an American school student

3. What you want to be when you grow up and how you will reach that goal

"Priming the Pump" for Composition Writing: Clustering

In *Writing the Natural Way*, a 1983 J. P. Tarcher publication, Gabriele Rico puts forth a method of "natural writing" that begins with wholeness and sparks the creative process. She calls the process "clustering." It consists of putting the topic in a word circled in the middle of a blank page, then clustering ideas that spill and radiate outward from the center. The process causes a shift from a sense of randomness to a sense of direction in preparation for writing a composition. The practice of the process with students, according to Rico, "demonstrates a coherence, unity, and sense of wholeness, a recurrence of words and phrases, ideas, or images that reflect pattern sensitivity; an awareness of the nuances of language rhythms; a significant and natural use of images and metaphors; and a powerful "creative tension."

This method used in the Pre-Writing step of composition writing (see "The Writing Process," chapter six) helps tremendously with "inventing or combining ideas" as it gives a visual organizational technique that helps students overcome the writer's block that a blank page sometimes projects. It gives a concrete tool to the otherwise abstract arrangement of ideas apart from outlining which requires organizational ability rather than fostering it.

"Any word can become a storm center of meanings, sounds, and associations, radiating out indefinitely like ripples in a pool. . . . A nucleus word or short phrase acts as the stimulus for recording all the associations that spring to mind in a very brief period of time." (Rico, pp. 29–30)

The "Clustering" exercise on p. 280 demonstrates the use of the technique in the Pre-Writing step and then the finished product:

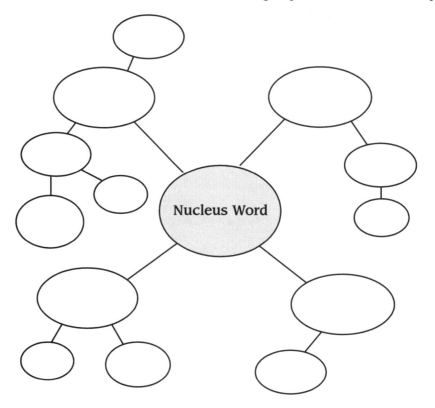

Concrete Poetry

By J. Barnes
Fourth Grade

Fourth Grade Letter-Writing
Williamsburg Field Study Summary

The essayist Francis Bacon wrote many years ago: "Reading maketh a man full, speaking—a ready man, but writing maketh a man exact!" A learning experience such as we had in Williamsburg on our Field Study with three historic interpreters was a very inspiring event. Williamsburg is a unique experience because there are no other resort areas in America that are as extensive in the recreation of life in America's colonial period. We saw, heard, touched, smelled, and even tasted colonial life yesterday in a way most American children don't have the privilege of doing. You learned many things that, if you don't record them now, will fade away from your memory.

As inspired scholars, let us summarize and record this tremendous learning experience by writing a letter. Pretend you are a young man or lady living in the Colony of Virginia and your parents have sent you to the College of William and Mary in Virginia's capital, Williamsburg. You have just arrived in Williamsburg from your plantation and now will write a letter to "Honor'd Papa" (much as John Q. Adams did when he was a young man), telling him about your adventure of traveling through the wilderness, of your impressions of city life and thanking him for the opportunity to study at the College with men such as George Wythe, Thomas Jefferson, and George Mason.

Write your summary in the form of a letter using the following guidelines:

1. Decide where your family plantation is and describe your journey to Williamsburg with your father's servant on board a carriage or coach. How long did it take? Who traveled with you? What did you see? What was the weather like? Where there any mishaps?

2. Describe your first impressions of Williamsburg. What is the basic layout of the city? What are the buildings like? How is life different or the same as life on your plantation? What is your favorite building and why? Did you see any Burgesses in town? Any signs of royalty? What kind of items are for sale in the General Store?

3. Describe your lodgings and roommate at college. Have you met any of the professors?

4. Thank your parents for the privilege of studying at the College of William and Mary.

5. Sign your letter.

6. You may illustrate your letter if you wish.

Student Work Inspired by Poetry

The fourth grade students presented the following work in history class in response to a lesson on colonial craftsmen that included the study of Longfellow's *The Village Blacksmith*. They were invited to write a composition or a poem describing the blacksmith.

The Village Blacksmith

[Notice use of Longfellow's vocabulary.]

A village blacksmith is a strong hard worker.
He works with his brawny arms.
He holds the sledge hitting the iron.
He works really hard all day trying to make
　　some use of the iron.
He is so very kind to the children that
　　come by each afternoon to try to catch the
　　sparks when he hits the iron with his sledge.

—Aaron

The Greatest Blacksmith

[Notice the rhythm inspired by Longfellow's art.]

This nice blacksmith
Fun and loving
Strong and tender,
See him coming
Down the road.
Let us greet him!
Come on, come on!
Let us meet him!
Bring a smile on your face!
Bring him toward the village place.

—Tasha

Fourth Grade
Colonial America Christian History Paper

*True education results in a free and independent man, able to exercise liberty of
conscience and who is well-developed in Christian character. Equipped with the tools
of lifelong learning, he is wholly literate and able to reason Biblically!*

—Carole Adams

Purpose

Learn how to research and write a paper
with guidance.

Study a specific area of interest in America's colonial period.

Due Dates

Selection of topic due February 4

Working outline of paper due February 14

Completed paper due February 27

Requirements

1. Cursive handwriting in black pen only;
   no computers, word processors, or
   typewriters to be used.

2. Title page to include:

   Title of paper

   Your name, grade, due date

   Subject and teacher

3. Text of paper should be written on one
   side of notebook paper: minimum of
   five (5) pages of text.

4. Vocabulary page defining any word
   you had to consult a dictionary to
   understand. Do not use words in this
   paper you do not understand!

5. Hand-drawn illustrations and maps

6. Bibliography: Alphabetized list of
   books, articles, and resources used to
   research and write the paper.

Text

1. Introductory paragraph to the period
   of Colonial America

2. Paragraph introducing the reader to
   your subject

3. Describe how your subject came to
   the colonies with a brief history of its
   development and growth in Europe.

4. Describe your subject.

5. Tell how the continent of North
   America affected the development
   and growth of your subject in the
   colonies.

6. Include the individuals God used in
   your subject.

7. Describe the influence of your subject
   on the growth of the colonies.

8. Did it help lay a foundation or hinder
   God's purposes for a new nation?

9. What particular character qualities
   would be needed?

10. Concluding paragraph

January 27, 1989

Dear Fourth Grade Parents,

This paper should reflect the student's ability to research and write about a subject that interests him with a minimum of help from his parents. The body of the paper is not to be copied text from resources. For some of the students this is a first step in researching and writing and may be difficult. Please assist your child only as necessary. I hope that this assignment will provide a learning process that will faithfully serve your child's love of learning and researching all his life.

Please know that I am assisting them in the classroom and have many resources available on the back table. Please don't hesitate to call upon me for any reason. I am happy to help in any way. The students are marbling paper in art class to use as covers for their papers. I will provide folders for each child.

Please initial at the bottom of the page indicating that you are aware of this project and return to me by February 4th. Please assist your child in selecting a topic and meeting the deadlines. Thank you for all you do at home to promote excellence in all that we do in the curriculum.

For Christ, His Story in America,

- -

Student's Name: _____

Topic: _____

Parent's Signature_____Date: _____

Fifth Grade Essay
Christian History Field Study Tour Evaluation
The Nation's Capital

This essay on our Christian History Field Study Tour of Washington, D.C., will be graded and weighted as a test score for this report card period. This essay will serve as a record of your tour with your classmates, which should be a special memory throughout your life as you recall all the delightful moments of touring your nation's capital as a young student. Of the three areas of "thinking governmentally"—**I plan** (legislative), **I do** (executive), and **I evaluate** (judicial)—only the evaluation is left to complete.

Please consider and ponder your responses carefully and remember to write in paragraph form using complete sentences. Begin each paragraph with a topic sentence, include supporting sentences, and end with a concluding sentence. Use your notes, your sketches, and any materials you collected on your tour.

Introductory Paragraph: Please give a brief history of your nation's capital, describing when it came into existence, where it is geographically located, and some of the interesting details of its design and basic architectural style.

Paragraph 2: Relate the date of your tour, with whom you toured, and describe the weather. Tell your overall impressions of the city. What was the spirit of the city—welcoming and friendly? uninviting and cold? bustling and busy? etc. What did you experience as you toured throughout the day?

Paragraph 3: Describe the three buildings of the three branches of government that we studied in history class: executive, legislative, and judicial. Relate some of the interesting details of touring these buildings. Did you see any external signs of the faith of your forefathers in them? Describe what you saw. Write details.

Paragraph 4: Describe your meeting with our U.S. Senator. Whom else did you meet or see of national prominence?

Paragraph 5: Describe the National Archives Building and the historic documents of liberty that you saw. What were your impressions of seeing these valuable and historic documents? To what extent has your nation gone to protect them from destruction? Why do you think this has been done?

Paragraph 6: Describe the monuments that you saw. What was your favorite one? Tell why. (You may want to quickly sketch it.)

Paragraph 7: Summarize the day in Washington, D.C. Why is Washington, D.C., described by many as the most beautiful capital of any nation in the world? Relate your favorite moment of the day. How did we experience the influence of secular humanism that George Washington and Thomas Jefferson would not have experienced? What is the solution to restoring our nation's character back to its Christian foundation? How do you think God would like to use you in this way?

Paragraph 8: Conclusion.

The Research Paper

1. In the fifth grade, students should be taught and guided by the teacher through the process of drafting and completing a research project with the goal of writing a research paper independently in the sixth grade.

2. The goals of the guided research paper are to:

   a) Teach students how to research and write about a topic with the minimum of adult help;

   b) Provide a learning experience that will teach students the process of researching to serve them all their life.

3. The body of the paper is not to be copied text from resources. This may prove to be difficult at first for many students.

4. Guidelines for the teacher:

   a) Select a general topic from the history or science curriculum and type a list of suggested titles.

   b) Type an overview of the research paper listing the requirements and each component with its due date, providing adequate time to complete each component.

   c) Send a parent letter home with the overview alerting parents about the assignment and requesting their involvement.

   d) Visit a large library and teach students how to use the library.

   e) Help students locate books and resources in the library.

   f) Teach students how to collect facts and bibliographic information on note cards.

   g) Provide class time to draft the outline, giving assistance.

3. Text requirements:

   a) Introduction

   b) Body of Text

   c) Conclusion

4. Final draft requirements:

   a) Title Page

   b) Outline used as the Table of Contents

   c) Text of the paper (which may be typed by the student) double-spaced on one side of the paper with pages numbered.

   d) Five (5) page minimum of text

   e) Christian history timeline

   f) Bibliography page to include three (3) sources

   g) Report cover

5. See the following pages for sample assignments.

Fifth Grade
History Research Project
American Enterprise and Invention

Subject

American Enterprise and Invention

Tools of Research

Library books, encyclopedias, articles on subject, Webster's 1828 *Dictionary*, notes from class, index cards

Requirements

March 22	Select topic after discussion with parents. _____Parents please initial and return by March 23.
March 23	Visit the library with a teacher for books and resources.
April 10	Working outline with note cards and bibliography cards
April 17	Rough draft including outline and bibliography
April 24	Assignment Due!

Final Draft Requirements

1. Title page

2. Outline used as a Table of Contents

3. Text of the paper (which may be typed by student) double-spaced on one side of paper with pages numbered

4. Five (5) page minimum of text

5. Illustrations (hand-drawn only)

6. Christian History Timeline

7. Bibliography page to include three (3) sources

8. Report cover

Text Requirements

1. Introduction: Introduce reader to the period of America's history in which the flowering of our Republic occurred; describe it and the internal causes and external effects. Define enterprise and invention and the history of the explosion of creativity in the United States.

2. Body of Text: Brief history of chosen subject to include the need, the idea, the development of the invention or product; inventor and his character; a Christian history timeline; a description of the invention; illustration(s).

3. Conclusion: Describe whether the invention had a positive or a negative effect in fulfilling God's ordained purposes for this nation; the influence of the chosen subject on America and her citizens; did it aid in advancing or hindering the Gospel and liberty for the individual?

Suggested Topics
(Student may select another subject with approval.)

1. A Great American Character and His Influence: Thomas A. Edison; Charles Lindbergh; Eli Whitney, etc.

2. Contrasting Two Captains of Industry: Eli Whitney and J. D. Rockefeller, etc.

3. Fathers of American Industry and Their Influence: Samuel Slater, E. I. duPont, Eli Whitney, Robert Fulton, John Stevens, Cyrus McCormick, etc.

4. The Locomotive and Its Effect on Travel in America

5. Elias Howe and the Sewing Machine

6. Alexander Graham Bell: Father of the Telephone

7. Charles Goodyear: Father of the Rubber Industry

8. Thomas Edison: Father of the Electrical Industry

9. Eli Whitney and the Cotton Gin

10. The Wright Brothers and the Airplane

11. Charles and Frank Duryea and the Gasoline Car

12. Cyrus McCormick and the Reaper

13. John Deere and His Singing Plow

14. Lee de Forest: Father of the Radio

15. The Electrical Revolution: Henry, Farraday, Morse, Edison, Tesla

16. Samuel Morse and the Telegraph

17. The Development of the Ironclads and Their Effect on America

18. Westinghouse and the Air Brake

19. Simon Lake: The Development of the Submarine

20. Edwin Drake and the Petroleum Industry

21. Charles Martin Hall and the Aluminum Industry

22. David Wilkinson: Father of the Machine Tool Industry

23. The Role of Women in American Industry and Enterprise

24. John Stevens: Father of American Railroads

25. The Development of Mass Production and the Assembly Line

26. John Audubon: American Painter

27. The History of Illustration in America: Pyle and Wyeth

28. The Flowering of the Printed Word in America

Sample Student Composition from Clustering Exercise

Assignment:

Using a character in *Ivanhoe*, show the need for a written law and limited government in England.

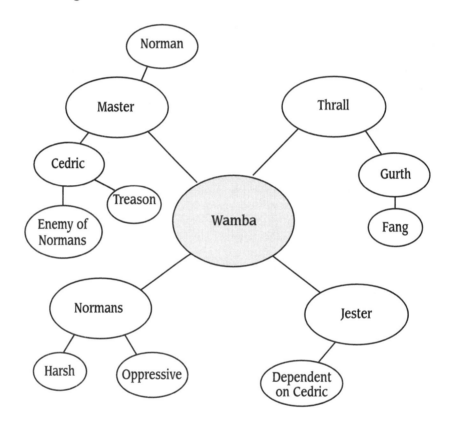

The Cruel Normans

I am Wamba, a thrall of Cedric the Saxon. I have come to you to complain about the oppression and unnecessary harshness of the Normans. My fellow swineherd, Gurth, has experienced a great deal of this conflict. The claws of his dog, Fang, have been cut off by the Normans. Now he can no longer herd his sheep. The king does not realize that the food on his plate comes from the slaving Saxons!

My master is an "enemy" of the Normans and is quite boisterous about it. There is a chance he could be killed for treason or some other accusation. Then I would be out of a job, and since I'm a jester, jobs would be scarce. If that happened, I would be out of money, food, and a roof over my head. So I continue my complaint about the Normans ruling a Saxon-inhabited country. The need for law to make justice for all is needed in England.

—S. Morse
Sixth Grade

Seventh Grade Oration
"Friendship"

People might ask what friendship is. In his original dictionary, Noah Webster said, "True friendship is a noble and virtuous attachment." Noble and virtuous means having general moral excellence, knowing and doing what is right and good. That means that in order to have a friendship that will last, you need to have dignified attachment with a friend.

The Bible also tells us that Abraham is repeatedly called a friend of God. We know that Abraham had a covenant with God. A covenant is a promise, an enforceable agreement, a vow made by both parties. God knew he could depend on Abraham, and Abraham knew he could trust in God. So friendship does require honesty, diligence, and love, a deep caring for the well-being of another. Proverbs 17 says "a friend loveth at all times." This isn't always easy and requires commitment and determination.

It's important to take time in choosing your friends. You must see how they act, if they're someone you would want to be like. Look for common interests like sports, favorite school subjects, or hobbies. It says in Proverbs 18:24 that, "A man that hath friends must show himself friendly. . . ." To be a friend it helps to have good eye contact, this shows openness and interest as does being a good listener. Make sure your body language is positive, show interest in what the other person has to say. Show respect for others and their opinions and make sure that it's not a one-way conversation. The exchange of ideas will benefit you both. These social skills will help your communication, and without communication you can not have a relationship with God or anyone. Proverbs 18:24 goes on to say, "There is a friend that sticketh closer than a brother." This means Jesus is our truest and closest friend so that you should also be searching and striving to get closer to God.

Friends find ways to support and help each other. Friends share in the joy of your triumphs and soften the sting of defeat. The joy shared by friends is joy doubled. This world would be a lonely place without friends. I thank God for friends.

C. Carroll
1998

High School Portfolio Project

Christian History Research Paper and Dramatic Presentation

The Portfolio Project represents each high school student's scholarship and study of universal history, literature, and the fine and performing arts, as well as his proficiency in written and oral communication. It is designed to challenge each student to draw upon his creativity, individual giftings, Biblical reasoning, and communication skills. The Portfolio Project is a multi-disciplinary academic assignment which is designed to:

- Build scholastic productivity and enterprise within the character of each student;

- Lead the student toward independent thinking and problem solving;

- Develop the habit of using primary sources in research and study;

- Interweave the disciplines of literature, historical research, the fine and performing arts, and writing in completing a research paper and a dramatic presentation;

- Provide the student with the opportunity to refine communications skills in a creative avenue that best reflects his God-given talents and individuality;

- Provide an opportunity to learn how to work collegially on an assignment.

The subject for research must employ documented primary sources in the written paper as well as the script. It should reflect God's hand in history, indicating whether the event or character advanced or hindered the Gospel and liberty for the individual.

The Portfolio Project format may be a monologue or a dialogue, written creatively to be presented dramatically. The student(s) must create a simple backdrop, use appropriate props and costume(s) that depict authenticity, and weave the fine

arts into the presentation in some way. A Prologue should precede the dramatic presentation.

The student should select the topic for the Portfolio Project first and then base the research paper upon this topic. The English teacher will teach "How to Develop a Thesis," as well as "How to Write a Research Paper Using the A.P.A. Format." Time is given in the weekly schedule for research and writing. Students should plan to devote time to locating primary source documents either through the teacher or local libraries.

The sixteen-week Portfolio Project includes:

1. Research Paper, designed to cultivate and refine the following skills:

    a) Developing a thesis: selection should be approved by the first month of school.

    b) Researching from at least three primary sources: the student will learn how to locate and use them.

    c) Writing a six-page research paper (plus title page, abstract, reference page, and any appendixes) using the A.P.A. format. (One of the books read may be used for the quarterly book review English requirement.)

    d) Due end of the semester

2. Portfolio Project—To be created and documented after the research paper is completed for a ten-minute dramatic presentation:

    a) The theme should reflect God's hand in history, be written from a Providential view, and indicate whether the chosen event advanced or hindered the Gospel and liberty for the individual.

b) Format: monologue or dialogue in two separate presentations:

(1) Written Presentation: should follow the A.P.A. format, with title page, abstract, prologue and script, and should include character(s), staging, props, costume(s), and music; list of references; appendix(es) including the cost to produce.

(2) Dramatic Presentation to the Class: should include prologue, monologue or dialogue; staging which should be simple and depict authenticity, and include literature, music, and art woven into the presentation; a simple costume fashioned and worn depicting authenticity.

c) Written presentation and oral presentation.

The Portfolio Project should be organized, formatted, and typed for a ten-minute presentation in the following way:

1. Written Presentation: Each of the following lettered items represents a new page in the written presentation to include a title centered at the top of the paper.

    a) Title Page: The format for Portfolio Project Title Page is the same as the Research Paper and should follow the A.P.A. Manual. If two or more students have collaborated, each student must sign the title page after his typed name.

    b) Abstract: The abstract is a 100 to 125-word synopsis of the Portfolio Project formatted the same way as for a Research Paper. It should include the historical setting, event, character(s), and primary sources incorporated.

c) Prologue: The purpose of the prologue is to link the student's Research Paper (with complete title and date of paper) to the Portfolio Project and should briefly explain why the theme of the Portfolio Project was chosen.

d) Script: The script should be written in conversational style. Primary sources must be included. When quoted verbatim, a reference citation (A.P.A. format) should follow.

e) Treatment: Each of the following items should be left-hand justified and underlined on the page. The student should briefly describe or list the necessary items for each category: Character(s); Staging; Props; Costumes; Music.

f) References

g) Appendix(es), including cost sheet

2. Dramatic Presentation: Each student will present his portfolio project to the class. A separate grade will be given for the dramatic presentation. Several will be selected to be presented to the entire high school. The staging should be designed so that backdrop and props can be assembled for presentation in two minutes.

    a) Prologue: The student(s) will begin by introducing the audience to the historical setting, event, character(s), and primary sources incorporated.

    b) Monologue or Dialogue: The monologue or dialogue should be delivered with dramatic elocution. The student may not read his or her typed copy "word for word." Occasionally looking at the script for cues is acceptable.

High School Thesis

*The Principle Approach® High School Thesis
is dedicated to and guided by these ideals:*

Y ou go to a great school not so much for knowledge as for arts and habits; for the habit of attention, for the art of expression, for the art of assuming at a moment's notice a new intellectual position, for the art of entering quickly into another person's thoughts, for the habit of submitting to censure and refutation, for the art of indicating assent or dissent in graduated terms, for the habit of regarding minute points of accuracy, for the art of working out what is possible in a given time, for taste, for discrimination, for mental courage, and for mental soberness.

—William Johnson Cory, 1823–1892,
English Poet, Master at Eton

One of the most critical changes we have witnessed in American education has been the change away from the reasoning, writing, reflecting ability so prominent in the generations that produced the Declaration of Independence, the Constitution of the United States of America, the Monroe Doctrine, and other documents. This ability to define a philosophy of government in writing was the result of a colonial education in principles, leading ideas, and their application to the field of civil government—America's unique contribution.

—Rosalie Slater,
Architect of The Principle Approach,
Christian History of the American Revolution

The High School Thesis is the culminating academic experience for each graduating senior. Its purpose is to guide the Principle Approach senior through the experience of developing, researching, writing, and defending a personal position on a worthy idea in a way that manifests his or her Biblical worldview and Christian scholarship, thus equipping the student for a lifetime of presenting and defending his faith and worldview. Each senior is assigned a Thesis Advisor who is a StoneBridge faculty member. The role of the Thesis Advisor is to "walk the student through the process" of researching and writing a thesis and to assist the student in preparing for the oral presentation and defense. The thesis research paper and oral presentation are graded and recorded on the student's permanent record.

Defined in Webster's 1828 *Dictionary*:

Thesis, n. [L. *thesis*; Gr. , a position, from to set]

1. A position or proposition which a person advances and offers to maintain, or which is actually maintained by argument; a theme; a subject.

2. In *logic*, every proposition may be divided into *thesis* and *hypothesis*. Thesis contains the thing affirmed or denied, and hypothesis the conditions of the affirmation or negation.

The basic requirements of the High School Thesis are for the senior to:

1. Research, write, and submit in typed A.P.A. format a twenty (20) page thesis;

2. Prepare and deliver a twenty-minute oral presentation of his thesis to the Thesis Advisory Council;

3. Orally defend the position by fielding Thesis Advisory Council questions.

Thesis Objectives

1. Enter a mentoring relationship which provides an avenue for fostering inspiration and guides the development, writing, and defense of the student's thesis.

2. Enable a season in the life of the student for discovery:

   a) Pivotal point in the student's life where childish thinking advances into the world of adult ideas and thinking;

b) First philosophical contribution;

c) Affect his own culture;

d) Original thinking

3. Demonstrate the mastery of Christian scholarship through the 4-R's: Research, Reason, Relate, and Record.

4. Produce a polished presentation and oral defense for future scholarly discourse.

Format

1. High School Thesis presented and assigned to the students at the conclusion of their junior year.

2. Thesis selected and presented to the Advisory Council in September of the senior year.

3. Advisor and mentoring schedule assigned during the senior year.

4. Four-R the thesis: Research, Reason, Relate, and Record.

5. Written thesis submitted mid-May.

6. Position defended orally before the Thesis Advisory Council.

7. Several theses selected by the Thesis Advisory Council to be presented orally to the High School student body.

8. Completion transcribed on the high school diploma and academic transcript.

APPENDIX

References and Resources
Where no publication information is given, any edition is acceptable; Foundation for American Christian Education is cited as F.A.C.E.

Abe Lincoln Grows Up, Carl Sandburg. Harcourt, Brace & World, 1954.

Abigail Adams: First Lady of Faith and Courage, Evelyn Witter. Milford, Mich.: Mott Media, 1976. [See F.A.C.E.'s *Abigail Adams Teacher Guide* by Rosalie J. Slater.]

The Abolition of Man, or Reflections on Education with Special Reference to the Teaching of English in the Upper Forms of Schools, C. S. Lewis. New York: Macmillan Publishing Co., 1947.

Abraham Lincoln, Ingri and Edgar Parin d'Aulaire

Aesop's Fables. Introduction by G. K. Chesterton. Franklin Watts, 1969.

The Agony and the Ecstasy, Irving Stone

All God's Children and Blue Suede Shoes: Christians and Popular Culture, Kenneth A. Myers. Wheaton, Ill.: Crossway Books, 1989.

Alone, Admiral Richard E. Byrd

American Dictionary of the English Language, Noah Webster. 1828 facsimile ed. San Francisco: F.A.C.E., 1967.

American History in Verse. Edited by Burton Stevenson. Greenville, S.C.: Bob Jones University Press, 1975.

An American Life, Ronald Reagan. New York: Simon and Schuster, 1990.

American Literature: A Study of the Men and the Books That in the Earlier and Later Times Reflect the American Spirit, William J. Long. Boston: Ginn & Co., 1913, 1964.

The American Pageant: A History of the Republic, Thomas A. Bailey. Boston: D. C. Heath & Co., 1956.

America's Spelling and Reading with Riggs. Beaverton, Oreg.: The Riggs Institute, 1992.

The Annotated Mother Goose. Introduction by William S. and Ceil Baring-Gould. [Out-of-print]

The Annotated Shakespeare, A. L. Rowse. 1978.

The Anti-Federalists and the Constitutional Convention Debate. Edited by Ralph Ketchum.

Apollo to the Moon, Gregory P. Kennedy. New York: Chelsea House Publishers, a division of Main Line Books Co., 1992.

The Art of Persuasion, Linda Bridges and William F. Rickenbacker. National Review Book, 1991.

The Autobiography and Other Writings by Benjamin Franklin. Edited by Russel B. Nye. Boston: Houghton Mifflin Co., 1958.

Bambi, Felix Salten

A Basic History of the United States, Carson. 5 vols.

The Bay Psalm Book

Beacon Lights of History, John Lord. 1885. New York: William H. Wise & Co., 1920. [10 to 15 vols. depending on edition; out-of-print but available through book search.]

Bede's Ecclesiastical History of the English Nation. New York: Dutton, 1970.

Ben Hur: A Tale of the Christ, Lew Wallace

Benjamin Franklin, Ingri and Edgar Parin d'Aulaire. Doubleday & Co., 1950.

Benjamin West and His Cat, Grimalkin, Marguerite Henry. Illustrated by Wesley Dennis. Indianapolis: Bobbs Merrill Co., 1947. [See F.A.C.E.'s *Benjamin West Teacher Guide* by Rosalie J. Slater.]

Beowulf. Translated by Burton Raffel. New York: Mentor, 1963.

Bequest of Wings: A Family's Pleasure with Books, Annis Duff. Viking Press, 1954 [out-of-print].

Berlin Diary, William L. Shirer. 1941.

The Bible [in various versions]—the source and seedbed of every field of study. The Dickson New Analytical Study Bible [KJV] is recommended for its historic perspective.

[B & C] *The Bible and the Constitution of the United States of America*, Verna M. Hall and Rosalie J. Slater. San Francisco: Foundation for American Christian Education, 1983.

The Bible in English Literature, Edgar Whitaker Work. New York: Fleming H. Revell Co., 1917.

The Big Fisherman, Lloyd C. Douglas

The Book of Abigail and John: Selected Letters of the Adams Family, 1762–1784. Edited by L. H. Butterfield, Marc Friedlaender, and Mary-Jo Kline. Cambridge, Mass.: Harvard University Press, 1975.

The Book of Life. Arranged and edited by Newton Marshall Hall and Irving Frances Wood. 8 vols. Chicago: John Rudin & Co., [1923–1952 editions are recommended].

Canterbury Tales, Geoffrey Chaucer

Captain John Smith's America. Edited by Lankford.

Carry On, Mr. Bowditch, Jean Lee Latham. Houghton Mifflin Co., 1955. [See F.A.C.E.'s *Carry On, Mr. Bowditch Teacher Guide* by Rosalie J. Slater.]

The Children's Poets, Walter Barnes. Yonkers-on-Hudson: World Book Co., 1932.

A Child's Garden of Verse, Robert Louis Stevenson. 1885.

A Child's History of England, Charles Dickens. New York: The American News Co., 1880; Edited by John Richard Green. New York: Harper and Brothers, 1894.

Christian History. Periodical published by Christianity Today, Inc. For subscription information, call 800-873-6986, or write to P.O. Box 11618, Des Moines, IA 50340. The past 50 issues (12 years) are now available on a multi-media CD-ROM, call 800-806-7798.

[C & P] *The Christian History of the American Revolution: Consider and Ponder.* Compiled by Verna M. Hall. San Francisco: F.A.C.E., 1976.

[CHOC I] *The Christian History of the Constitution of the United States of America*, Vol. I: *Christian Self-Government.* Compiled by Verna M. Hall. San Francisco: F.A.C.E., 1960.

[CHOC II] *The Christian History of the Constitution of the United States of America*, Vol. II: *Christian Self-Government with Union.* Compiled by Verna M. Hall. San Francisco: F.A.C.E., 1962.

Christianity and the Constitution: Faith of Our Founding Fathers, John Eidsmoe. Grand Rapids, Mich.: Baker Books, 1987.

"Christopher Columbus: Christ-Bearer to the New World." F.A.C.E. syllabus by Rosalie J. Slater.

Christopher Columbus, Mariner, Samuel Eliot Morison. 1942. New York: A Meridian Book, New American Library, 1983.

Cinnabar, the One O'Clock Fox, Marguerite Henry. Illustrated by Wesley Dennis.

The Classic Fairy Tales. Compiled by Iona and Peter Opie.

The Classic Myths in English Literature and in Art, Charles Mills Gayley. 1911. Waltham, Mass.: Ginn and Co., 1967. [Based on Bulfinch's Age of Fable, 1855]

The Closing of the American Mind, Alan Bloom. Simon and Schuster, 1987.

Cobblestone, the History Magazine for Young People. Cobblestone Publishing, Inc., 7 School Street, Peterborough, NH 03458-1454, 800-821-0115. Secular presentation.

Come Over and Help Us, Rosalie Slater. San Francisco: F.A.C.E. [A drama based on John Eliot and Daniel Gookin]

The Coming of the Pilgrims, Told from Governor Bradford's First-hand Account, E. Brooks Smith and Robert Meredith. Boston: Little, Brown & Co., 1964.

The Complete Poetical Works of John Milton. Edited by Douglas Bush. Boston: Houghton Mifflin Co., 1965.

The Complete Works of Charles Dickens. Centennial edition, 36 vols. Geneva: Edito-Service, n.d.

Composition and Rhetoric, for Higher Schools, Sara E. H. Lockwood and Mary Alice Emerson. Boston: Ginn & Co., 1903.

The Country of the Pointed Firs, Sarah Orne Jewett. New York: Anchor Books, 1989.

The Courtship of Miles Standish, Henry Wadsworth Longfellow. [See poem and teacher's guide by Elizabeth L. Youmans.]

C. S. Lewis, Speaker and Teacher, Carolyn Keefe. Zondervan, 1971.

David Copperfield, Charles Dickens

Dear and Beloved Physician, Taylor Caldwell

Death Comes to the Archbishop, Willa Cather

The Deerslayer, James Fenimore Cooper [See F.A.C.E.'s *Deerslayer Teacher Guide* by Rosalie J. Slater.]

The Diary, Samuel Pepys

The Diary of Anne Frank, Anne Frank.

Discovery, Richard E. Byrd

Divine and Moral Songs for Children, Isaac Watts. [First printed in 1715.] Edited by Carris J. Kocher. Evensville, Tenn.: Cumberland Missionary Society, 1991.

Doorways to Poetry, Louis Untermeyer. Harcourt, Brace & World, 1938.

Drums, James Boyd. New York: Scribners, 1936.

The Education of James Madison: A Model for Today, Mary-Elaine Swanson. Montgomery, Ala.: Hoffman Education Center for the Family, 1992.

The Elements of Style, William Strunk, Jr. and E. B. White. Macmillan Publishing Co., 1972.

Emma Willard's Universal History [Photographic reproduction of *A System of Universal History in Perspective* by Emma Willard, 1839]. Denver, Colo.: The Mile-Hi Evangelist Press, 1974. Write to P.O. Box 275, Denver, CO 80201.

English Literature: Its History and Its Significance for the Life of the English-Speaking World, William J. Long. Boston: Ginn and Co., 1909, 1945.

Enjoyment of Literature, Ralph P. Boas and Edwin Smith. Harcourt, Brace, & World, 1934. [Out-of-print, but available through book search.]

Essays Old and New. Edited by Robert U. Jameson. 3d ed. New York: Harcourt, Brace & World, 1957.

An Etymological Dictionary of Modern English, Earnest Weekley. Dover Publications, 1967.

Everyday Life in Roman and Anglo-Saxon Times, M. and C. Quennell

Exodus, Leon Uris

The Faerie Queene, Edmund Spenser

Fairy Tales, Hans Christian Andersen

A Family Program for Reading Aloud, Rosalie June Slater. 2d ed. San Francisco: F.A.C.E., 1991.

Famous Authors for Young People, Ramon P. Coffman and Nathan G. Goodman. New York: Dodd, Mead & Co., 1943.

Famous British Poets, Sybil Norton and John Cournos. New York: Dodd, Mead & Co., 1952.

The Famous Literature of England and America. Philadelphia, Pa.: American Book and Bible House, 1899.

Favorite Poems, Old and New, Helen Ferris. Doubleday, 1957.

Fieldbook of the Revolution, Benson Lossing

Footprints of Time, Charles Bancroft. 1879.

Foxe's Book of Martyrs, John Foxe. Edited by Marie G. King. Old Tappan, N.J.: Fleming H. Revell Co., 1968, 1981.

The Genesis Flood, Henry Morris and John C. Whitcomb. Grand Rapids, Mich.: Baker Book House, [1961].

"The Gentle Boy," Nathaniel Hawthorne

Geoffrey Chaucer of England, Marchette Chute. E. P. Dutton, 1936.

George Washington, a Biography, Washington Irving. Edited and abridged with an introduction by Charles Neider. New York: Doubleday & Co., 1976.

The Glory and the Dream: Abraham Lincoln, before and after Gettysburg, Michael A. Musmanno. The Long House, 1967.

The Golden Treasury of the Best Songs and Lyrical Poems in the English Language, Francis Turner Palgrave. Oxford University Press, 1861; The Golden Treasury. American ed. Macmillan Co., 1928, 1956, 1967.

Grandfather's Chair, Nathaniel Hawthorne. 1841.

Great Men and Famous Women. Edited by Charles F. Horne. 10 vols. New York: 1894.

The Greek Treasure, Irving Stone

Grimms Fairy Tales. Pantheon Books, 1944.

Gulliver's Travels, Jonathan Swift

A Handbook to Literature, William Flint Thrall and Addison Hibbard. New York: Odyssey Press, 1936.

Hans Brinker, or the Silver Skates, Mary Mapes Dodge. [See F.A.C.E.'s *Hans Brinker Teacher Guide* by Rosalie J. Slater.]

Heidi, Johanna Spyri [See F.A.C.E.'s *Heidi Teacher Guide* by Rosalie J. Slater.]

The Home Book of Great Poetry, a Treasury of over One Thousand Favorite Poems. Compiled by Burton E. Stevenson. New York: Galahad Books, a division of Budget Book Service, 1995.

The Home Book of Verse for Young Folks, Compiled by Burton Egbert Stevenson. 1929. Holt, Rinehart and Winston, 1967.

The House at Pooh Corner, A. A. Milne

How Should We Then Live? The Rise and Decline of Western Thought and Culture, Francis A. Schaeffer. Old Tappan, N.J.: Fleming H. Revell Co., 1976.

How to Speak, How to Listen, Mortimer J. Adler. Macmillan, 1983.

How to Teach Spelling, Laura Rudginsky and Elizabeth Haskell. Cambridge, Mass.: Educator's Publishing Service, 1984.

Ideas Have Consequences, Richard Weaver. Chicago: University of Chicago Press, 1948.

Idols for Destruction: The Christian Faith and Its Confrontation with American Society, Herbert Schlossberg. Nashville, Tenn.: Thomas Nelson, 1983.

Idylls of the King, Alfred Lord Tennyson

The Iliad, Homer

Ivanhoe, Sir Walter Scott. [See F.A.C.E.'s *Sir Walter Scott Teacher Guide* by Rosalie J. Slater.]

Johann Sebastian Bach: The Boy from Thuringia, Opal Wheeler and Sybil Deucher.

John of the Mountains: Journals of John Muir

The Journal of Major George Washington. Facsimile edition published by the Colonial Williamsburg Foundation, Williamsburg, Va.; distributed by the University Press of Virginia, Box 3608, University Station, Charlottesville, VA 22903.

The Kid's Study Bible, NIrV. Zondervan, 1996.

Knickerbocker's History of New York, Washington Irving

The Lady of the Lake and Other Poems, Sir Walter Scott. [See F.A.C.E.'s *Sir Walter Scott Teacher Guide* by Rosalie J. Slater.]

The Last of the Mohicans, James Fenimore Cooper

Lavender's Blue: A Book of English Nursery Rhymes. Compiled by Kathleen Lines. New York: Oxford University Press, 1990.

Leif, the Lucky, Ingri and Edgar Parin d'Aulaire

Lessons in English, Sara E. H. Lockwood. Boston: Ginn & Co., 1890.

Letters from a Farmer in Pennsylvania, John Dickinson

The Life and Writings of Cicero

The Life of Columbus, Washington Irving

Life of Johnson, James Boswell

The Life of King Alfred, Asser

The Life Application Bible, King James Version

Lion of God, Taylor Caldwell

The Lion, the Witch, and the Wardrobe, C. S. Lewis

The Literature of the Bible, Leland Ryken. Grand Rapids, Mich.: Zondervan Publishing House, 1974.

Little House in the Big Woods, Laura Ingalls Wilder. [See F.A.C.E.'s *Little House Teacher Guide* by Rosalie J. Slater.]

Little Women, Louisa Alcott. [See F.A.C.E.'s *Little Women Teacher Guide* by Rosalie J. Slater.]

Lives of Bradford and Winthrop, Cotton Mather, Old South Leaflet No. 77. Boston: The Old South Association, 310 Washington Street, Boston, MA 02108.

Magnalia Christi Americana, Cotton Mather

The Making of American California: A Providential Approach, Dorothy Dimmick. Gilroy, Calif.: 1960.

Marguerite de Angeli's Book of Nursery and Mother Goose Rhymes. Doubleday & Co., 1979.

Matthew Fontaine Maury: Scientist of the Sea, Frances Williams

Matthew Henry's Commentary on the Whole Bible. Old Tappan, N.J.: Fleming H. Revell Co., n.d.

Men of Iron, Howard Pyle. New York: Airmont Books, 1965. [See F.A.C.E.'s *Men of Iron Teacher Guide* by Rosalie J. Slater.]

Men under the Sea, Edward Ellsberg. Westport, Conn.: Greenwood Press, 1981.

The Merchant of Venice. Adapted by Jennifer Mulhern. Silver Burdett Press, 1988.

Miracle at Philadelphia, Catherine Drinker Brown. Boston, Mass.: Little Brown & Co., 1973.

Morte d'Arthur, Sir Thomas Malory

Mother Carey's Chickens, Kate Douglas Wiggin. 1910. San Francisco: F.A.C.E. reprint, 1991.

My Antonia, Willa Cather. Boston: Houghton Mifflin Co., 1918.

Narrative of the Captivity and Restoration of Mrs. Mary Rowlandson

The Noah Plan History and Geography Curriculum Guide, Elizabeth L. Youmans. F.A.C.E., 1998.

The Noah Plan Literature Curriculum Guide, Rosalie J. Slater. F.A.C.E., 1997.

The Noah Plan Reading Curriculum Guide, Second Edition, Martha Shirley. Chesapeake, VA: F.A.C.E., 2005.

Noah Webster: Father of the Dictionary, Isabel Proudfit. Julian Messner, 1942.

Norton's Anthology of English Literature. Edited by M. H. Abrams et al. New York: W. W. Norton & Co., 1987.

The Notorious Jumping Frog of Calaveras County, Mark Twain

Now I Can Read Favorite Bible Stories, Rhona Pipe. Nashville, Tenn.: Thomas Nelson, 1995.

The Odyssey, Homer. Translated by Edward Fitzgerald.

The Odyssey of Homer. Translated by George Herbert Palmer. 1884. Cambridge, Mass.: The Riverside Press, Houghton Mifflin Co., 1949.

Of Plimoth Plantation, William Bradford. [See F.A.C.E.'s *Providential History Teacher Guide* by Rosalie J. Slater.]

The Oregon Trail, Francis Parkman

The Outcasts of Poker Flat, Bret Harte

The Outline of Literature. Edited by John Drinkwater.

Out of the Silent Planet, C. S. Lewis

The Oxford Book of Children's Verse. Edited by Iona and Peter Opie. Oxford: Oxford University Press, 1971.

The Oxford Book of English Verse, 1250–1918. Edited by Sir Arthur Quiller-Couch. Oxford: Clarendon Press, 1939.

The Oxford Companion to the English Language. Edited by Tom McArthur. Oxford: Oxford University Press, 1992.

The Oxford Dictionary of English Etymology. Edited by C. T. Onions. Oxford: Oxford University Press, 1995.

The Oxford Dictionary of Nursery Rhymes. Edited by Iona and Peter Opie. Oxford: Oxford University Press, 1951.

The Oxford Nursery Rhyme Book. Compiled by Iona and Peter Opie. Oxford: Oxford University Press, 1967.

The Oxford Shakespeare: The Complete Works of William Shakespeare. Edited by W. J. Craig. Dublin: Trinity College, 1905.

Paddle-to-the-Sea, Holling Clancy Holling. 1941. Boston: Houghton Mifflin Co., 1969.

Paradise Lost, John Milton. Viking Portable.

Patton: A Genius for War, Carlo d'Este. New York: Harper Collins Publishers, 1995.

Peter Pan, James M. Barrie

The Pilgrim's Progress, John Bunyan

Pillar of Iron, Taylor Caldwell

Pinocchio, Carlo Lorenzini Collodi. [See F.A.C.E.'s *Pinocchio Teacher Guide* by Rosalie J. Slater.]

Plimoth Plantation Day Packet, Elizabeth L. Youmans. F.A.C.E.

Pocahontas, Ingri and Edgar Parin d'Aulaire

Providential History Teacher Guide, by Rosalie J. Slater. F.A.C.E.

The Poems of Phillis Wheatley. Edited by Julian D. Mason, Jr. Chapel Hill, N.C.: University of North Carolina, 1966; 1989.

The Poetical Works of Longfellow. Houghton Mifflin Co., 1893; Cambridge edition, 1975.

Poetry selections from the works of:
Blake, William
Browning, Elizabeth Barrett and Robert
Bryant, William Cullen
Burns, Robert
Byron, George Gordon
Carroll, Lewis
Coleridge, Samuel Taylor
De la Mare, Walter
Dickens, Charles
Dickinson, Emily
Donne, John

Eliot, T. S.
Emerson, Ralph Waldo
Field, Eugene
Frost, Robert
Holmes, Oliver Wendell
Kipling, Rudyard
Longfellow, Henry Wadsworth
Lowell, James Russell
Milton, John
Poe, Edgar Allan
Rossetti, Christina
Sandburg, Carl
Scott, Sir Walter
Shakespeare, William
Shelley, Percy Bysshe
Stevenson, Robert Louis
Tennyson, Alfred Lord
Watts, Isaac
Whitman, Walt
Whittier, John Greenleaf
Wordsworth, William

Pride and Prejudice, Jane Austen

The Prince, Niccolo Machiavelli

Principia, Sir Isaac Newton

Quo Vadis? Henryk Sienkiewicz

A Reader's Guide to Religious Literature, E. Beatrice Batson. Chicago: Moody Press, 1968.

Reading between the Lines: A Christian Guide to Literature, Gene Edward Veith, Jr. Crossways Books, 1990.

The Real Personages of Mother Goose, Katherine Elwes Thomas. New York: Lothrop, Lee & Shepard Co., 1930.

Reminiscences, Douglas MacArthur

The Republic, Plato

The Rime of the Ancient Mariner, Coleridge

The Robe, Lloyd C. Douglas

Robinson Crusoe, Daniel Defoe [See F.A.C.E.'s *Robinson Crusoe Teacher Guide* by Rosalie J. Slater.]

The Roots of the American Republic, E. C. Wines. 1953. Reprint, Marlborough, N.H.: Plymouth Rock Foundation, 1997.

Rudiments of America's Christian History and Government, Rosalie J. Slater and Verna M. Hall. 2d ed. San Francisco: F.A.C.E., 1994.

The Scarlet Pimpernel, Baroness Orczy

Secret Garden, Frances Hodgson Burnett.

Select Translations from Old English Prose. Edited by Albert S. Cook and Chauncey B. Tinker. New York: Gordian Press, 1968. Reprint of 1908 ed.

Seven Came Through: Rickenbacker's Full Story, Captain Edward V. Rickenbacker. Doubleday & Co., 1943.

The Seven Laws of Teaching, John Milton Gregory. Baker Books, 1995.

Shakespeare's Knowledge and Use of the Bible, Charles Wordsworth. London: Smith, Elder Co., 1864.

A Short History of England, Edward P. Cheyney. 1904. Boston: Ginn and Co., 1960.

A Short History of the English People, John Richard Green. New York: Harper & Bros., 1882, 1894.

Short Stories. Edited by H. C. Schweikert. Harcourt Brace Jovanovich, 1934. [Out-of-print, but available through book search.]

Sir Walter Scott: Wizard of the North, Pearle Henriksen Schultz. New York: Vanguard Press, 1967. Reprinted by F.A.C.E. in 1998 [See F.A.C.E.'s *Sir Walter Scott Teacher Guide* by Rosalie J. Slater.]

The Sketch Book, Washington Irving

Songs of Innocence and Songs of Experience, William Blake

A Sound Curriculum in English Grammar: Guidelines for Teachers and Parents, Kenneth Oliver. Occasional Paper 23. Washington, D.C.: Council for Basic Education, 1975.

The Source, James A. Michener

Spelling and Reading with Riggs, Teacher's Edition. Myrna McCulloch. Beaverton, Oreg.: K & M Publishing, 1989.

The Spirit of St. Louis, Charles A. Lindbergh. [See F.A.C.E.'s *Spirit of St. Louise Teacher Guide* by Rosalie J. Slater.]

The Spy, James Fenimore Cooper

Stories from Shakespeare, Marchette Chute. World Publishing Co., 1956.

The Story of English, Robert McCrum, William Cran, and Robert MacNeil. New York: Elisabeth Sifton Books, Viking Penguin, 1986.

The Story of King Arthur and His Knights, Howard Pyle. New York: Charles Scribner's Sons, 1903; Dover [facsimile] edition, 1965.

The Story of My Life, Helen Keller

The Story of the Bible, Edgar J. Goodspeed. Chicago: University of Chicago Press, 1936. [Previously published as *The Story of the Old Testament*]

Strong's Exhaustive Concordance of the Bible

A Study of Fairy Tales, Laura F. Kready. Introduction by Henry Suzzallo. Cambridge, Mass.: Riverside Press, 1916.

The Tale of Peter Rabbit, Beatrix Potter

A Tale of Two Cities, Charles Dickens. 1859.

Tales from Shakespeare, Charles and Mary Lamb, Everyman, 1990.

Tales of the Alhambra, Washington Irving

The Talisman, Sir Walter Scott

[T & L] *Teaching and Learning America's Christian History: The Principle Approach®*, Rosalie J. Slater. San Francisco: F.A.C.E., 1965.

Those Who Love, Irving Stone. Garden City, N.Y.: Doubleday & Co., 1965.

The Thread That Runs So True, Jesse Stuart

Three Revolutions, Stefan T. Possony, ed., including Friedrich Gentz's essay translated from German by John Quincy Adams. Chicago: Henry Regnery Co, 1959.

Trailblazer of the Sea, Jean Lee Latham

Treasure Island, Robert Louis Stevenson

The Tree of Liberty, Elizabeth Page. Holt Rinehart & Winston, 1969.

Uncle Remus, Joel Chandler Harris

Up from Slavery, Booker T. Washington

The Uses of Enchantment: The Meaning and Importance of Fairy Tales, Bruno Bettleheim. New York: Knopf, dist. by Random House, 1976.

Voyages of the English Nation, Richard Hakluyt

The Walls of Windy Troy: A Biography of Heinrich Schliemann, Marjorie Brayer

Wheeler's Graded Studies in Great Authors: A Complete Speller. Chicago: W. M. Wheeler & Co., 1899.

Why Johnny Can't Read: And What You Can Do about It, Rudolf Flesch. New York: Harper & Row, 1955, 1983.

Why Johnny Still Can't Read: A New Look at the Scandal of Our Schools, Rudolf Flesch. New York: Harper & Row, 1981.

The Wind in the Willows, Kenneth Grahame

Winnie the Pooh, A. A. Milne

A Wonder Book, for Girls and Boys, Nathaniel Hawthorne. New York: Airmont Books, 1966.

Words Every College Student Should Know, Kenneth A. Oliver.

The Works of Anne Bradstreet. Edited by Jeannine Hensley. Cambridge, Mass.: The Belknap Press of Harvard University Press, 1967.

The Works of James Russell Lowell. Boston: Houghton, Mifflin and Co., Riverside Press, 1899.

World History, a Christian Interpretation, Albert Hyma

The World of Captain John Smith, Foster

Write for College, a Student Handbook. Patrick Sebranek, Verne Meyer, and Dave Kemper. Wilmington, Mass.: Write Source/Houghton Mifflin Co., 1997.

The Writing Road to Reading™, Romalda Spalding. New York: William Morrow Co., 1990.

The Writings of Kate Douglas Wiggin. Boston: Houghton Mifflin Co., 1917.

The Young Explorer's Bible, NIV. Zondervan, 1995.

The Young Reader's Bible (70 Bible Stories), Bonnie Runo and Carol Reinsma. Standard Publishing, 1994.

NOTE: For rare or out-of-print volumes mentioned in this guide, try the internet site **www.bibliofind.com.**

A Basic Annotated Bibliography for High School English Teachers

Prepared by Mr. Jeffrey L. Black, American Heritage Christian Schools
September 10, 1977

Introductory Comments: The works by Webster are out-of-print, except those with the publishing information. All annotations in quotation marks about him are taken from Miss Slater's biography of Noah Webster in the Webster's 1828 Dictionary (1967 facsimile reprint by F.A.C.E.) unless otherwise noted. This is only a preliminary working bibliography. It is inadequate but a good start.

The difficulty in finding traditional, standard, classical grammars of English was clearly stated in a letter to me (dated May 25, 1977) from Kenneth Oliver, Professor of English and Comparative Literature at Occidental College. Professor Oliver is the only college teacher I am aware of who is committed to basic education in teaching English. I quote him at length.

"There is no grammar series that I could recommend wholeheartedly. For the past several decades, the concept of grammar has been bruited about and a lot of junk has been published but none has found really widespread approval. Perhaps the best is the series by Paul Roberts, but it is fading in popularity and is not, in my judgment, a workable series. Nor do I know of any that I would care to recommend.

"There are good things about grammar and language in general which could be highly useful for a teacher to know. Among these I would include John Conner's A Grammar of Standard English (the first thirty or so pages are excellent), and The English Language, Form and Use, by William Chisholm, Jr. and Louis T. Milic, which gives a good general perspective on English as well as information about words, syntax, figurative language, and style. Pommer and Sales's The Use of Language is old (about 1950–55) but is sound and interestingly developed.

"The most complete grammar is probably Otto Jespersen's four-volume Modern English Grammar. The enclosed bibliography (far from complete) suggests others that are well-known for one reason or another.

"I wish you well with your studies and in your teaching. At present, a good teacher of English needs to be able to develop his own grammatical assignments and exercises—until some better texts are published.

"For further bibliography, I would suggest you check with a professor of English sympathetic with basic education, or a local university library—using great discernment."

The Other Recommendations of Kenneth Oliver:

A. From his booklet A Sound Curriculum in English Grammar, pp. 33, 40:

1. Oliver, Kenneth. *Our Living Language*, revised and enlarged. Los Angeles, Calif.: Occidental College, 1962.

2. Oliver, Kenneth. *Words Every College Student Should Know*.

3. Partridge, Eric. *Origins, a Short Etymological Dictionary of Modern English*.

4. Skeat, *Concise Etymological Dictionary of the English Language*.

B. From Books for College Libraries, "Modern European Languages," pp. 37–38:

5. Jespersen, Otto, 1860–1943. *A Modern English Grammar on Historical Principles*. London: G. Allen & Unwin Ltd., 1928– ; 1. English language-Grammar, Historical; 2. English language-Syntax.

6. Sweet, Henry, 1845–1912. *A Short Historical English Grammar*. Oxford: Clarendon Press, 1892; an abridgment of the historical portions of the author's New English Grammar, cf. Pref. 1. English language-Grammar, Historical; 2. English language.

7. Jespersen, Otto, 1860–1943. *Essentials of English Grammar*, University of Alabama Press [1964]. (Alabama linguistic and philological series), "A one-volume grammar embodying the principles explained in 'The philosophy of grammar' and partly carried out in the four volumes of my 'Modern English grammar'"; 1. English language-Grammar—1870–1950.

8. Quirk, Randolph. *A Grammar of Contemporary English* (by Randolph Quirk and others). London: Longman [1972]. 1. English language-Grammar—1950.

9. Zandvoort, Reinard Willem, 1894– . *A Handbook of English Grammar*, 3d ed. Englewood Cliffs, N.J.: Prentice Hall, 1966.

C. From The New Encyclopedia Britannica:

10. Whitehall, Harold. *Structural Essentials of English* (1956).

11. Hill, A. A. *Introduction to Linguistic Structures: From Sound to Sentence in English* (1958).

12. Sledd, J. H. *A Short Introduction to English Grammar* (1959).

13. Long, R. B. *The Sentence and Its Parts* (1961).

14. Roberts, Paul. *English Sentences* (1962).

15. Joos, Martin. *The English Verb* (1964).

16. Gleason, H. A. *Linguistics and English Grammar* (1965).

17. Stageberg, N. C. *An Introductory English Grammar* (1965).

18. Darbyshire, A. E. *A Description of English* (1967).

19. Quirk, R. et al. *A Grammar of Contemporary English* (1972).

20. Strang, B. M. H. *Modern English Structure*, 2d ed. rev. (1968).

The Recommendations of Mr. Jeffrey L. Black:

D. *General Texts and Curriculum Guides*

21. Hodges, John C.; Whitten, Mary E.; and Connolly, Francis X. *Harbrace College Handbook*, 5th ed. New York: Harcourt, Brace & World, 1941 [1962]. Probably the most widely used standard, college text. May be used with upper-level high schoolers.

22. Oliver, Kenneth. *A Sound Curriculum in English Grammar: Guidelines for Teachers and Parents*. Occasional Paper Number Twenty-three. Washington, D.C.: Council for Basic Education, 1976. Order from The Council for Basic Education, 725 Fifteenth St., N.W., Washington, D.C. 20005. A very concise, clear summary of the leading principles of grammar and how to break these principles out through the grades.

23. Rogers, Ruth and Stewart, Paul R. *Keys to Good English*. Oklahoma City: The Economy Company, 1965. 6 books. A rather intense and advanced series of text workbooks. One for every grade, grades 7–12. It contains extensive exercises, which are more challenging than most texts, but lacks sufficient explanation. With proper background, explanation and lecturing, and for students with an excellent elementary school foundation, this series might be used with great profit. The Economy Company also publishes "Keys to English Masters—The 70 Series."

24. Webster, Noah. *A Grammatical Institute of the English Language:* I. The American Spelling Book, 1783. II. The Improved Grammar of the English Language, 1784. III. An American Selection of Lessons in Reading and Speaking, 1785. Out-of-print. Miss Slater: "These volumes republished again and again became the basis of an American system of education and their influence grew with the history of the young republic." Dr. Harry Warfel: "By his Institute (speller, grammar, reader) he had supplied the correct standard for language in our schools, given a religious tone to all our textbooks, and had fostered patriotic pride."

E. *Study Habits and Thinking*

25. Flesch, Rudolf. *The Art of Clear Thinking*. New York: Collier-Books, Collier-Macmillan, 1969. Principles of clear thinking. If we can get ourselves, then our students, to think straight, we will be a long way toward advancing American Christian scholarship and civilization.

26. Kornhauser, Arthur W. *How to Study: Suggestions for High-School and College Students*. Chicago: The University of Chicago Press, 1966. The standard, classic small primer on the subject. Authoritative. It has been reprinted twenty-three times since 1924. Excellent bibliography.

27. Roth, David M. *Memory Course: A Simple and Scientific Method of Improving the Memory and Increasing Mental Power*. Hackensack, N.J.: Wehman Bros., 1969. I have never used it, but it was highly recommended to me in grad school. Probably the most sound, well-known method.

28. Staton, Thomas F. *How to Study*. 5th ed. Montgomery, Ala.: How to Study, 1968. Instructor's guide comes with it. Good, simple guide based on P (preview), Q (question), R (read), S (state), and T (test).

29. Staubach, Charles N. *How to Study Languages*. Ann Arbor, Mich.: The George Wahr Publishing Co., 1952. By a Professor of Romance Languages, University of Michigan. Deals with exercises, verbs, vocabulary, grammar, reading, study habits.

30. Woodley, Colin E. *How to Study and Prepare for Exams*. New York: A Signet Book, The New American Library, 1961. "A comprehensive guide on how to study, do research, read and take notes . . . for all students from secondary school to college. Complete with schedules, time tables, and aids for specialized study."

F. *Phonology (pronunciation and speaking), Orthography (spelling), and Penmanship*

31. Brown, Grace M.; and Hulbert, Michael J. *Letters, Sounds and Words*. 2d ed. Dubuque, Iowa: Kendall/Hunt Publishing Co., 1976. For students with a good foundation in The Writing Road to Reading, this would be a helpful text for more advanced phonics. Developed by Dr. Grace Brown especially to teach foreign students at The City College of San Francisco, it is a very original and enjoyable approach. Some progressive techniques, but nevertheless some effective exercises.

32. Morrison, J. Cayce, and McCall, William A. *Morrison-McCall Spelling Scale for Grades 2 to 8*. New York: Harcourt, Brace & World, 1951. Eight lists of fifty words, ranging from very simple to difficult, selected to measure spelling ability and progress. May be used repeatedly through the grades. Full explanation on how to use it for objective results. Recommended in The Writing Road to Reading.

33. Orton, Dr. Samuel T. *Reading, Writing and Speech Problems in Children*. New York: W. W. Norton and Co., 1937. This authoritative work is the scientific basis of Spalding's The Writing Road to Reading. Orton was an "eminent neurologist and brain specialist," lecturer at The Columbia College of Medicine, and experienced English teacher. "His theory of the functioning of the brain in speaking, writing, and reading and his practical means to prevent or overcome confusions were clear, logical and highly effective in practice." This is suggested reading for those concerned with the relation of reading and neurology.

34. Spalding, Romalda Bishop, and Spalding, Walter T. *The Writing Road to Reading: A Modern Method of Phonics for Teaching Children to Read*. 2d rev. ed. New York: William Morrow & Co., 1969. Large phonogram cards are helpful but not crucial since they can be cut out of the book. Former Vice-President of The Reading Reform Foundation says this is the purest and most direct system of phonics. Scientifically-based on Dr. Orton's research. Thousands of teachers have used it and not one has ever been reported abandoning it, who gave it a fair and full try.

35. Webster, Noah. *The Elementary Spelling Book, Being an Improvement on The American Spelling Book*. Latest rev. ed. New York: American Book Company, 1908. Miss Slater: "Noah Webster's The American Spelling Book, the famous 'blue-backed speller,' set a publishing record unlikely to be equalled by any school text in America. Over a period of one hundred years more than one hundred million copies were worn out by Americans as they learned their letters, their morality and their patriotism." Jefferson Davis (1859): " 'Above all other people we are one, and above all books which have united us in the bond of common language, I place the good old Spelling-Book of Noah Webster. We have a unity of language no other people possess, and we owe this unity, above all else, to Noah Webster's Yankee Spelling-Book.' " The 1843 edition "contained a section entitled Precepts Concerning Social Relations in which are described qualities which a young man should identify in his future life partner." This book also contained A Federal Catechism, which gave monumental backing to the "Republican Principles under the New Constitution." A Federal Catechism contained 'a short explanation of The Constitution of the United States of America, and the Principles of Government.' Among those subjects specifically taught was a discussion of the 'defects of democracy' and a definition of a 'better form of government,' namely, that of a 'representative republic.' Students learned that the United States is 'a federal representative republic,' and that the states are all governed by constitutions that fall under the name of representative republics."

G. *Reading*

36. Mortimer, J. *How to Read a Book: The Art of Getting a Liberal Education*. A Clarion Book. New York City: Simon and Schuster, 1967. Director of The Institute for Philosophical Research and (I believe) the editor of the Great Books series. Though a liberal, he appreciates basic education. Hailed universally among educators as the leading work on the subject.

37. Center, Stella S. *The Art of Book Reading*. New York: Charles Scribner's Sons, 1952. "A guide for the intelligent reader who seeks in books better understanding and greater enjoyment, by a former director of The Reading Institute of New York University." Harold L. Roth, Library Journal: "the author . . . presents a method of approach to the problem of reading critically, and well-based on her experience in teaching people of all ages to read. . . . Reading material is divided into type classes, i.e. essays, plays, poetry, etc. with excellent examples . . . to show how to read."

38. Flesch, Rudolf. *Why Johnny Can't Read and What You Can Do about It*. New York: Harper & Row, Publishers, Perennial Library, 1966. The controversial work that set progressive "Look-Say" education on its head and exposed the foolishness and destructiveness of all non-pure phonic systems. Flesch has been a leading refuter of "Look-Say" since 1955. Should be read for perspective on the modern pure phonics vs. "Look-Say" debate.

39. McCall, William A., and Crabbs, Lelah Mae. *Standard Test Lessons in Reading*. New York: Teachers College Press, Columbia University, 1974. About eighty pages/book. A series of five books to cover reading from grades 2–12. Each book has about eighty three-minute reading lessons. The student must read and answer questions over a paragraph. Excellent for plotting reading growth week-by-week through the grades.

40. Webster, Noah. *An American Selection of Lessons in Reading and Speaking.* 1785. Out-of-Print. Miss Slater: This work "included many patriotic selections taken from the speeches, addresses, and writings of Washington, Hancock, and others, as well as the Declaration of Independence, addresses from Congress, and poems and epics written to celebrate American events. These were calculated to improve the minds and refine the taste of youth; and also to instruct them in Geography, History, and Politics in the United States. To which is Prefixed, Rules in Elocution, and Directions for expressing the principal Passions of the Mind."

H. *Prosody (syllabication, accentuation, versification)*

41. Curry, Robert L., and Rigby, Toby W. *Reading Independence through Word Analysis: A Pre-Test and Manual for Improving Word Analysis Skills.* Columbus, Ohio: Charles E. Merrill Publishing Company, 1969. Basic guide with exercises to the principles (rules) of syllabication and accentuation.

I. *Lexicology (meaning of words) and Etymology (origin history and formation of words including prefixes and suffixes)*

42. *The Compact Edition of the Oxford English Dictionary*—Complete Text, Reproduced Micrographically. 2 vols. New York: Oxford University Press, 1971. Reproduction of the original 13-vol. ed. with four pages from the original on a page. The only complete and scholarly lexicology of every word in the English language since 1250. Contains half a million words, with complete etymologies and quotations of classics wherein they are found, complete bibliographies. Both proper and common names. Helpful for any words Webster's 1828 does not contain and for further explanation of those he includes.

43. Fernald, James C. *Standard Handbook of Synonyms, Antonyms, and Prepositions.* Book-of-the-Month Club: "As useful as a Dictionary. Contains eight thousand synonyms and three thousand antonyms; also indicates the correct prepositions to use with many of the words listed."

44. Jespersen, O. *Growth and Structure of the English Language.* Cambridge University, one of the world's top-flight secular universities, lists only this grammar for the B.A. in English recommended reading. (The Cambridge University Handbook, 1970–71, p. 200.)

45. Johnson, Samuel. *A Dictionary of the English Language*, 1755. A scholar's dictionary, unlike Webster's dictionary which was designed for the common person. The first full attempt to record and define the words of English.

46. Oliver, Kenneth. *Words Every College Student Should Know.* Oliver, in A Sound Curriculum . . . , p. 40, says: "It is, as far as I know, the first purely analytical dictionary, defining words by prefix(es), stem(s), and suffix(es)."

47. Partridge, Eric. *Origins, a Short Etymological Dictionary of Modern English.* Oliver, in A Sound Curriculum. . . , p. 40, says that this work is "an exceptionally fine source" for exercises on related word stems, "since it gathers words into families according to the stems or roots and then explains the development of each word."

48. *Concise Etymological Dictionary of the English Language.* Oliver, A Sound Curriculum . . . , p. 33: "excellent for adult beginners."

49. *Thorndike's Word Book.* Report of the five thousand most commonly used words in English.

50. Trench, Richard Chenevix. *Deficiencies in Our English Dictionaries.* Written by the celebrated Irish Bible scholar (1807–1886), born in Dublin, Ireland, who wrote some poems, including "Some Murmur When Their Sky Is Clear."

51. Trench, Richard Chenevix. *Select Glossary of English Words.*

52. Trench, Richard Chenevix. *The Study of Words.*

53. Webster, Noah. *A Compendious Dictionary of the English Language.* 1806. Miss Slater: "The foundation of his own American Dictionary." This was the first English lexicon which began "the identification of an American language as distinct from that of England. . . . The Compendious Dictionary built upon and expanded the work of an English schoolmaster, John Entick, who had published The New Spelling Dictionary of 1784." Webster's knowledge of ten languages enabled him to greatly expand and improve on it. A collector's item. In the preface, "Webster set forth his proposals for a gradual reform of spelling, and an Americanization of Pronunciation, including the addition of some words unique to Americans." Webster: "Compiled for the use of the common schools in the United States."

54. Webster, Noah, *An American Dictionary of the English Language*, 1828 facsimile edition. Republished in facsimile edition by Foundation for American Christian Education to Document and Demonstrate: I. The Unique Nature of Our Form of Government and of Our Civil Institutions which "Requires an Appropriate Language of the Definition of Words"; II. "To the Youth of the United States the Definition of Language"; III. To All Americans "That the Principles of Republican Government Have Their Origin in the Scriptures"; Prefaced by an Article: "Noah Webster, Founding Father of American Scholarship and Education," by Rosalie J. Slater, M.A., Anaheim, Calif.: Foundation for American Christian Education, 1967. 2 vols. in one. "The first dictionary identifying America as a Christian form of government. Biblical definitions and examples." Noah Webster's American Dictionary of the English Language: Intended to Exhibit: I. The Origin, Affinities and Primary Signification of English words, as Far as They Have Been Ascertained; II. The Genuine Orthography and Pronunciation of Words, according to the General Usage, or to Just Principles of Analogy; III. Accurate and Discriminating Definitions, with Numerous Authorities and Illustrations, to which Are Prefixed, An Introductory Dissertation on The Origin, History and Connection of the Languages of Western Asia and of Europe, and a Concise Grammar of The English Language. Webster studied twenty-six languages and fourteen areas of learning to write it. Contains clear etymologies, incisive objective definitions, abundant Scriptural references, superlative governmental, theological, Biblical character, and educational definitions. The only American Christian dictionary ever produced. Authored by the Father of American Christian Education and Scholarship.

55. Webster, Noah. *Dissertations on the English Language.* 1789. Out-of-print. Based on his master's thesis on the relationship of literature and Christianity. This work "led him into his profound study of etymology and philology and caused him ultimately to master more than twenty-six languages." The work states the need for an independent nation to have its own language system. He proposes "universal undisputed practice" and the "principle of analogy," as the governing principles in the proper development of a language within the fixity of linguistic standards and purity. The work then explains how a language can both grow and maintain purity simultaneously. This work should be absorbed by all concerned about this problem in light of the modern demoralization of English.

56. Webster, Noah. *Synopsis of Words in Twenty Languages.* 1825. As far as I know, this work was never published. It was the basis of his American Dictionary. It contained words from most Indo-European languages. It "became a useful tool with which he was able to trace the primary meaning of a word from its source, or head-waters, through the various tributaries of its meaning. This exactness in defining the original idea of the word freed the lexicographer from dependence on synonyms as substitutes for exact meaning."

J. *Syntax (relation of words to each other for meaning: Units of speech, phrases, clauses, and sentences)*

57. Magee, Ethel B., et al. *A Brief Review of English Grammar with Supplementary Exercises.* Rev. ed. Los Angeles, Calif.: Schwabacher-Frey, 1925. Typical of the older grammars, this brief work is a helpful tool for review and exercises.

58. Quackenbos, G. P. *An English Grammar.* Belton, Texas: School Supply, (1862). Standard, classic, traditional American high school grammar. The only reprint available that I am aware of.

59. Scott, Fred Newton, and Buck, Gertrude. *A Brief English Grammar.* Chicago: Scott, Foresman and Company, 1905. A basic grammar, useful on the Junior High level.

60. Webster, Noah. *Rudiments of English Grammar: Being an Abridgment of the Improved Grammar of the English Language.* New-Haven: Dunie & Peck, 1831. A grammarian's gold-mine. Out-of-print. Most of it has been republished in the F.A.C.E. 1967 facsimile reprint of Webster's 1828 dictionary in the section entitled "Philosophical and Practical Grammar, etc."

61. Webster, Noah. *The Improved Grammar of the English Language.* 1785. Out-of-print. Miss Slater: This work "contained the Scriptural admonition: 'Train up a child in the way he should go, and when he is old he will not depart from it.' His Spellers, Grammars, Readers, Histories, and Dictionaries all implemented this Thesis. The examples, illustrations, and definitions used in his volumes were replete with ideals of virtue and industry, of piety and patriotism." Buy it if you can find it.

K. *Punctuation: Mechanics, and Form*

62. *Manual of Standard Usage in Written Work—Junior and Senior High Schools.* A Bulletin for Students. Bulletin No. 157. Authorized by the Board of Education. Dallas, Tex.: Dallas Independent School District, June 23, 1965. Basic, overall guide. Especially good on punctuation, and form. Excellent guide for mechanics of writing. May be used back-to-back with William Strunk's Elements of Style.

63. Turabian, Kate L. *A Manual for Writers of Term Papers, Theses, and Dissertations.* 3d ed., rev. Chicago: The University of Chicago Press, 1967. Very popular guide on the details of the form, quotations, footnotes, bibliography, typing, etc. of college and grad students. Needed for upper level high school teacher when dealing with finer points.

L. *Writing: Research (term paper), Original, Reflective, Analytical, and Connective*

64. Cooper, Charles W., and Robins, Edmund J. *The Term Paper: A Manual and Model.* 4th ed. Stanford, Calif.: Stanford University Press, 1967. The simplest guide, containing all the basic steps with adequate explanation. Excellent for teaching the basics of how to write a term paper. May also be used as a student guide.

65. Flesch, Rudolf. *How to Be Brief: An Index to Simple Writing.* New York: Harper & Row, 1962. Especially helpful for the verbose and wandering writers.

66. Flesch, Rudolf. *The Art of Readable Writing.* New York: Harper & Row, 1949. An enjoyable and direct guide to the subject.

67. Hansen, Travis L. and Gray, Lee Learner. *Writing the Research and Term Paper.* Bronxville, N.Y.: Cambridge Book Company, 1969. An excellent basic guide, containing the step-by-step process, mechanics and an example of a research paper. Elementary. Good for junior high lectures.

68. Markman, Roberta H., and Waddeli, Marie L. *Ten Steps in Writing the Research Paper.* Woodbury, New York: Banon's Educational Series, 1971. "Arranged to lead the student step-by-step through the writing of a research paper from finding a suitable subject to checking the final copy. Easy enough for the beginner, complete enough for the graduate student." Fuller than Cooper & Robins.

69. Strunk, William, Jr. *The Elements of Style.* With Revisions, an Introduction, and a chapter on Writing by E. B. White. New York: The Macmillan Company, 1972. "An old stand-by on how to write a composition, dealing with elementary rules of usage, principles of composition, form, words and expressions commonly misused, and an approach to style. The best thing I know of for teaching upper level highschoolers to write. White: "It was Will Strunk's . . . attempt to cut the vast tangle of English rhetoric down to size and write its rules and principles on the head of a pin. . . . In its original form it was a forty-three page summation of the case for cleanliness, accuracy, and brevity in the use of English. Today, fifty-two years later, its vigor is unimpaired, and for sheer pith I think it probably sets a record that is not likely to be broken. . . . Seven rules of usage, eleven principles of composition, a few matters of form, and a list of words and expressions commonly misused—that was the sum and substance of Professor Strunk's work. . . . In the English classes of today,

'the little book' is surrounded by longer, lower textbooks—books with permissive steering and automatic transitions. . . . [This book] still seems to maintain its original poise, standing, in a drafty time, erect, resolute, and assured. I still find the Strunkian wisdom a comfort, the Strunkian humor a delight, and the Strunkian attitude toward right-and-wrong a blessing undisguised." (pp. vii–xiii, passim.)

M. *Pedagogy (how to teach literature and language)*

70. Evans, Bertrand. *Teaching Shakespeare in the High School*. New York: The Macmillan Company, 1966. Written by a practical teacher and lover of Shakespeare, who says: "I am convinced that Shakespeare is far and away the most important author who can be studied by high school students. . . . He is indispensable." (p. 1) Evans goes on to substantiate this point and then to explain what to avoid and how to teach students to love and understand Shakespeare by direct reading, study, and reflection of the original. Deals with the place of activities, units, forms, which plays to read and when, bibliography and notes on nine plays.

71. Highet, Gilbert. *The Immortal Profession*. Book-of-the-Month-Club: "A collection of stimulating essays on 'the joys of teaching and learning' by the renowned author, critic and classical scholar. 'Superb, humane, civilized . . . offers the rewards of the company of a richly furnished mind.' —Wall Street Journal." These next four I know nothing about and therefore cannot recommend personally. Nevertheless, it is an important area and these books may give sound direction. I suggest they be carefully evaluated at a library or bookstore before being purchased.

72. Fomler, Mary E. *Teaching Language and Literature*. Newark: McGraw-Hill, 1966.

73. Guth, Hans P. *English Today and Tomorrow*. Englewood Cliffs, N.J.: Prentice-Hall, 1964.

74. Hook, J. N. *The Teaching of High School English*. 3d ed. New York: The Ronald Press Co., 1965.

75. Loban, Walter; Ryan, Margaret; and Squire, James R. *Teaching Language and Literature*, Grades 7–12. New York: Harcourt, Brace & World, 1961.

N. *Literature and Special Reference Works*

76. Batson, Beatrice. *A Reader's Guide to Religious Literature*. Chicago: Moody Press, 1968. Batson-Britisher; literature professor at Wheaton College, Ill. "This handbook examines the writings of representative authors (of a distinct God-oriented position) from the early middle ages to the 20th century. Outstanding literary works such as Augustine's Confessions, Dante's Divine Comedy and Milton's Paradise Lost receive proportionately more consideration. The concentration is on authors whose frame of reference and writing have been molded by some form of Christianity. Each chapter begins with a study of the historical and cultural context of the works included in that chapter. There are also biographical sketches of the authors. The work is fully documented in footnotes and a helpful bibliography for future study is appended."

77. Bullinger, E. W. *Figures of Speech Used in the Bible—Explained and Illustrated*. Grand Rapids, Mich.: Baker Book House, 1968. Unfortunately out-of-print again. "It is a complete and detailed study of the figures of speech used in the Bible. . . . It has never been duplicated or equaled in point of thoroughness and detail." It contains over 217 figures, with the proper Greek or Latin pronunciation of the figures and the English equivalent, its etymology and copious examples of the figure in Biblical passages (five thousand total) fully quoted, giving full explanation where necessary. The figures are clearly defined and distinguished. A "must" tool for every serious student of poetry.

78. Guyot, Arnold. *Physical Geography*. New York: Ivison, Blakeman and Co., 1885. Photographically reproduced from the original in the Print Shop of Pacific Coast Bible College, 1100 South Valley Center, San Dimas, CA 91773. The consistently Christian interpretation of world geography with Asia as the continent of origins, Europe as the continent of development of civilization, and America as the fullest flowering of a Christian civilization.

79. Rose, Tom. *Economics: Principles and Policy from a Christian Perspective*. Milford, Mich.: Mott Media, 1977. The book does what the title says. It is strong on application to contemporary problems. Very practical. Excellent background for interpreting literature with economic themes, such as Robinson Crusoe.

80. Thrall, William Flint and Hibbard, Alan. *A Handbook to Literature*. Revised and enlarged by C. Hugh Holman. New York: The Odyssey Press, 1960. Every literature teacher should own it. It is the standard reference tool on all types of terms (linguistic, historical, formalistic, etc.) related to literature with thorough descriptions of the qualities of literary aspects. It contains sections on "Some Standard Works on English and American Literature" and "Outline of Literary History, English and American." Thoroughly cross-referenced.

O. *Literature and the Bible*

81. Dwight, Timothy. "A Dissertation on the History, Eloquence and Poetry of the Bible" in *The Christian History of the American Revolution: Consider and Ponder*. Compiled by Verna M. Hall. San Francisco: Foundation for American Christian Education, 1976. Delivered at the Public Commencement at New Haven, 1772. Dwight shows the superiority of the Bible over the classic ancients like Homer and Virgil. He deals with Biblical forms of literature, such as the ode, pastoral, elegy, dramative and epic poem, and various figures of speech.

82. Hoare, W. H. *The Evolution of the English Bible*. J. Murray, 1901. How we received The Book of Books, which has influenced English and American literature, history, and government more than any other.

83. Moulton, R. G. *The Literary Study of the Bible*. 1900. Very fine work on literary forms.

84. Ryken, Leland. *The Literature of the Bible*. Grand Rapids, Mich.: Zondervan Publishing House, 1974. Ryken says: "I have written for readers who wish to fit biblical literature into their experience of literature generally. . . . This is why I have related biblical literature to the main works of classical, English, and American literature rather than to the more esoteric sources known only to biblical specialists." The book is an excellent introduction not only to biblical literature, but also to literature generally. It contains chapters on "The Story of Origins," "Heroic Narrative," "The Epic of the Exodus," "Biblical Tragedy," "The Book of Job," "The Lyric Poetry of the Psalms," "God, Worship and Nature in the Psalms," "Biblical Enconium," "The Song of Solomon," "Biblical Pastoral," "Wisdom Literature," "Biblical Satire," "The Gospel as a Literary Form," "Biblical Parable," "Epistle and Oratory in the New Testament," "The Book of Revelation." It also contains a "Glossary of Literary Terms" and Scripture and Subject indexes.

85. Smith, Wilbur M. "A Bibliography of the Influence of the Bible on English Literature (and, in part, on the Fine Arts)." Fuller Library Bulletin, ix-x (January–June, 1951). Write to the Librarian, Fuller Theological Seminary, P.O. Box 750-M, Pasadena, California for a duplicate copy.

86. Work, Edgar Whitaker. *The Bible in English Literature*. New York: Fleming H. Revell Company, 1917. Out-of-print. Rather superficial. Does not deal with the relationship of government, Christianity, and English literature. Primarily a brief history of the Christian English writers and the Biblical themes and allusions in their literature. Very rich source of bibliography.

P. *Literature and American History*

87. Baldwin, Alice M. *The New England Clergy and the American Revolution*. New York: Frederick Ungar Publishing Company, 1958.

88. Bancroft, George. *History of the United States*. 10 volumes. Little, Brown and Company, 1866. Excellent full history on America.

89. Frothingham, Richard. *The Rise of the Republic of the United States*. Little, Brown and Company, 1890. The best single-volume work.

90. Hall, Verna M., Comp. *Self-Government with Union*. Volume two of *Christian History of the Constitution* Series. Edited by Joseph Allan Montgomery. Introduced by Felix Morley. San Francisco, Calif.: The American Christian Constitution Press, 1962. "This volume continues the documentation of America's Christian philosophy of government as understood by our Founding Fathers prior to the Constitution. The emphasis is upon Biblical Christian unity as the basis of American political union."

91. Hall, Verna M., Comp. *The Christian History of the American Revolution: Consider and Ponder*. With an Index of Leading Ideas by Rosalie J. Slater. San Francisco, Calif.: Foundation for American Christian Education, 1976. This is the first of "a series of volumes dealing with America's historic Christian stand against tyranny." It is "illustrated with historical documents and works of American art. (It includes) biographies of writers and artists" and a Scriptural index. It is "a Scriptural invitation to American Christians to reflect upon the uniqueness of American History as it relates to the liberty of the Gospel (internal) and its effect upon the formation of the American Christian Republic (external)." This volume deals with the ten-year Constitutional Debate, 1765–1775, which "enabled the Colonists to identify in their lives and writings the Biblical principles of a Christian republic, the highest form of civil government." The volume includes many sermons of the clergy which show their understanding of the key principles of Christian government.

92. Hall, Verna M., Comp. *The Christian History of the Constitution of the United States of America: Christian Self-Government*. Introduction by Felix Morley, edited by Joseph Allan Montgomery. American Revolution Bicentennial Edition. San Francisco, Calif.: Foundation for American Christian Education, April 19, 1975. "The emphasis in this volume is upon Christian self-government, tracing the Chain of Christianity® moving westward to establish America."

93. Johnson, Edward. *Wonder-Working Providence, 1628–1651*. Edited by J. Franklin Jameson. Barnes and Noble, 1952.

94. Slater, Rosalie J., and Hall, Verna M. *Rudiments of America's Christian History and Government: Student Handbook*. San Francisco, Calif.: Foundation for American Christian Education, 1968, 1994. "A work-text for junior and senior high school students."

95. Slater, Rosalie J. *Teaching and Learning America's Christian History: The Principle Approach®*. Foreword by Mark Fakkema. San Francisco, Calif.: Foundation for American Christian Education, April 19, 1975. The authoritative work on "The Principle Approach," the historic philosophy and method of American Christian Education. "A Christian Education Guide for home, church, and school indicating how the Biblical principles from Christian History can be taught in all grades and subjects. Includes a Christian History Study Course."

96. Webster, Noah. *History of the United States*. 1832. Expresses his "American Constitutional Principles." It was "a widely used text in American schools. Webster had been the first to introduce the study of American History into schoolbooks. The importance of this volume was its recording of America's Christian History as Webster traced the hand of God and the relationship of America to Christianity and the Bible." No doubt, this would be an excellent companion volume for teaching American literature. Out-of-print. Another important work to reclaim.

Q. *Literature and English History*

97. Green, John Richard. *Conquest of England*. 1883.

98. Green, John Richard. *History of the English People*. Harper and Brothers, 1886.

99. Green, John Richard. *Short History of the English People*. 1898. The best one-volume background work.

100. Green, John Richard. *The Making of England*. 1882.

101. D'Aubigne, J. H. Merle. *The Reformation in England*. 2 vols. Edited by S. M. Houghton. London: Banner of Truth Trust, 1963. First published in 1866–78 as Books VI, VIII, and XV of the History of the Reformation in Europe in the Time of Calvin.

R. *Literature and European and Universal History*

All of the universal histories are out-of-print and written from the Providential Approach. I have not worked with them personally, but they have been highly recommended to me.

102. Bancroft, Charles. *Footprints of Time*. R. T. Root Publishing Company, 1879. Excellent. Providential universal history. May be used back-to-back with English literature as the Chain of Christianity® moving westward base.

103. D'Aubigne. *History of the Reformation*.

104. Durwy, Victor. *Universal History*.

105. Fisher, George. *Universal History*.

106. *Harper's Dictionary of Classical Literature and Antiquities*.

107. Lord, John. *Universal History*. Lord was a minister.

108. Rawlinson, George. *Universal History*.

109. Rollin, Charles. *Ancient History*. 1730. It gives the Christian basis of every subject, including English literature and language, as it developed historically.

110. Hollin, Charles. *Universal History*.

111. Webster, Noah. "Dissertation . . . Upon The Universal Diffusion of Literature, As Introductory to The Universal Diffusion of Christianity." Unpublished Webster's Thesis, Yale College, c. 1783. This has never been published to my knowledge. From the title it looks to be a diamond mine for the American Christian approach to literature. A duplicate copy may perhaps be requested by writing to Yale University or to New York Public Library. One statement convinces one of its superior worth: "This country must in some future time, be as distinguished by the superiority of her literary improvements, as she is already by the liberality of her civil and ecclesiastical constitutions." This work was a "challenge to English grammarians" and it "brought him into confrontation with the many theories of orthography, pronunciation, definition, and grammar."

112. Willard, Emma. *A System of Universal History in Perspective*. Illustrated by a Chronological Picture of Nations, or Perspective Sketch of the Course of Empire, in a series of maps, giving the Progressive geography of the world. Photographically reproduced from the original. Denver, Colo.: The Mile-Hi Evangelist Press, 1974. It may be obtained from the publisher, P.O. Box 275, Denver, CO 80201. This work was published by F. J. Huntington & Co., N.Y. in 1939.

S. *Literature and Noah Webster*

Noah Webster is given a separate section because of his unique importance and because of the wide variety of his works.

113. Webster, Noah. "A Collection of Papers on Political, Literary and Moral Subjects." 1843. This would be worth looking into.

114. Webster, Noah. *Diary*. 1790 ff.

115. Webster, Noah. *Elements of Useful Knowledge*. c. 1785. Contained "the history and geography of the United States."

116. Webster, Noah. *Moral Catechism*. c. 1785.

117. Webster, Noah. The Holy Bible, Containing the Old and New Testaments, in the Common Version, with Amendments of the Language. 1833.

118. Webster, Noah. *The Peculiar Doctrines of The Gospel, Explained and Defended*. c. 1810.

119. Webster, Noah. *To the Friends of Literature in the United States*. 1807.

120. Webster, Noah. "Value of The Bible, and the Excellence of the Christian Religion: For the Use of Families and Schools." 1834. This was Webster's companion piece to his edition of the Bible.

T. *The Cambridge and Oxford Reference Works* These are very scholarly and factually reliable; they contain rich background materials and brilliant insights. But beware of their secularism and humanism in literary criticism, interpretation, and philosophy of education, government, and literature. The Cambridge works are published by the Cambridge University Press, Cambridge, England. The Oxford works are published by the Clarendon Press, Oxford, England (Oxford University Press).

121. Harvey, Paul. *The Concise Oxford Dictionary of English Literature*. 1957.

122. *The Oxford Companion to American Literature.*

123. *The Oxford Companion to Classical Literature.*

124. *The Oxford Companion to English Literature.*

125. *The Oxford Companion to the Theatre.* Excellent for background on Shakespeare and other leading dramatists.

126. Sampson, George. *The Concise Cambridge History of English Literature.* 1961.

127. *The Cambridge History of English Literature.*